many current analyses of the dynamics of the Palestinian uprising *(intifada)* and Israel's brutal tactics to suppress it, generally ignore the role of Zionism's exclusivity which makes Jews "more equal than all others" in Israel. Emotional parochial reactions to past persecutions of Jews and Zionist claims that its "Jewish" state provides Jews with a haven from discrimination have usurped the more complex, objective analysis of the sources of anti-Semitism. Increasing evidence that the basic ideology and policies of political Zionism are the cause, not only of the Palestinian uprising, but also of serious conflicts among Israeli Jews is generally ignored. But the lack of public focus on the discrimination inherent in Israel's political and legal structure does not diminish the forcefulness of the anti-Zionist argument: that preferential legal treatment of a single ethnic/religious group violates the human rights of the indigenous population; that the values of political/national Zionism and the policies of its state are incompatible with the democratic tradition and the enduring universal and spiritual values of Judaism, Christianity and Islam; that leaders of such high religions are morally obligated to stand in judgment on the Zionist politics and policies of Israel.

The essays were written by Jews, Christians and Muslims as a tribute to Rabbi Elmer Berger for diligently defending, for over forty years, the great spiritual values of the Jewish faith against the onslaught of an ideology that falsely equates political Zionism with Judaism and has corrupted the universal moral truths of the sister religions of "the Book."

Elmer Berger 1908—

Anti-Zionism

Analytical Reflections

Editors:
Roselle Tekiner
Samir Abed-Rabbo
Norton Mezvinsky

Amana Books
P. O. Box 678
Brattleboro, Vermont 05301

PUBLISHED BY AMANA BOOKS,
58 ELLIOT STREET
BRATTLEBORO, VERMONT 05301
MANUFACTURED IN THE UNITED STATES OF AMERICA

ISBN 0-915597-73-X

1 3 5 7 9 10 8 6 4 2

CONTENTS

THE CONTRIBUTORS

Elmer Berger was ordained a rabbi in 1932 and served congregations in Michigan before helping to found the American Council for Judaism. He is now president of American Jewish Alternatives to Zionism (AJAZ) which regularly publishes *Report,* an analysis of news of the Middle East, written by Dr. Berger. He is author of *The Jewish Dilemma, A Partisan History of Judaism, Judaism or Jewish Nationalism, Who Knows Better Must Say So, Letters and Non-Letters, Memoirs of an Anti-Zionist Jew* and numerous articles and pamphlets.

Naseer Aruri is Professor of Political Science at Southeastern Massachusetts University. He is author of *Jordan: A Study in Political Development; Enemy of the Sun: Poems of Palestinian Resistance;* and numerous articles on human rights, the Palestine question, Lebanon, Islam and U.S. policy in the Middle East. He is editor of *Middle East Crucible: Studies on the Arab-Israeli Confrontation and Occupation: Israel Over Palestine.*

Roselle Tekiner is Adjunct Professor of Anthropology at Eckerd College in Florida where she teaches courses on Middle East cultures. She has written several articles on institutionalized discrimination in Israel based on analyses of Israel's "fundamental" laws.

Shaw Dallal, a native of Palestine, has a doctorate from Cornell Law School. He was law clerk to N.Y. Supreme Court Justice Richard J. Cardamone and legal counsel to OAPEC. He is Adjunct Professor of International Business and Relations at Utica College of Syracuse University. He has written extensively on the Middle East.

Benjamin M. Joseph was one of the first Israeli draft resisters. He emigrated to the United States in 1976 and earned a Ph.D. in political science at the Graduate Center of City University of New York. He is author of *Besieged Bedfellows: Israel and the Land of Apartheid.*

W. Thomas Mallison is an International Law Consultant and Emeritus Professor of Law at George Washington University Law Center, Washington, D.C. **Sally V. Mallison** was formerly Research Associate in the International and Comparative Law program at George Washington University Law Center and is now an International Affairs Consultant. Their books include *The Palestine Problem in International Law and World Order.* They have been consultants to AJAZ since its inception.

Cheryl A. Rubenberg is Associate Professor of International Relations in the Political Science Department at Florida International University.

She is author of *Israel and the American National Interest: A Critical Examination; The Palestine Liberation Organization: Its Institutional Infrastructure;* and numerous articles on U.S. policy in the Middle East and Palestinian human rights.

Ruth Mouly has taught Political Science at Reed College, Portland State University, Colorado Woman's College, City College of New York and the University of Pittsburgh. She has written and published in the areas of religion and foreign policy. She is doing research at the University Center for International Studies, University of Pittsburgh, on Christian fundamentalism as it pertains to support for Israel.

Israel Shahak is Professor of Organic Chemistry at the Hebrew University in Jerusalem and chairman of the Israeli League for Human and Civil Rights. Born in Warsaw into a religious family and surviving imprisonment in the Poniatowo and Bergen-Belsen Nazi concentration camps, he came to Palestine in 1945. Throughout his life he has been a student of Judaism and Jewish history. He has achieved an international reputation as a commentator on Israeli Jewish society.

Norton Mezvinsky is Professor of History at Central Connecticut State University in New Britain, Connecticut. He teaches courses that deal with the history of Judaism, the modern Middle East and certain aspects of United States History. He has written and published in each of these areas and has studied Zionism for over three decades.

INTRODUCTION

This book is a testament to the long and honorable tradition of op-position to political/national Zionism. It includes current evaluations of Israel, the political entity Zionism established in the Middle East, which has long benefited from wide admiration and support. The state was unilaterally established in 1948 and was generally hailed as the fulfill-ment of "the Zionist dream" to build a utopian society. Jews would live there as the majority, free from anti-Semitic injustices, free to create a humanitarian, benevolent peace loving democracy that would be a "light unto the nations." There were a few dissenting voices warning of prob-lems a "Jewish" state would create for Arabs and for Jews but they received virtually no media coverage. They faded away almost com-pletely after 1967 as Israel's spectacular military victory over the Arab states was euphorically celebrated.

Not only the popular media contributed to the idyllic, almost sacro-sanct image of Israel. Scholarly publications appeared, analyzing nearly every aspect of government, society and politics. For the most part, they optimistically expressed faith that Israeli industry and ingenuity would overcome problems the "Jewish" state would face. The United States government responded to Israel with abundant financial subsidies. Pri-vate sources contributed substantially to the realization of Zionism's pub-licly declared goals. Little reason was offered to question Israel's Zionist ideology and policies.

Israel's invasion of Lebanon in 1982 was a significant turning point after several decades of massive American public support of Israel. As television viewers watched Israel's daily bombardment of Beirut and its suburbs and the consequent suffering and deaths of civilians, articles appeared speculating about what happened to "the Zionist dream."

The *intifada* began at the end of 1987. Palestinians rose up in frus-tration and anger after twenty years of occupation. Much of the world witnessed Israel's brutal tactics to halt stone throwing and quell dem-onstrations. Soldiers tear gassed participants, systematically broke their bones, destroyed their homes, shot and often killed them. Palestinians accused of instigating protests were deported, some without any due process, including those who advocated civil disobedience instead of violence. Unpleasant facts could no longer be glossed over by self declared leaders of the "American-Jewish community." Previously staunch uncritical supporters of Israel began openly to criticize the Israeli government. Dissenting voices grew louder as American journalists joined the bandwagon. Media exposure of Israel's "iron fist" policies from 1982 to 1988 revealed a radically different image than had long been presented.

A growing body of literature now challenges long standing myths of the Israeli government's benevolent and humanitarian motives. There is also some illumination and analysis of Israel's sophisticated public relations efforts that succeeded in building faith in Israeli "democracy." But there is little analysis of Israel's Zionist infrastructure as the possible cause of Israel's failure to live up to the high expectations of her supporters.

When commentators speculate about the causes of Israel's present problems and the decline in her image, they sidestep the most glaring evidence. They ignore that a "Jewish democracy" is a contradiction of terms; that undemocratic measures are necessary when preferential rights are conferred on a single ethnic/religious group; that the fulfillment of the "Zionist dream" is a daily living nightmare for the indigenous Palestinian population. "The fading of the Zionist dream," or Israel's "loss of her soul," is how it is often put. A superficial diagnosis is that Israelis "lost their way," which ignores the fact that repressive policies are necessary in the overall Zionist strategy to maintain a state for "the Jewish people in a land where others recently lived as the majority population." Israel has not lost its way, but in the pursuit of its goals has lost much of its sentimentalized reputation. Analysis of Zionist ideology, the linear progenitor for the political and legal structure of Israel, is continually avoided in explanations for Israel's now highly visible actions and the decline of its popular image.

The major premise of this volume of essays is that the historical continuity of classic Zionist ideology is responsible for many of the serious socio-economic and political problems confronting Israel. It is not, as many commentators maintain, rejection of the fundamental values of Zionism that has tarnished the country's image abroad. It is political/national Zionism itself, as enunciated by Theodor Herzl in his 1897 book, "Der Judenstaat" and pursued diligently by the Zionist establishment. Herzl believed that anti-Semitism would inevitably pervade all nations, making it necessary for all Jews—"the Jewish people"—to have their own state where they would create and maintain a permanent majority. Herzl's ideology later motivated Israel's lawmakers to structure the state to provide preferential treatment for Jews in a land where another religious and ethnic group had lived as the majority until Zionist policies and actions put many to flight.

There has always been opposition to political Zionism but most public resistance collapsed during and after the demonic anti-Semitic Nazi campaigns. Sympathy for Hitler's victims created a groundswell of popular support for perceived Zionist objectives. Contrary to the popular opinion that Zionism would solve "the Jewish problem," a relatively small segment of Jews emerged in the early 1940's with a program designed to continue the democratic tradition of anti-Zionism. Rabbi Elmer Berger was among those who insisted that the answer to Hitler and the terror of anti-Semitism was not the withdrawal and isolation of Jews in a separate state where they would have preferential national and political rights at the expense of Palestinians. They advocated instead the implementation of genuine democratic rights for all people in all nations. Consequently, a key plank in the platform of these anti-Zionist Jews was that the peace agreements following World War II recognize Palestine as a democracy in which all citizens, regardless of religious faith or ethnic origins, would enjoy full equality of rights and obligations.

Elmer Berger's emergence as a leader in a national anti-Zionist campaign was an outgrowth of his commitment to the historic position of Reform Judaism that Jews are a religious community, not a nation. As rabbi of a congregation in the late 1930's, he began publicly to challenge demands of the World Zionist Organization for United States support of a "Jewish" state. He later became one of the founders, among 32 other Reform rabbis, of the American Council for Judaism and one of its principal ideological architects. At its peak, this anti-Zionist organization had as many as 50,000 members.

While continuing his opposition to a "Jewish" state on religious grounds, Dr. Berger's perspective expanded to include resistance to the increasing Zionist domination of American Jewish institutions. He also began to concern himself with the adverse political impact of the new state upon both American interests in the Middle East and upon Palestinians. Since 1968 he has continued his concerns as president of *American Jewish Alternatives to Zionism*. During his forty-five year career as an anti-Zionist advocate and writer, he has continually emphasized that Judaism is entirely separate from the politics of the Zionist state and should be kept separate; that the values of Zionism are incompatible with the values of Judaism. He insists that a clearly understood distinction between Judaism and Zionism would help to clarify many major issues in the Israeli/Palestinian conflict.

The initial essay in this volume, "Zionist Ideology: Obstacle to Peace," was written by Dr. Berger in 1981. We have chosen it from his voluminous works because it reflects both the theological roots of his lifelong commitment to an anti-Zionist position and his prophetic predictions of the drastic consequences for Middle East peace that would result from establishment of a Zionist state. He analyzes fundamental Zionist ideology and the way in which it has been translated into the political reality of Israeli domestic and international policies, including Knesset legislation. The essays that follow were written as a tribute to Elmer Berger for his integrity, his scholarship and his courage in championing the cause of national self-determination for the Palestinian people and diligently defending the values of Judaism.

Naseer Aruri discusses anti-Zionism as a secular, democratic alternative to Zionism. He shows that its fundamental and enduring democratic principles are in contrast to the principles of Zionism which is responsible for the establishment of an undemocratic, exclusivist state recognizing only Jews as its nationals.

Roselle Tekiner analyzes Zionist "fundamental" laws as the basic cause of Israel's prolonged "Who is a Jew?" controversy. Because these laws confer "national" benefits only on those Israeli citizens who are eligible for "Jewish nationality" (members of "the Jewish people"), it is of crucial importance for an Israeli citizen to be officially recognized as a Jew.

Shaw Dallal traces the continuous, historical betrayal by England, Zionism and the State of Israel of the human rights and civil liberties of the Palestinians. Dallal supplies extensive documentation from primary sources to show that the betrayal is due to dereliction of the "great powers," including the United States.

Benjamin Joseph analyzes the symmetry in ideology and practice between Israel and South Africa, showing that the Zionist system of Israel and the apartheid system of South Africa are equally discriminatory. He provides many examples of mutually beneficial practical collaborations.

Sally Mallison and W.T. Mallison demonstrate with abundant documentation and commentary that the United States government treats Israeli Zionist institutions in this country as if they are legitimate, voluntary organizations of American citizens, while obstructing the operation of legitimate organizations opposed by Israel. This is accomplished through discriminatory application of its own laws and failure to honor commitments made in international agreements. The Mallisons focus on the efforts of Congress to force closure of information offices of the Palestine Liberation Organization.

Cheryl Rubenberg comprehensively surveys United States interventions and "peace proposals" for the Palestine problem. She begins with the "lost" King-Crane Commission Report under Woodrow Wilson and ends the dismal historical record with George Shultz's "peace plan" of

1986-1987. The consistent flaws in virtually all these efforts is that, in one way or another, they are predicated on values which are antithetical to United States interests in the Middle East and values of all democratic societies.

Ruth Mouly examines Christian beliefs—fundamentalist, moderate and liberal—that are translated into uncritical support of the State of Israel. Numbering many millions, Christian Zionists are formidable allies of Israel. She also discusses Christian denominations whose political opinions on the Palestine problem are antidotes to those of Pat Robertson, Jerry Falwell, and other fundamentalist preachers.

Israel Shahak traces the ways in which Jewish bureaucracies have opposed the opportunities democratic societies have provided Jews to be free human beings. This continues in recent years as political/national Zionism serves as a force to inflict tragic, mortal injury on Palestinians by exploiting the vestigial insecurity which is understandably still latent in many Jews. With an encyclopedic knowledge of the history of Polish Jews and the literature of Judaism, he details the obstacles Zionism has consistently raised against the emancipation of Jews and Judaism. In a large sense, much of Shahak's essay is a version of the Old Testament struggle between priest and prophet.

Norton Mezvinsky discusses the anti-Zionist tradition in Reform Judaism. From the late 1800's to the late 1930's, Reform institutions resisted national Zionism and the idea of a "Jewish state." Instead they championed emancipation of Jews wherever they were still excluded from benefits of democratic ideals. But motivated by the tragedy of Europe's Jews in the 1930's and 1940's, and shaken by the disciplined assaults of Zionists, resistance began to erode. By the time the Zionist state was established, the institutions of Reform, except for a minority of rabbis and laymen, had become supporters of the exclusivist, discriminatory, particularist state.

Zionism cannot be fully understood in terms of a dream to end the suffering of Jews. As these essays point out, a state established and maintained for a single ethnic/religious group requires undemocratic methods to suppress the rights of the indigenous population. Writing from the perspective of different disciplines and dealing with various aspects of Zionism, the authors are on common ground in recognizing the humanitarian, democratic principles of anti-Zionism as a guide to ending the Israeli/Palestinian conflict. It is our hope that this volume will help speed the time when a just and durable peace will succeed the protracted conflict and help restore to Judaism its historic place of respect as a depository for some of the great, spiritual values of civilization.

1

ZIONIST IDEOLOGY: OBSTACLE TO PEACE

ELMER BERGER

I. "The Missing Link"

It is a platitude—after more than 30 years—to describe the so-called "Arab/Israel" confrontation with discouraging adjectives such as "stubborn," "intractable," "resistant to normal diplomacy." More pessimistic observers often use depressing terms like, "insoluble," "irreconcilable," "irrational." U Thant, when he was Secretary General of the United Nations, called it a new "hundred years war." Whichever of these usual descriptions is preferred is eloquent testimony to failed diplomacy—of all kinds, good and bad—in the search for a formula to terminate the hostilities. "The Camp David process" is the latest performance. It was launched with great eclat in 1978-79. It is now clear that even if "the process" produces the much heralded "comprehensive peace" it will be only after profound alterations of the formula blue-printed at the renowned Presidential hide-away.

Despite this dreary record of three decades of failure the conventional diplomats persist in promoting formulas which, for the most part, are warmed-over versions of previous failures. Hope seems to spring eternal that drawing a border here rather than there, a quibble for some vague amelioration of the tragedy of Palestinians (called "refugees" by the more mendacious or innocent), some re-cycled system of guarantees for Israel's "security," or some internal political transformation in either the Zionist state or one of the confrontation Arab states will be the magic formula. In other words, a careful study of the dozens of formulas and modalities with which some serious and some cynical statesmen have attempted to substitute peace for the continuing war, provides evidence that when all the sales talk is illuminated by knowledge of the historic, organic causes of the problem, nothing new has been added. The same old pieces have simply been moved about on the same old board. All the games so far have ended as a draw.

One element common to all these failures is that none has formally included Zionism in the agenda of issues to be negotiated. This is a strange "oversight" because, from the very beginning of the Palestine problem. in the Balfour Declaration era, the Zionist organization was party to the negotiations. The Zionist Organization/Jewish Agency for Palestine negotiated with the United Nations during the partition debate in 1947-48. The "Declaration of the Establishment" of the State of Israel specifies "the Zionist Movement" as one of the "establishers." And the organic relationship of the government of the state and the World Zionist Organization is evident in the daily coordination of activities of the two and is detailed in formally enacted Israeli law .[1]

One of the reasons for this diplomatic reticence about Zionism is that the World Zionist Organization (the progenitor of the Zionist State of Israel) sedulously cultivated confusion about several different and often contradictory varieties of the phenomenon.

Undeniably, "Zion" (and not necessarily Zionism) is one of the *sancta* of traditional or orthodox Judaism. This Zion, in its authentic, orthodox meaning, is a theological—not a political/nationalistic—concept. In God's wisdom, when "the people" morally merited it, God would usher in the millennium by sending the messiah to lead "the children of Israel" back to Zion. Distilling this "future hope" out of a correct interpretation of relevant Old Testament texts, these orthodox Jews understood the ancient Israelites and Judeans lost the Holy Land because they had sinned. They had gone "whoring" after other gods and engaged in a long list of injustices towards fellow humans. Judaism is a "covenant" religion. The covenant changed from age to age, but it was always a contract between "the people" and God. God "promised" the land and would prosper them in it *if* "the people" rigorously fulfilled the precise moral and ethical stipulations of the covenant as it was interpreted by "God's prophets" in any particular age. Micah spoke for all the prophets when he warned (III: 9-10:12), "Zion will be plowed" and "Jerusalem shall become a heap" because the people "abhor justice and pervert all equity." Only God—not men or any combination of men—could make the judgment of whether or not the conduct of the people had reached the point of moral excellence to repair the covenant and so clear the way for God to restore them to the land.

Interpreted in this accurate sense, not even the enormous tragedy of the Holocaust could authenticate "the return." The Zionist exploitation of the tragedy perpetrated by Nazism is a better-than-average expedient to explain the establishment of the Zionist state. But it is a human explanation, not the fulfillment of Divine purpose. And the established state is anything but "a house of prayer for all peoples." (Isaiah LXVI:7.)

It is crucial to recognize that the decisive, definitive factor distinguishing this religious/messianic Zionism from the political/territorial Zionism which built the Israeli state is the austere, stringent morality which is embraced in the unquestionable authority of God. God—not men—will determine the time and appoint the leader for "the return" as it is conceived as a sacrament for some Jews.

Perhaps the most authentic—certainly the most dramatically visible—observers of this tradition in Judaism are the *Neturai Karta* (Guardians of the City) in Jerusalem itself. Rabbi Avram Blau was acknowledged as a leader of this group. The story is told that when the Israeli general in command of the troops who invaded Jerusalem in the 1967 fighting met Blau on the street leading to the quarter where the *Neturai Karta* was concentrated, the general expected a hero's welcome. He advised Blau that his congregants could now fulfill their spiritual dream of praying at the "Wailing" or West Wall. But the Rabbi responded to these "good tidings" with a stern rebuke. "When God prepares the way and commands we will go," he is reported to have said. "But we will not go at the invitation of your soldiers." The story may be apocryphal, but it could well have happened. It accurately reflects the substance of the religious Zionism of these devout Jews.

One of American Judaism's most distinguished theologians, Dr. Jakob Petuchowski, has said of such Jews—many of whom came to Zion even before there was a Zionist state—

> Politically . . . they had no aspirations whatsoever. On the contrary, they deemed all efforts directed at creating a Jewish State in Palestine to be sinful interference with the messianic time-table of Almighty God.[2]

There are legitimate, *theological* disagreements with this orthodox doctrine. Some of those disagreements are found among Jews themselves. Probably the most unequivocal theological dissent was proclaimed in 1885 in a credal declaration issued by a group of Reform Jewish rabbis in Pittsburgh, Pennsylvania. Known as the Pittsburgh Platform, it stated:

We consider ourselves no longer a nation but a religious community. And therefore expect neither a return to Palestine, nor a sacrificial worship under the administration of the sons of Aaron, nor the restoration of any of the laws concerning the Jewish state.

Anti-Zionism and opposition to a Zionist state has been—and is—therefore a legitimate position in Judaism. There were—and are—Jews who, far from incorporating political Zionism as a part of their faith, have regarded it as a moral imperative to stand in opposition.

It would be less than candid to leave the implication that the demonstrable existence of this anti-Zionist tradition implies indifference to the fate of humans now comprising the majority population of the Israeli state. Historically, the general perception of the *Yishuv* (the Jewish population of Palestine at any given time) was one of "refuge" from the oppressive societies of Eastern and Central Europe and later, of course, in an intensified version after the rise of Hitler. This remains the dominant image among the majority of western European and American Jews. Most do not belong to any Zionist organization. Most would accept the description of "non-Zionist," however vague this term is to the point of meaninglessness. They have also sometimes been called "philanthropic Zionists." On the whole, they are sadly uninformed—or misinformed—about the specifics of the political issues of the Palestine problem. "Arab" information, by and large, has been both inadequate and inept. Responsible anti-Zionist information by Americans (or western Europeans) has been plagued by lack of resources and consistently overshadowed by heavily financed and expertly designed Zionist propaganda. Lacking effective presentation of their own official positions, Arabs have been victimized by Zionism's representation of them in the worst possible stereotypes of their humanity and aspirations.[3] The PLO is "dedicated to terrorism for the sake of terror." The Arab states are determined "to drive the Jews into the sea." Israel's obstructionist policies in every effort to attain a peace are always reasonable precautions for Israel's "security."

Even this abbreviated delineation of this most prevalent attitude among Jews suggests that none of these positions should be invested with the sanctity of religious doctrine. They are defensive positions. They react to real or Zionist-fabricated threats to what is now a significant number of Jews whose existence in a part of Palestine is a fact of history and of *realpolitik*. "Philanthropic Zionists" do not perceive any Arab resistance to Zionism as a threat to *their* legitimate rights. For the most part, these Jews do not fully comprehend the significance of the Zionist state's gratuitous, legislative grant *to them* of Zionist national/political rights and obligations. Where even partial comprehension exists these Jews reject the grant, once they understand it as a form of "dual nationality" fused into their Judaism.

Clarification of these matters is important so that knowledgeable and responsible critics of past and present policies of the Zionist state may feel free to speak their judgments, uninhibited by the Zionist-nourished misrepresentation accusing such critics of attacking legitimate rights of Jews or derogating some authentic sacrament of Judaism. Free, informed and civil debate of the political issues will be as helpful to these "philanthropic" Jews as to the rest of the world, now acutely concerned with Middle East peace. In fact, since Jews have been more directly the targets of Zionist propaganda and therefore—after the Palestinians themselves—the greatest victims, releasing constructive critics of destructive Israeli policies from any sense that they are contributing "anti-Semitic" injury to Jews may be more helpful to these Jews than to others. Such a release from a sense of guilt could recruit new, informed, responsible participants in the expanding public debate about Palestine and Middle East peace. New participants would accelerate clarification of the specifics of the political issues, providing guidance for and impact upon wider audiences, including many of these "non-Zionist" "philanthropic" Jews. This, in turn, would inevitably influence politicians and decision makers of the "great powers" who so heavily influence policy. And these, in turn, might then be relieved of the hobgoblin of the Zionist-concocted myth of a "Jewish people" holding one-dimensional, homogeneous political views and prepared to operate as a blackmailing, political lobby. A sequence of such developments would provide the optimum of freedom for the inevitable and expanding political debate over resolution of the Middle East's oldest and so far most intractable problem. And such free debate is also the minimal necessity for most of the political leaders of the West who are more often followers of unreliable public opinion polls and submissive servants of the loudest, special pleaders than genuinely creative leaders.

This brief exploration of religious motivations and of the doctrine of messianic Zion would be incomplete without mention of the "fundamentalists" or "biblical literalists" of various denominations of Christianity. These Christians also consider the "return of the Jews" to the Holy Land to be a divinely ordained ingredient of the millennium. They are among the most formidable advocates and defenders of the policies of the Zionist state. In Holland, for example—until the most recent months—their *religious* predilections played an important role in determining the pro-Israeli policies of The Netherlands' government. In the United States—and throughout much of the world—Billy Graham's equating of the Zionist state with the fulfillment of Old Testament prophecy has been a political factor of considerable consequence. There is concern in some quarters of the United States now that the so-called Moral Majority, composed largely of such Biblical "literalists," spearheaded by the Reverend Jerry Falwell, may have influence on Ronald Reagan's approach to the Arab/Israel/Palestinian problem. Mr. Falwell was one of the reverend gentlemen who, this past year, was reported to have said, "God does not hear the prayers of Jews." Nothing daunted by his arrogant effrontery, the Zionists—ever alert for *political* advantage—invited Mr. Falwell to be an honoured guest at a banquet featuring Mr. Begin.

There are, of course, theological differences separating these fundamentalist Christians from the messianism of some traditionalist Jews. The Jewish millennialists hold that first the messiah will come and lead "the children of Israel" back to Zion. Their Christian counterparts believe the restoration of "the Jewish people" to the Holy Land is only one integral part of the preliminaries to the return of Jesus who will then be acknowledged by all humanity—including Jews—as *the messiah*. The fundamental fallacy of this brand of Christian theology is the same as that of the "theology" of the Zionist propagandists who deliberately attempt to confuse the authentic, spiritual messianism of some Jews with the secular political policies of the Zionist state. Neither insists upon the explicit moral stipulations of the contractual covenant with which the Old Testament prophets delineated the God/man relationship. In other words, the decisive distinguishing element of *God's* determination that "the people" are *morally* prepared for "the return" is, by no accidental oversight, noticeably absent. *Jewish* Zionist neglect of this part of the contract is understandable as a cynical, political deception. The lapse by Christian fundamentalists is explainable by the presumed chronology of their theology. The moral perfection of humans will not precede the "second coming." This idyllic state will exist only after Jesus is again active on earth in His resurrected messianic role. He will then lift from all who recognize Him the burden of their sins. So, in the two faiths, the order of "redemption" is reversed. And in this sense, the Christian fundamentalists are somewhat more consistent with their theology than the Zionist "theologians" are in the context of Judaism. The latter are hard-pressed to demonstrate that the ethics and morality of the mortals living now in Israel are so superior to the virtues of the rest of humanity that God would now be justified to declare the millennium is at hand and Menachem Begin, or the Gush Emunim are representatives of the true messiah!

Leaving aside these speculations in theological imponderables, however, the fact is that the messianists and millennialists—both Christian and Jewish—operate with their own expertise in the field of *religion*. Their debate and dialogue are legitimate in the context of theology. They both address the imponderables of life usually regarded as the prerogatives of religion: questions of God's will, of man's spiritual aspirations and the criteria for ultimate truth. These are not questions to be resolved by boundary adjustments, superior armaments or the election of one kind of *human* sovereignty over another. Genuinely religious men and women may invoke God's guidance to assist in finding the closest human approximation of justice or truth in resolving these mundane matters. And the earnest, agonizing efforts of men of real integrity to find the best, possible human formula for such problems may be ennobling examples of human striving to do God's will. But neither the mortal players nor the results should be cavalierly equated with the Divine Plan. To attempt to proscribe the struggle, the debates which accompany human efforts to reach the greatest possible justice and the nearest approach to truth in answer to these earthly problems by having some mortal assert he or she has the authority to seal any one, human design with the insignia of God is arrogance in the superlative degree and a profanation of any of mankind's great religions. Any who attempt to foreclose debate of such political questions by claiming divine sanction for *their* particular answers do, indeed, "take the name of the Lord in vain."

Mindful of these religious/theological commitments of both some Christians and some Jews, and distinguishing between these matters of religion and the substantive, political issues of territory and political rights which comprise "the Palestine problem," students of and commentators on international affairs may—even have a moral responsibility to—speak their minds on the merits of the cases of the several parties to the conflict. An additional caveat is for the commentary to be responsibly buttressed by ascertainable facts. Then, partisanship is not only permissible. It, too, becomes a moral responsibility with respect to each facet of the complex problem. It is in this spirit, hoping to contribute to the free atmosphere congenial to democratic debate and dialogue that the following analysis of the role of Zionist ideology as an obstacle to peace is offered.

The fact that, from the very beginning of international recognition of the territorial/political claims of Zionism it was considered essential to establish safeguards for the rights of indigenous Palestinians and anti-Zionist Jews in countries other than Palestine, is self-evident proof of the potential of Zionism for political and territorial aggression.

The Balfour Declaration offered the British Government's "favor" for "a national home for the Jewish people." The extent of the "favor" was specifically restricted by the provision:

[It] being clearly understood that nothing shall be done which may prejudice the civil and religious rights of existing non-Jewish communities in Palestine or the rights and political status enjoyed by Jews in any other country.

When Sir Mark Sykes first showed the text of the Declaration to Chaim Weizmann, he said, anticipating Weizmann's elation, "It's a boy". But Weizmann later recorded in his autobiography,

Well—I did not like the boy at first. He was not the one I expected.[4]

The disappointment can be explained only by the restrictions placed upon Zionism. The stipulated protection of the rights of the "non-Jewish communities" meant a dilution of Zionism's aspirations for a "Jewish state"; and the safeguards for the "rights and political status" of Jews in countries other than Palestine diluted the Zionist assertion that all Jews shared a common *national* identity. The negotiating history of the Declaration and the final text both testify to the historic fact that the British government, anti-Zionist Jews and advocates of the rights of the Palestinian Arabs all recognized the threat inherent in Zionism's ideology to the rights of native Palestinians, as well as the threat to Jews, in any country, who rejected the Zionist claim that identification as a Jew automatically included acquisition of whatever Zionist political/national rights and obligations might follow recognition of the Zionist Organization as party to an international, political agreement.

If demolition of the Zionist Organization had accompanied the Declaration of the state's establishment in 1948 the threats of further aggression against the rights of native Palestinians and Jewish citizens of countries other than Palestine might—probably would—have been liquidated. Native Palestinian Christians and Moslems of Palestine would still have objected to the partition of their country. But the demographic mix of the "Jewish state" proposed in the 1947 United Nations recommendation would have included so significant an Arab minority that the Zionist ideologists who took over the government would have been unable, in a democratic society, to structure a state so uninhibitedly Zionist/ "Jewish" nationalist as the present state of Israel. And without the local Zionist groups operating within the disciplines of the World Zionist Organization in countries with large populations of Jews, there would have been no apparatus making demands upon non-Palestinian or non-Israeli Jews which compromised their "rights and political status."

But the Zionist movement was *not* demolished. On the contrary, its status, privileges and responsibilities were reinforced and increased. According to Article 4 of the Mandate, the activities of the Zionist Organization were "subject always to the control of the British Administration." But the Mandate was terminated in May of 1948. The termination ended any juridical recognition of an international status for the Zionist Organization. It had no "charter" legitimizing its operations in countries other than Israel and it had no status or designated program within the newly-declared Israeli state. It was, in other words, in limbo.

II. Filling the Vacuum

In negotiations extending over a period of about two years, the World Zionist Organization and the Israeli government formulated a legal relationship to replace the one which the expiration of the Mandate had terminated. The result was a law which the Knesset enacted in 1952. It is known as "The World Zionist Organization/Jewish Agency for Israel (Status) Law."

The "Status" law was a domestic, legislative act. It is one of Israel's "Fundamental" or "Basic" laws. Together with the "Law of the Return" and "The Law of Nationality" (now supplemented by the recent enactment declaring Jerusalem the capital of the Zionist state), these "fundamental" or "basic" legislative acts reflect the primacy of the state's "Jewish people" nationality commitment. The state has no constitution. But laws in this "fundamental" or "basic" category have the weight of constitutional law, differentiated from more transient, statutory legislation. In various ways, these laws make those accepted as "Jewish people" nationals—whether in Israel or elsewhere—"more equal than any others," to use Orwell's colorful phrase. Only Jews are admitted freely *as of right* under "Law of the Return." Only such immigrants, entering under this law, may claim the *right* of *automatically* acquiring Israeli citizenship. The immigrant must take the initiative to renounce this citizenship within a given period of time if he or she does not wish to acquire it.

The "Status" law expressed the Israeli government's interest in a continuing relationship with the world Zionist movement. It also detailed the substantive character of this relationship. Two more years of negotiation followed. These latter negotiations refined the specifications of the services the Zionist movement was expected to perform for the state. They also provided a mechanism for coordinating the functions of the Zionist movement with those of the government. This series of negotiations produced an instrument which is identified as the "Covenant." The "Covenant" transformed the "Status" law from a domestic, legislative act into a bi-lateral agreement. Inasmuch as the World Zionist Organization/Jewish Agency had long been recognized as a "public body," the "Covenant" actually elevated the "Status" law to the stature of international law. It joined the Zionist Organization and the government in a relationship which some scholars believe makes the Zionist Organization an organic part of the government. Others think the 1952 law and the 1954 Covenant make the Zionist Organization an agent of the government.[5]

Professor W.T. Mallison, Jr. concludes his definitive legal analysis of both the "Status" law and the Covenant with the observation that the World Zionist Organization/Jewish Agency had to be

> recognized as an integral part of a single Zionist- Israel sovereignty because of the effective control the Government exerts over it.

Dr. Mallison continues,

> The most compelling conclusion is that the Zionist-Israel sovereignty contains an Organization/Agency component which is, in some aspects, part of the Government and in others its captive public body. Whichever aspects predominate at a particular time and for a particular purpose, the component is nevertheless subject to effective control by the Government of Israel. The juridical effects of this study are not varied whether the Organization/Agency be appraised as a government, public body, or both. In any or all three of these appraisals of status, it remains a component of the single Zionist-Israel sovereignty.[6]

The predominantly important consequence of this organic, legal linking of the Zionist movement to the conventionally recognized government of the Israeli state is that the political/national substance which the dual sovereignty nourishes and operates is Zionism. The historical legislative record and the substance of the resultant enactments both demonstrate, beyond any doubt, that the state of Israel promoted, obtained and now sustains a system of extra-territorial nationality rights and obligations which it claims for all Jews, whether they live in the Israeli state, or elsewhere. The claim is in flagrant violation of the protective clause of the Balfour Declaration and, insofar as the Declaration is integral to any international law legitimacy for the existence of the state, it is also in violation of international law.

III. The Jewish People

The body politic for which the state claims to exercise many national responsibilities and from which it expects many national services is not limited to the conventionally recognized citizenry of the state. It is a claimed entity which historically Zionism has called "the Jewish people."

The first three paragraphs of the "Status" law leave no doubt.

1. The State of Israel regards itself as the creation of *the entire Jewish people*, and its gates are open, in accordance *with its laws, to every Jew* wishing to immigrate to it.

2. The World Zionist Organization, from its foundation five decades ago, headed the movement and efforts of *the Jewish people* to realize the age-old vision of the return to its homeland and, with the assistance of other Jewish circles and bodies, carried the main responsibility for establishing the State of Israel.

3. The World Zionist Organization, which is also the Jewish Agency, takes care as before of immigration and directs absorption and settlement projects in the State.[7] (Emphasis supplied)

The official *Israel Government Year-Book* for 1953-54 (p. 57) confirms the claimed relationship.

The World Zionist Organization-Jewish Agency for Eretz Israel Law 5713-1952 was of great constitutional importance. The Prime Minister, in submitting the Law to the Knesset, defined it as "one of the foremost basic laws." This Law completes the Law of the Return in determining the *Zionist* character of the State of Israel. The Law of the Return established the right of every Jew to settle in Israel, and the new *law* established *the bond between the State of Israel and the entire Jewish people* and its authorized institutions in matters of immigration into and settlement in Israel. (Emphasis supplied)

The official description of the legal relationship between the Zionist movement and the Israeli government, and the glimpse of the political/national substance of the implementing legislation, make it clear that Zionism is an important—even an over-riding—national interest of the Israeli state. It is, therefore, unrealistic to expect to negotiate with the Israeli state about anything—peace included—without taking Zionism into consideration even as it would be unrealistic to attempt to negotiate with any other state while ignoring or objecting, even implicitly, to the fundamental value-system of the particular state. No democratic state could be expected, voluntarily, to surrender its fundamental democratic values. No capitalist state can be expected, voluntarily, to abandon its commitment to free markets. No socialist state can be expected, voluntarily, to jettison its dedication to collectivist values. Self-proclaimed protestations of pragmatism to the contrary, it is unrealistic to expect the admitted Zionist state, voluntarily, to abdicate its perceived role as both the dynamo of Zionism and the beneficiary of the supra-national movement.

Whether or not such abandonment is essential to a peace between the Zionist state and its Arab neighbors depends, of course, on the substance and character of Zionist ideology. Regrettably, most examinations of the phenomenon have been done by, and their significance has been limited to academicians, theorists and others removed from the many negotiating formulas which, over the years, have been constructed in the search for peace. The accessible records of these many negotiations offer almost no evidence that the participating statesmen confronted this central factor. It is at least a credible deduction that all the formulas to manipulate territory, compromise formulas for establishing "the legitimate rights of the Palestinian people," schemes for guaranteeing security of "all states" in the area have failed because—by design or ignorance—this vital interest of one of the major parties has never been put on an agenda.

Any examination of Zionist ideology must begin with an exposition of the meaning of the claimed constituency of the Zionist state—"the Jewish people." The term is one of the most deliberately deceptive identifications of a subject of international law in the vocabulary of modern politics. In the first place, it is a fact that substantial numbers of Jews—perhaps a majority of all Jews in the world—categorically reject any identification which would include them as constituent parts of a separate "Jewish" nationality. There is a crucially important difference between the expression, "Jewish people" and "*the* Jewish people." [8] In Zionism, "the Jewish people" is the claimed nationality constituency. Consequently, it is necessary to know who or what "the Jewish people" is to comprehend the ideology with which Zionism proposes to meet the needs of this constituency, as Zionism perceives those needs. The functions and activities of the State of Israel—which is a Zionist state—are determined by these same Zionist perceptions.

In the Zionist/Israeli lexicon, "*the* Jewish people" has a much more precise meaning than is generally indicated in the casual usage employed in the conventional media or by politicians, or even by those reputed to be serious statesmen or diplomats. In official or authoritative Zionist legal/political instruments, "the Jewish people" is intended to mean much more than a loose, amorphous collectivity of individuals who are Jews with nationality rights and responsibilities equal to those of other citizens or residents of whatever country may be their domicile. Historically, the term was a deliberately chosen, ambiguous synonym for "Jewish nation." Theodor Herzl, the architect of the Zionism which was parlayed into the Zionist state—and later leaders and propagandists of the movement—knew the majority of Jews in emancipated societies rejected any concept which regarded them as a separate, political nationality. One of Herzl's basic dogmas, asserted in his classic, *The Jewish State*, was

We are a people—one people.

No doubt the founder of the political/national Zionist movement made the declaration with such unqualified dogmatism because the prevailing perception of Jews about themselves—and to a lesser extent perhaps, of others' about Jews—was different from the concept he offered of a separate nationality. But the perception of Jews as a national entity was indispensable to Herzl's embryonic campaign to obtain a turf for the "Jewish" nation he wanted to believe existed and which he wanted the international community to recognize. That Herzl—and his colleagues of the time—knew no such entity existed is evident in the Basle Program which was the operative platform for the Zionist movement until it was superseded by the Biltmore Program of 1942. The Basle Program was adopted at the First Zionist Congress in Basle, Switzerland in 1897. It recommended a four-part strategy for eventual realization of the movement's ultimate objective "to create for the Jewish people a home in Palestine secured by public law." The third of these strategies was

The strengthening and fostering of Jewish national sentiment and consciousness.[9]

The declaration of the necessity to develop programs for "national . . . consciousness" was an admission that "the Jewish people" nationality did not yet exist. It needed to be created.

It is not necessary for present purposes to engage in the polemic of whether or not such a nationality entity exists even now. It is sufficient to acknowledge that, despite consistent historic rejections of the concept by many Jews, the international community of nations has often acted *as if* the entity does exist.

Chaim Weizmann rejoiced at such international perception as early as 1922. The Balfour Declaration and the Mandate had textually acknowledged the existence of Jews who rejected Zionist nationality and who respected the "civil and religious rights" of Palestinian Arabs. Both documents, therefore, were less qualified in their commitment to full Zionist aspirations than Zionist leadership had hoped. In an address to an annual meeting of the Zionist Conference in Carlsbad, Germany on

August 25, 1922, Weizmann, who had been a principal negotiator for the Declaration and the Mandate, told this group of disappointed followers:

> The value of the Mandate, apart from being a great success of Zionism, consists in the *recognition of the Jewish people*. This is of immense value, which will bear fruit and will open up new perspectives as yet hidden from our weak eyes. . . .[10] (Emphasis supplied)

Recognition of this "Jewish people" nationality concept is the first priority of Zionism's diplomacy. It is the cornerstone of the Zionist state's system of nationality rights and obligations. Appreciation of the centrality of this factor is indispensable to any assessment of Israel's long-range adaptability to the Middle East. It is therefore indispensable to any evaluation of any formula touted to solve the Palestine problem with the desired "just and enduring peace."

IV. Who Qualifies?

Such an evaluation must begin with the determination of who is included in this alleged nationality entity. It is self-evident that *the* crucial qualification is identification as a "Jew." The criteria for determining this identification are imprecise. For most of its history as a political/territorial movement, Zionism has been tormented by this question of, "Who is a Jew?"

In 1947, the Jewish Agency representative, testifying to the United Nations Special Committee on Palestine, said,

> Technically and in terms of Palestine legislation the Jewish religion is essential.[11]

"Palestine legislation" at the time, of course, was Mandate law. The Jewish Agency's own definition was broader. According to the same report, the Agency spokesman said,

> Generally we accept as Jews all who say they are Jews . . . all who come and say they are conscious of being Jews are accepted.

Zionist authorities, both political and legal, left no doubt that Jews— however defined—were to possess rights which were not possessed by others. So, for example, Dr. Ernst Frankenstein argued,

> The Mandate admits only one collective right, viz., that of the Jewish people to its National Home, while such rights as are pro-

vided in the Mandate in favour of the non-Jewish inhabitants of Palestine are individual rights. Under the Mandate, a non-Jew who is not an inhabitant of Palestine has no right to be admitted to the country. It is true that Article 2 of the Mandate speaks of the National Home "as laid down in the preamble"; it then upholds the reservation of the "civil and religious rights of existing non-Jewish communities of Palestine" contained in the Balfour Declaration. But the right of a people to a land is, without any doubt, not a civil or religious, but a political right. (Emphasis supplied) [12]

Zionist ambiguity in defining "Jew" however, did not long survive the termination of the Mandate. Once the state was established, the authority of government was no longer divided between the Mandatory and the Zionist Organization. *Israeli* law then clarified the Zionist definition of "Jew." Raphael Patai is not unfriendly to either Zionism or its Middle East state. In *The Jewish Mind*, published in 1977, Patai reviewed the historic confusion over the term "Jew." He says:

> All that, however, is a thing of the past. At the present, the most important legal context in which the question of who is a Jew must be answered is the Law of Return enacted by the Knesset (parliament) of the State of Israel on July 5, 1950. The main provision of this law states,
>
> "Every Jew has the right to come to this country as an immigrant". The term "Jew" in the law is vague; it is not clear whether it is used in a strictly religious or an ethnic sense.

Patai continues:

> The halakhic (rabbinical law) definition of a Jew as a person who either was born of a Jewish mother or has converted to Judaism was adopted by the Knesset in 1970. . . .

Patai then acknowledges that the dispute narrowed to what constituted proper conversion. But he notes that the disputants all agree the common feature

> [was] the requirement that a formal conversion take place which could be effected only by a rabbi.[13]

In the juridical system of the Zionist state, therefore, religion—either actively practised or assumed as an inheritance through the mother—is the *sine qua non* of membership in "the Jewish people."

The Knesset action of 1970 was actually anticipated in 1963 in the widely publicized, so-called "Brother Daniel" case. Oswald Rufeisen had been born a Jew and converted to Catholicism. He was denied the *right* of immigration to Israel as a Jew with the consequent automatic acquisition of citizenship. The decision was made by the Supreme Court. Subsequently, Rufeisen acquired citizenship by naturalization. Whether he—or his offspring—qualify as members of "the Jewish people" or as non-"Jewish people" nationals of Israel is uncertain.

V. "More Equal Than Others"

The question is neither irrelevant nor theoretical. Two practical consequences for Mr. Rufeisen, or other non-"Jewish people" nationals of the Zionist state, or of Palestine, depend upon the answer.

First, Mr. Rufeisen, or any Christian or Moslem who is a citizen of Israel but who does not qualify for membership in "the Jewish people," lives in a status inferior to anyone who qualifies by the law of the Zionist state as a "Jewish people" national, *even though he or she may be a citizen of another state*. This is the point at which *any Jew*, whose credentials are accepted by the Zionist state for membership in the synthetic, nationality entity called "the Jewish people," enjoys a status superior to even a non-"Jewish people" citizen. One of the state's foremost legal authorities, Dr. Nathan Feinberg of the Hebrew University in Jerusalem, put it this way:

> The right to the National Home is granted to the Jewish people as a whole, and not to any part of it; it is granted not to Zionists or to Jews who have settled in Palestine or who will settle there, but to all Jews wherever they may be.[14]

In other words, *all Jews*, wherever they may be, qualify as "Jewish people" nationals. But "questionable" Jews, like Mr. Rufeisen, may not—and certainly Christian or Moslem nationals of the Zionist state do not—qualify.

Dr. W. T. Mallison, Jr., has described the situation as one in which Jews, regardless of their conventionally recognized citizenship, are presumed *by the Zionist state* to possess a "functional second nationality by virtue of their religion." People who are Jews but citizens of another state may enjoy *in the Zionist state* certain advantages which are not enjoyed by citizens of this state who cannot qualify as "Jewish people" nationals. Since the criterion of "Jewish people" membership is either religion or race by virtue of descent from a mother recognized to have been Jewish, the state is either theocratic or racist. By definition, it must violate the human rights of those under its jurisdiction who cannot qualify as "Jewish people" nationals. Given this condition *in law* it follows almost inexorably that, *as a matter of policy*, the state must resort to any strategy which will guarantee a *permanent* majority of "Jewish people" nationals.

Whatever the causes of the "Arab refugee" problem in 1948-49, it was commitment to this Zionist nationality concept which motivated Israel's consistent rejection of the annual United Nations resolutions requiring Israel to offer the "refugees" repatriation. It is the same ideological commitment which, following the 1967 war and occupation of Arab territory, now confronts the Zionist state with a situation which many Zionists see as a dilemma. Anthony Lewis, one of the more perceptive columnists of *The New York Times*, put it this way:

> A substantial number of Israelis have come to feel that the Begin policy of indefinite control over the occupied territory would face Israel with a terrible choice: to absorb the one million Arabs in the occupied territory and thus dilute the Jewish character of the state, or else to hold those Arabs in something less than full citizenship and thus corrupt the idealist vision of Zionism.

> A noted Israeli historian, Jacob Talmon, wrote before his death last summer that "the attempt to rule a million Arabs against their will may make our beautiful dreams of national and spiritual renewal seem ridiculous." He also disagreed with the argument that continued occupation of the West Bank would strengthen Israel's security. To take on "the rebellious hostility of a subjected population," he said, would be "to sit deliberately on a volcano."[15]

To this point in its history, the Zionist state has solved the dilemma by refusing the Palestinians—non-"Jewish people" nationals of the country—the universally recognized right of repatriation on the one hand, and by repression of the "new refugees" in the territories occupied in the 1967 war on the other. Such policies are the source of Talmon's (and other "idealistic" Zionists') concerns that Zionism's "beautiful dreams" may prove "ridiculous."

VI. "Jewish People" Obligations

Every nationality both conveys rights and exacts obligations. Zionist nationality is no different. The first three paragraphs of the "Status" law set out "Jewish people" nationals' "rights" in the Zionist state. Paragraphs 4 and 5 set out the corresponding obligations. They also appoint the Zionist Organization as the agent of the state charged with responsibility for supervising the discharge of these "obligations" by "Jewish people" nationals, wherever they may live. The Zionist Organization accepted the assignment in the "Covenant," negotiated with the Israeli government and signed by both parties in 1954.

The resulting "condition on the ground," so to speak, produces the second condition in Israel in which "Jewish people" nationals are differentiated from non-"Jewish people" Israelis or Palestinians.

Paragraph 5 of the "Status" law is perhaps most revealing of the way in which the exclusivist, discriminatory character of Israel's Zionist-ideology/nationalism creates a condition of incompatibility with any state in which—at least in the ideal of law—national rights and obligations are shared by all citizens regardless of race, religion or ethnic origin. The incompatibility escalates to open hostility with the contiguous Arab states which are predominantly Moslem with significant minorities of Christians. And the hostility takes on the character of persistent, virulent belligerency among the Palestinians who have been either displaced or live under repressive occupation in the occupied territories or in the inferior status of second class citizens in pre-June 1967 Israel. Paragraph 5 states:

> The mission of gathering in the exiles, which is *the central task* of the State of Israel and the Zionist movement in our days, requires constant efforts by the Jewish people in the Diaspora; the State of Israel, therefore, expects the cooperation of all Jews, as individuals and groups, in building up the State and assisting the immigration to it of the masses of the people, and regards the unity of all sections of Jewry as necessary for this purpose.[16] (Emphasis supplied)

To understand this paragraph, a semantic exposition of traditional Zionist language is necessary. "Exiles" are all Jews living outside of Palestine or the state of Israel. "Diaspora" means any place other than Palestine or Israel in which Jews live.

These clarifications make clear the political significance of this section of the "Status" law. An Israeli "Fundamental" law declares the state's "central task" is to "ingather the exiles." The rationale for the law is classical, Herzlian Zionist ideology. Herzl's conception of the world as incurably anti-Semitic was the genesis for the Zionist mission of saving "the Jewish people" by "ingathering" its constituency from the "anti-Semitic" nations and establishing them in a nation-state of their own.

It follows inexorably that a state committed to this "central task" rather than to the protection and welfare of *all* of *its* citizens will allocate its resources accordingly. It cannot meet its perceived and legislated "central" obligation as the "savior" of one classification of people, dispersed world-wide and nominated as its beneficiaries because of their religious faith or ethnic/racist descent and, at the same time, provide all of its resident nationals with the benefits of its resources on a basis of complete equality. The two conceptions of the functions of statehood are—and must be—mutually incompatible.

The organic relationship established in the "Status" Law and the Covenant between the Zionist Organization and the government provides the *modus operandi* which the Zionist state employs to supervise the disposition of the resources of "Jewish people" nationals put at the disposal of the state to implement its "central task." Paragraph 4 of the "Status" Law provides:

> The State of Israel recognizes the World Zionist Organization as the authorized agency which will continue to operate in the State of Israel for the development and settlement of the country, the absorption of immigrants from the Diaspora and the coordination of the activities in Israel of Jewish institutions and organizations active in those fields.

Within the meaning of Paragraph 5, the World Zionist Organization operates in the state *only for Jews*. It services the state's declared, principal function of "ingathering the exiles." Benefits deriving from the operation of the Zionist Organization are limited—in the Zionist state—only to "Jewish people" nationals. But the Zionist Organization is mandated by the state's government to perform this function. It is clear, therefore, that the *official* policy of the state is discriminatory. The state employs the infrastructure of the Zionist Organization to put policies of discrimination in place and in other than an officially declared and overt manner.

This convenient arrangement illuminates the significance of references in official records of the World Zionist Organization to "Jewish housing," "Jewish agriculture," "Jewish education," "Jewish labor" and so on, to include many social and economic functions of modern governments. It is a clever ruse, little understood or, at least little exposed and taken into account by those who persist with adulatory observations about the practice of human rights in the Zionist state and the state's civility and peaceful intentions. In practice the system works fairly simply. Normal treasury funds of the government may be allocated among all citizens with no more than customary, bureaucratic inequities. But the not inconsiderable funds of the Zionist Organization are employed for "Jewish people" enterprises. They provide "Jewish people" recipients considerable economic and social advantages.

VII. How It Works

Sabri Jiryis is a Palestinian lawyer who practised in Israel and is now living in Beirut. In his definitive book, *The Arabs in Israel*,[17] he provides a number of examples of how the system works. Tobacco is a major crop of Arab farmers. As in many countries, the marketing of tobacco is regulated by the government. Arab tobacco, bought by "Jewish" companies, was paid for at a rate of 64.4% *less* than what was paid "Jewish" farmers. The difference is accounted for by the fact that "Jewish" farmers dispose of their crop to Alei Tabac. Alei Tabac is owned by the Jewish Agency/World Zionist Organization. According to Jiryis,

> The Jewish Agency does not deny the practice, claiming that it was created to help Jews and no one else.[18]

Jiryis says the same condition prevails for two other important crops— olives and olive oil.

In a state where by law the government is a partner with an institutional infrastructure committed to serving one part of the population on the basis of its religious faith it is not surprising that discrimination is not limited to the market place. Social and political attitudes are also affected.

In a *Foreword* to the Jiryis book, Noam Chomsky provides an accurate summary. He says, speaking as a Socialist Zionist,

> Responsibility for development is assigned in large measure to the Jewish Agency . . . that operates in the interests of Jews with a budget on roughly the scale of the development budget of the government. By such means as these, the state has succeeded in directing resources to Jewish citizens without technically introducing legal discrimination— though in fact . . . segregation and other discriminating practices are founded in the legal system itself.[19]

In the Zionist state—as indeed in many countries—application of "law" is not always determined by the language employed in "the legal system." Administration of the law can—and very often does—bend the intent of the system, even where the intent is to distribute the benefits and powers of the state equitably among its citizens. In the Zionist state the very intent—by definition— is to favor the maintenance and reinforcement of the "Jewish character" of the society.

The treatment of Arabs in the Galilee is one of the most flagrant examples. The demographic facts, including the higher birthrate among Arabs than among Jews, presented a grave threat to the continued domination of the state by Zionist ideology, with its primary concern for

"Jewish people" nationality. Israel's Northern District Commissioner of the Ministry of Interior, noted that in 1976, "the natural growth of the Arab population in Israel is 5.9% in comparison with 1.5% of the natural growth of the Jewish population per annum."[20] Ominously, for planners of a *Zionist* state, with this disparity in the growth rate, "the Arabs will constitute more than 51% of the population of the district in 1978."

The Koenig Plan recommended several strategies for making the lives of the Arabs of the Galilee sufficiently difficult to encourage their emigration. One of these was "to limit the number of Arab employees to 20%" in any "factory . . . in critical regions."[21]

Another strategy was to be applied in the field of education:

> To make it easy for the Arabs to go abroad for studying and to make it difficult for them to return and to find a job—that policy might help their emigration.[22]

The economy and the educational system of the Zionist state are heavily subsidized by Jewish Agency/Zionist funds from abroad. They are allocated, according to the Status Law and the Covenant, by the prescribed combination of representatives of the government and the Agency. The government is, therefore, party to such recommendations offered by one of its appointed officials.

The cities of Acre and Nazareth, with concentrated Arab populations, presented the most imminent threats to Zionist-state planners. In Nazareth, the government/Zionist organization combined, using discriminatory allocation of Zionist/government funds, put in place some of the most severe forms of discrimination against Arabs. Some Israelis speak quite candidly of the results as an integral part of "Judaization of the Galilee."

The keystone of the plan to "Judaize" the Galilee was to build what came to be called "Upper Nazareth." In 1948-49, Nazareth was almost totally an Arab city. Upon the hills surrounding the old city, the government and the Jewish Agency employed Zionist funds, designated for the apparently harmless purpose of building "Jewish" housing, to construct the new city.

> It was built upon thousands of acres of land which were expropriated high-handedly . . . taken by force from the Arab settlements, particularly Nazareth and neighbouring Rana.[23]

Not "a single unit of habitation" has been built in Arab "old Nazareth" since 1966. In Upper Nazareth meanwhile, Zionist/government funds have constructed a plethora of new housing. No Arab is permitted to purchase or rent any of the units despite the fact that—at least until recently—a number of them have been uninhabited. In old Nazareth, by contrast,"there is a grave and chronic housing crisis". The government even "offered publicly to buy any flat in Upper Nazareth which 'becomes empty' at any price offered for it, so it will not fall into Arab hands."[24]

Consequently, "old Nazareth" has become a virtual slum. The condition is intended to be a "persuader" helping to dislocate Arabs from one of their more concentrated population centers in the Galilee. And, ever conscious of "public relations," the contrast between "Jewish" Upper Galilee and the old city is an example of Arab "inferiority" which zealous official tour-guides do not hesitate to make clear to the innocents abroad in the "Holy Land."

Despite this built-in bias, which is consistent with the Covenant and the Status Law's commitment to "ingather the exiles," the state is failing in the attainment of its "central task." Emigration—not immigration—figures are at a peak. In August of 1980, *Yediot Aharanot*, a popular Israeli newspaper, reported that there are "100,000 Israeli passport holders living in Los Angeles, California alone." "A senior consular official" of Israel in that city complained because 2,000 emigres arrive "each month."[25] And an Associated Press story, datelined Tel Aviv, reported in December that,

> Jewish immigration, a cornerstone of Israel's existence, has fallen to the lowest level in 12 years and the number of Jews leaving Israel is on the increase.[26]

The same report noted the official figures of the Ministry of Immigration revealed that 22,000 immigrants "are expected this year, 1980," compared with "37,200 in 1979."

A lengthy article in *Ma'ariv*, usually considered to be Israel's most conservative newspaper, and perhaps the most widely read, on September 10, inventoried some of the benefits offered "Olim" (Jewish immigrants) in an effort to increase *Jewish* immigration. For example:

> While Israeli Arabs are unemployed or consigned mostly to menial, low-paid jobs if they are not self-employed, the wages of "post-graduate Olim" are supplemented "up to 90% of the average wage in the market." This benefit from Zionist/government funds is assured for a year after entry and "in most cases is continued for five years or more." The bonus is consistent with Paragraph 4 of the Status Law which specifies that "absorption of immigrants from the Diaspora" is one of the functions for which the government recognizes the World Zionist Organization as "the authorized agency."

The same *Ma'ariv* article reports housing benefits held out as bait for new immigrants. Israeli Arabs, concentrated in villages for the most part and barred from buying, leasing or renting property on some 85% of Israeli land,[27] generally suffer with sub-standard housing, few utilities and excessive rents. But Amidor, "the Israeli government company" providing "housing services under the Housing Ministry," has many "goodies" for Olim. A Tel Aviv "flat" which an Oleh may rent for "1,820 Israeli pounds a month" would bring 6,000 pounds on "the market."[28]

> Those who rent a flat through the free market enjoy a subsidy from the Absorption Ministry up to 80% for five years.
> . . . There are thousands of empty flats *waiting for Olim* in various development towns, among them, Beit Shean, Upper Nazareth, Kiriyat Shimona, Dimona, Ashdod. . . . (Emphasis supplied).

The *Ma'ariv* article lists other inducements provided Olim by the co-ordinated Zionist Organization/government subsidies to attract the "exiles."

It is probably small comfort to the Israeli Arabs that many long-time Jewish nationals of Israel are complaining about the high priority assigned to immigration. Whether or not they fully comprehend, they are complaining against a basic commitment of a state which regards "the Jewish people"—and not only the Jews of Israel and certainly not the "non-Jewish people" Israelis—to be its national constituency. And the Zionist state has solemnly declared in its "fundamental law" that redemption of "the Jewish people" from "exile" is its "central task."

In a monograph published in 1969, Jiryis detailed other examples of Zionist discrimination against Israeli Arabs during the years 1948-1966.[29] All involved Zionist Organization/governmental decisions in the allocation of the funds coordinated according to the Status Law for the purpose of encouraging immigration of Jews and their absorption into the Zionist society. Among these were:

> Failure to extend electricity lines to Arab villages. Failure to provide post offices to most Arab villages, while some Arab villages, including Bedouin encampments have no postal service whatsoever. Only one quarter of all Arab villages had telephone service. Health services inferior to those provided Jews.

Jiryis summarized the 1966 situation as follows:

> A comparison between the services provided to Arabs and Jews shows how great the discrimination has been. Arab standards approach those of Jews only in the case of prison services; there are many more Arab prisoners than Jewish prisoners.

In the more complete study, published in 1976, Jiryis admits some improvements had been made for some Arabs in some of these services. But the fundamental disparity remains. Jiryis concludes the later volume, saying:

A basic fact that emerges from a study of the history of the last quarter of a century is that the Arab in Israel has been and continues to be a "different" citizen,"non-Jewish," belonging to the goyim and excluded from the rights enjoyed by Jewish citizens. This distinction, which affects every aspect of Arab life, has been *officially implemented* from the establishment of Israel to the present.[30] (Emphasis supplied)

The Zionist state, in other words, consistently puts a higher national interest priority on absorption of "the Jewish people"—those who have already come from a wide disparity of national backgrounds as well as those still to be recruited from "exile"—than upon equality for the "non-Jewish people" nationals who remained in the state after 1948-49. And this "central task" of the Zionist Organization/government combine is certainly rated a higher national priority than the inalienable right of any of the displaced Palestinians, now scattered among many nations in enforced "exile." Jiryis sees this declared central purpose of the Zionist state as a major factor which has

helped to keep the Palestine problem alive both inside and outside Israel. The Palestine question seems to have returned to its point of origin, proving to the Arabs in Israel that their problems cannot be solved until the case of Palestine as a whole is resolved.[31]

VIII. The Source of Conflict

However disappointing to the Camp David followers, that conclusion is inescapable. They persist in attempting to find "security" for the Zionist state and peace in the Middle East by Israeli withdrawal from Sinai, in an Egyptian agreement to sell Israel oil, in superficial cultural exchanges between Egypt and Israel, and in formulas for Palestinian "autonomy" which are insulting to Palestinian national dignity and self-consciousness. What many Camp David advocates are not admitting—perhaps not seeing—is that anything less than a comprehensive peace, including the right of the Palestinian nation to an independent state of its own, is also to invite increasing disorder instead of security for the Zionist state.

Given the legislated commitment of the state of Israel to the fundamental concept of primacy for Zionism's "Jewish people" nationality, there is no way the state can implement human rights in any of the commonly accepted definitions of the term. And violence inexorably follows violations of human rights if the consequent injustices are not eradicated by peaceful processes and established by law. When the deprived victims are of one ethnic group, with familial and national or ethnic ties to neighbouring states, the violence has great potential for internationalization. Conceptually, this is the kernel of the Zionist/Palestinian/Israeli/Arab conflict.

It is a sad commentary that for more than sixty years, the reputed statesmen of the world have either accepted—or appeared to accept—at face value the standard Zionist apologetics offered to justify Israel's Zionist commitment for any given period of its history. The most prevalent excuse today attributes Israel's aggressive exclusivism to the state's necessity for both internal and external security. But history supplies abundant evidence to the contrary. Nationalist territorial Zionism's dehumanizing of Arabs has *not* been in response to or defense against Arab inhumanity to Jews. The accurate statement of the equation is quite the other way around. It has been the sometimes gradualist, sometimes cataclysmic translation into practice of Zionism's ideology which has generated Arab hostility. Arabs are humans, capable of rational thought and the determination of self-interest. It follows that the declared source of their sustained hostility is no mere political rationalization to disguise sinister designs or to make some inherent racial or religious prejudice appear more palatable, Nor was the sixty-year old conflict originally spawned and later nourished by disagreements over merely territory or about the possible demographic mix of "Arabs" and "Jews" in what might have been an independent Palestinian state. *The source of conflict was always Zionism.* There was Arab resistance to Zionist aggression from the earliest days of the Zionist Organization's implementation plans when the majority population was "Arab," and there was no dispute about territory as such. The now generally recognized failure of the so-called Camp David "Framework" can be attributed essentially to the fact that it proceeded on the superficial assumption that only issues of politics or territory, somewhat complicated perhaps, but only politics and territory were involved. *No* formula has ever worked peace in Palestine. From the very beginning—starting with the first Zionist Commission which went to Palestine even before the Mandate legitimized the Balfour Declaration—all formulas have failed because of Zionism's insistence upon its hard-core racist and/or theocratic yardsticks to determine full participation in the society which Zionism contemplated.

Unless this is understood, a "peace" formula which might otherwise be regarded to offer rationally acceptable compromises on territory or on a form of Palestinian autonomy, may simply allow the paranoid abnormal ideology of Zionism to seep into crevices instead of being heavy-handedly imposed in the style of Mr. Begin. A specific, current example is the *apparently* innocent demand that "Jews" be permitted to trade in land and reside in the West Bank. Zionists want the world to believe this demand represents only a simple problem of human rights in which an individual's religious faith should create no social or political disabilities. But such simplicity is not the whole truth. The rest of the truth is that the appellant making this demand is the very one which declares every Jew is a constituent of "the Jewish people," possessing nationality rights in and owing nationality obligations to the Zionist state. Even in ideal conditions of peace, no state is legally or morally obligated to accept inhabitants who are presumed to have such operative foreign attachments. The objectionable character of the demand is aggravated when those foreign attachments are saturated with an ideology as xenophobic, as paranoid, as racially or theocratically exclusivist as Zionism is today.

Menachem Begin is no Zionist edition of a Darwinian sport. He *is* authentic Zionism. If he had not won the election in 1977, he would have surfaced sooner or later. If he had not existed, the dynamics of the movement would have created him. There has not been an American president—and perhaps no statesman of other nationality—who has not needed to be told that this ideology, with its built-in paranoia and inherent anti-Arab commitment, is at the root of Arab inability to make further compromises about either territory or the "inalienable rights" of the Palestinians. Statesmen and diplomats of all kinds have needed—and still need—to be impressed with both the character of this ideology and its central role in determining Israeli policies. Only one American Secretary of State ever approached an exposition of the obstacle to Middle East peace which is inherent in Zionist ideology. When John Foster Dulles returned from the Middle East in 1953, he advised the American people "the Arabs fear Zionism more than Communism." His Assistant Secretary, Henry Byroade, expanded on the idea in two statements which are unique in all the official American rhetoric and among declarations by authorities of other nations. Byroade advised Israel to become a Middle Eastern state and to "cease regarding itself the center or nucleus of a world wide grouping of people of one religious faith." The savagery of the Zionist/Israeli attack on Byroade measured how close he came to the raw nerve of the indefensible ideology of the Zionist state. Anti-Zionists applauded the effort to distinguish between a normal Israel and a Zionist Israel.

Nor, judging by the available records, have "Arab" statesmen or diplomats competently and consistently informed the world of the dimensions of the obstacle to peace which Zionist ideology presents. Perhaps because they have been most egregiously injured by Zionism, some Palestinian spokesmen have addressed the issue. In an authoritative article in the *Journal of Palestine Studies*,[32] Sabri Jiryis, who is also a member of the PLO National Council, candidly wrote:

> The Palestinians may, in certain circumstances, be ready to seek a settlement in the area to which Israel is a party. But they are not prepared to conclude an agreement recognizing the legitimacy of Zionism; no Palestinian Arab can ever accept as *legitimate* a doctrine that he should be excluded from most parts of his homeland, because he is a Christian or Muslim Arab, while anyone of the Jewish faith anywhere in the world is entitled to settle there. Realism may require recognition of the existence of a Jewish state in Palestine and that this fact be taken into account in seeking a settlement. But this can never mean approving the expansionist and exclusivist tendencies of Zionism.

IX. "Twas Ever Thus"

The constancy of Zionist ideology as the ultimate fermentation-agent of Israel policy is illustrated in recently published English translations of parts of Moshe Sharett's diaries. Moshe Sharett was Israel's first Foreign Minister and, for a brief period, its Prime Minister. He was regarded as a "dove" by many innocents in the days when Ben Gurion was considered the number one hawk. But the diaries dispute this theory. Sharett's objectives were essentially the same as those of the flamboyant Ben Gurion. Sharett simply favored different, more gradual, more subtle tactics. He filled diaries with agonizing and indecision as well as with reflections of his reluctance to engage in public debate with the charismatic first Prime Minister. The time is 1955. The setting is that the United States is still interested in cultivating Abdel Nasser's friendship. The United States was prepared to offer Israel a security guarantee coupled with an attempt to persuade Nasser to make peace.

On August 14, Nasser indicated he was interested in "normalizing relations with Israel." In other words, conditions were favourable for a settlement. But the Zionist ideologues did not wish a settlement. An important consideration in the sequence of events is that the Israeli population was enjoying a growing sense of prosperity and security. This did not suit the Zionist ideologues who believed the people's teeth should be set on edge so that when the opportunity came, the country might be ready for Israel's next move to expand. The immediate territorial target was Gaza. The political objective was to disrupt the growing rapport between the United States and Nasser. Sharett's diary, for May 26, 1955, records the thinking of some of those who orchestrated Israeli attitudes and also influenced world opinion. The principal spokesman for the opponents of the possible peace was Dayan. And the diary reports

> We do not need (Dayan said) a security pact with the United States. Such a pact will only constitute an obstacle for us. We face no danger at all of an Arab advantage of force for the next 8-10 years. Even if they receive massive military aid from the West, we shall maintain our military superiority thanks to an infinitely greater capacity to assimilate new armaments. The security pact will only handcuff us and deny us freedom of action, and this is what we need in the coming years. Reprisal raids which we couldn't carry out if we were tied to a security pact are our vital lymph. First (the reprisal raids) make it imperative for the Arab governments to take strong measures to protect the borders. Second, and that's the main thing, they make it possible for us to maintain a high level of tension among our population and the army. Without these actions we would cease to be a combative people and without the discipline of a combative people we are lost. . . . We have to cry out that the Negev is in danger so that angry men will go there.

Sharett then adds his own comments:

> The conclusions from Dayan's words are clear: This state has no international worries, no economic problems. The question of peace is nonexistent. It must calculate its steps narrow-mindedly and live on its sword. It must see the sword as the main, if not the only instrument with which to keep its morale high and to retain its moral tension. Towards this end it may, no—it *must*— invent dangers and to do this it must adopt the method of provocation and revenge. . . And above all—let us hope for a new war with the Arab countries so that we may finally get rid of our troubles and acquire our space. . . . Ben Gurion himself said it would be worth while to pay an Arab a million pounds to start a war.[33]

The eternal, Zionist dialectic again! If the people are not obsessed with fear, create conditions to frighten them. If there are no visible enemies—create them! Ignore any hand outstretched in friendship, for the friendship can dissolve the ideology. The analogy to recent Israeli conduct is obvious. Conventional compromises of the conventional issues of peace will achieve nothing more than another precarious armistice. Arabs were the victims of Zionism before there was Zionist sovereignty over territory and before law, canonized in the Zionist state, formalized Zionism's racism into Israeli nationalism. Arabs know best in all the world the essence of this bitter conflict. But they have been unable, or unwilling, to articulate their concern and to identify this parochial, Zionist ideology as the malignancy metastasizing into every one of the more ephemeral issues and making them unresponsive to normal, diplomatic treatment.

This Arab failure, plus the resistance of western "statesmen," refusing to hear or see for political reasons, plus the persistence, inventiveness and opportunism of Zionist/Israeli propaganda have produced in much of the world a one-dimensional judgment of the Arab/Palestinian/Israeli/ Zionist conflict. In the west, most of what the average citizen knows about "Arabs" he knows from Zionist, or Zionist-indoctrinated sources. It is symbolic of the false dilemma into which this knot-hole vision of the conflict has directed the world that the Palestinian aspiration of a democratic, secular, unitary state is commonly viewed with trepidation, if not outright abhorrence. The unspoken reason, of course, is not that Jews would be exterminated or "driven into the sea." The reason is that such a state would exorcise Zionism and its synthetic "Jewish people" nationality together with its expansionist, extra-territorial claims to part (or under Begin, all) of Palestine. That the democratization of any society and the elimination of extra-territorialism are regarded generally as desirable attainments in normal international relations never seems to trouble the myopic supporters of Zionist/Israel.

There are a few lines in Orwell's *1984* which are suggestive of the process which has produced this "doublethink" on so ubiquitous a scale.

> "Don't you see that the whole aim of Newspeak is to narrow the range of thought?", one of the technocrats serving Big Brother asks of a colleague. In the end we shall make thought-crime impossible, because there will be no words in which to express it. Every concept that can ever be needed will be expressed by exactly *one* word, with its meaning rigidly defined and all its subsidiary meanings rubbed out and forgotten. . . . Every year fewer and fewer words, and the range of consciousness always a little smaller . . . the Revolution will be complete when the language is perfect. . . . By the year 2050 . . . not a single human being will be alive who could understand such a conversation as we are having now.

That rather accurately describes what Zionist propaganda has done— at least in the western world—over the last half century. Paradoxically, this ethno-centered, exclusivist, aggressive ideology has been widely accepted as a benevolent, liberating, progressive phenomenon. Not until its true character is fully understood and the wider horizons of the human dimensions of the total confrontation with "the Arabs" are adequately perceived, will the ever "smaller range of consciousness" be replaced with the elevated vision needed to create the so far elusive but eminently desirable "just and enduring peace."

NOTES

1. "The World Zionist Organization/Jewish Agency for Israel (Status) Law," enacted by the Knesset in 1952 and a "Covenant" between the Zionist Organization and the government adopted in 1954. Both of these political/ national instruments are analyzed in this pamphlet.
2. Jakob J. Petuchowski, *Zion Reconsidered*, Twayne Publishers, Inc., N.Y. 1966, p. 41. Dr. Petuchowski's book is a thorough analysis of the differences between Theodor Herzl's state/political/territorial Zionism and the traditional Zion of orthodox Judaism. For a briefer analysis of the same subject, see Elmer Berger, *Prophecy, Zionism and the State of Israel*, American Jewish Alternatives to Zionism, 501 Fifth Avenue, #2015, N.Y. 10017. The pamphlet is available upon request.
3. Jack G. Shaheen, "The Arab Sterotype on Television". *The Link*, Americans for Middle East Understanding, 475 Riverside Drive, N.Y. 10027, Room 771. April/May 1980, Vol. 13, No. 2. For additional information about distortions of the Arab image in the media, contact American-Arab Anti-Discrimination Committee, 4201 Connecticut Ave. N.W. Suite 500, Washington, D.C. 20008.
4. Chaim Weizmann,*Trial and Error: The Autobiography of Chaim Weizmann*, 1949, Harper & Brothers, p. 208.
5. For substantiation of the statements made in these paragraphs, see, "The Legal Problems Concerning the Juridical Status and Political Activities of the Zionist Organization/Jewish Agency: A study in International and United States Law", W. T. Mallison, Jr., *William and Mary Law Review*. Vol. 9, Spring, 1968, No. 2 pp. 556-629. Professor of International Law, The George Washington University, Washington, D.C.
6. *Ibid*. p. 608.
7. Joseph Badi, Ed., *Fundamental Laws of the State of Israel*, Twayne Publishers, N.Y. 1961, p. 285.
8. It is curious how often in Zionist history the definite article "the" has played an important political/legal role. The Balfour Declaration, for example, referred to "*a* national home for the Jewish people". The generally accepted version of Resolution 242 omitted the definite article before the language, "territories occupied in the recent conflict". The result of the deliberate use of "a" instead of "the" in the Balfour Declaration was an interminable debate about whether the "national home" was to be considered a repository of Zionist rights and obligations for *all* Jews or simply one collectivity of Jews among many, in many other nations, with Palestinian nationality attachments limited only to those Jews who opted for Palestinian citizenship. The deliberate omission of the "the" in Resolution 242 has been the source

of continuing debate as to whether Israeli military forces are required by the resolution to withdraw from *all* territories occupied in 1967 or whether the extent of required withdrawal is negotiable. The deliberate Zionist use of "the" before "Jewish people" is intended to imply clearly that all Jews are constituents of *one* entity which is to be invested with the political/territorial/national rights which are the essence of Zionism. Few statesmen and almost no commentators or media personalities make the distinction.

9. Nahum Sokolow , *History of Zionism*, Longmans, Green & Co., London, England, 1919, Vol. 1, p. 268. For a detailed examination of the legal and political steps taken by the Zionist movement to establish the concept of "Jewish people" nationality in international law, see W. T. Mallison, Jr.,"The Zionist—Israel Juridical Claims to Constitute 'the Jewish people' Nationality Entity and to Confer Membership in It: Appraisal in Public International Law", *The George Washington Law Review*, Vol. 32—June, 1964—November 5, Washington, D.C., pp. 983f. See also, Elmer Berger, *The Jewish Dilemma*, Devin Adair, N.Y., 1945, pp. 71ff.

10. *Chaim Weizmann*: Tribute in Honour of His Seventieth Birthday. Ed. Paul Goodman, Victor Gollancz, Ltd., London, 1945, p. 179.

11. *The Jewish Yearbook of International Law*, 1948, Rubin Mass, Jerusalem, 1949, p. 18.

12. *Ibid.*, p. 40.

13. Raphael Patai, *The Jewish Mind*, Charles Scribner's Sons, N.Y. 1977, pp. 22;23.

14. *Op. cit. Jewish Yearbook of International Law*, p.

15. *The New York Times*, November 17, 1980, p. 19.

16. *Op. cit. Fundamental Laws of the State Of Israel*, p. 285.

17. *Monthly Review Press*, New York and London, 1976. See particularly pp. 161ff.

18. *Ibid*: p. 216.

19. *Monthly Review Press*, New York and London, 1976, p. XII. Precise figures for Zionist contributions to the state are difficult to obtain on a current basis. *The Israel Yearbook*, (1978), contains an article, "Thirty Years of Achievement" by the Treasurer of the Jewish Agency, Arye L. Dulzin. (pp. 43-53).
"In the past 30 years . . . the Jews of the world, through the campaigns of the United Jewish Appeal in the United States and the Keren Hayesod in 62 other nations have contributed . . . over 5.7 billion dollars."

20. "Northern District" is essentially the Galilee. The report is unofficially known as "The Koenig Plan", after Israel Koenig, the Commissioner of the district. The report was supposed to have been "secret", but was leaked to the press in Israel. The complete text, in translation, has been published in a pamphlet, "Palaces of Injustice", Americans for Middle East Understanding, Room 771, 475 Riverside Drive, N.Y. 10027. Available on request.

21. *Ibid*: p. 11.

22. *Ibid*: p. 13.

23. For details see, *The Non-Jew in the Jewish State*, p. 73. This is a collection of articles published in the Israel press, edited and prepared and privately distributed in translation, by Dr. Israel Shahak, 2 Bartenura Street, Jerusalem, Israel. Dr. Shahak is Professor of Chemistry at the Hebrew University.

24. *Ibid*: p. 74.

25. "America: The Golden Ghetto", *Yediot Aharanot*, August 29, 1980. Translated and published in *Israeli Mirror*, Suni News Service, 21 Collingham Rd., London, England, No. 526, November 4, 1980.
26. *Associated Press*, "Movement of Jews to Israel is Down", *Sarasota Herald-Tribune*, Sarasota, Florida, December 16, 1980, p. 4-A.
27. Uri Davis and Walter Lehn, "And the Fund Still Lives", *Journal of Palestine Studies*, The Institute for Palestine Studies and Kuwait University, P.O. Box 11-7169 Beirut, Lebanon, Vol. VII, No. 4, Summer, 1978, p. 23.
28. At the present writing the Israeli pound is equal to 2-3 cents of American money, with an inflation rate of 135% per annum.
29. Sabri Jiryis, *The Arabs in Israel*, 1948-1966, The Institute for Palestine Studies, Ashqar Bldg. Clemenceau St., Beirut, Lebanon, p. 172ff. This monograph should not be confused with the more complete survey of the same title, published later and cited below.
30. Sabri Jiryis, *The Arabs in Israel*, Monthly Review Press, N.Y., 1976, p. 235.
31. *Ibid*. p. 239.
32. Sabri Jiryis, "Political Settlement in the Middle East", *Journal of Palestine Studies*, P.O. Box 11-7164, Beirut, Autumn, 1977, Vol. VII, No. 1, pp. 3-25.
33. Livia Rokach, *Israel's Sacred Terrorism*, A Study Based on Moshe Sharett's "Personal Diary" and Other Documents, Association of Arab-American University Graduates, Inc., Belmont, Massachusetts, 1980, P.O. Box 456, Turnpike Station, Shrewsbury, Massachusetts, 01545, p. 44.

2

ANTI-ZIONISM: A DEMOCRATIC ALTERNATIVE

NASEER H. ARURI

Zionism emerged and took shape under the influence of 19th century European nationalism and colonialism. It endeavored to establish a Jewish state by colonizing a territory away from Europe. While there is abundant literature on the similarities between Zionism and colonialism, there is hardly any work which examines the relationship between anti-Zionism and anti-colonialism. If Zionism was the product of the same milieu which generated regressive ideological movements, then can it be said that anti-Zionism was an integral part of the world-wide movement of opposition to colonialism? Correspondingly, if Zionism is regressive, oppressive, segregationist, exploitative, then can we say that anti-Zionism is progressive, integrationist, pluralistic, egalitarian, liberationist, and humanistic? If *herrenvolk* democracy is the logical outcome of Zionist colonization, then is genuine democracy likely to be the product of anti-Zionism?

To answer these questions, it is necessary to examine the writings of anti-Zionists during the past century. The available literature of anti-Zionism reflects a diversity of perspectives, methods of struggle and proposed solutions to the Jewish question as well as to the Palestine/Israel conflict. The writings bear the influence of the environment, of the time, and the realities of international politics. But, while anti-Zionism is not monolithic, it is not without a common denominator. Its opposition to the establishment of an exclusive Jewish state with its supra-nationality claim, and its insistence on de-Zionization as the means to co-existence, assert its identity and substantiate its coherence as a philosophy and a vision. Within this broad framework, two major trends of anti-Zionism may be discerned. The first is rooted in a largely non-ideological humanist democratic tradition. The second falls between the ideological and the semi-ideological. It is based on a socio-political analysis of the context in which Zionism has grown and culminated in the state of Israel. It is reconstructionist in that a thorough-going transformation of Israeli society is seen as the only viable alternative to the present system, which is deemed to bear the seed of its own destruction.

Despite the divisions of anti-Zionist writings into two broad groups, the demarcation lines which separate them are generally but not strictly drawn. Yet, the distinctions are sufficiently clear to justify the categorization. In as much as Zionism was seen as a Jewish problem, most of the critiques of Zionism in these categories belonged inevitably to Jewish writers and political leaders. Anti-Zionists had to diagnose the disease, prescribe remedies, and identify alternatives. This study will address the various trends within the anti-Zionist movement, and make an assessment of its responses and the extent to which they coalesced on the democratic-humanist alternative. The thrust of this essay then, will be the contributions of anti-Zionism to a democratic-humanist philosophy. Given that the definitions of democracy abound, the concept will be viewed simply in terms of such notions as the equal protection of the law, equal worth and equal dignity; open, pluralistic, non-racist institutions, and a liberationist environment.

Anti-Zionism is a positive concept despite the "anti"; in fact, since Zionism itself is a negative ideology, the two negatives in the term "anti-Zionism" translate into affirmation. It proposes to cure the ills of Zionism, which was in essence the offspring of negative movements, ideologies, outlooks and practices, which belong to the 19th century. German nationalism with its emphasis on the Fatherland, blood and manifest destiny equipped Zionism with much of its ideological arsenal.[1] The resurgence of European colonial imperialism in the late 19th century served as an incubator for the state of Israel, while Orientalism, the concept of the white man's burden, and apartheid offered inspiration, theoretical guidance and concrete models. For example, the colonial character of the Zionist movement was freely admitted by Zionists; in fact, the first society established in 1861 in Frankfurt-an-der-Oder was named the "Society for the Colonization of the Land of Israel."[2] The Twelfth Zionist Congress set up a "Colonization Department"; the villages established by Zionist settlers in Palestine were called "colonies," and the term Yishuv itself, denoting the entire body of Jews in Palestine, meant "settlement." Chaim Weizmann compared his experience with that of the French 'colons' in Tunisia when he referred to a conversation with Lord Cecil:

> I ventured the opinion that the Zionist Organization had—even then—done more constructive work in Palestine than the French in Tunisia.[3]

And when Herzl was trying to secure Bismarck's blessings for the Zionist project in Palestine, he wrote: "Who will dare to call my plan a pretty dream after the greatest living empire builder has stamped his approval on it"?[4] Cecil Rhodes was another role model and source of inspiration for the father of Zionism, who appealed for his help:

> I need you . . . you are being invited to help make history . . . it is not in your accustomed line; it doesn't involve Africa, but a piece of Asia Minor, not Englishmen, but Jews. But had this been on your path, you would have done it by now. . . . How then do I happen to turn to you, since this is an out of the way matter for you? How indeed? Because it is something colonial.[5]

Zionism was thus firmly grounded in the negative ideologies of late 19th century Europe, a fact that became a source of concern to Jewish leaders who had to ponder its effect on Jewish values, traditions and behaviors, as well as on the Palestinian Arabs and the areas surrounding Palestine.

That concern began to grow as the Zionist movement ignored the existence of the native Palestinian, declared the people non-people and proclaimed their land "empty," in accordance with the applied deformities of 19th century European scientific achievements to the Asian and African continents. Achad Ha'-Am, who was committed to the establishment of Jewish colonies in Palestine, exemplifies that concern. For him, a "return to Zion" was to be seen in the context of developing "a cultural life of Jewry and the spiritual regeneration of Judaism." [6] He cautioned against "national egoism" [7] and was troubled by the violations of the rights of the Palestinians and the impact of these violations on the moral fabric of the Jewish community. Referring to his brethren's transgressions, he wrote in 1891:

> Serfs they were in the land of the diaspora, and suddenly they find themselves in unrestricted freedom, and this change has awakened in them an inclination to despotism. They treat the Arabs with hostility and cruelty, deprive them of their rights, offend them without cause and even boast of these deeds; and nobody among us opposes this despicable and dangerous inclination.[8]

Twenty-two years later, after witnessing the unfolding of the scheme to conquer the land and labor, he wrote protesting the boycott of Arab labor:

> Apart from the political danger, I can't put up with the idea that our brethren are morally capable of behaving in such a way to humans of another people, and unwittingly the thought comes to my mind: if it is so now, what will be our relation to the others if in truth we shall achieve at the end of times power in Eretz Israel? And if this be the "Messiah": I do not wish to see his coming.[9]

He died in 1927, a disappointed man with a broken heart, outraged by the cycle of violence which the Zionism that he supported had introduced:

> My God, is *this* the end? . . . Is this the dream of our return to Zion, that we come to Zion and stain its soil with innocent blood? It has been an axiom in my eyes that the people will sacrifice its money for the sake of a state, but never its prophets. . . .[10]

In 1951, long before the rule of Menachem Begin and Ariel Sharon, Hans Kohn wrote that Achad Ha'-Am "might have felt today even lonelier among the Zionists than he did during his lifetime."[11] The irony of all this was that Achad Ha'-Am was a Zionist, a nationalist writing his indictments of Zionism in the 1920s, not in the 1980s when Zionism became more fundamentalist, chauvinist and expansionist. Despite the fact that he was a Jewish nationalist in the modern political sense of the word, he nevertheless "reflected the Jewish state as an immediate object of national policy"[12] and did not cherish the prospect of Jewish resources and energies being directed towards the creation "of a little state which would again become a football of its strong neighbors. . . ."[13] The "return to Zion" which he had sought was not an end in itself; rather, a means to "rekindle the spiritual heritage and the ethical traditions of Judaism"[14] to create a Jewish cultural renaissance. He disagreed vehemently with the "return" scheme of the First Zionist Congress:

> In Basel, yesterday, I sat lonely among my brothers, like a mourner at a wedding. . . . This new enthusiasm is an artificial one, and the result of treacherous hopes will be despair. . . . The salvation of Israel will come through prophets, not through diplomats![15]

Achad Ha'-Am's attitude toward the Palestinian Arabs, while different from that of the anti-Zionist, expressed the benevolence of conquerors, but also exhibited some commitment to co-existence and mutual respect. While emphasizing Jewish "historical rights" in Palestine, he recognized that for Palestinian Arabs "too, the country is a national home." According to Hans Kahan, neither community was viewed by the "agnostic Rabbi" as having exclusive rights:

> If you build your house not in an empty space, but in a place where there are also other houses and inhabitants, you are an unrestricted master only inside your own house. Outside the door, all the inhabitants are partners, and the management of the whole has to be directed in agreement with the interests of them all.[16]

Anti-Zionism and the Democratic Humanist Tradition

Humanist anti-Zionism has its roots in a tradition of universalism, which had a deep antipathy to chauvinistic nationalism. Jewish anti-Zionist writers who fell in this category were imbued with a spirit of openness, which reflected a commitment to a common humanity and pluralist existence. One can easily detect across the spectrum a trace of Gandhism, a trace of Quakerism, a broadly socialist line. A secular approach intermeshed with spirituality, which is more akin to liberation theology than to conventional religiosity, can be discerned in the contributions of Jewish humanists. Their world outlook was decidedly universalist and integrationist, in the broad sense of the term, where common aspirations and common destinies preceded particularistic concerns and tribalistic sentiments. To most of them, the Jewish people constituted a community but not a Jewish nation. "I recognize the sense of community among Jews; I reject the ethnic basis of Jewish life," wrote Morris Lazaron in the *Atlantic Monthly* in 1944.[17] There was a strong indictment of this nationalism with German rather than French antecedents in their writings. They shunned ghettoism and recognized the kinship between Zionism and its presumed protagonist, anti-semitism. The alternative to a world full of these regressive, reactionary, and dehumanizing instruments of retardation was an open society in Palestine or elsewhere, based on the ideal of freedom, of civil and political liberty, the free flow of ideas as well as the unrestricted movement of people and mixture of races.

One variant of humanist democratic anti-Zionism which addressed the Jewish question called for a secular, fully-integrated, liberal existence. Two Jewish immigrants to America from eastern Europe exemplified this trend, Rabbi Isaac Wise (1819–1900), and Professor Morris Cohen (1880–1947). Unlike Achad Ha'-Am, a nationalist in his own way, Rabbi Wise held that Judaism was a religion, not a nationality. Outside the synagogue, Jews were to be fully integrated exactly like other Americans. Of the First Zionist Congress and Theodor Herzl, Rabbi Wise said quite bluntly:

> The false Messiah who appeared from time to time among the dispersed and suffering remnants of Judah, had no religious purpose in view; all of them were political demagogues, or patriotic fantasts, with as much religious zeal as was deemed requisite to agitate the Jewish mind and to win the goodwill of the masses and its leaders for the proposed political end, which was the restoration of the Jewish nationality and the *conquest of Palestine*.[18]

Wise's alternative outlet for Jewish energies in the United States instead was the path of integration. That required renouncing past political allegiances and becoming a fully equal member of the American nation.

Professor Morris Cohen viewed Zionism as a nationalist philosophy, inherently dangerous to liberalism. Irrespective of the motives for the "return to Zion," religious or political, the final outcome was far from worthy. They were all rationalizations of a flawed proposition: that Jews are inassimilable, either because they are a peculiarly gifted oriental people or because they are like all other people who have a home of their own, hence their need for a home too. Such opposition to assimilation "would make the salvation of Jews, as well as non-Jews, depend on general enlightenment."[19]

Cohen pursued complete individual liberty for Jews and non-Jews alike. But he wrote that nationalistic Zionism demands not complete freedom for the Jews, but group autonomy, and it was in the latter concept where he perceived the malaise. Not only was it incompatible with "Americanism," but it was also the cornerstone of a chauvinistic and a closed society. It infringed on the freedom of religion, in as much as it denied the right of a person born a Jew to abandon the religion and fall on the dictates of his/her own conscience. The end result of Zionism, whether in the diaspora or in Palestine, was ghettoism:

> Indeed, how could a Jewish Palestine allow complete religious freedom of intermarriage, and face non-Jewish immigration, without soon losing its very reason for existence? A national Jewish Palestine must necessarily mean a state founded on a peculiar race, a tribal religion, and a mystic belief in a peculiar soil, whereas liberal America has traditionally stood for separation of church and state, the free mixture of races, and the fact that men can change their habitation and language and still advance the process of civilization.[20]

He dismissed the notion that Palestine was the unique arena from which Jews can contribute to civilization or fulfill their lives in accordance with Jewish tradition. "There is not a single opportunity offered by Palestine that is not open, to a larger extent, in America,"[21] he wrote. The nightmare of Zionism, in that regard, was its fear of "America's ideal of freedom," which, according to him, derived from a lack of confidence on the part of Zionists in the ability of Judaism to "hold its own in the open field."[22]

While Cohen's writings revealed admiration for the scientific achievements of Jews and horticultural innovations in Palestine, nevertheless these achievements "did not presuppose the establishment of a Jewish state."[23] In fact, he said that they may be extended in the future "within the framework of a non-sectarian state that allows equal rights to all Jews, Christians, Mohammedans, and atheists alike."[24] Here lies an explicit endorsement of what was to become the platform of the Palestinian national movement in the aftermath of the Arab-Israeli war of June 1967. If that compatibility is not exact in terms of the letter, it is so at least in spirit. Cohen wrote these words in 1946 as part of a disavowal of some views that have been falsely associated with his anti-Zionist stance. His explanation expressed a single standard of rights and an indictment of unreasonable classification based on religion or ethnicity:

> In the first place it should be made clear that one need not be a Zionist to protest against British laws and regulations which, in defiance of international compacts, deny to would-be immigrants the right to enter Palestine merely because they are Jews. Laws that discriminate against any creed are abhorrent to the conscience of liberal humanity, whether they are the Nuremberg Laws of Hitler, the British laws limiting Jewish immigration and land purchases in Palestine, or the United States immigration laws which make ancestry the test of admissibility to our shores. . . . Tribalism is a creed that leads to grief and massacre, whether it bears the label of Zionism, Aryanism, Anglo-Saxon America, or Pan-Islam.[25]

Whether or not Cohen anticipated Palestinian dispossession partly as a result of Jewish immigration to Palestine and land acquisition there, is a matter for speculation. He was obviously concerned whether the very concept of a Jewish state in Palestine would admit of the equality which was at the core of his philosophy. That state, which would be based on mystic ideas of 'Blood and Soil' may not allow a non-Jew to hold office, to become 'president of the Republic' or even to be included in the equality of the right to immigration:

> Certainly I could never bring myself to support efforts to establish a Jewish state which would not be in accord with the democratic principle of separation of church and state, and equality of civil, religious and economic rights to all inhabitants regardless of race and creed.[26]

Apparently, Cohen had no faith that a Jewish state, by its very definition, would be capable of guaranteeing such principles. He might have, in fact, anticipated the United Nations General Assembly resolution 2159 of 15 October 1975, which determined that "Zionism is a form of racism and racial discrimination."[27] Here is what he wrote about the racist character of Zionism in his book, *The Faith of A Liberal*:

> Zionists fundamentally accept the racial ideology of the anti-Semites, but draw different conclusions. Instead of the Teutons, it is the Jew that is the purer or superior race. All sorts of virtues, idealism, etc., are the characteristic qualities of its spirit. Only in Palestine can this spirit find root, and only in the Hebrew language its adequate expressions. The scientific adequacy of the ethnologic, historic, and philosophic evidence by which all this is supported, would be beneath contempt. . . . Nevertheless, these beliefs are radically false and profoundly inimical to liberal or humanistic civilization. History, and Jewish history, especially, shows that the claim to purity of race on the part of any civilized people is entirely mythical.[28]

Cohen adhered tenaciously to the idea of population mixtures and group communication as essential to the advancement of civilization. Cross fertilization of ideas and the synthesizing of an endless variety of concepts could only be promoted by an atmosphere of openness and complete tolerance:

> No great civilization could ever achieve, except by a mixed people freely borrowing from others in religion, language, laws, and manners. The Jews were such people when they produced the bulk of Biblical literature, and they certainly increased their contribution to civilization when they left Palestine and mixed with other people.[29]

Other Jewish figures shared Cohen's reservations about the anti-democratic and closed character of Zionism, and his sensitivity to its theoretical contradictions. They, consequently, envisaged alternative socio-political visions compatible with universal humanistic values.

Morris Jastrow warned the 1919 Paris Peace Conference against the 'reactionary' nature of political Zionism, and opposed a Jewish state in Palestine on the grounds that such an "anti-democratic" policy constituted a "plan of segregation."[30] Instead, he recommended a single pluralist state:

> The obvious form that the reconstruction of Palestine after the war should take on is the creation of a Palestine state based on *all* the nationalities there congregated, and not a Jewish state which, if it means anything at all, would place the emphasis on a state formed of a *single* nationality . . . the logic of the situation, therefore suggests that the remaining tenth of the Jews, who for one reason or the other, will desire to settle in Palestine, forming with the other a single political *entity* which would constitute the Palestine nation.[31]

The idea of a bi-national self-governing entity was also espoused by Judah Magnes and Brit Shalom (League of Peace), which he established to promote Arab-Jewish understanding. This was a cause which he continued to struggle for and died for, in New York in 1948, pleading for it with President Truman.

Judah Magnes described his formula as "political parity and numerical parity for the two nationalities."[32] He opposed partition on the grounds that it would mean "intensification of chauvinism on both sides."[33] He abhorred the regressive nationalism which was prevalent in 19th century-early 20th century Europe, and which gave rise to fascism, but he perceived the universalist value of liberation in Arab nationalism:

> I sympathize with Arab nationalism as I sympathize with every freedom seeking endeavor.[34]

After he resigned from the Zionist Organization in 1915, he wrote, "I have left the desire for the new shining secular nationalism. I want the international, the human."[35] He recorded his apprehension about the effect of political Zionism on the indigenous Palestinian Arabs in the following words:

> Will the Jews here [Palestine] in their efforts to create a political organism become devotees of brute force and militarism as were some of the late Hashmoneans? We seem to have thought of everything except the Arabs. . . . If we have a just cause, so have they. If promises were made to us, so were they made to the Arabs. If we love the land and have a historical connection with it, so too the Arabs. . . . If we wish to live in this living space, we must live with the Arabs, try to make peace with them. . . . We stand over against the great Arab democracies as interlopers. . . . We must look

for an entente cordiale. Not upon the basis of force and power, but upon that of human solidarity and understanding. . . . Is our nationality like that of all the nations, pagan, and based upon force and violence, or is it a spiritual nationality? The right of the Jew does not confer the right of political majority.[36]

Magnes worked together with Éugene Debs and Norman Thomas—the American Socialist leaders—with the American Civil Liberties Union, and other U.S. socialists and trade unionists. He was an anti-war activist, a humanist and anti-imperialist. He expressed his unhappiness with the Balfour Declaration, which he characterized as "imperialism's iniquitous gift to the Jewish people."[37]

The eminent scientist Albert Einstein was also an adherent to the idea of bi-nationalism, while he supported cultural Zionism. He recorded his opposition to the partition of Palestine in eloquent and unequivocal terms:

I should much rather see reasonable agreement with the Arabs on the basis of living together in peace than the creation of a Jewish state. Apart from practical considerations, my awareness of the essential nature of Judaism resists the idea of a Jewish state, with borders, an army, and a measure of temporal power, no matter how modest. I am afraid of the inner damage Judaism will sustain—especially from the development of a narrow nationalism within our own ranks, against which we have already had to fight strongly, even without a Jewish state. We are no longer the Jews of the Maccabee period. A return to a nation in the political sense of the word, would be equivalent to turning away from the spiritual-ization of our community which we owe to the genius of our prophets.[38]

Hans Kohn, the eminent historian and expert on nationalism, and Hannah Arendt, the renowned philosopher and historian, were also among the champions of bi-nationalism. According to Hans Kohn, Zion-ism grew out of German romanticism with its emphasis on the Father-land, destiny, blood, manifest destiny, chosen people, and the organic folk community. He considered that concept of folk nationhood based on "biological determinism" as incompatible with French nationalism and the spirit of the Enlightenment.[39] Moshe Menuhin wrote that Kohn made clear the "degeneration of political nationalism from a movement for the assertion of individual liberty and the rights of the citizen against his government . . . into degenerative, depraved, and predatory aggres-sive political nationalism."[40] This diagnosis of Zionism was undoubtedly a major factor influencing Kohn's support for Brit Shalom and its objective of bi-nationalism.

Similarly, Hannah Arendt saw Zionism, with its uncritical acceptance of German-inspired nationalism, as a philosophy which explains people "not in terms of political organizations, but in terms of biological superhuman personalities."[41] For her, Herzl was the epitome of the reactionary underdog who saw reality not in terms of differences in class structure, in political parties or movements, but in terms of unchanging and unchangeable bodies of people who showered hostility upon Jews. The world's political forces were separated into two categories in accordance with how they related to Jews. This Manichean outlook led the Zionists to seek and develop their own isolated organism—"inside the closed walls of a biological entity"—an entity destined to be closed and intolerant to non-Jews, perhaps not unlike the Puritan society in New England. Arendt reveals the parochial anti-liberationist character of Zionism in the negotiations carried out by Herzl, in which Jewish demands were unrelated to other events, trends, or the destinies of other people:

> Herzl was careful not to tie the claims for Jewish liberation to the claims of other peoples. He was even ready to profit by the minority troubles of the Turkish empire and he offered the rulers of that empire Jewish aid in coping with them.[42]

This Zionist collusion against the Armenian victims of Turkey was seen by Arendt as the logical outcome of Zionism's outlook on life. She makes a passionate appeal for abandoning that reality, which has become a nightmare and for moving in the direction of embracing a common humanity:

> Only when we come to feel ourselves part and parcel of a world in which we like everybody else, are engaged in a struggle against great and sometimes overwhelming odds . . . only when we recognize the human background against which recent events have taken place . . . only then will we be able to rid the world of its nightmarish quality. That quality . . . can inhibit all action and exclude us altogether from the human community.[43]

In addition to her concern about the effect of political Zionism on Jewish values and behavior, Arendt expressed concern about the adverse effect of the Zionist program on the lives of the indigenous Palestinian Arabs. Commenting on the resolutions adopted at the 1944 Convention of the American Zionist branch of the World Zionist Organization in Atlantic City, Hannah Arendt said the following:

... American Zionists from left to right adopted unanimously ... the demand for a 'free and democratic Jewish commonwealth ... [which] shall embrace the whole of Palestine, undivided and undiminished.' ... The Atlantic City Resolution goes even a step further than the Biltmore Program (1942), in which the Jewish minority has granted minority rights to the Arab majority. This time the Arabs were simply not mentioned in the resolution, which obviously leaves them the choice between voluntary emigration or second-class citizenship. It seems to admit that only opportunist reasons had previously prevented the Zionist movement from stating its final aims.[44]

The Germanic quality of Herzl's nationalism disturbed other Jewish writers, whose commitment to common plurality and democratic existence moved them to oppose Zionism. William Zuckerman expressed real apprehension in a 1934 article in the *Nation* that Zionism was heading towards fascism. He wrote that "Fascism is too glaring a fact of Jewish life for denials. . . . Jews . . . are stricken with the virus of fascism."[45] He perceived a Teutonic rather than an Italian origin for that fascism. As in Germany, the driving force was a "strong feeling of national wrong," and the source of recruitment was the "nationalistic youth." Even its forces, "like those of the Nazis, are also divided into storm troops (*Brith-Trumpeldor*) and bodyguards (Brith Chail)."[46] Zuckerman cautioned against the consequences of that emerging fascism:

> If Zionism shows itself as blind as German nationalism and, impelled by legitimate national grievances and economic despair, opens the door to fascism among Jews, the moral disintegration which will set in will not be less than that which led to the establishment of the Bronn Houses and concentration camps, the crime of Zionism will be even greater, for it has already the lesson of German nationalism before it, and there is no excuse for ignorance and blindness now. . . .[47]

Like Arendt, William Zuckerman was disturbed by the same nightmarish quality of Zionism, its isolationism, exclusiveness, and narcissistic ethnocentrism:

> These people come to Palestine not with the old idea of transforming their own lives, but with the idea of transforming the country to fit their old economy; not to escape from the ghetto, but to transplant it; not to build a new home on entirely new social foundations, but to resurrect the old one—the ideal of the middle class fascist the world over. . . . They come to Palestine not because of

any idealism . . . because that is the only country where they can have a fascism of their own. . . .[48]

The dangers of nationalism claimed the attention of other prominent Jewish writers like Maxime Rodinson and I.F. Stone. Rodinson pointed out the similarities between the assertions of Zionists and those of anti-Semites:

> But in the end, who is it that claims that the Jews are eternally rooted in their Jewishness, despite all the efforts of those who do not desire to belong to a Judaic religion or a Jewish people? Don't Zionists do this? Don't anti-Semites do it too? And who is it that affirms that the Jews are aliens in the countries outside Israel in which they live and that they must return to this, their only 'home-land'? Don't anti-Semites say it too? . . . Herzl, the founder of po-litical Zionism said this without embarrassment.[49]

But Rodinson distinguished between this kind of nationalism to which Zionism belongs and the liberating nationalism, which promotes inde-pendence and struggles against oppression. While Zionism achieved its principal objective—the creation of a Jewish state in Palestine—it did not, however, solve the "Jewish" problem, but aggravated and created another problem, the Palestine problem, and in turn "spread hatred of the Jews into the Arab countries where anti-Semitism was previously unkown".[50] Further dangers of this narrow nationalism were enumer-ated by Rodinson: The success of Zionism which created the Palestine problem "contributed to strengthening the most reactionary forces in the Arab countries . . . has afforded the imperialist powers myriad op-portunities to peddle their support and weaponry in the Middle East . . . enabled the most chauvinistic and retrograde orientations to gain ground . . . [and led to] a policy of preventive aggression abroad and discriminatory legislation at home . . . encouraging a racist and chauvinistic mentality that impels society down the road of social regres-sion." [51]

I.F. Stone expressed serious apprehension about the adverse effect of this narrow nationalism on Jewish values. He found its racist character and its glaring double standard particularly abhorrent:

> For Israel is creating a kind of moral schizophrenia in world Jewry. In the outside world, the welfare of Jewry depends on the main-tenance of secular, non-racial, pluralistic societies. In Israel, Jewry finds itself defending a society in which mixed marriages cannot be legalized, in which non-Jews have a lesser status than Jews, and in which the ideal is racist and exclusionist. Jews might fight else-

where for their very security and existence-against principles and practices they find themselves defending in Israel. Those from the outside world, even in their moments of greatest enthusiasm amid Israel's accomplishments, feel twinges of claustrophobia, not just geographical but spiritual. Those caught up in Prophetic fervor soon begin to feel that the light they hoped to see out of Zion is only that of another narrow nationalism. Such moments lead to a re-examination of Zionist ideology.[52]

Anti-Zionism: Plans of Reconstruction

In addition to the spiritual anti-Zionists, the integrationists and the anti-nationalists, there are others who are neither Marxists nor religious, who oppose Zionism simply on moral grounds, on whether it is right or wrong. There are also humanists whose opposition emphasizes the concepts of equality for every single human being.

It is generally conceded in their writings that the Palestinian Arabs have suffered a great historical injustice as a result of the creation of Israel, on Arab Palestinian territory, and that the state of Israel, as it is presently constituted, cannot allow redress. A just solution must, therefore, be based on the principle of equal rights for all inhabitants of Palestine-Israel, regardless of religion, race or date of arrival in the country. Only they have the right to determine the future of their country and shape its institutions. The existence of two identifiable communities, one Arab and one Jewish in Palestine, is recognized as a basic fact. Yet, it is agreed that one community must not oppress the other or deny it fundamental rights to life, liberty or property. Hence, a just solution will inevitably require a thoroughgoing transformation of the way by which Israeli Jews live and organize their society. This transformation requires a qualitative change in that society and involves a basic revision of the manner by which values are allocated, including the abandonment of those values and institutions which violate the principle of equal protection of the law.

We shall refer to this category as "reconstructionist," in view of the imperative to restructure the two communities and to reorder the pattern of their relationship. The various plans represented in this category show slight variations with regard to the desired structural relationship of the two communities, but whether the goal is one unitary state of Muslims, Christians and Jews, or several loosely federated structures, or a bi-government country, the common denominator is equal rights and equal justice for all.

A basic premise of these proposals is that any just solution of the Palestine conflict must take into account that Zionism is a major cause of that conflict, and that the conflict itself resulted from the creation of Israel, which constituted an attack on Arab rights. The expulsion of the Palestinian people and the expropriation and confiscation of their property are the central issues of that conflict. Restoration of these basic rights is recognized as a prerequisite to a just solution. A general framework for reconstruction, which projected a democratic, secular state in Palestine, was advanced by the national movements. It postulates that "the establishment of a progressive, open society for all Palestinians (Jews, Christians and Muslims) is the only humanitarian and permanent solution to the problem. It is advanced as a logical alternative to 'throwing the Arabs to the desert' or 'throwing the Jews in the sea.' "[53] All Jews, Muslims and Christians living in Palestine or those who were forcibly exiled from it will have the right to Palestinian citizenship. The plan guarantees the right of all exiled Palestinians to return to their land, and it repudiates all religious and other discriminatory tests for citizenship. The principle of equal rights for all is advocated in the spheres of politics, economics, culture, and religion.

Proponents of the single state solution assert that the target of the revolutionary struggle in Palestine is a *system*, and not a religious or racial community. The system will function and persist only in so far as the oppressed group—Palestinian Arabs and Israeli Jews—are willing to acquiesce in their oppression. As a system, the Zionist structure cannot be half-destroyed; it must be confronted in its totality with the view of dismantling its very institutions that account for discriminatory practices. Compromises which do not involve a basic restructuring of the system or a re-examination of its principal assumptions will not alter the existing relationship of the two communities in a significant way, and could only benefit one community to the detriment of the other. The future must, therefore, be sought by those inhabitants who, irrespective of their race or creed, would strive for a dignified existence and equal justice for all.

Noam Chomsky advanced the view that the claims of national rights to the same territory by Jews and Arabs are equally valid. A federal framework is the most suitable structure for reconciling the "just demands" of each national group for self-government and cultural autonomy. Specifically, he recommended "two federated republics with parity, a guarantee of a high degree of autonomy combined with significant economic integration, highly permeable boundaries, and an ending of all legal ties to outside elements (the world Jewish community and Pan-Arab ties).[54]

Chomsky admits that this binational society must be considered a long-range program and must be based on the common pursuit of socialism, which would become the new common bond between Jews and Arabs. "It should also aim to overcome the paralyzing and destructive tendency of people to identify themselves solely, or primarily, as Jews or as Arabs, rather than as participants in a common effort."[55]

While both the PLO single state plan and Chomsky's federated republic agree in their endorsement of equal rights and rejection of exclusionary laws and practices, they nevertheless collide over the question of whether Jews are entitled to national rights. The PLO doctrine recognizes that the Jewish community in Israel is entitled to religious, cultural and political autonomy. This doctrine was superseded by the two-state solution which began to emerge in 1974 and is broadly accepted in the Palestinian community as the basis for a political settlement. It denies however, that this community has national rights. The projected democratic secular state of Palestine would consist of Muslim, Christian and Jewish citizens and not of two national groups, one Arab and one Jewish. For Chomsky, this scheme is analogous to that of a Jewish state with an Arab minority: "The PLO speaks of a democratic secular state within the framework of comprehensive Arab unity, offering to Israeli Jews no prospect other than that of a tolerated minority granted civil rights within an 'Arab nation'. . . . Jews, in contrast, are denied any national rights within this scheme."[56]

The concept of bi-nationalism received initial endorsement from Uri Davis, an Israeli who started out as a "moderate" Zionist, but moved away to an anti-Zionist position and "in parallel, but separately, from pacifist positions to non-pacifist positions."[57] He was influenced by the civil rights movement in the United States in the 1960's, and by the words of Martin Buber, Martin Luther King, Mahatma Gandhi and Elmer Berger. At the start of his career, he had this to say about the notion of bi-government in Palestine:

> I would contend that freedom and justice can be established equally for both peoples only in terms of an egalitarian (socialist) bi-governmental country wherein Israeli Jews, wherever they live, are equal participants in the Israeli-Jewish government, and Palestinian Arabs wherever they live, be it Tel Aviv or Nablus, are equal participants in the Palestinian-Arab government.[58]

Davis' plan conceded equal rights for all, including "equal economic rights (socialism)," "equal cultural and religious rights," "equal rights of residence and immigration," and "equal political rights of self-determination." [59] Both Davis and Israel Shahak, the noted Israeli human rights activist and survivor of a Nazi concentration camp, disapprove of the state of Israel as it is presently constituted because it is "based on *apartheid* directed against Arabs."[60] Redress might only be obtained upon the reconstitution of "Palestine-Eretz-Israel" into two states in which human rights will be superior to the states' right of sovereignty. Basic to their plan is the unconditional repatriation of Palestinian refugees to their land and property:

> It is, in our judgment, the indisputable right of the Palestinians to return to their ancestral homes in Palestine, irrespective of whether these homes are in the territories of Israel proper or in the post-1967 occupied territories. We also must point out . . . that we support this right even in the cases where the existing state of Israel has destroyed the home, razed the cemeteries and violated the mosques in question. We recognize that in some cases the houses of Palestinians are now occupied by Jews, let alone the innumerable cases where these have been destroyed. The right of the Palestinian whose house is occupied or has been destroyed, to be given a human habitation as near to his ancestral home as possible is, in our opinion, unquestionable.[61]

Under Davis' plan, a majority of Palestinian refugees would be living in Israel proper, but they would not necessarily be under the jurisdiction of the Israeli state. They would exercise their rights of citizenship in the Palestinian Arab state while living in territory held by Israel.

Like Chomsky, Davis disagreed with the PLO doctrine, which envisaged a democratic secular state as part of a unified Arab nation. He argued that in such a state, Israeli Jewish citizens would have no reason to expect better treatment than that accorded to the Palestinian Arab citizens prior to 1967, by the "democratic secular Jewish state as described in the Israeli declaration of independence."[62]

Davis, however, moved away from his earlier attachment to a bi-national government. In an address to the 17th session of the Palestine National Council, which convened in October 1984 in Amman, Jordan, he said that the only legitimate and viable alternative to the present state of Israel is a "government of Palestinians, Arabs and Jews, who will faithfully represent the interests of this land."[63] He even called on the Palestine National Council to open its ranks to "Palestinian Jewish membership" under the same criteria that determine the quota for representation of the West Bank and Gaza constituencies. He also proposed that PLO statistics record the number of Palestinians as approximately 8 million, of which 3.5 million are Palestinian Jews and 4.5 million are Palestinian Arabs. His prerequisites for a settlement that would secure equality of individual and collective rights under the law to Jews and

Arabs in Palestine are: return, self-determination, and the establishment of an independent Palestinian state on Palestinian national soil. He placed emphasis on return not only to territories occupied in June 1967, but to areas occupied in 1947-48 such as Acre, Haifa, Jaffa and Beersheba. Unless this internationally accorded right is applied, these refugees have the right to "reassert their presence in the homeland from which they are excluded, if necessary by military means and *armed struggle*, and that we must support them morally and materially in that struggle."[64] (Emphasis mine)

His terms of reference are incompatible with the continued existence of Israel as a Jewish state, hence, "it is only at the anti-Zionist margins of the Israeli Jewish society and polity that the Palestinian Arab can, and does, meet the Israeli-Jew as a comrade in a common struggle."[65] Correspondingly, the contributions of anti-Zionism to democracy and equality can be compared to those of the white citizens of South Africa who are anti-apartheid.

Israel Shahak views the question from the same perspective which characterizes the egalitarian and liberationist tendencies of anti-Zionism. His *sine qua non* is the principle that just states "must belong to their citizens, with no restrictions placed on any race, religion or nationality."[66] Accordingly, he condemns the whole idea of a Jewish state as unjust, and he views the Law of Return as causing "the greatest discord between Jews and Palestinians."[67] The alternative to this system for Shahak is a struggle to establish a "lasting concord between Jews and Palestinians." He said, "I believe that the principle of equal justice for every human being, if taken seriously and not merely declaimed, can form the basis of such a concord."[68] He outlined three problems connected with this principle of equal justice: The first is the problem of terror and the need for disassociation from Israeli state terrorism against the Palestinian people, and "indiscriminate terror carried out by Palestinian organizations."[69] The second problem is the proposed political structure espoused by both sides, which Shahak finds anti-democratic:

> I condemn the whole idea of the Jewish state as unjust . . . the infamous Law of Return . . . by the same token I oppose the notorious Paragraph Six of the 1968 Palestinian Covenant. . . . Just as I am against a "Jewish state," I am against an Arab state as well. . . . The struggle must be common in humanity, common in principle, common in equality. Only such a way is possible.[70]

The third problem, which relates to his ideal pursuit of justice for every human being, is a tendency to pursue allies who cling to the Arab past and to the Jewish past:

The principle of equal justice is not found in the Jewish past; nor is it found in the Arab past. The roots of this principle do not go further back than the American and the French Revolutions. . . . King David and King Solomon may have been poets and prophets, but they were also tyrants. . . . I admire many aspects of the Arab heritage, but I do not accept the rule of Caliph Haroun al-Rashid . . . our beginnings are in "liberty, equality, fraternity" and "government of the people, for the people, and by the people." Allies who are devoted exclusively to the past are dangerous and must be repudiated.[71]

He recognizes that the road is long; yet he is convinced that it is "long but short" and will lead to the "common aim: to lasting cooperation between the Jewish community and the Arabs in the Middle East."[72]

Shahak often equates Zionism with Nazi racism. He sees Israel as consisting of Jews and non-Jews, similar to Nazi Germany:

You have separate tables for dying Jewish infants and dying non-Jewish infants and so on. This is Nazification of Jewish society. . . . If one can learn anything from the Nazi experience, it is that one should be against Nazism. And I am against Nazism, whether German, Jewish, or Arab.[73]

His condemnation of fanatical racism on the part of some Jews also extends to participation in "white lies" about Jews:

Very many non-Jews (including Christian clergy and religious laymen, as well as some Marxists from all Marxist groups) hold the curious opinion that one way to "atone for the persecution of Jews is not to speak out against evil perpetrated by Jews . . . the crude accusation of "anti-Semitism" (or, in the case of Jews, "self-hate") against anybody who protests at the discrimination of Palestinians or who points out any fact about the Jewish religion or the Jewish past, which conflicts with the "approved version" comes with greater hostility and force from non-Jewish "friends of the Jews" than from Jews.[74]

The foregoing excerpts from Shahak's writings on the possibilities of concord in Palestine, racism, anti-Semitism, and chauvinistic nationalism reveal his unshakable commitment to the principle of equal justice for every single human being. In the contribution of Israel Shahak, anti-Zionism is unambiguously democratic, humanistic, and pluralistic.

Shahak's commitment to a democratic polity, based on equal justice and a single standard of human rights, was voiced earlier by Dr. Elmer

Berger, the leading Jewish anti-Zionist in the United States. He was the founder of the American Council for Judaism and was for many years its Executive Director. In 1955, he was appointed Executive Vice President, in which position he served until 1968, when he disagreed over policy matters with the Council's leadership. He believed that it was impossible to adhere to the universal and moral values of Judaism and to overlook Israeli aggression against the recognized rights of the Palestinian people.

Convinced that there was no use in trying to reconcile the irreconcilable, he organized the American Jewish Alternatives to Zionism, Inc.(AJAZ). Through AJAZ and its educational program, Dr. Berger was able to renew and reassert the message which characterized his professional life and career: That peace in the Middle East requires the application of Judaism's commitment to truth and justice and the abandonment and rejection of Zionism's commitment to Palestinian dispossession, dispersion, and disinstitutionalization. AJAZ rejects categorically and emphatically the claim by Zionism and the State of Israel that all who profess Judaism as their faith automatically and involuntarily constitute a national entity called the "Jewish people." Under Israeli law, all constituents of this "Jewish people" nationality entity are Israeli nationals with rights and obligations.[75] This is the meaning of the claim that Israel is "the sovereign state of the Jewish people"—a claim which confers upon Israel an extra-territorial jurisdiction over Jews wherever they may be.

Dr. Berger has spent a lifetime fighting against this conception of the Jews. He and Professor Thomas Mallison obtained an official rejection of this "Jewish people" nationality claim in international law, from the U.S. Department of State in 1964. Dr. Berger's opposition to this concept is very significant and has far-reaching consequences. It is consistent with the humanitarian programs that are the hallmark of his career and the essence of the movement with which he has been identified. It is an affirmation of the right of Americans, identified as Jews, to reject Israel's claim of extra-territoriality; by declaring their anti-Zionism, they affirm the democratic principle of the separation of church and state. By so doing, they also remind their own government in Washington that any aquiescence in this Zionist/Israeli claim of extra-territoriality is incompatible with American constitutional proscription of unreasonable classification. Therefore, to be anti-Zionist on these grounds is to uphold the 14th Amendment to the U.S. Constitution, which prohibits the government from distinguishing among Americans on the basis of religious belief. Rabbi Berger has consistently reminded the government that its aquiescence in this extra-territoriality claim would seriously infringe upon the Constitution, because membership in this so-called "Jewish people" nationality entity, as defined by Israeli law, is determined by either religious or racial criteria.

This lifetime endeavor by Dr. Berger is not to be mistaken for an esoteric, intellectual, jurisprudential exercise. It is, in fact, the epitome of committed scholarship, which is rooted in the concepts of pluralist existence and common humanity. These concepts have the attributes of integration equality for every human being, and democracy for everybody—not only for a select body of citizens.

Dr. Berger's committed scholarship offers Palestinian Arabs and Israeli Jews a way out of the morbid Hobbesian existence in which they find themselves. It challenges the Israeli objective of segregating American Jews and retarding their integration into American society; it also demonstrates that the distinction between Judaism and Zionism is a prerequisite for achieving true democracy in Israel. Only if Israel were to be de-Zionized, will it be able to trade a genuine democracy for the present *herrenvolk* democracy.

Dr. Berger's scholarship also vindicates the democratic, secular, unitary solution proposed by the Palestinian national movement. He was not discouraged by those who abandoned that vision, condemning it as an impractical solution, utterly unsuitable for our imperfect world. He was not deterred by the emasculation of that vision and by its removal from the diplomatic agenda of the Middle East. His adherence to that vision can only be attributed to a vested interest in the only possible humanitarian solution—the only alternative to the current system, which Shahak describes as apartheid. This system makes its Jewish citizens and potential citizens, who have never even lived in the state, more equal than those who have a recognized claim to Palestinian nationality. In that sense, Dr. Berger perceived Zionist legislation as more grotesque than apartheid in South Africa. In a speech to the African National Congress and the November 29th Committee (April 15, 1986), he said:

> I have often wondered why Americans, from the presidents to the most common citizens, have given the back of our hand to the original PLO proposition for a democratic secular unitary state. Surely in any other troubled place in the world, we would give our blessings to an insurgency with such commitment. It may be too late for now to realize a unitary state in Palestine. . . . But we free citizens can still exercise our freedom to influence aid to Israel upon a reformation of its Zionist, separatist system of inequality

practiced against its "non-Jewish people" citizens. We can challenge those who stridently shout "terrorist" at the Palestinians, who resent the second class treatment of their brothers and sisters living in the Zionist state and who are being dehumanized in the territories Israel continues to occupy in defiance of the decent opinions of mankind.[76]

To those Americans who have grown accustomed under the Reagan impact to equate the struggle for Palestinian self-determination with terrorism, Rabbi Berger asserted that the principal source of violence and instability in the Middle East is the fact that Palestinian rights remain unfulfilled and that the struggle for liberation is distinct from terrorism:

The critical mass in that struggle is *not* terrorism, but the lack of an attainable peace ... there is a qualitative difference between terrorism for terror's sake of gangs, like the Baader Meinhof group or the Red Brigade, on the one hand, and on the other hand, many others who have resorted to violence because the movers and the shakers have shut them out of the conventional procedures for negotiating and talking about grievances. And in this category of humans excluded from recognition of their total humanity and deprived of even the fragile structures devised for civilized and peaceful adjudication of international confrontations, like Abou Ben Adam, the Palestinians lead the list.[77]

The humanistic universalism which characterizes the works of Hannah Arendt, William Zuckerman, Hans Kohn, Morris Cohen, Elmer Berger and others whose work constitutes the bulk of our study, is also reflected in the work of Cheryl Rubenberg. In the preface to her major study, *Israel and the American National Interest*, she sets the tone of the book—a tone marked by a firm commitment to equality, human dignity, and a single standard of rights:

I fully recognize the necessarily subjective nature of my values, which essentially center around justice and justification. I reject the narrow world views of religion, ethnicity and nationalism. I believe we live on a very small planet and that regardless of the color of our skin, our place of birth, or our language, we are all of equal worth and equal dignity, entitled to live with the full measure of that dignity, dominated, repressed, and exploited by no one. I recognize that these values inform my view of the world and color my scholarship. Thus, for example, I cannot look at the Palestine-

Israel conflict and not see the Palestinians, both Muslims and Christians, as fully human and with the same inherent dignity as Jews. I cannot condone the domination, displacement, dispossession and subordination of one people by another. I cannot accept the notion of racial, ethnic, or religious superiority.[78]

Rubenberg appeals to Americans—Jews and Christians, who make the huge aid programs to Israel possible—to break their silence in the face of Israeli violation of the human rights of Palestinians: "The suffering of Palestinians cries out for our attention and amelioration."[79] But a permanent solution to the Palestine/Israel conflict can only be achieved within the framework of a democratic polity:

> In Israel, Palestinians must become full citizens in a genuinely democratic state wherein all citizens share equally in human and civil rights values. Discrimination based on nationality and religion is the antithesis of democracy.[80]

Anti-Zionism: Visions of A Socialist Society

The Israeli Socialist Organization (ISO) rejects the very concept of Israeli nationalism altogether. It views Zionism as the principal obstacle to a socialist revolution in Israel and rapprochement with the Arab world. It advocates Israeli-Arab unity in the framework of a socialist federation in the Middle East. Even prior to the June 1967 war, an ISO pamphlet called for that unified socialist republic:

> Only through a clear and firm rejection of Zionism and *any other sort of Israeli nationalism* (there is a non-Zionist type) can a link be established between revolutionaries inside Israel and those acting through the Arab world. Such a link is necessary for achieving the historical task confronting revolutionaries in this area in the next few decades: namely, that of establishing a unified Socialist Republic from the Atlantic Ocean to the Persian gulf.[81]

De-Zionization is considered by ISO as a prerequisite for a democratic solution. Israel must undergo a profound revolutionary change which will transform it from a Zionist state claiming jurisdiction over the Jews all over the world, into a socialist state that represents the interest of the people who live in it. De-Zionization requires the end of all relations of economic, military and political dependence on the United States, including the financial and political ties between Israel and the U.S. Jewish community. In his book, *The Other Israel*, Arie Bober identified the demand for de-Zionization as the centerpiece of the Israeli-Socialist Organization's program:

> One point of the de-Zionization program is the call for the formation of an independent, militant, trade- union organization based on committees democratically elected in the work places. . . . Another demand of the de-Zionization program calls for the separation of religion and the state. . . . An immediate logical consequence of the demand for secularization is the demand for the abrogation of the law of return, which depends on the religious definition of 'Jew.'[82]

Thus the ISO program calls for a total restructuring of the Israeli state at the level of its institutions, laws and practices, as well as that of its foreign relations. Eli Lobel, another Israeli socialist, supports this analysis:

> The problem has international dimensions, and the struggle against Zionism must therefore be waged on an international level. Concretely, this implies international popular support for the struggle to achieve a united Jewish-Arab, revolutionary Palestine—a step toward or a part of a Middle Eastern socialist federation, regardless of whether the majority is Arab or Jewish, and without racial or ethnic discrimination.[83]

While Israeli socialists are generally in harmony with the anti-nationalist, democratic, and humanitarian aspects of anti-Zionism, they also emphasize the necessity of struggle against imperialism. They go beyond the concern for the fate of Jews in western communities and the impact of Israeli legislation on their social and legal conditions. They see the task of these communities as consisting of mobilizing the Jewish masses against imperialism, a political task rather than a private or personal matter. They remind Jewish communities outside Israel of A. Leon's analysis of the social and economic role, which their predecessor played in a declining feudalism, and they caution them to avoid their link with a declining imperialism.

The re-emergence of Palestinian revolutionary struggle in the aftermath of the 1967 war was seen by Israeli socialists as an opportunity to realize their objective, a federation of socialist states in the Middle East. On the one hand, their struggle is internationalist and anti-imperialist, hence it requires a *revolutionary* Palestinian ally; on the other hand, the struggle must be based on the recognition of the right of Israelis to self-determination:

> A conquered and oppressed people has the right and duty to resist and to struggle for its freedom. The means and methods necessary and appropriate to such a struggle must be determined by this people itself. . . . While recognizing the unconditional right to resist occupation, we can only support those (Palestinian) organizations, which, in addition to resisting occupation, also recognize the right to self-determination of the Israeli people; on this basis, the struggle of the Palestinian people can become a common struggle of Arabs and Jews for a common future in this region.[84]

Conclusion

Our study has shown that throughout the past century there was a steady stream of anti-Zionist literature, which offered an alternative to the scheme of Theodor Herzl and Chaim Weizmann. The dissenting notions and heretical views cited here represent a mere sample of anti-Zionists, whose quarrel with Zionism was rooted in deep philosophic disagreements. Their work exhibits a broad consensus favoring a democratic, pluralist, integrationist polity. Hence, their view of the world provoked a collision with the very concept of Israeli statehood which was, by definition, exclusivist, segregationist and anti-democratic, particularly for the natives. That collision was more typical of anti-Zionists of the pre-state period. Their antipathy to Germanic nationalism, which was one of the factors that promoted two world wars, triggered a sense of clear and present danger. As an offspring of that particular brand of nationalism, Zionism was seen as a future instrument of strife and violence.

The early anti-Zionists rejected the ethnic basis of Jewish life, the "ingathering" idea, and the claim to racial purity as concepts leading to ghettoism, which would inhibit inter-group tolerance and communication. They perceived a kinship between the advocates of a state for the Jews and the anti-Semites who consider Jews alien in the countries in which they lived, unassimilable and incapable of becoming full members of the community outside an Israeli state.

This rejection of the ghetto was in itself an affirmation of a progressive nationalism which was thoroughly pluralist, vigorously democratic, and largely secular. The idea of separation of religion and state was promoted by secular and religious anti-Zionists alike. The barring of "unreasonable classification" and the endorsement of "equal protection" permeated the thought of anti-Zionists throughout the entire period under study.

While the post-state anti-Zionists shared the humanist and democratic grounding of the pre-state anti-Zionists, their attention was nevertheless focused on the proper modalities of repair. Since the state became a physical reality, the emphasis had to be placed on controlling the damage, correcting the injustice and creating the bases for a brighter future. The works of contemporary anti-Zionists endeavor to reconstitute political life in Palestine/Israel to make it more compatible with the democratic, secular, pluralist character of anti-Zionism. But in the end the work of the contemporary as well as that of the early anti-Zionists are reflections of the same humanist liberationist edifice. There is a common thread which ties them together as an integral whole and which gives them a legacy that is more consonant with the tenets of a progressive order.

NOTES

1. Some would argue that the Holocaust gave great impetus to Zionism. For a critique of that view, see Boaz Evron "Learning the Wrong Lessons From the Holocaust" *Journal of Palestine Studies*.
2. On the colonial nature of Zionism, see the excellent study by Fayez Sayegh, "The Non-Colonial Zionism of Mr. Abba Eban," *Middle East Forum* Vol. XLII No. 4, 1966, pp. 49-50.
3. Chaim Weizmann, *Trial and Error: An Autobiography* (New York, Harper 1949) p. 191.
4. *The Complete Diaries of Theodor Herzl* (ed.) R. Patai (New York: Herzl Press, 1960) p. 120.
5. *Ibid.* pp. 1193-1194.
6. Abdelwahab Elmessiri. *The Land of Promise: A Critique of Political Zionism.* (New Brunswick, N.J.: North America 1977), p. 59.
7. Hans Kohn. "Achad Ha'-Am: Nationalist with a Difference" *Commentary.* Vol. XI, no. 6 (June 1951).
8. Gary Smith, *Zionism, The Dream and the Reality* (New York, Harper & Row, 1974), p. 31.
9. *Ibid.* p. 32.
10. *Ibid.* p. 36.
11. *Ibid.* p. 37.
12. According to Sir Leon Simon. "Achad Ha'-Am" *Encyclopedia of Zionism and Israel.* Vol. I.
13. Quoted in Moshe Menuhin. *The Decadence of Judaism In Our Time.* (Beirut: Institute for Palestine Studies, 1969) p. 61.
14. *Ibid*, p. 60.
15. *Ibid*, p. 62.
16. Quoted in *Ibid*, pp. 65-66.
17. Reprinted in Gary Smith, *op.cit.*, p. 101.
18. *Ibid*, p. 304.

19. Quoted in Smith, *op.cit.*, p. 49.
20. *Ibid*, p.51.
21. *Ibid*.
22. *Ibid*, p. 52.
23. *Ibid*, p. 55.
24. *Ibid*.
25. *Ibid*, pp. 54-55.
26. Morris R. Cohen, "A Dreamer's Journey" (Boston: Beacon Press, 1949), p. 227. Quoted in Menuhin, *op.cit.*, p. 308.
27. U.N. General Assembly Document No. A/C. 3/L.2159, 15 October 1975.
28. Quoted in Menuhin, *op.cit.*, p. 308.
29. *Ibid*, p. 309.
30. M. Jastrow, "Zionism and the Future of Palestine", (New York, 1919) Appendix. His statement to President Wilson for conveyance to the Paris Conference.
31. Quoted in Smith, *op.cit.*, pp. 40-41.
32. Smith, *op.cit*, p. 114.
33. *Ibid*, p. 115.
34. Menuhin, *op.cit.*, p. 319.
35. *Ibid*, p. 316.
36. Menuhin, *op.cit.*, p. 317.
37. *Ibid*, p. 315.
38. Quoted in Menuhin *op.cit.*, p. 324.
39. Elmessiri, *op.cit.*, p. 27.
40. Moshe Menuhin, *Jewish Critics of Zionism*.
41. Michael Selzer (ed), *Zionism Reconsidered; The Rejection of Jewish Normalcy*, (New York: Macmillan, 1970), p. 241.
42. Martin Buber, "Nationalism", a translation of an address delivered by Mr. Buber on the 5th of Sept., 1921 in Karlsbad, and appeared in the English in *Israel and the World: Essays in a Time of Crisis*. (New York: Schocken Books, 1948) quoted in Smith, *op.cit.*, p. 77.
43. *Ibid*, p. 78.
44. Hannah Arendt, "Zionism Reconsidered", *Menorah Journal*, vol. XXXIII, No. 2, (Autumn 1945).
45. William Zuckerman, "The Menace of Jewish Fascism", *The Nation*, 25 April 1934.
46. *Ibid*.
47. *Ibid*.
48. *Ibid*.
49. Maxime Rodinson, *Cult, Ghetto, and State: The Persistence of the Jewish Question*, (London: Al Saqi, 1983), p. 13.
50. *Ibid*, p. 112.
51. *Ibid*.
52. Menuhin, *op.cit.*, p. 210.
53. "Towards the Democratic Palestine", *Free Palestine*. Vol. 2, No. 2, (June, 1970), pp. 6-7.
54. Noam Chomsky, "A Radical Perspective", *The Arab World: From Nationalism to Revolution*, eds. Abdeen Jabara and Janice Terry (Wilmette, Ill.: Medina University Press, 1971) p. 190.
55. Noam Chomsky, "A Radical Perspective", *The Arab World: From Nationalism*

to Revolution, eds. Abdeen Jabara and Janice Terry (Wilmette, Ill.: Medina University Press, 1971) p. 191. Chomsky expounded his ideas in two articles: "Dark at the End of the Tunnel", *Ramparts*, Jan. 1973, pp. 38-55; and "Breaking The Mideast Deadlock II, The Prospects", *Ramparts*, April 1975, pp. 31-61.

56. "Breaking the Mideast Deadlock II, The Prospects," *Ramparts*, April 1975, pp. 31-61.

57. Uri Davis, *Israel: An Apartheid State*, (London: Zed Press, 1987), p. 102.

58. Uri Davis,"An Exchange on Israel and the Palestinians", *New York Review of Books*, Feb. 10, 1972, p. 33.

59. *Ibid*, p. 33.

60. Uri Davis and Israel Shahak, "An Open Letter to the War Resistors League on the Middle East", The Middle East Peace Organizer, (San Francisco, April, 1975); see Uri Davis' later work *Israel: An Apartheid State*, (London: Zed, 1987). See also Israel Shahak, "A Summary of the System of Legal Apartheid". "The Shahak Papers" reprinted in PHRC *Palestine Human Rights Newsletter* (Chicago, Nov. 1987).

61. Uri Davis and Israel Shahak "An Open Letter To The War Resistors League on the Middle East" *The Middle East Peace Organizer* (San Francisco, April 1975).

62. Uri Davis,"An Exchange on Israel and the Palestinians".

63. Davis, *Israel: An Apartheid State*, p. 103.

64. *Ibid.*, p. 11.

65. *Ibid.*, p. 96.

66. Israel Shahak, "Equal Justice for Every Human Being," Information Papers No. 11, *Arabs and Jews: Possibility of Concord*, Association of Arab-American University Graduates, 1974, p. 27.

67. *Ibid.*

68. *Ibid*, p. 25.

69. *Ibid*, p. 26.

70. *Ibid*, p. 27.

71. *Ibid*, p. 28.

72. *Ibid*, p. 29.

73. Quoted in Charles Glass, "Jews Against Zion: Israeli Jewish Anti-Zionism," *Journal of Palestine Studies*, Vol. V, Nos. 1 & 2 (Winter 1976), pp. 77-78.

74. *Ibid*, p. 41.

75. For an analysis of the concepts of "nationality" and "citizenship" in Israeli law, see Roselle Tekiner's excellent study "On The Inequality of Israeli Citizens," *Without Prejudice*, EAFORD, Washington, D.C., Vol. 1, No. 1, pp. 48-57.

76. Text in American Jewish Alternatives to Zionism, Inc. *Back to Some Basics*, Report #51, p. 51.

77. From a speech to the American and Arab Friendship Society delivered at Ohio State University, Columbus, Ohio, May 15, 1986, Text in *Ibid.*, pp. 64-65.

78. Cheryl Rubenberg, *Israel and the American National Interest* (Urbana and Chicago: University of Illinois Press, 1986). p. XIII.

79. Cheryl Rubenberg, "Palestinian Human Rights Under Israeli Rule," *Church and Society*, March/April 1987. p. 32.

80. *Ibid.*

81. Israel Socialist Organization, *Some Remarks Concerning the Left in Israel*, Tel Aviv. January, 1967. p.15.
82. Arie Bober, *The Other Israel: The Radical Case Against Zionism*, (New York, Doubleday, 1972), pp. 202-203.
83. Ahmad El Kodsy and Eli Lobel, *The Arab World and Israel* (New York: Monthly Review Press, 1970), p. 132.
84. From a statement by the Israeli Socialist Organization (ISO) dated May 1968. Quoted in *Ibid.*, p. 136.

3

THE "WHO IS A JEW?" CONTROVERSY IN ISRAEL: A PRODUCT OF POLITICAL ZIONISM

ROSELLE TEKINER

"Who is a Jew?" is an explosive political issue in Israel. Angry shouts and recriminations reverberate through the halls of the Knesset as Israeli politicians vigorously debate how the law should define a Jew for the purpose of nationality registration. With the public passionately taking sides, the controversy has several times dominated the news for months and reached such huge dimensions that it threatened to topple several governments. The longstanding argument is between religionists and secularists[1] who have never been able to agree nor to compromise their differences on this issue. The religionist position is that a Jew must be defined according to religious law. Only those who fit the definition, that is, by birth to a Jewish mother or converted to Judaism, may acquire nationality status in Israel. Secularists disagree. They insist that Jewish identification for nationality purposes is not a matter of religion.

Secularists, who support a secular state, are in the majority. They include not only the large part of the population who never attend religious services, but also many who are religiously observant, but nonetheless want Israel to be a secular state. Religionists are primarily Orthodox Jews who want Israel structured according to rabbinic laws of Judaism and therefore demand that the official definition of a Jew be a religious one. They have consistently wielded political power far out of proportion to their numbers through a system of rabbinical courts and political coalitions with Labor and Likud. Because neither of these two major political parties has ever had a clear-cut working majority, they often make *quid pro quo* arrangements with leaders of religious parties. Secularist Knesset members,therefore, often find themselves supporting religionists' objectionable demands for the sake of garnering sufficient votes for their own political priorities.

During the early years of Israel's existence, the issue of who is a Jew, as a matter of Israeli public law, lay dormant. Religionists and secularists alike were motivated to build a Jewish state and the biological and/or religious credentials of immigrants were not scrutinized to determine whether he or she truly qualified as a Jew according to religious law. They were not asked to submit proof that their maternal antecedents were Jews by birth nor were converts rejected if their conversion was not conducted according to Orthodox ritual. The public controversy now plaguing Israel began in 1958 when the Interior Ministry issued guidelines for registering a Jew in the Population Registry. The new ruling stated that no proof other than a registrant's declaration be required for registration as a Jew under "nationality."

The religionists were enraged at this official public flouting of the religious definition of a Jew, although it had been quietly disregarded all along in the interest of populating the state with Jews. Religionist agitation finally forced a reversal of the ruling and in 1960 a religious requirement was officially instituted for nationality registration as a Jew. This in turn enraged secularists, who insisted that the Jewish state was a secular state and that nationality status in Israel had nothing to do with observance of Judaism. Thus began the neverending controversy polarizing Israeli society.

There have been a number of court challenges to the definition of a Jew, all of which have been bitterly fought and all of which have been won by the minority religionists.[2] Each new victory increased secularists' resentment of dominant religionist influence in government affairs. Hostility of one group against the other is increasing, often erupting into physical violence. In Jerusalem, religionists throw stones at cars traveling on the Sabbath to express disapproval of violations of religious law. Orthodox rabbis and their followers have disrupted services at Reform synagogues. There were reports in American newspapers during the summer of 1986 that religious zealots were defacing and burning secular structures, and secularists were retaliating by damaging and defacing synagogues. There is dismay in Israel and among Israel's supporters everywhere that disagreement over the definition of a Jew has turned Jews against Jews.

The issues underlying the "Who is a Jew?" controversy are puzzling to those living in a country where religion and ethnic origins are not official government concerns. Frequently reminded by public officials, journalists and scholars that Israel is a democratic nation like their own, Americans in particular have reason to wonder why there is so much fuss about an apparently abstract issue. It seems that either the rabbis are perversely digging up problems for secularists to solve or that Israeli politicians have inexplicably made a theological issue a matter of profound public concern. Or because Israel is said to have been created as a haven for homeless Jews, it may be wrongly assumed that a stringent definition of a Jew is necessary to curtail too strong an influx of immigrants to the little state. Although the media report the controversy, many journalists seem neither to understand the cause of the conflict nor its full consequences. Reports often make it seem that immigrants who sue for official recognition as a Jew are doing so solely to avoid naturalization proceedings; that they are suing for the right given by the Law of Return only to officially recognized Jews, to obtain citizenship automatically. Or an inadequately informed reporter tells his readers that success of Orthodox demands to narrow the definition of a Jew would mean that Israel would not recognize most American Jews as Jews.[3] Neither conclusion is warranted by the facts.

Certain basic information about the legal and political structure of Israel is required in order to understand the serious practical considerations that motivate immigrants to sue the government to gain official recognition as a Jew. Those who fail to qualify for citizenship under the Law of Return, such as non-Jewish spouses of Jews or children of Jewish fathers and non-Jewish mothers, are entitled by law, unless they convert to Judaism, only to a second-class citizenship status, the same as Israel gives indigenous Palestinians. When Israeli Jews take sides and create a public controversy over a matter that does not concern them personally, they are motivated primarily by concern over separation of "church" and state. The facts surrounding the fights in Israel over the definition of a Jew have been so well obscured by religious and political rhetoric that attention has been successfully diverted from the unique features of the state structure that generated the problem and continue to nurture it.

Israel was constructed on a model provided by political Zionism, the basic premise of which is that Israel is "the State of the Jews." Although the mechanisms that must operate to maintain a state for any one particular religious or ethnic group are incompatible with modern concepts of democracy, Israel is nonetheless consistently characterized, within and outside the country, as a democratic state. A possible incompatibility between the principles of Zionism and the principles of democracy rarely seems to occur to many of those who try to analyze Israel's problems. Although an increasing number of books and articles severely criticize Israel's policies, and some attribute problems to institutions that constitute the organizational apparatus of the state,[4] the ideology of Zionism remains virtually immune from open criticism.[5] A likely reason is that many Americans perceive "Zionism" solely as a religious or humanitarian concept. This erroneous perception inhibits critical discussion, and therefore public awareness, of the discriminatory nature of Zionism, the principles of which provide the foundation of the structure of the state of Israel. Unlike pro-Zionist literature that often receives enthusiastic reviews in major book review publications, even when without merit,[6] writings that openly criticize Zionism are seldom reviewed for the general reader, whatever their merits. But for the American public to understand why the definition of a Jew has assumed major proportions, dividing Israel into warring factions, it is necessary to be informed about the nature of Zionism. The strategies to achieve and maintain a Zionist "State of the Jews" are the root cause of the "Who is a Jew?" controversy.

Origins and Early Development of Political Zionism

Zionism is a political nationalist movement, the name of which relates to the Bible's references to Zion. According to religious Zionism, at a time God chooses, when the obligations of the Covenant are met, He will return Jews to a utopian Zion. Adoption of the name "Zionism" for a political nationalist movement implies that political Zionism and religious Zionism have the same origin and share the same goals.

The ideology of political Zionism was systematized by Theodor Herzl and published in his book, *Der Judenstaat*, in 1895. It outlines a plan for resolving what he called "the Jewish problem" by establishing a "state of the Jews." His plan is based on two main premises: 1) that Jews throughout the world comprise a nation despite their centuries-long dispersion, and 2) that anti-Semitism is a permanent incurable affliction of mankind, making it impossible for Jews ever to assimilate into a country other than their own. Starting with these debatable assumptions, he argued that Jews are entitled to a territory to fulfill their alleged national aspirations free from prejudice and discrimination.

Herzl was not a religious Jew. Herzlian Zionism, while incorporating religious concepts into the political ideology, did not stress adherence to Judaism in promoting the concept of a Jewish nation in exile. Many traditional Jews were alienated by the omission. For them, "return to Zion" is a messianic religious concept, not a political one, and a Zionist state means a state God promised if Jews fulfill their covenantal obligations to obey His laws. Early in the Zionist movement, some Orthodox Jews developed a strong organized opposition to a Jewish State, regarding the founders of political Zionism as evil men presuming to the role of God by trying to hasten the redemption of the Jews.[7] These religious Zionists were strong anti-Zionists in the political sense of the term "Zionism."

Reform Judaism also opposed Herzl's "state of the Jews," but on grounds different from those Orthodox Jews who opposed political Zionism for theological reasons only. One basis of Reform Judaism, which blossomed in the nineteenth century, was opposition to the messianic concept of a return to Zion. Before Herzl proposed his plan for a Jewish nation, Reform Jews regarded themselves solely as a religious community, their national identification deriving from their domicile countries, not their religious beliefs. It was therefore in keeping with their basic philosophy that the Central Conference of American rabbis announced in 1898 their opposition to Herzl's attempt to establish a Jewish state. It was re-emphasized at the Conference that Judaism is neither political nor national, but spiritual. Reform Jews were anti-Zionists in both the religious and political sense of the term "Zionism." They rejected the concept of Zion as a geopolitical location to which Jews would be returned, either by God or by Theodor Herzl and his followers.

There was still strong Jewish opposition to Zionism when Chaim Weizmann became the acknowledged leader of the Zionist movement during world War I. The objections of Orthodox, Reform and secular Jews threatened his efforts to convince the western powers that Jews were united in support of a Jewish state. He expressed concern that the British government would ask him to identify his Zionists, when he was unable to furnish an impressive list because so many Jews were openly opposed to a Jewish national movement.[8] He also coined the term "non-Zionism" as a device to draw support from indifferent Jews. The term suggests that support for a Jewish state need not mean acceptance of the Zionist concept of a second nationality for Jews. "Non-Zionism" succeeded in gaining support for a Jewish state from many Jews who opposed Zionism because they rejected the idea of national attachment to a state other than their own, but who were justifiably concerned about the welfare of persecuted Jews.

Weizmann inherited the problems of Herzl, who had also been conscious of the lack of a sufficient following of Zionists to carry through his program. The platform of Herzl's first Zionist Congress, held in Basle in 1897, declared that Jewish national sentiment and consciousness must be fostered. Recognition of a need to foster Jewish national consciousness indicates that a Jewish nation in exile was a wish awaiting fulfilment, not a reality. The Zionist leadership was prepared for a great deal of patient effort to develop the spirit of Jewish nationalism that they claimed, with inadequate justification, already existed. These efforts had still not succeeded when Weizmann was demanding a territory for Zionism's "Jewish nation" from the allied powers during World War I. Weizmann followed Herzl in avoiding the term "Jewish nationality" in public documents, knowing it to be unpalatable to Jews who were satisfied with a single nationality status in their domicile countries. Both substituted the euphemism "the Jewish people," for it implies to many diaspora Jews an ethnic or religious identification rather than a political nationality which many reject. The verbal camouflage continues today. One rarely hears about "Jewish nationality," even though it is a legal supra-citizenship status in Israel which political Zionism claims applies to all Jews in the world and which gives them rights and obligations denied Israeli citizens who are not Jews. The preferred, less controversial expression to refer to Zionism's alleged nation of Jews is "the Jewish people," a term long used popularly to refer to Jews, but not as a national entity inscribed in law.

The rising tide of anti-Semitism in Europe diluted opposition to political Zionism. In 1937 the Central Conference of American Rabbis reversed the 1898 stand of Reform Judaism by supporting a "Jewish homeland as a haven of refuge for the oppressed and as a center of Jewish culture and spiritual life." This was far from an endorsement of a Jewish nation-state in Palestine, but was a significant step towards an eventual, almost total surrender to Herzlian Zionism. A segment of the Orthodox Jewish rabbinate also reacted to anti-Semitism by abandoning objections to political Zionism and supporting the claim for a Jewish state.

Anti-Semitism and compassion for its victims were the principal factors leading Orthodox, Reform, Conservative and secular Jews into the Zionist fold. The Holocaust later wiped out almost all opposition. Hitler's genocidal program created an emotional climate which contributed to Herzl's plan to isolate Jews in a country of their own where Zionist ideology claimed they would be protected from anti-Semitism. Nazism underlined the threat of danger to Jews outside Israel, a threat that was an important element of Herzlian Zionist ideology and has been successfully used to strengthen the concept of "aliya" (immigration of Jews to Israel), which is the ultimate aim of Zionism.

Herzl's plan for a state of the Jews was realized in 1948 with the establishment of the state of Israel. The name is historically related to the tribes united under David and Solomon, who were called "children of Israel." Taking the name of the old biblical kingdom for the name of the state implies that contemporary Jews are lineal biological descendants of the biblical tribes and therefore heirs to the land of Palestine, as promised by God in chapter 12 of Genesis. But even if the biblical "Promise" were a valid basis for a land claim in the twentieth century, the fact is that Jews have divided and subdivided themselves into many different lines of descent as they lived in different places among biologically diverse people throughout the world.

Building A Democratic Facade for A Jewish State

After the Zionists attained their "state of the Jews," they were faced with the practical problem of structuring the state to satisfy religionists, to whom a Jewish state meant a state following the tenets of Judaism, and secularists, who wanted a democratic state for Jews, free of religious domination.

The first document issued by the new state was the Proclamation of Establishment in 1948, stating "full social and political equality of all citizens without distinction of religion, race or sex." This statement is in the spirit of a secular democracy, for it appears to guarantee full rights to non-Jews, but it is not a law and has no legal force. Nonetheless, the document is consistently invoked as evidence that Israel is a genuine democracy, misleading much of the world, including many Israelis themselves, into believing that, at least in principle, Israel stands for equality of all citizens. The Proclamation of Establishment is a standard pro-Zionist reference to rebut charges that Palestinian Arabs are legally discriminated against in Israel, despite the fact that equality of Jewish and non-Jewish citizens is negated by "fundamental" laws that were enacted after the state was established.

During the several years after Israel's birth, attempts were made to draft a constitution to satisfy the divergent views of religionists and secularists, but it proved to be an impossible task. Although it was agreed that Israel should be a Jewish state, there was serious controversy over a constitutional definition of a Jew. Religionists insisted that, for nationality purposes, a Jew should be defined according to Orthodox rabbinic law as one born of a Jewish mother or converted to Judaism. Secularists rejected this religious definition but could offer no satisfactory secular definition of a Jew. There was also disagreement about the meaning of conversion. The Orthodox rabbinate does not recognize other than an Orthodox ritual conversion, meaning that those converted by a Reform or Conservative rabbi would not be admitted to Israel as citizens with full nationality rights. The interrelated problems of defining a secular Jew, and of writing a democratic constitution that would incorporate and publicly declare a principle of Jewish exclusivity, resulted in abandonment of the project.

In place of a constitution, three "fundamental" laws were enacted by the Knesset, the Israeli parliament. The Law of Return gives all Jews in the world the right to enter Israel without formalities. The Law of Citizenship provides for the acquisition of Israeli citizenship. The Status Law authorizes the world Zionist Organization/Jewish Agency to assist immigration and development of the country. In the absence of a constitution, the rights of citizens must be gleaned from these laws, which are written in ambiguous language replete with biblical expressions and with many terms of referral to Jews, but containing no definition of a Jew. The controversial issue of who officially qualifies as a Jew in the state of Israel was left open to various and often conflicting interpretations.

The Law of Return is not a conventional immigration law, but a nationality law, for the right to enter a country freely is conventionally the right only of the nationals of that country. Therefore, despite the absence of the word "nationality" (Hebrew: "le'um") in its title, the Law of Return is a nationality law. It gives all Jews nationality status in the state of Israel, whether or not they are citizens of other countries and whether or not they ever intend to "return" to Israel in the literal sense of the term.

The expression "return" is borrowed from Holy Writ. Its origin is the biblical concept of the return of a morally reconstituted "people of Israel" to Zion, once the Covenant between them and God is restored.[9] "Return" is consistently used in Israeli law to imply that Jews are in exile anywhere but in Israel. Using language that associates the state of Israel with the biblical nation of Israel serves the propaganda claim that criticism of Israel is criticism of the religion of the Jews, and it is therefore anti-Semitic to criticize the Israeli government. The accusation of anti-Semitism is a powerful weapon, often used to mute critical analysis of Israel's discriminatory state structure and discredit political opposition to Israel's policies.[10]

There is another practical consequence of the use of "return" in the title of Israel's foremost law, instead of the more appropriate term, "nationality." It avoids spotlighting Zionism's claim that all Jews are nationals of Israel and alienating those who object to a second nationality, gratuitously legislated for them, as Jews, in a state other than the one in which they hold citizenship. The word "return" emphasizes that Israel is the homeland of all Jews and that when they enter, they are not immigrating, but returning from exile. Without specifically stating so, the Law of Return gives all Jews nationality rights in the state of Israel and effectively bars non-Jews from those rights.

The Law of Citizenship sets forth procedures for Jews and non-Jews to obtain Israeli citizenship. Authoritative books written by reputable legal scholars consistently translate the Law of Citizenship incorrectly into English as "Law of Nationality."[11] The translation conveys the mistaken impression that "nationality" and "citizenship" are interchangeable terms in Hebrew, as they are in English, when they are not. In the United States, all nationals are citizens and all citizens are nationals, "nationality" applying to all who meet requirements for United States citizenship. But in Israel, "nationality" (Hebrew: "le'um") and "citizenship" (Hebrew: "ezrahut") are two separate, distinct statuses, conveying different rights and responsibilities. Because the Law of Return implicitly bars non-Jews from nationality rights, Palestinian citizens, who are Moslems or Christians, can never be nationals. But Jews who are citizens of other countries are nationals of Israel and they automatically become citizens of Israel when they "return." The translation of the Law of Citizenship as "Law of Nationality" conveys the false impression that this law gives nationality rights to Jews and non-Jews, when, in fact, it is the Law of Return that confers a nationality status upon Jews—and Jews exclusively.[12] The Law of Citizenship calls the former "citizens by return," to distinguish Jewish citizens from non-Jewish citizens. There is nothing in the text of the law to indicate that the rights of "citizens by return" differ in any way from other citizens, making it appear that "by return" is a kind of honorary designation without legal significance.

The distinction between "nationality" and "citizenship," cleverly concealed by faulty translations and by words and phrases that deviate from conventional usage, is a mechanism to carry out legalized discrimination against non-Jewish citizens. It creates a unique extra-territorial Jewish nationality status that gives Jews of all countries rights in the state of Israel that are permanently denied non-Jewish citizens. The first two "fundamental" laws, the Law of Return and the Law of Citizenship, form the legal foundation for carrying out discriminatory practices against non-Jews. The third "fundamental" law, the World Zionist Organization/ Jewish Agency Status Law, establishes the operating mechanisms for discrimination.[13]

The Status Law creates a partnership between the State of Israel and the World Zionist Organization to develop the state for "the Jewish people." [14] The law states that the "mission of gathering in the exiles" is the "central task of the State of Israel and the Zionist Movement." The language used is not the legal language in which the laws of secular states are usually written. The words and phrases often seem to mean something other than their legal meaning. "Mission" sounds as if it refers to a humanitarian effort to rescue persecuted homeless Jews. "Exiles" conveys the impression that reference is to those who are banished from or not integrated in the societies in which they live. But "exile" in the Israeli/Zionist lexicon means a Jew not living in Israel. "Gathering in" suggests that Israel's central task is to provide a sanctuary for the persecuted, when its legal meaning is to bring Jews to Israel, where Israeli citizenship will be automatically granted.

The central task of a democracy should be to serve all citizens, but it is evident, when legal meanings are disentangled from the euphemisms, that Israel's highest priority goal is to import a select group of persons who, according to conventional concepts, are foreigners. Camouflaged with expressions of humanitarianism, the state's chief task, to serve "the Jewish people," seems, on the surface, to be compatible with the position that Israel is a democracy. The sanctimonious language of the Status Law makes it appear that "Jewish national" institutions, serving only Jews, are not under government control but are philanthropic institutions, a ruse that is apparently an attempt to exonerate a purportedly democratic government from discriminatory practices against Palestinian citizens. It has successfully inhibited analyses of the relationship between the government and the World Zionist Organization that might expose the partnership role of the government in implementing developmental projects that benefit only Jewish citizens. But the Status Law makes the World Zionist Organization/Jewish Agency integral elements of the governmental apparatus. These organizations are not the independent philanthropic agencies they are propagandized to be. The United States tacitly approves of the deception by granting them tax deductible status, despite the fact that, for many practical purposes, their operations are controlled by Israeli government officials.

Had discrimination against Palestinians been written into Israeli law as specifically as discrimination against Blacks is written into South African law, outside support would surely be jeopardized. Therefore, pro-Zionist strategies have successfully turned popular attention away from similarities between Israel's and South Africa's apartheid systems. Israel's leaders have always been aware that world sympathy hinges on perception of Israel as a democracy.

Israel and South Africa both have a Population Registry Law providing for registration of the entire population by the Secretary of the Interior. In South Africa the classification is racial; in Israel it is a "nationality" classification. Every individual in both South Africa and Israel is officially registered in a particular group that can be used to determine social, economic and political status. There is no secret about the fact that the purpose of the classification in South Africa is to give Blacks an inferior status. As a result, South Africa is almost universally denounced as a racist state. John Dugard, professor of law at the University of Witwatersrand in South Africa, describes South Africa's Population Registry Law as "the cornerstone of the whole system of apartheid."[15]

Israel's Population Registry Law also provides a foundation for discrimination—not on the basis of race, for Arabs and Jews are not racially separate—but on the basis of "nationality." "Israeli" is not an acceptable designation of nationality for purposes of registration. If it were, both Jewish and Arab citizens would qualify for nationality rights, which would contravene the Law of Return that provides no nationality rights for non-Jews. The only acceptable response for Jews is "Jewish nationality," officially placing them in a separate category from Arab Palestinians. A consequence of the Status Law's division of functions between the World Zionist Organization/Jewish Agency and the government is that only Jews qualify for "national" benefits, such as participation in "national" housing, "national" land or "national" labor.

The intricately interwoven provisions of the three "fundamental laws" place non-Jewish Israeli citizens in an inferior social, economic and political position. The Population Registry Law serves to implement their discriminatory provisions, thus providing the cornerstone of the Zionist system of apartheid.

M. Gouldman states in *Israeli Nationality Law* that the main purpose of the Population Registry law is to collect statistical data.[16] This implies that Jewish nationality has no legal significance but is an ethnic identification, as it was under the Ottoman Empire's millet system, and still is in some Eastern European and Middle Eastern countries.[17] The statement is as deceptive as other tactics which convey the false impression that Israel is a genuine democracy. The absence of reference to "nationality" in the Law of Return, erroneous translations of the Law of Citizenship as "Law of Nationality," and institutions created by the Status Law to benefit only Jews, are all part of a strategy that camouflages Israel's discriminatory state structure.

One must be impressed by the intellectual effort that went into the cleverly ambiguous wording of the "fundamental laws."[18] The language so successfully obfuscates their discriminatory provisions that much of the world has accepted at face value the statement of citizen equality in the Proclamation of Independence. A widely held false assumption that the government operates on the democratic principle of equal rights is an effective shield against recognition that the publicized fights for official recognition as a Jew are, in reality, fights for first class citizenship rights. If a misled public does not know there are two categories of citizenship in Israel, one for Jews and the other for non-Jews, the clue for understanding the reasons for the "Who is a Jew?" controversy is missing. When the central task of a state is to import persons of a select religious/ethnic group, and to develop the country for their benefit alone, it is crucially important to be officially recognized as a *bona fide* member of that group.

"Fundamental" Laws Boomerang

When second class citizenship for non-Jews became part of the grand plan to make Israel a Jewish state with a majority Jewish population, Palestinian citizens were the intended victims. The Population Registry registered their nationality as "Arab." This officially placed them in a category that made them ineligible for nationality rights in the state of Israel and therefore ineligible for benefits from the Zionist Organization's subsidies to "national" institutions, which provide many services normally the responsibility of a government.[19]

For a decade after the state of Israel was established, the procedures of the Population Registry accommodated the goal shared by all Zionists, religionist and secularist, to "ingather the exiles" to build a Jewish State. Clerks registered the nationality of an immigrant as "Jew" on the basis of the registrant's statement. As a general rule, proof of eligibility was not demanded to make one eligible for automatic citizenship (by return) and full nationality rights in the state of Israel, as provided in the Law of Return and the Law of Citizenship. But in 1958, when the Interior Ministry issued a directive officially stipulating that the word of a registrant is sufficient for registration as a Jew under "nationality," two members of the National Religious Party threatened to resign in protest. Although the directive did nothing to change established practice —a simple declaration had always been acceptable— the crisis erupted because the directive tried to formalize existing procedures. When the fact became publicized that "Jewish nationality" could be acquired by persons who did not meet the qualifications for Jewish identity under religious law, religionists took a stand against the Interior Ministry's attempt to put a stamp of approval on the practice. Secularists took the opposite position, upholding the Interior Ministry's decision. What started as a minor administrative problem mushroomed into highly emotional Knesset debates about how to define a Jew, bringing to public attention for the first time the gravity of this issue.

Secularist objection to the religious definition of a Jew is not a question of faith or morals, for religionists are not insisting that official recognition as a Jew requires profession of the Jewish faith. A person having a Jewish mother may be an atheist and still be recognized as a Jew. Only when one's mother is not Jewish is a religious conversion required by religious law. Therefore, religionists support the position that an atheist born of a Jewish mother is entitled to Jewish nationality in the state of Israel, whereas his non-Jewish wife and their children (probably also atheists) are expected to embrace Judaism to be entitled to similar political rights.[20] This incongruous situation is the most common cause of immigrants' challenges to Population Registry procedures. If they are denied official Jewish identification, they are not only cut off from Jewish nationality benefits, but their children, whom they will likely bring up in the same non-religious tradition as themselves, will be unable to marry Jews without first undergoing a ritual Orthodox conversion.[21] Many who take a secularist position on the issue of nationality rights maintain that a father should count as well as a mother in determining nationality and that a ritual conversion is not necessary for official identification as a Jew. They argue that limiting Jewish identification to the religious definition creates an obstacle to populating the country with Jews and contravenes the central task of the state to encourage "aliya," or Jewish immigration.

The religious faction won not only the first serious debate but all subsequent legal challenges to the religious definition of a Jew. Public controversy was often avoided by encouraging a controversial applicant to submit to an Orthodox conversion and settle the matter quietly. But some who failed to qualify according to the religious definition, but nonetheless regarded themselves or their children as Jews, rejected the hypocrisy of such conversion for the purpose of acquiring nationality rights.[22] Each challenge reaching the courts kindled another "Who is a Jew?" heated public controversy. Each victory of the religious faction increased resentment against their dominant religious influence in government affairs and contributed to a smouldering groundswell of popular discontent. Secularists have always been the majority in the Israeli government and therefore in a position to overrule demands of religious bloc representatives seeking to impose religious law, but they are caught in a trap of their own making. They exploit religious sentiment and symbols to win outside support for their Jewish state, but object to "the Jewish people" being defined religiously. They also promote Israel as a secular state for both foreign and domestic consumption. Many Israelis were therefore not well informed about religious requirements for nationality acquisition until the question "Who is a Jew?" became a major political issue after 1958. A religious definition of a Jew disregards reality, for most Israeli Jews are not religious and do not pretend to be. Having taken government pronouncements at face value, many found it ridiculous that religion should be the basis of Israel's Jewish nationality status.[23]

There was total surrender to the religionists' demands in 1970 when the Law of Return was amended to incorporate a religious definition of a Jew. The amendment states that a Jew is "a person who was born of a Jewish mother or has become converted to Judaism and who is not a member of another religion."[24] According to Akiva Orr's study of changing Jewish identity, many Israelis became disillusioned and angry when their political leaders were unable to offer a secular definition of a Jew, despite Israel being constantly promoted, within and outside the country, as a secular democratic state. Orr states that many young people began to question publicly the basis for their Jewish identity.[25] Disillusionment of secular Jews as a consequence of the religionists' many victories may be one of the many causes of increasing emigration.

The religious definition of a Jew can no longer be challenged on legal grounds. Still, the fighting between the religious and secular factions has not ceased. The serious "Who is a Jew?" debates now concern the definition of conversion. Because the Orthodox rabbinate recognizes only its own definition of traditional belief as authentic Judaism, Reform and Conservative rabbis are not recognized as rabbis in Israel. Therefore, some Jews are deprived of religious leadership of their choice. Determined to further denigrate Reform and Conservative Judaism, the religious faction is vigorously continuing its campaign to have the legal definition of a Jew changed once again.[26] They want the law to specify that conversions to Judaism be conducted according to Orthodox ritual. Success of these efforts will result in further restrictions on qualifications for nationality status in Israel by definitively eliminating converts to Reform and Conservative Judaism.

Resentment of the continuing imposition of Orthodox religious rules on a secular majority has been going on since the beginning of the state. Emotions are increasingly inflamed to the extent that people are sometimes fighting it out in the streets over their opposing views about the role of religion in Israel. Riot policemen with tear gas, clubs and water hoses are sometimes required to break up so-called "Sabbath wars."[27] The social fabric of Israel is disintegrating because of "fundamental" laws that were written to discriminate against Palestinians. Jews are becoming increasingly victimized by Israel's discriminatory laws.

Solving the Problem of Jewish Identity

Studies were conducted in Israel in 1965 and 1974 to determine the factors contributing to self-identification as a Jew. The subjects of the first study were 3,679 eleventh graders (16 to 17 years old) from 117 schools. The 1965 study was replicated in 1974 with a sample of 1,875 eleventh graders from 35 schools. Simon Herman, social psychologist at the Hebrew University in Jerusalem, reported and analyzed the results.[28] The respondents were divided into three categories according to a definition of themselves as either religious, traditional or non-religious. In answer to the question, "Are we in Israel an inseparable part of the Jewish people throughout the world or do we belong to a separate people formed here — Israelis?" 96% of the religious, 87% of the traditional and 76% of the non-religious in the 1974 study identified with "the Jewish people" throughout the world. The results differed little from those of 1965. The replies to this and other questions indicated that religion is the most important element of identity as a Jew. Herman wrote, "The Jewishness of even non-religious Jews cannot be completely divorced from its religious association. . . . There is strictly speaking no secular Jewishness."[29]

The concept of Israel as the state of an extra-territorial nation of Jews is the foundation of the legal, political and social structure. The state was founded on the basic principle of Herzlian Zionism that Jews are one people with a common history and destiny. The Zionist premise of the existence of a political, national entity called "the Jewish people" is incorporated into Israel's fundamental laws. It is therefore a justifiable cause of concern that a large segment of the Israeli Jewish population considers itself separate from the Israeli government's claimed constituency of all Jews throughout the world. Although the 24% of non-religious, 13% of traditional and 4% of religious Israelis who do not identify as part of "the Jewish people" represent a minority of the total population, the process of secularization is increasing in Israel. Even children of religiously observant parents are increasingly less likely than their parents to attend synagogue services and pass the ancestral faith on to their own children. With a growing proportion of the population fitting into a non-religious category, which the studies show to be weakest in self- identification as a member of "the Jewish people," non-identifiers with Zionism's basic premise can be expected to grow. Herman recognized this as an acute problem for Israel, pointing out that "awareness of the problem has stimulated a search in some quarters for paths to an intensified Jewishness which is in keeping with the Jewish historical tradition and yet can be followed by young Israelis who are not strictly observant."[30]

The core of this "acute problem" is the Zionist premise on which the state of Israel was built, that Jews throughout the world are more united with each other in national aspirations than they are with their own countrymen. On the basis of this dubious concept of national Jewish unity, Israel's lawmakers created an extra-territorial political nationality entity, "the Jewish people," adopting the expression that had long been applied to Jews on the basis of shared cultural characteristics derived from their ancestral religion. For many secular Jews, derivations from Judaism, such as religious symbols, festive celebrations and identification with Holocaust victims[31] are the only cultural characteristics separating them from their non-Jewish countrymen. These "Jewish" characteristics are often but a small part of a total cultural identity, most elements of which are unrelated to being Jewish. Unable to arrive at anything more realistic than religious ties to suggest Jewish national unity, religious symbolism and expressions were adopted for official use and programs instituted to perpetuate memories of the Holocaust. In general, non-religious Jews did not object to the implied relationship between their religious backgrounds and national ties to Israel, provided they were not coerced into abiding by religious rules. But the studies show that this acquiescence failed to develop into a Jewish national allegiance among non-religious Jews, even within Israel. Many Israeli Jews, never having experienced anti-Semitism, do not have a feeling of solidarity with victims of the Holocaust.[32] When events forced a definition of a Jew into the limelight, they became polarized over the issue of the role of religion in society, increasing the need to find a non-religious source of identity to support Zionism's claim of a "nation of Jews."

The concern Herman calls "an acute problem" is in fact a continuation of a chronic one—how to transform Jews, who are products of a variety of cultures and range in religious beliefs from atheism to ultra-Orthodoxy, into an integrated nation. Finding the path to Jewish identity, necessary for a Jewish state to flourish, has long strained the ingenuity of pro-Zionist thinkers and tacticians. With religious Jews adamant that only Judaism defines a Jew, one solution would be to attempt to strengthen Judaism among non-believers. But this is apparently regarded as an unrealistic endeavor. An alternative is to find within the Jewish historical tradition a source of unity that can be made to appeal to those who have abandoned faith in Judaism as well as to those for whom religious faith is the source of their identity.

The concept of a Jewish race fulfills the requirement Herman set, that a solution be in keeping with the Jewish historical tradition, for tradition says that Jews are descended from Abraham. Many secularists as well as religionists cite God's promise to the children of Abraham to justify the establishment of the state of Israel in Palestine and the occupation of territories acquired in the 1967 war. The West Bank is referred to by most Israeli politicians by the biblical names "Judea and Samaria." The statement often made by Jewish settlers in the occupied territories, that God gave them the land, is an affirmation of traditional Jewish history that Abraham is the father of all Jews. A recent presentation of Jewish history as a unilinear development from the biblical nation of Israel to the contemporary state of Israel was highly praised by many reviewers.[33]

Race has often been a powerful unifying force and an effective ideological spur to nationalist movements. Whether announced biological relationships are real or feigned, a belief in blood brotherhood helps to mobilize people toward common goals. To promote racial unity for purposes of national unification, Kemal Ataturk, the first president of the Turkish Republic, motivated Turks to consider themselves a separate race. In reality, however, Turks are the product of a number of different tribes who migrated from Central Asia and further mixed with a variety of people in Anatolia. But the anthropological facts did not deter Ataturk from sponsoring studies to demonstrate the purity of a Turkish race and demanding sacrifices from his countrymen in the name of racial unity in order to assist his westernization program.

A notorious example of an evil political misuse of the concept of race was Adolf Hitler's promotion of a pure "Aryan race," endangered by intermixture with "inferior" races. That there is neither an Aryan race, nor inherently inferior and superior races, did not inhibit him from having millions of persons massacred to purify the "human race." Facts have usually not been a deterrent to development of a concept of racial unity to support national goals. The difference between Ataturk's motivation compared with Hitler's shows that promotion of the concept of race among people who are racially diverse does not necessarily have an evil motivation or lead to disastrous results.

The concept of a Jewish race is not incompatible with conventional religious history, for God, in "choosing" the Jews, made them a "unique" people. But there are strong deterrents to seriously promoting biological uniqueness of Jews. The world well remembers the consequences for Jews of the Nazi promotion of the idea that Jews are biologically different from other people. Assiduous pro-Zionist efforts, within and outside Israel, to keep the memory of the Holocaust alive, have made it almost unthinkable for Israelis to adopt Hitler's propaganda line—that Jews are racially separate from non-Jews and that a Jew is definable by blood lines. Furthermore, many reliable studies show that Jews are not now, and never were, distinguishable as a racial group.

In his classic study, "The Jewish People: A Biological History," the distinguished anthropologist Harry Shapiro demolished theories of a Jewish race with archaeological, skeletal, linguistic, historical and literary data.[34] He showed that even the early Hebrews were not racially different from surrounding populations and that Jews interbred with non-Jews throughout history, despite religious taboos against intermixture. Inter-marriages as well as the taking of captured non-Jewish women as wives are mentioned in the Bible. After the Jews were exiled by the Romans in 70 A.D., they dispersed widely and settled among non-Jews of various physical types. Although they were set apart as Jews by traditional customs, intermixture was not uncommon. Shapiro concluded that throughout the ages, Jews absorbed biological characteristics from the groups among whom they settled, either through marriage, illicit sexual contact or rape. This and other attacks on the Jewish race concept call attention to the greater biological resemblances between Jews and some of the non-Jewish populations among whom they once lived than exist between widely dispersed Jewish populations.[35]

The conclusion of Shapiro and many others, that Jews do not constitute a race, has been accepted as valid by the scientific community. The idea of a Jewish race was shown to be a false concept that was often used as a pseudo-scientific rationale for anti-Semitism. During the last several decades, no responsible writer or speaker used the term "Jewish race" to a knowledgeable audience. To do so would certainly have aroused a serious challenge. If the concept of a Jewish race is now to be successfully promoted, two main tasks must be accomplished. Credible evidence must be presented to invalidate the results of the early studies. And to avoid a charge of racist motivations, it must be shown that the concept of a Jewish race does not imply racial superiority, nor lead to racist persecutions, as happened under Hitler. Efforts in these directions are underway in Israel.

In "A New Look at Jewish Genetics", Batsheva Bonne-Tamir, chairman of the Department of Genetics of the Tel Aviv University School of Medicine, reported that results of recent research in population genetics disagree with "those researchers who rejected the notion that there is a separate Jewish race."[36] She addressed the reasons for the disagreement, explaining that an anti-racist trend existed during the 1960's which inspired a UNESCO publication, "The Problem of Race in Modern Science." She specifically referred to Harry Shapiro's article, "The Jewish People: A Biological History,"[37] as influenced by a trend of political thinking of the time that there was no separate Jewish race. She further pointed out, to explain the contradictory results, that the earlier studies relied on single genetic markers, such as ABO blood types, which cannot provide an accurate answer. Also, that data on Jewish populations now available in Israel are far more reliable than what was available several decades ago. In sum, a political trend of the time, inadequate data and unreliable methodology resulted in the wrong conclusion that there is no separate Jewish race. The Israeli studies, on the other hand, according to Bonne-Tamir, are reliable because they use multiple genetic markers (many of which were previously unknown), they employ large representative and random samples, and the ethnic origin of the sample populations were accurately determined. This information was given to Israeli readers. The article was written in Hebrew and published in an Israeli popular science magazine. Newspapers reported the findings of a Jewish race to the Israeli public.[38]

Five years later, an article titled "Genetic Links for Scattered Jews" appeared in *Nature*, an unspecialized British science journal which publishes reports of ongoing research in all fields. Referring to continuing genetic studies of Jewish populations, the article begins with the statement:

> Preliminary studies using DNA sequences as a new and sophisticated tool for genetic analysis tend to support the conclusion drawn from earlier investigations that the Jews, even after being scattered around the world for two millennia, remain—to a significant degree—genetically distinctive.[39]

This view, attributed to Bonne-Tamir, can mean nothing other than an affirmation of a Jewish race, for a race—to a biologist—is a population that is genetically distinctive to a significant degree. To avert criticism from those who might suspect the motives of those who claim there is a Jewish race, the article goes on to say that Bonne-Tamir's view is not to be rejected as racist doctrine, for she does not suggest "that Jews are better or worse for having a common genetic heritage. She simply points to the evidence that it exists."[40]

This denial of racist motives rests on a definition of racism that arose from the Nazi model, a necessary ingredient of which is an allegation that one group is biologically superior to another. However, this feature need not be present in a policy of discrimination recognized as racist today. If it is required that oppressors must label their victims inferior to themselves, most official acts of discrimination could not be correctly called "racist." For example, South Africa does not justify apartheid laws by declaring that Blacks are inferior to Whites, nor does Israel attribute racial inferiority to Arabs to justify discriminatory policies. And Great Britain does not say that Asians are racially inferior when immigration restrictions are placed on them. Post-World War II policies of discrimination are more subtle than were those of the Third Reich, for governments try to avoid having world opinion place them in that infamous category as they carry out policies of discrimination. A charge of "racism" is deflected by discriminating without offering a motive, or pretending motivations other than biological inferiority. However, the act of discrimination, as a systematic policy, is racist, according to the generally accepted definition of racism today, as discrimination on grounds of race or national or ethnic origin.[41] There is good reason for denying racist motives. The concept of a Jewish race may not, in itself, be racist, but the danger exists that some might think it is. Because the existence of a Jewish race was the alleged "scientific" basis for Nazi massacres of Jews, the surprising statement that a Jewish race has now been discovered to be the reality Hitler claimed it to be, is a strong reminder of the tragic consequences of racism. Those who fear that a revival of a Jewish race concept might lead to disastrous results for Jews or others, far outnumber those who care how a Jew is officially defined in Israel.

It is noteworthy that, as the level of reader sophistication increases, claims of a Jewish race disappear. In the professional international genetics journal in which the study was published, the authors state that the purpose of studying the genetics of the Jews was not to determine whether a Jewish race exists, but rather was a systematic study of genetic polymorphic systems, using data collected on immigrant Jewish populations.[42] There is good reason to assure colleagues that the participating researchers were not motivated to revive the concept of a Jewish race, for the project would be highly unlikely to receive favorable review and the subsequent funding it enjoyed.[43] Race classifications were abandoned in science several decades ago, not only because they were used as a pseudo-scientific basis for racist doctrines, but also, increasing evidence had accumulated that the traits used to differentiate populations were not genetically stable and therefore not reliable.[44] Today, racial classifications are regarded as irrelevant to any major scientific concern.

Bonne-Tamir's criticism in *Mada* of the methodology and sampling of the earlier studies may be justified, but pointing out their inadequacies does not validate either the methods or samples of her own studies. She is correct in stating that a single genetic marker does not constitute a reliable guide to racial differences, but neither do multiple genetic markers. Using many, each of which is not exempt from non-hereditary influences, does not add up to the scientific reliability Bonne-Tamir implies for her own research results. As for the increased reliability of conclusions derived from large representative and random samples, her study was faulted on statistical grounds by the one article in a professional journal that investigated some of the results.[45]

Bonne-Tamir claims that careful determinations of ethnic origins of the Israeli samples make the Tel Aviv University studies more reliable. But there is a question as to the selection of the non-Jewish samples in the studies to which she refers. Jews now living in Israel were compared with non-Jews in the countries from which they had recently emigrated.[46] But in order to reach a valid conclusion that Israeli Jewish populations are free from "non-Jewish genes," they should be compared also with non-Jewish populations among whom their more distant ancestors lived. Historical evidence was disregarded. In a review of historical events relevant to the genetics of the Jews, there is no reference to interbreeding between Jews and non-Jews,[47] although there is abundant historical evidence that the genetics of Jewish populations were considerably modified through the centuries by proselytism, intermarriages and extramarital sexual relationships, both violent and voluntary.[48] By ignoring historical evidence, the primary source of information from which we can learn when and where taboos against intermixture were minimal or non-existent, the studies failed to explore the likely sources of the non-Jewish biological influences that Shapiro and others wrote about. It does not follow from a claim, even if it were proved, that a particular Jewish population is significantly different from recent non-Jewish neighbors, that the Jewish population is not carrying genes resulting from earlier intermixture during a more tolerant era.

There is truth in Bonne-Tamir's statement in *Mada* that an anti-racist trend existed after World War II. Some scientists were indeed motivated to enter the discussion of a Jewish race in order to demolish the concept underlying Hitler's massacre of Jews. It is also true that scientific interest in race studies ceased afterwards, which might seem to suggest that the trend waned after the goal was achieved of disproving the existence of a separate Jewish race. But the loss of scientific interest in classifying people racially was not totally due to the political, racist uses that had been made of racial classifications. A more important cause was the discovery that the physical characteristics of a population change through time even when there is no intermixture with other populations. Race classifications lost their attraction for tracing migrations and micro-evolutionary changes.

Even if the early studies were motivated by political considerations, it does not necessarily follow that the results are wrong. The important consideration is that politics should not influence the conclusions derived from the results. Bonne-Tamir implies that contrary conclusions, arrived at through new and improved methods of genetic analysis, support her allegations of a built-in bias in the old studies and suggests that her own research was not politically motivated. But these allegations do not invalidate the early studies. The sound historical, archaeological and linguistic evidence of intermixture is totally ignored in defending the reliability of the new studies, as if all previous evidence was rendered irrelevant by new genetic technology. It is highly questionable that the Israeli studies accomplished what it is said they accomplished, that is, the determination that Jews are genetically distinctive. An absence of political bias in one's own study is not established by attributing bias to studies that arrive at contrary conclusions.

Summary and Conclusions

The seeds of Jewish infighting were sown when the state was established on the Zionist principle that Israel is "the state of the Jews," with laws to provide exclusive benefits for Jewish citizens. Singling out Jews for a nationality status denied others, but without legally defining a Jew, opened the way for disputes about qualifying criteria. The minority position, that a Jew must be defined by religious law, has consistently prevailed over the majority view that religion and nationality must remain separate. Each religionist victory increases hostility between the two factions.

The single most important clue to understanding the significance of the "Who is a Jew?" controversies is the difference in Israeli law between "citizenship" and "nationality." Without knowing the implications of Jewish nationality compared with Israeli citizenship, it is difficult to understand the protracted, intense controversies which prompt immigrants to endure long court battles to gain legal acceptance as a Jew. When Zionist legislation made identification as a Jew the sole criterion of nationality in Israel, the intent was to exclude Arabs in order to establish a privileged status for Jews. But the strategy backfired when religionists exerted their influence to put a religious definition of a Jew into law. As a result, some Jews also began to feel the sting of Israel's discriminatory Zionist-inspired legislation. With religion the sole legal criterion for possession of full nationality rights, persons who do not fit the legislated religious definition of a Jew must accept a second class citizenship, much the same as Arabs. The disqualified are primarily the non-Jewish wives of Jews and their children. And if Orthodox Knesset members succeed in amending the Law of Return once again, those converted to Judaism by Reform and Conservative rabbis will also be disqualified, unless they agree to an Orthodox ritual conversion. Despite their being relatively few in number, the plight of Jews rejected for nationality status has often caused secularists, on the basis of principle, to be pitted against religionists in public debate about who is a Jew.

The results of the studies of Jewish identity show that there is still a need to strengthen national allegiance to the Zionist-created "Jewish people" state, even for many Jews born in Israel who have no political ties to other countries. The Israeli school children who stated their loyalty to be to Israel rather than to "the Jewish people," represent a continuing threat to the basic Zionist concept of a Jewish nation without borders with headquarters in Israel. In an attempt to counter this threat, the pattern set by early Zionists of putting Zionist ideology above the facts is still being followed.

Promoting the idea of a Jewish race to help solve the identity crisis is as contemptuous of fact as promoting Israel as a democracy where all citizens are equal. Instead of expending intellectual resources on the never-ending job of patching up cracks in the shaky foundation on which Israel was built, Israel's laws should be de-Zionized. If Zionism's false concept of an extra-territorial Jewish nation were repudiated and replaced with a truly democratic Israeli nation-state, religion and/or ethnicity would no longer either qualify or disqualify a person for nationality rights. Replacing Zionist "fundamental" laws with a constitution guaranteeing equal rights for all citizens might make Israel the democratic state it now falsely claims to be. If all citizens—regardless of religious faith—were truly equal under the law, there would no longer be political or legal incentives for arguing about who qualifies as a Jew.

NOTES

1. Although it is a gross over-simplification to divide Israeli society into two sectors as regards any domestic policy, the terms "religionist" and "secularist" are used throughout this paper for convenience in distinguishing those who advocate religion as the basis of national rights and obligations, and those who reject religion as the determining criterion for nationality. The terms are not intended to imply that one group follows Judaism and the other does not. Even a rabbi can be a secularist in the sense the term is used here. "Religionist" and "secularist" contrast those who hold differing political attitudes on the question of official criteria for nationality status.
2. See Oscar Kraines, "Landmark Cases and Incidents," 22-76, in*The Impossible*

Dilemma: Who is a Jew in the State of Israel, New York, Bloch Publishing Co., 1976.

3. For example, *Minneapolis Star Tribune,* September 6, 1987.

4. See Ian Lustick, *Arabs in the Jewish State,* University of Texas Press, 1980.

5. Writers rarely criticize Zionism openly and directly as the foundation of Israel's discriminatory political, legal and social structure. Simha Flapan, for example, in *The Birth of Israel,* Pantheon Books, 1987, systematically destroys the credibility of myths that have shaped Israeli policies from the very beginning of the state, myths that are based on the ideology of Zionism. Nonetheless, a continuing commitment to socialist Zionism prompts him to state, "I have never believed that Zionism inherently obviates the rights of the Palestinians, and I do not believe so today." (p.11). *The Israeli Connection,* Pantheon Books, New York, 1987, by Benjamin Beit-Hallahmi, is one of the few books published by an establishment United States press that outspokenly questions the morality of Zionism. W. Thomas and Sally Mallison, *The Palestinian Problem in International Law and World Order,* Longman, Essex, England, 1986, also do not mince words regarding the responsibility of Zionist ideology for the Middle East conflict.

6. Joan Peters, *From Time Immemorial,* 1984, claims that there were few Arabs in Palestine before the end of the nineteenth century and that Arabs were later drawn there by economic benefits provided by Jews. The book, which reinforces the myth of "a land without people for a people without land," was highly praised in major book review publications as a responsible denial of Palestinian land claims in Palestine. After examining her assertions and statistics, competent scholars such as Norman Finklestein, then a graduate student at Princeton University, Albert Hourani, a historian at Oxford University, and Yehoshua Porath of the Hebrew University, among others, declared that her documents and statistics were misrepresented. Her book was called "preposterous" and "worthless."

7. Emile Mamorstein writes in *Heaven at Bay, The Jewish Kulturkampf in the Holy Land,* London, Oxford University Press, 1969, p.79,

> With regard to the Zionists what shall I say and what am I to speak? There is great dismay also in the Holy Land that these evil men who deny the Unique One of the world and His Holy Torah have proclaimed with so much publicity that it is in their power to hasten redemption for the people of Israel and gather the dispersed from all the ends of the earth.

8. Paul Goodman, *Chaim Weizmann, a Tribute on His Seventieth Birthday,* London, Victor Gollancz Ltd., 1945, p.199.

9. Elmer Berger has pointed out in many lectures that the Land of Israel was promised to the children of Israel only if they fulfilled the Covenant to obey His laws.

10. Paul Findley,*They Dare to Speak Out,* Lawrence Hill & Co., Westport, Connecticut, 1985, relates many cases of intimidation by pro-Israel activists and suppression of free speech through accusations of anti-Semitism.

11. Joseph Badi, ed.,*Fundamental Laws of the State of Israel,* Twayne Publishers, N.Y. 1961; M.D. Gouldman,*Israel Nationality Law,* Hebrew University, Jerusalem 1970; O. Kraines, op. cit.

12. This is not to imply that all authors who refer to Israel's "Law of Nationality"

do so to deceive. When scholars refer to the original translation, they may unintentionally reinforce what may have been a deliberate intent to obscure the difference between a citizenship and a nationality status.

13. For further comments on effects of "fundamental" laws, see Roselle Tekiner, "Jewish Nationality Status as the Basis of Institutionalized Racial Discrimination in Israel," in *American Arab Affairs*, Summer 1986, pp. 79-98 and "On the Inequality of Israeli Citizens," in *Without Prejudice*, vol. 1, No.1, 1987, pp. 48-57.

14. See Chapter 2, "The Juridical Status and Political Activities of the Zionist Organization/Jewish Agency," in W. Thomas and Sally V. Mallison, *The Palestine Problem in International Law and World Order*, Essex, England, Longman, 1986.

15. John Dugard, *Human Rights and the South African Legal Order*, Princeton University Press, 1978, p.60.

16. M.D. Gouldman, op. cit., p.29.

17. Under the millet system, religious groups were divided into nations on the basis of religion. Each was under separate jurisdiction of its own religious leader. The Muslim millet had a higher standing within the empire than the others.

18. It may not be fair to credit Zionist thinkers with the original idea of creating two categories of citizenship for the purpose of providing legal benefits to one category alone. There is a prototype of the distinction between "ezrahut" and "le'um" in the Nuremberg laws. "Law for the Protection of German Blood and Honor," refers to "Staatsangehoerige" (members of the state) "of German blood," which implies that at the time there were "Staatsangehoerige" who did not have German blood, i.e., Jews. A law subsequently enacted, "The Reich Citizenship Law," designated German (blooded) "Staatsangehoerige" as "Reichsbuerger" (citizens of the Reich). Because Jews could not be "Reichsbuerger," they were ineligible for civil service positions and were soon stripped of all rights as members of the state.

19. For a discussion of the operations of the "national" institutions, see Ian Lustick, op. cit., 97-109. For the handicaps the subsidies place upon Arabs, see Sabri Jiryis, *The Arabs in Israel*, Monthly Review Press, New York and London, 1976.

20. The "Brother Daniel case" proved an exception to the religionist position that, born a Jew, one remains a Jew for life. Oswald Rufeison was born to a Jewish mother in Poland, converted to Catholicism and was ordained a friar. When he immigrated to Israel, he tried to register as of Christian religion and Jewish nationality. His request for Jewish nationality was denied and he was told to apply for citizenship through naturalization. Rufeison did not get much religionist support, for apparently a Christian Jew is a far greater contradiction than an atheist Jew. If religious law were strictly upheld by religionists, they would have supported Rufeison's claim. When the court ruled against Rufeison, religious groups hailed the decision, while many secularists decried it. Although contrary to religious law, the court decision constituted legal confirmation that religious belief, if not strict Halachic law, is the basis of nationality in Israel. For details, see Akiva Orr, "The UnJewish State: The Politics of Jewish Identity in Israel," London, Ithaca Press, 1982, pp. 91-98.

21. There is no civil marriage in Israel. The Law of Marriage and Divorce gives

the rabbinate jurisdiction over marriage regulations, which strictly follows the religious prohibition against intermarriage. If the state is criticized for violations of human rights implicit in this law, reponsibility can be passed to the rabbinate.

22. The Shalit case of 1969 provided the first major public dispute after the court declared against Rufeison. Mrs. Shalit, the non-Jewish wife of a non-religious Jew, refused to convert to Judaism to obtain nationality rights for herself and her children. For details, and references to other cases, see Oscar Kraines, op. cit., pp. 46-53.

23. See Akiva Orr, op. cit., pp. 91-97.

24. The last phrase was probably added to the religious definition as a consequence of the "Brother Daniel" case of 1962. See footnote #20.

25. Akiva Orr, op. cit., 95-97.

26. *The New York Times* of July 9, 1987 reported that three bills redefining a Jew in a way that would have denied the legitimacy of Reform and Conservative Judaism were very narrowly rejected by the Knesset.

27. "Police and Religious Clash Again in Jerusalem,"*The New York Times*, August 30, 1987.

28. Simon N. Herman, *Jewish Identity, A Social Psychological Perspective*. Sage Publications, Beverly Hills and London, 1977.

29. Ibid; see also Simon N. Herman, *Israelis and Jews*, Random House, New York, 1970.

30. Herman, op. cit. 1977, p. 201.

31. The roots of the Holocaust are religious. Anti-Semitism flourished long before race differences were systematized. Racist theories based on physical differences were "scientific" rationalizations of deep Christian prejudices against the Jews on theological grounds.

32. Georges Tamarin, *The Israeli Dilemma: Essays on a Warfare State*, Rotterdam University Press, 1973.

33. Paul Johnson,*History of the Jews*, Harper and Row, 1987.

34. Harry Shapiro, "The Jewish People: A Biological History," UNESCO, New York, 1960.

35. See also Raphael Patai and J.P. Patai-Wing, *The Myth of a Jewish Race*, Scribners, New York, 1975, a comprehensive report of sources of non-Jewish mixture in Jewish populations.

36. Batsheva Bonne-Tamir, *Mada*, v.24, #4-5, 1980. *Mada* is a Hebrew science journal published under the auspices of National Council for Research and Development, the Israel Academy of Sciences and Humanities, Bar-llan University, Ben Gurion University, the Hebrew University, Jerusalem, The Technion, Israel Institute of Technology, and the Weizmann Institute of Science.

37. Harry Shapiro, op. cit.

38. The following information appeared in an article in *Davar*, an Israeli daily newspaper, on August 9, 1981:

> Genetic research done in Israel during the past ten years shows that the genetic differences between Jews of various communities are usually smaller than differences between Jews and non-Jews from the same country. For example, Jews who originated in Poland are like Jews who originated in Yemen from a genetic point of view much more than they are like Christian Poles. Among Ashkenazi Jews the

foreign genes constitute less than 10%. The external physical differences that can be seen between Jews of various communities, such as hair color, develop mainly because of environmental influence (climatic factors such as the sun) and not the hereditary balance.

On November 8, 1981, the following article, under the heading of "With tears and sweat we will build our race," appeared in "Davar", written by Aaron Meged, a prominent Israeli journalist:

In our bitter fight against the race theories of H.S. Chamberlin and the Nazi, Alfred Rosenberg, the theories that brought terrible disasters to us, that allocated evil characteristics to all of us and being naturally inherited ones, so that no Jew could escape them, we tended to disregard totally the existence of biological characteristics that are common to all Jews. The Hebrew Encyclopedia, while dealing with the term, "the people of Israel," dwells lengthily on this problem, whether the Jews are a "race," and claims that mixed marriages, conversions, rape, etc., over generations during which Jews were living among other peoples, have eroded their biological characteristics and eliminated the unity of the race. But just as archaelogy is not a precise science, so it is with the science of genetics. Findings change; conclusions change. In a few days, an international genetics congress will convene in Jerusalem and Professor Arie Shinberg from Tel Aviv University will say that "genetic research done in this country by various scientists proved that there is a great genetic bond within the Jewish people among all its communities; Ashkenazi, North African and other." He will add that the results of this research are astonishing because for years we accepted the idea that among the various communities of Jewish people there are different genes as a result of assimilation in other nations.

39. Nachemia Meyers,"Nature," v. 314, March 21, 1985, p. 208.
40. *Ibid.*
41. According to a United Nations General Assembly resolution of 1965 and a 1987 ruling of the United States Supreme Court, the term "racism" includes discrimination based on ethnic origin.
42. B. Bonne-Tamir, B. Karlin and R. Kenett,"Analysis of Genetic Data on Jewish Populations, I. Historical Background, Demographic Features and Genetic Markers," in *American Journal of Human Genetics* 31, 1979, p. 325.
43. In addition to funding by Israeli institutions, the article acknowledges grants from the United States National Institute of Health, the National Science Foundation and the German Volkswagen Foundation.
44. F. Boas, *Changes in Bodily Form of Descendants of Immigrants*, Columbia University Press, 1912; M. Goldstein, "Demographic and Bodily Changes in Descendants of Mexican Immigrants," *Institute of Latin-American Studies*, 1943; G. Lasker, "Migration and Physical Differentiation," *American Journal of Physical Anthropology*, vol. 4, 1946, 273-300. H. Shapiro, *Migration and Environment*, Oxford University Press, 1939. F. Weidenreich, "The Brachycephalization of Recent Mankind," *Southwestern Journal of Anthropology* vol. 1, 1945, 1-54.
45. N.E. Morton, R. Kenett, S. Yee and R. Lew, "Bioassay of Kinship in Populations of Middle Eastern Origin and Controls," *Current Anthropology* 23, no.2, April 1982, 157-167.

46. S. Karlin, R. Kenett and B. Bonne-Tamir, "Analysis of Biochemical Genetic Data on Jewish Populations: Results and Interpretations of Heterogeneity Indices and Distance Measures with Respect to Standards," *American Journal of Human Genetics* 31, no.3, May 1979, pp. 341-365; S. Karlin, D. Carmelli and B. Bonne-Tamir, "Analysis of Biochemical Genetic Data on Jewish Populations. III. The Application of Individual Phenotype Measurements for Population Comparison." *American Journal of Human Genetics* 34, 1982, pp. 50-64.
47. B. Bonne-Tamir, B. Karlin and R. Kenett, op. cit., 324-339.
48. See Harry Shapiro, 1960, op. cit., and Raphael Patai and J. Patai-Wing, op. cit.

4

THE QUESTION OF PALESTINE: PALESTINIAN ATTITUDES TOWARD CIVIL LIBERTIES AND HUMAN RIGHTS

SHAW J. DALLAL

Historical Introduction

The problem of Palestine has played a significant role in shaping Palestinian attitudes toward civil liberties and human rights. These attitudes stem from the early Arab national movement and can be traced back to the Syrian national movement in 1847.[1] In his classic work, *The Arab Awakening*, George Antonius writes:

> The story of the Arab national movement opens in Syria in 1847.... (p.13) The rule of tolerance established ... had one unpremeditated result: it opened the door to Western missionary enterprise; and, by so doing, it gave free play to two forces, one French and the other American, which were destined between them to become the foster parents of the Arab resurrection.... (p.35) Meanwhile, the missionaries were rapidly opening schools in various parts of Syria. Their first foundations were in Beirut, Jerusalem and the Lebanon....[2]

"Syria" was defined by the General Syrian Congress, which convened in Damascus on July 2, 1919, with delegates from Lebanon and Palestine,[3] as having the following boundaries:

On the north, the Taurus Range; on the south, a line running from Rafah to al-Jauf and following the Syria-Hejaz border below Aqaba; on the east, the boundary formed by the Euphrates and Khabur rivers and a line stretching from some distance east of Abu Kamal to some distance east of al-Jauf; on the west, the Mediterranean Sea.[4]

Thus, at the time, Palestine was an integral part of Syria under Ottoman domination.

The resolutions of the General Syrian Congress represent the first documented statement on civil liberties and human rights supported by a Palestinian delegation. These resolutions unmistakably reflect French and American influences:

> We, the undersigned, members of the General Syrian Congress . . . composed of delegates from three zones, namely the southern (Palestine), eastern and western . . . with credentials . . . to represent the Moslem, Christian and Jewish inhabitants of our respective districts . . . submit the following . . . before the American Section of the Inter-Allied Commission. . . . We desire the Government of Syria to be . . . based on *principles of democratic and broadly decentralized rule* which shall *safeguard the rights of minorities*, and . . . we protest against Article XXII[5]of the Covenant of the League of Nations which relegated us to the standing of insufficiently developed races requiring the tutelage of a mandatory power. . . . We reject the claims of the Zionists for the establishment of a Jewish commonwealth in that part of southern Syria which is known as Palestine. . . . *Our Jewish fellow-citizens shall continue to enjoy the rights and to bear the responsibilities* which are ours in common. . . . We desire that there should be no dismemberment of Syria, and no separation of Palestine or the coastal regions in the west or the Lebanon from the mother country. . . . The lofty principles proclaimed by President Wilson encourage us to believe that the determining consideration in the settlement of our own future will be *the real desires of our people* . . . we would not have risen against Turkish rule under which we enjoyed civic and political privileges, as well as rights of representation, had it not been that the Turks denied us our right to national existence. . . .[6] (Emphasis added)

These appeals made in the early part of this century represented and perhaps still represent the perceptions and the attitudes of the people of southern Syria (Palestine) toward civil liberties and human rights. These attitudes were intensified by a history of bad faith and double dealing perpetrated against the Arabs in general and the Palestinian people in particular by the Government of Great Britain during World War I subsequent to an Agreement concluded by the British Government and the Arabs. The Agreement was concluded in the form of diplomatic notes exchanged between Great Britain, represented by the High Commissioner of Egypt, Sir Henry McMahon, and the Arabs, represented by Sharif Hussain, the Sharif of Mecca. These notes defined the boundaries of an independent Arab state including Palestine, pledged to the Arabs by the Government of Great Britain.[7]

The first note from the Sharif of Mecca to Sir Henry McMahon was dated July 14, 1915. In it, the Sharif stated:

> Whereas the entire Arab nation without exception is determined to assert its right to live again in freedom and administer its own affairs in name and in fact. . . . For these reasons, the Arab nation has decided to approach the Government of Great Britain with a request for the approval, through one of their representatives if they think fit, of the following basic provisions. . . . Great Britain recognizes the independence of the Arab countries . . . the two contracting parties undertake, in the event of any foreign state attacking either of them to come to each other's assistance with all the resources of their military and naval forces. . . .[8]

On August 30, 1915, Sir Henry McMahon sent a reply to the Sharif of Mecca in which he stated:

> In earnest of this, we hereby confirm to you the declaration of Lord Kitchener as communicated to you . . . in which was manifested our desire for the independence of the Arab countries and their inhabitants. . . .[9]

Further communications took place, in which the boundaries of the independent Arab state were agreed upon.[10]

On December 13, 1915, Sir Henry McMahon sent the following assurance to the Sharif of Mecca:

> In these circumstances, the Government of Great Britain have authorized me to declare to your Lordship that *you may rest confident that Great Britain does not intend to conclude any peace whatsoever, of which the freedom of the Arab peoples and their liberation from German and Turkish domination do not form an essential condition* . . .[11] (Emphasis added)

This assurance, however, was in direct conflict with the Sykes-Picot Agreement.[12]

On January 1, 1916, the Sharif of Mecca wrote to Sir Henry McMahon the following:

Your excellency may rest assured, and Great Britain may rest assured, that we shall adhere to our resolve to which reference has already been made . . . Your statement that you do not wish to impel us to hasty action which might obstruct the success of your objectives render further explanation superfluous, except that we shall have to let you know in due course our requirements in the way of arms, ammunition and so forth. . . .[13]

On January 30, 1916, Sir Henry McMahon responded:

The Arab countries are now associated in that noble aim which can be attained by uniting our forces and acting in unison. . . .[14]

When the Supreme Council of the Inter-Allied Forces met in Paris on March 20, 1919 at the conclusion of World War One to consider the Sykes-Picot Agreement,[15] President Wilson proposed setting up an Inter-Allied Commission to investigate the wishes of the inhabitants of Palestine. The Inter-Allied Commission, also known as the King-Crane Commission, made its recommendations on August 28, 1919.[16] In dealing with the civil liberties and the human rights of the people of Palestine, the Commission stated:

. . . The Commissioners began their study of Zionism with minds predisposed in its favor, but the actual facts in Palestine . . . have driven them to the recommendation here made. . . . President Wilson laid down the following principles. . . . The settlement of every question, whether of territory, of sovereignty, of economic arrangement, or of political relationship upon the basis of the free acceptance of that settlement by the people immediately concerned, and not upon the material interest or advantage of any other nation. . . . If that principle is to rule, and so the wishes of Palestine's population are to be decisive as to what is to be done with Palestine, then it is to be remembered that the non-Jewish population of Palestine—nearly nine-tenths of the whole—are emphatically against the entire Zionist programme. . . . The Peace Conference should not shut its eyes to the fact that the anti-Zionist feeling in Palestine and Syria is intense and not lightly to be flouted . . . it would intensify, with a certainty like fate. . . . There would then be no reason why Palestine could not be included in a united Syrian state, just as other portions of the country. . . .[17]

Great Britain's involvement in the fate of the people of Palestine continued until it gave up its mandate over Palestine on May 15, 1948, after the United Nations decreed the partition of Palestine into two states, one Arab and the other Jewish, while providing that the area of Jerusalem would have an international status.[18]

At the end of World War II, violence intensified in Palestine. During the British election campaign of 1945, the Labor Party made election promises to scrap the "British statement of policy on Palestine" of May 14, 1939, referred to as "The White Paper." Among other things, that document stated:

> The alternatives before His Majesty's government are either (i) to seek to expand the Jewish National Home indefinitely by immigration, against the strongly expressed will of the Arab people of the country; or (ii) to permit further expansion of the Jewish National Home by immigration only if the Arabs are prepared to acquiesce in it. The former policy means rule by force. Apart from other considerations, such a policy seems to His Majesty's government to be contrary to the whole spirit of Article 22 of the Covenant of the League of Nations. . . . His Majesty's government are determined to check illegal immigration . . . nor will they be under any obligation to facilitate the further development of the Jewish National Home by immigration regardless of the wishes of the Arab population. . . .[19]

After the Labor Party came to power on July 27, 1945, however, it reversed its position and declared its support for "The White Paper." An Anglo-American Committee of Inquiry was then established to formulate a common Anglo-American policy on Palestine. Its recommendations were released on November 13, 1945. Among other things it provided:

> . . . . Palestine alone cannot meet the emigration needs of the Jewish victims of Nazi and Fascist persecution; the whole world shares responsibility for them. . . . We, therefore, recommend that our governments together . . . should endeavor immediately to find new homes for all such "displaced persons," irrespective of creed or nationality. . . . We regard it as essential that a clear statement . . . that Jew shall not dominate Arab and Arab shall not dominate Jew in Palestine. . . . That Palestine shall be neither a Jewish state nor be made an Arab state . . . but a state which guards the rights and interest of Moslems, Jews and Christians alike; and ac-

cords to the inhabitants, as a whole, the fullest measure of self-government. . . ."[20]

In February of 1947, Britain's attempt to reconcile Palestinian demands with Zionist demands in Palestine collapsed. The Labor Government of Great Britain therefore decided to refer the Palestine dispute to the General Assembly of the United Nations, which convened in special session at Britain's request from April 28 to May 15, 1947.[21]

On May 15, 1947, the General Assembly created UNSCOP, the U.N. Special Committee on Palestine, which consisted of representatives from eleven small states selected on a basis of geographic distribution. They were intended to be neutral, and were given "the widest powers to ascertain and record facts, and to investigate all questions and issues relevant to the problem of Palestine. . . ." UNSCOP was instructed to "prepare a report . . . and . . . submit such proposals as it may consider appropriate for the solution of the problem . . . not later thanSeptember 1, 1947".[22]

UNSCOP, by a majority vote, submitted to the General Assembly a proposal for the division of Palestine into two states, one Jewish, consisting of 56 percent of the area of Palestine, and one Arab, consisting of 44 percent of the area of Palestine. The two states were to remain in economic union. The city of Jerusalem and its immediate environs were to have a special international body controlling it. The General Assembly adopted this proposal, with minor modifications, on November 29, 1947.[23]

The Palestinians, who constituted two-thirds of the population of Palestine[24] and who owned more than ninety-three percent of the lands of Palestine,[25] were infuriated at the inequity of the Partition Plan. Unaware of the military capabilities and preparedness of the Jewish minority, they vowed to prevent the implementation of the Partition Plan.[26]

The Zionist Military Program

Zionist para-military organizations had been in existence since the late 1870's. These organizations eventually "fathered the organization of Jewish guardsmen, 'Hashomer,' which was founded in 1907 and which was precursor to Haganah."[27] The Haganah, which was created in 1917,[28]

was in action between 1936 and 1939. During the 1939-45 war, individual members and groups of Haganah had experience of armed action in the Jewish Brigade; in independent Jewish units;

in special operations with British forces in the Middle East and Western desert; and in parachute missions in Europe and the Balkans.[29]

After World War II, the Haganah continued as a military force in Palestine—"born, reared, developed and armed in absolute secrecy."[30]

Thus when the United Nations passed the resolution which partitioned Palestine in November 1947, the Haganah was a disciplined, battle-tested and well-equipped military establishment.[31]

The Palestinian military forces, on the other hand, were not in existence. Palestinian uprisings had always taken the form of guerrilla action, conducted spontaneously. They were not organized on a permanent basis. The Palestinian uprising of 1936-39 had been crushed at the hands of the British forces. After World War II, therefore, the impoverished Palestinians were no match for the Zionist forces.[32]

When the hostilities between the Palestinians and the Zionists broke out in December of 1947, the "appropriate moment" for the violent uprooting of the Palestinians by the Zionists seemed to have arrived. The Zionists thus unleashed their military program. They began their raids on isolated undefended villages in an effort to terrorize the Palestinian inhabitants, who began to flee their homes and farms at the advance of Zionist forces. Massacres of innocent civilians began to take place, as in Deir Yassein,[33] where the whole population of that village—men, women and children—was massacred in cold blood. The massacre of Deir Yassein was conspicuous, not because it was unique,[34] but because of its impact as Menachem Begin, the perpetrator of that outrage, boasted:

> . . . In the result it helped us. Panic overwhelmed the Arabs of Eretz Israel. . . . Arabs throughout the country, induced to believe wild tales of 'Irgun butchery,' were seized with limitless panic and started to flee for their lives. This mass flight soon developed into a maddened, uncontrollable stampede. Of the about 800,000 Arabs who lived on the . . . territory of . . . Israel, only 165,000 [remained]. The political and economic significance of this development can hardly be overestimated.[35]

Begin's elation at his success in contributing to the displacement of the Palestinians was shared by Israel's first president, Chaim Weizmann, who was said to be a "rational" elder statesman. In describing Weizmann's happiness with the displacement of the Palestinians, James G. McDonald, the United States' first Ambassador to Israel, wrote:

> Dr. Weizmann, despite his ingrained rationalism, spoke to me emotionally of this 'miraculous simplification of Israel's tasks.'[36]

Some American Jews, however, were repulsed by what the Zionists did to the Palestinians, as attested to by the following passages by an American Jewish writer in 1949:

> Now that I've traveled every corner of this country, it has become clear that the Israeli troops must have been decidedly tough even with non-combatant Arabs during the war. There are . . . too many dynamited, desolated native villages where little or no fighting occurred. The Jews simply came in and smashed the place. . . . Israel knows and laments Dir Yassin, where Irgun massacred . . . men, women and children. Native fear of more Dir Yassins must be added to all the other reasons for the mad flight of the Arab people. . . . I am shaken by the expressions of grief and shame I have privately received from non-political but prominent Israelis whose personal integrity is beyond question. 'The Israeli soldier has looted, burned, and slaughtered,' I have been told. . . . It is even hinted that certain officers actually ordered their troops to let themselves go. . . .[37]

Filling the Vacuum

After expelling hundreds of thousands of Palestinians from their homes and lands, the Israelis tried to fill the evacuated land with new Jewish settlers. Most American and European Jews, however, showed little interest in emigrating to Israel, despite the pressure exerted upon them. In the early fifties, in the United States in particular, the Israelis exerted unusual pressure on the American Jewish community to emigrate to Israel. In a speech in the Knesset on December 13, 1951, David Ben-Gurion asserted that "mass immigration sources were drying up." He expressed frustration over "how to induce American Jews to come when there was no whip cracking over their heads." Ben-Gurion continued:

> They went bankrupt since the establishment of the Jewish state. There were not five leaders who got up to go to Israel after the state was established. I don't maintain they would have been followed by masses, but they would have proved that Zionism was not void of meaning at least in the eyes of its leaders.[38]

Israel's campaign for American Jewish immigrants may not have succeeded dramatically. Its campaign for Jewish immigrants from the Arab states, however, received a large measure of success. But some of the methods used in that campaign were often violent and underhanded, as Israel turned to the Arab Jewish communities in Iraq, Morocco, Yemen, Syria, Egypt and other Arab countries.

For example, in April of 1950, the Jewish community of Iraq was suddenly subjected to "anti-Jewish" violence of inexplicable origin. It is now known that on the last evening of Passover of that year, about fifty thousand Iraqis of the Jewish faith, in accordance with an ancient tradition, were promenading in Baghdad along the Tigris River. A car sped along the river and hurled a bomb which exploded on the pavement. No one was hurt, but the Iraqi Jewish community was petrified. Rumors began to circulate that a fanatic Iraqi Moslem organization was planning a massacre of Iraq's Jewish community. The whole matter seemed incredible because these more than 130,000 Iraqi Jews had lived in Iraq with their Moslem and Christian brethren for centuries. Leaflets then began to appear urging Iraq's Jews to flee to Israel.[39] Thousands panicked and began to sign up for emigration. The bombings intensified. Several Iraqi Jews were killed. Tens of thousands of Jews then began to flee their native Iraq. By 1951, most of Iraq's Jews had fled Iraq in panic, abandoning their prosperous businesses, homes, property, and heritage. Only about five thousand Iraqi Jews remained in Iraq.[40]

Fifteen people were later arrested in connection with the bombings. It has been established that Israel's Haganah, under the leadership of David Ben-Gurion and Yigal Allon, smuggled arms and bombs into Iraq and admitted to have thrown the bombs at their Jewish brothers.[41] In reporting the exodus of Iraq's Jews, Wilbur Crane Eveland, a former CIA representative, wrote that three months before he arrived in Iraq in 1950, a bomb had exploded "outside a Passover gathering" which led 10,000 Iraqi Jews to emigrate to Israel. "Just after I arrived in Baghdad," Eveland wrote:

> . . . . an Israeli citizen had been recognized in the city's largest department store: his interrogation led to the discovery of fifteen arms caches brought into Iraq by an underground Zionist movement. In attempts to portray the Iraqis as anti-American and to terrorize the Jews, the Zionists planted bombs in the U.S. Information Service Library and in synagogues. Soon leaflets began to appear urging Jews to flee to Israel. . . . Although the Iraqi police later provided our embassy with evidence to show that the synagogue and library bombings, as well as the anti-Jewish and anti-American leaflet campaigns, had been the work of an underground Zionist organization, most of the world believed reports that Arab terrorism had motivated the flight of the Iraqi Jews whom the

Zionists had "rescued" really just in order to increase Israel's Jewish population.[42]

The United States Department of State knew about these events.[43] Years later the chief Rabbi of Iraq, Sasson Khedourri, stated:

By mid 1949, the big propaganda guns were already going off in the United States. American dollars were going to save Iraqi Jews— whether Iraqi Jews needed saving or not. There were daily "pogroms" in *The New York Times* and under datelines which few noticed were from Tel Aviv. Why didn't someone come to see *us* instead of negotiating with Israel to take in Iraqi Jews? Why didn't someone point out that the solid, responsible leadership of Iraqi Jews believed this [Iraq] to be their country? . . . The Iraqi government was being accused of holding the Jews against their will. . . . The government was whip-sawed . . . accused of pogroms and violent actions against Jews. . . . But if the government attempted to suppress Zionist agitation attempting to stampede the Iraqi Jews, it was again accused of discrimination.[44]

The Public Relations Offensive

The Israelis then proceeded to convert villages and lands of the ousted Palestinians into Jewish settlements.[45] They embarked on a ruthless public relations campaign,[46] informing the world that the Palestinians had voluntarily left their homes, that the Arab countries had expelled their Jewish populations, and that Israel was facing a challenge which threatened its very existence.[47] Nearly forty years after those fateful events, historians and scholars are gradually beginning to unravel the falsehoods which the Israelis have succeeded in spreading, especially in the United States.

The *Manchester Guardian Weekly*, of London, recently wrote:

A young Israeli scholar has driven a coach and horses through the traditional Zionist explanation of the creation of the Palestinian refugee problem with his discovery of a contemporary classified intelligence document assessing that 70 percent of the first wave of the great Arab exodus in 1948 resulted from Jewish military action.

The document, a secret Israeli army intelligence report dated June 30, 1948, goes out of its way to point out that the mass flight was against the wishes of Palestinian leaders and neighbouring Arab states. . . .

For almost four decades, the official Israeli explanation of the exodus has been that the Palestinians were told to leave by their own leaders and by other Arab countries. . . . But the 1948 report, which gives a detailed analysis of the reasons for the flight . . . does not mention any such instructions. . . .

Dr. Benny Morris believes that the story of Arab radio broadcasts ordering or asking Palestinians to leave their homes . . . solidified over the years, into a convenient myth that became the basis of subsequent Israeli propaganda. . . .

'People's minds have been warped by 40 years of nonsense,' he says. . . .[48]

Dr. Benny Morris affirmed the statement of the *Manchester Guardian Weekly* in a recent article in *The Middle East Journal*:

By early spring 1948, fear and Jewish military pressure prompted Arab villagers in large numbers to begin moving out of the areas allocated to the Jewish State in the 1947 U.N. Partition Plan. The burning of fields and the attacks on cultivators were among the pressures that led to the exodus. During May 1948, with most of the Arabs having left the Jewish-held areas, the Yishuv organized the harvesting of many of the abandoned Arab fields. Over the summer, in various areas, the often hungry and destitute exiles, playing a cat-and-mouse game with the Israel Defense Forces (IDF), infiltrated through Israeli lines back to their fields to salvage some of the crop. Jewish fears that, if allowed to succeed, these temporary, economically motivated forays would be transformed into a permanent refugee 'return' led to hard and fast orders to IDF units along the ceasefire lines to prevent such forays with fire. . . .[49]

Yet for years the Israelis and their supporters have been telling the world that the Palestinian exodus from Palestine was either voluntary or at the behest of their leaders.[50]

An official pamphlet dated 1953 of the Israeli government on the refugees emphatically stated that the Arab exodus followed "express instructions broadcast by the president of the Arab Higher Executive (the Mufti)."[51] A few years later, Abba Eban told the U.N. that the refugee problem was "the responsibility of the Arab governments,"[52] who had created it. This charge was repeated in a handbook published by the Israeli Information Service in 1967: "If the Arab states had not waged open war on Israel on the morrow of its establishment in May 1948, the Arab refugee issue would never have risen."[53] In 1973, these allegations were repeated by Samuel Katz in his book, *Battleground*, which was recommended as "a very valuable source of reference," and which would give "a most informed understanding of the situation in the Middle East."[54] Katz wrote:

> . . . . the Arab refugees were not driven from Palestine by anyone. The vast majority left, whether of their own free will or at the orders or exhortations of their leaders. . . .[55]

Another renowned public relations specialist, Jon Kimche, insisted in his famous book, *Seven Fallen Pillars*, that:

> . . . . there can be no question that the great mass of refugees left their homes at a time when they were not compelled to do so, at the urging and behest of the Arab League leaders. I watched that process myself. . . .[56]

The tragedy of the Palestinians is Israel's responsibility in three respects: First, Israel uprooted them from their homes and lands by violent means. Second, Israel launched a vicious and effective public relations campaign creating an indelible myth which is repeated until this day. The essence of this myth is that the Palestinian exodus was either voluntary or the responsibility of the Arab states which invaded Israel on May 15, 1948, states which, through broadcasts from Arab radio stations, encouraged the Palestinians to leave their land. Third, Israel denied the Palestinians the right to return to their homes once acts of hostility had ceased.

With respect to the violent uprooting of the Palestinians, in addition to Menachem Begin's boastful assertions that the Zionists terrorized the Palestinians "into a maddened, uncontrollable stampede,"[57] the late Count Folke Bernadotte (who, ironically, himself later fell victim to the Zionist acts of terror about which he reported) wrote in 1948:

> The exodus of Palestinian Arabs resulted from panic created by fighting in their communities, by rumors concerning real or alleged acts of terrorism, or expulsion. . . . There have been numerous reports from reliable sources of large scale looting, pillaging and plundering, and of instances of destruction of villages without apparent military necessity.[58]

Bernadotte's report of 1948 is now confirmed by "a report by the Israel Defense Forces intelligence branch called *The Emigration of the Arabs of Palestine in the Period 1/12/1947-1/6/1948*."This is the period which preceded the Arab armies' invasion of Palestine. During this period also "approximately half the refugees left Palestine."[59] The report states that 72 percent of the Palestinian refugees left as a direct result of Zionist military action. Others left because of "general fear" or "Zionist psychological warfare."[60]

With respect to the myth of Arab radio broadcasts and other pieces of "disinformation" alleging that the Palestinian exodus was the responsibility of Arab leaders, David Gilmour, in his recent article in *Middle East International*, wrote:

> Central to the thesis that the Palestinians were ordered to leave their homeland is the allegation that the Mufti and other leaders broadcast these orders over the wireless. It is a charge regularly made by Zionist apologists . . . and, more recently, Joan Peters in an inaccurate and shamelessly dishonest book, *From Time Immemorial* . . . Dr. Childers had gone to Israel to search for the evidence of the broadcasts. As the Israelis were unable to produce it, he decided to examine the American and British monitoring records of all Middle East broadcasts throughout 1948. He reported that 'there was not a single order, or appeal, or suggestion about evacuation from Palestine from any Arab radio station, inside or outside Palestine, in 1948. There is repeated monitored record of Arab appeals, even flat orders, to the civilians of Palestine to *stay put*'. . . .[61]

The uprooting of Palestinians from their homes and properties and the transformation of Palestine into Israel in 1948 has thus intensified the Palestinians' concern with civil liberties and human rights.

Contemporary Palestinian Attitudes Toward Civil Liberties and Human Rights

Contemporary attitudes of the Palestinian people toward civil liberties and human rights are often expressed in the writings of scholars and poets.[62] They reflect their preoccupation with the entire question of Palestine. An eloquent statement of the feelings of some Palestinians about civil liberties and human rights was made by the late Dr. Fayez A. Sayegh, a Palestinian scholar who grew up in Tiberias. This statement in particular reflects the impact of the Israel-Palestine problem on the author's thinking. He wrote:

Men who cannot and will not surrender to one another may be inspired to surrender together to a higher vision—and in that surrender find freedom and fulfillment, as well as reconciliation.

To accomplish this end, the vision must have the excellence to inspire and the power to command devotion.

As the longing for peace cannot overpower or replace craving for justice, the vision of peace must offer justice as well, or else forfeit its very credentials.

A vision of a just peace cannot be meek, overawed by current reality, proclaiming: Whatever is is here to stay.

It must have the boldness to question and the fortitude to challenge every being, if founded on injustice. Nor can it be purely restorative, proclaiming, 'Whatever was shall be resurrected in identical form.' It must dare to deviate from the past and create a modified future.

A bold vision of a just peace must also be morally uplifting. It must inspire men to brotherhood, when exclusionism sets them apart; to compassion, when vengefulness rages; and to giving and sharing, whether of their acquisitions or of their birth- right, when rapaciousness or cupidity prevail.

And it must be spiritually uplifting also. It must proclaim the primacy of the human person over the politico-juridical abstraction of statehood.

If the men and women of Israel also come to see their destinies in terms of such a vision—opting for peace and justice for all, in new Palestine—the ingenuity of statecraft and diplomacy (local, regional and international) will not be incapable of devising the procedural and programmatic formulas necessary for bringing about its realization, perhaps in our day.

Whenever it comes about, however, a new and glorious day will dawn. The Holy Land will become also a land of creative brotherhood, a land of triumph over the seemingly impossible and a land of righteous peace.[63]

Perhaps the best elucidation of the attitudes of the present Palestinian leadership about civil liberties and human rights in the light of the problem of Palestine was made by Yasser Arafat, Chairman of the Palestine Liberation Organization,[64] in an address to the United Nations which was probably prepared for him and reflects the thinking of some of the finest Palestinian minds of our time.[65] In this address, delivered on November 13, 1974, Arafat declared:

> The roots of the Palestinian question reach back into the closing years of the nineteenth century . . . the period during which Zionism . . . was born . . . as Palestine was usurped and its people hounded from their national homeland . . . theology was utilized against our Palestinian people. . . . When it is proposed that Jews solve the Jewish problem by immigrating to and forcibly settling the land of another people - when this occurs exactly the same position is being advocated as the one urged by anti-Semites against Jews. . . .

> Palestine was the cradle of the most ancient cultures and civilizations. Its Arab people were . . . setting an example in the practice of freedom of worship, acting as faithful guardians of the Holy places of all religions. . . . While we were vociferously condemning the massacres of Jews under Nazi rule, Zionist leadership appeared more interested at that time in exploiting them . . . in order to realize its goal of immigration into Palestine. . . . If the immigration of Jews to Palestine had had as its objective and goal of enabling them to live side by side with us, enjoying the same rights and assuming the same duties, we would have opened our doors to them, as far as our homeland's capacity for absorption permitted. Such was the case with the thousands of Armenians and Circassians who still live among us in equality as brethren and citizens. But that the goal of this immigration should be to usurp our homeland, disperse our people, and turn us into second-class citizens—this is what no one can conceivably demand that we acquiesce in or submit to. . . . We are struggling so that Jews, Christians and Moslems may live in equality enjoying the same rights and assuming the same duties, free from racial or religious discrimination. . . . How can one describe the statement by Golda Meir which expressed her disquiet about the Palestinian children born every day? They see in the Palestinian child . . . an enemy that should be exterminated. . . . For years, our population has been living under martial law and has been denied the freedom of movement . . . at a time

when an Israeli law was promulgated granting citizenship to any Jew anywhere who wanted to emigrate to our homeland. Moreover, another Israeli law stipulated that the Palestinians who were not present in their villages or towns at the time of the occupation were not entitled to Israeli citizenship. . . . For we deplore all those crimes committed against the Jews, we also deplore all the real discrimination suffered by them because of their faith. . . . So let us work together that my dream may be fulfilled, that I may return with my people out of exile, there in Palestine to live . . . in one democratic state where Christian, Jew and Moslem live in justice, equality, fraternity and progress. . . . I proclaim before you that when we speak of our common hopes for the Palestine of tomorrow, we include in our perspective all Jews now living in Palestine who choose to live with us there in peace and without discrimination. . . . We offer them the most generous solution, that we might live together in a framework of just peace in our democratic Palestine. . . . We do not wish one drop of either Arab or Jewish blood to be shed . . . [such bloodshed] would end once a just peace, based on our people's rights, hopes and aspirations had been finally established. . . . Only then can Jerusalem resume its historic role as a peaceful shrine for all religions. . . .[66]

Very few Americans heard or read Mr. Arafat's address.[67] His pleas for a democratic state where Jews and Arabs would live together in peace and equality were ignored.[68] The Palestinians thus found themselves continuing to struggle against people who claim, yet defy, an ethical imperative: "Justice, justice shalt thou pursue, that thou mayest live."[69]

The late William Hugh Brownlee,[70] commenting on the Palestinians' attitude toward civil liberties and human rights wrote:

The greatest hopes for the area are the democratic ideals cherished by the Palestinians, who seek liberty and justice for all. The Israelis should listen to them and sit down to a peace conference with them—including Palestinian representatives from both inside and outside the country. The greatest impediment to peace in the area today is the unwillingness of the Israelis and other Zionists to recognize the inalienable rights of the Palestinians.[71]

Even one of the founders of the state of Israel, Nahum Goldmann, once stressed that the Zionists "should never have lost sight of the fact that a territory belongs to the majority of the population that lives there."[72] Goldmann's assessments, however, were too little and too late. The Zionists, in any event, had not even heeded the earlier warnings, whether sincere or not, of their renowned leader, Chaim Weizmann, who asserted that the Palestinians "were as good Zionists as we are; they also loved their country and they could not be persuaded to hand it over to someone else."[73] Weizmann had recommended that the Zionists, in establishing a Jewish state, should seek "friendly relations"[74] with the Palestinians. As stated earlier, even he later acquiesced in Israel's deeds, when he became Israel's first president.[75]

The Zionists thus gave the people of Palestine the choice of "emigration or second-class citizenship."[76] They rejected the belief that:

> ... Arab-Jewish cooperation ... is not an idealistic daydream ... without it the whole Jewish venture in Palestine is doomed. ...[77]

The injustices perpetrated by the Israelis against the Palestinians helped to shape the attitudes of the Palestinians toward civil liberties and human rights. Mahmoud Darwish, a Palestinian poet, epitomized these attitudes in the following poem:

> As long as a hand-span of my land remains
> As long as I have an olive tree —
> A lemon tree —
> A well — and a cactus plant
> As long as I have but a single memory
> A tiny library
> A grandfather's picture — and a wall
> As long as Arabic words are uttered
> And folk songs are sung
> In my land
> Scribes of poetry
> Tales of Antar Al-Abse
> Epics of the wars against Persia and Rome
> As long as I possess my eyes
> Lips and hands
> My own — self!
> I shall declare in the face of my foe!
> A fierce struggle of liberation
> In the name of free men everywhere
> Workers — Students — and poets —
> I shall declare —
> And let the cowards — enemies of the sun
> Be satisfied of the bread of shame ...[78]

But basic violations of Palestinians' civil liberties and human rights continue unabated.[79] Israel has devised agencies, laws and regulations aimed at dislodging the Palestinians from their farms and lands.[80] An Israeli official can take a Palestinian's land when he decides that the land has not been "properly" cultivated,[81] or when it is needed for "immigrants,"[82] or "wounded veterans."[83] By dispossessing the Palestinians of the land they need for their very survival, the Israelis not only have intensified the Palestinians' demands for justice; they, in fact, have made the Palestinians stubborn enemies of the Zionist Jewish state,[84] as the following poem by Tawfiq Zayyad, the Mayor of Nazareth, indicates:

> It is a thousand times easier
> For you
> To pass an elephant through the needle's eye
> To catch fried fish in the milky way
> To plow the sea
> To teach the alligator speech,
> A thousand times easier
> Than smothering with your oppression
> The spark of an idea
> Or forcing us to deviate
> A single step
> From our chosen march.
> Like twenty impossibles
> We shall remain in Lydda, Ramlah, and Galilee.
>
> Here upon your chests
> We shall remain
> Like the glass and the cactus
> In your throats
> A fiery whirlwind
> In your eyes.
>
> Here, we shall remain
> A wall on your chest.
> We wash dishes in the hotels
> And serve drinks to the masters.
>
> We mop the floors in the dark kitchens
> To extract a piece of bread
> From your blue teeth
> For the little ones.

> Here, we shall remain
> A wall on your chests.
> We starve,
> Go naked,
> Sing songs
> And fill the streets
> With demonstrations
> And the jails with pride.[85]

The Palestinians are convinced that Israel does not only aim to dispossess them of their land and livelihood, but also to deny them equal political and social status.[86] There are two sets of laws in Israel,[87] one for Israeli Jews and one for Israeli Arabs.[88] Israel has devised a segregated society by isolating the Israeli Arabs so that they cannot oppose Israel's human rights policies. It has deprived them of their land so that they will continue to be dependent on a segregated state.[89]

Travel permits are almost always denied to the Israeli Arabs, except for those going to work. This is in order to minimize contact between the Israeli Arab residents of various villages and towns, and in order to prevent Israeli Arabs from returning to their villages in order to reclaim their land, and to prevent organization among the Israeli Arabs.[90]

Israel's objective has been described as the "continuing *under development* of the Arab sector."[91] It is also the increased dependence of Arabs on the Jewish population.[92] The Israeli Arabs have no industry of their own, and have been relegated to the meanest unskilled occupations, such as laborers and janitors.[93]

Yet Israel receives billions of dollars of aid from abroad, particularly from the United States.[94] This aid has two sources, one from private Zionist organizations and one from U.S. treasury grants. Since Israel's establishment, private Zionist funds have been tax exempt in the United States. These tax exempt private funds from the United States have amounted to several billion dollars.[95] They are controlled by Zionist organizations and are utilized solely for the Jewish citizens of Israel. Israel's Palestinian citizens who are not Jews are excluded from the benefit of these funds. Furthermore, by virtue of Israel's "Status Law," the United Jewish Appeal and the Jewish Agency are instruments of the Israeli government. In a recent article, Roselle Tekiner wrote that:

> The Status Law legitimates an arrangement between the government and the World Zionist Organization/Jewish Agency, the effect of which is permanent discrimination against the non-Jewish sector of Israeli citizenry. . . .[96]

The discriminatory use of these tax exempt private funds is not only a violation of the moral spirit in which the tax exemption was provided, it is a manipulating mechanism which renders the government and the people of the United States, especially the American Jewish community, full, if unwitting, participants in those activities of the Israeli government which give preference to Israel's Jewish citizens over its non-Jewish citizens.

The aid from United States' treasury grants is, of course, controlled by the Israeli government. A very small portion of this aid is used for Israeli Arabs or for the Palestinians in the occupied territories.[97]

Israeli-Jewish villages and towns are supplied with water, electricity and paved roads. They are also supplied with the most modern equipment. None of these advantages are provided to the Israeli-Arab towns and villages, or to the occupied territories.[98] The Israeli government policies toward the Arab minority are

> ... characterized by economic discrimination, neglect, a studied attempt to prevent Arab-owned centers of economic power from emerging, and a conscious effort to create and sustain ties of dependence - dependence of Arabs on Jews. . . .[99]

The poet Samih al-Qassem exclaims:

> We, Isaiah's grandchildren,
> Call him.
> We call to his kindly face
> Trembling
> Behind a veil of tears . . .
> We call him — angrily crying;
> O Isaiah you have slept for centuries.
> In your absence the city became a harlot
> Its silver tainted Its wine diluted with water.
> Tell them
> O struggling Isaiah
> Of the widows' bereavement.
> Speak to them
> Of this land's disgrace.
>
> Alleluia.
>
> The messengers of peace
> Weep bitterly
> For the innocent,

Their heads cut off
By the enemies of man.

Mournful Isaiah,
Arise today and cry in this village
Tottering on the brink of destruction . . .

Arise today.
Go up
And cry in the streets of Tel Aviv:
Thousand woes to him
Who does not seek the Lord . . .

Beloved Isaiah,
From the land of the Arabs
Comes a message:
Men of Tima;
Give water to the thirsty
Who seek refuge.

Behind the wounds of the fugitives
Fleeing before the sword
And
Give the hungry
A piece of bread.

Courageous Isaiah - arise!
And the children of Palestine
Will play again
Without fearing the serpent's bite,
And sheep may live in the wolves' den.

Alleluia.

The nations will adjudge
That no rights are lost
And voices are not silenced.

Struggling Isaiah!
The swords will be turned into plowshares
And the spears of the people into scythes.
No nation will raise its sword against another,

That little ones may not know war
Or bloodletting.
Alleluia — Alleluia . . .[100]

The persecution of the Israeli Arabs is not accidental. It has been the policy of the state of Israel since its establishment.[101] As Fouzi El-Asmar[102] wrote:

I sit in preventive detention
The reason, see, is that I am an Arab.
An Arab who has refused to sell his soul
Who has always striven, sir, for freedom.
An Arab who has protested at the suffering
of his people
Who has carried with him the hope
of a just peace
Who has spoken against death
at every corner

Who has called for and has lived
a life of brotherhood
That is why I sit in preventive detention
Because I carried on the struggle
And because I am an Arab.[103]

In September of 1976, the Koenig memorandum[104]became public. In order to forestall the possibility of an integration of Israeli-Arabs within Israel, Koenig, who was appointed by the Labor government of Yitzhak Rabin, recommended more Jewish settlements in areas that were predominantly Arab. He recommended the reduction of the number of Israeli-Arab intellectuals because, he counselled, their intellect would be potentially dangerous. He wanted to channel Israeli-Arab "students into technical professions," because "the dropout rate is higher." He recommended making it easier for Arabs to study abroad and harder for them to return. Hiring of recent Israeli-Arab graduates should be made difficult. He also proposed a smear campaign against Israeli-Arab intellectuals. He recommended a reduction of Israeli-Arab financial savings.[105]

In discussing the serious health problems which the Israeli-Arabs are facing in the Galilee, "which are strangely out of place in Israel with its high level of medical technology," Michael Fischbach wrote recently in *Middle East International*:

Six major health problems have been identified in Galilee: the lack of central sewage systems; improper disposal of solid waste; the inaccessibility of medical centers; the imbalance in health service provision and utilization between the two sectors; special 'at risk' populations; and the health personnel resources imbalance. This is not to suggest that these are the only adverse conditions which Galilee villages face; these are merely the ones which can be quickly and easily addressed or which lend themselves to simple technical solutions. . . .[106]

Fischbach continued:

This is not merely oversight. The 1976 Koenig report, for example, a secret government memorandum on the problems posed by large number of Arabs in the Galilee, made the following suggestion. . . . Endeavor to have central institutions pay more attention to giving preferential treatment to Jewish groups or individuals rather than to Arabs. . . .[107]

The means employed by the Israelis in the subjugation of Israeli-Arabs go beyond the realm of political and social manipulation to include torture and outright murder. The massacre in the Arab-Israeli village of Kafr Kasim received publicity after a two-month-long attempt to cover it up failed. Forty-three Israeli-Arab men, women and children were massacred in cold blood for no apparent reason. The perpetrators, members of the Israeli Armed Forces, were sentenced to prison terms of seven to eighteen years. The officer in charge of the operation was freed however. On appeal, all prison terms were reduced. One year after sentencing, all the perpetrators were freed.[108] In eulogizing the victims of the village of Kafr Kasim, Rashed Hussein wrote:

> No monument — no flower — no memorial.
> No verses — no curtain.
> No blood-soaked rag
> From the shirt of our innocent brothers.
> No stones with their names carved on it.
> Nothing at all . . . what a disgrace!
>
> Their wandering ghosts
> Cut out tombs out of Kafr Kasim's rubble.[109]

In the West Bank and in the Gaza Strip, Israel uses the same methods it has been using against its Israeli-Arab citizens.[110] Yet the Hague regulations of 1907 and the 1949 Geneva Conventions provide for the sanctity of private property in occupied territories.[111] They condemn unilateral annexation of such territories as illegal.[112] They denounce collective punishment.[113] The Israelis, who are signatories to the above conventions,[114] have embarked on a settlement program in the occupied territories in order to create a Jewish presence there which would make it impossible for the Palestinians to control their own land. In 1983, Israel's army chief of staff, Rafael Eitan, was quoted by *The New York Times* as having said:

> When we have settled the [West Bank] all the Arabs will be able to do about it will be to scurry around like drugged roaches in a bottle. . . .[115]

Another official of the Jewish Agency wrote that Jewish settlements in the occupied territories have to be created

> between and around concentrations of Arab population in order to minimize the danger of the creation of another Arab state in these territories. By cutting the Arab population from each other by Jewish settlements, it will be difficult for them to create political and territorial unity. There should be no doubts about our intentions to hold on forever to Judea and Samaria.[116]

The limited sources of water in the West Bank have been allocated in a disproportionate way, favoring the Jewish settlements.[117] In fact, the Israelis have been diverting water from the West Bank to Israel itself, thus depriving the Palestinians of it.[118] Palestinian farmers are forbidden to dig new wells, while some of their old wells have been confiscated.[119]

The Palestinians in the occupied territories are also subjected to harassment, torture and murder. The human rights organization, Amnesty International, issued its first report in September of 1980, investigating Israel's heavy hand.[120] Israeli authorities denied the charges of torture and murder.[121] But Amnesty International reported that the Israeli authorities were unable to "provide a convincing refutation" of the Palestinians' charges.[122]

Felicia Langer, an Israeli attorney, has frequently reported on torture and brutality in the West Bank. These reports have been supported by Amnesty International and the Swiss League of Human Rights.[123] Amnesty International has described crowded prison conditions, bad food and inadequate medical care. Prisoners are tortured and beaten, often in the genitals. They are given pills that bring on hysteria and hallucinations. They are hung upside down. Noxious, poisonous gases are thrown in their cells or sprayed into their faces. Cigarettes are stubbed out on their bodies.[124] "Prisoners are being put to death. . . . This crime is occurring gradually and is being covered up efficiently."[125]

Israel Shahak, an Israeli scholar wrote:

The large majority of Jewish population in Israel does not want to know about the daily suffering of the Palestinian population in the territories. . . . Just as has been said in the Bible . . . they harden their hearts. . . .[126]

Another wrote:

Yet Israelis and American Jews troubled by the situation on the West Bank rarely criticize it because of what it is doing to the Palestinians. Terror, injustice, cultural genocide, and murder of Arabs count for very little in the west. . . . The most acceptable way to criticize Israel's Arab policies is to say they are bad for Israel. . . .[127]

Israel has thus been responsible for some of the most ruthless acts of a government in this century. It has usurped the Palestinians' lands, murdered and tortured them, maligned them, maligned their leaders, and claimed that the Israelis are victimized by the Palestinians. As Fouzi el-Asmar wrote:

> You came like a broken-winged bird
> and found the nest
> You felt around like a pharaoh's cat
> and you found warmth,
> and you drank from the well dug in the desert
> and you said: 'It is not enough.'
> We shared the pieces of bread falling from
> the greedy table of the lords,
> and you said: 'Nonsense,
> It won't suffice that I simply drink
> from the well,
> I should own that well
> and eat all the pieces of bread
> falling from the greedy table of the lords,
> and put out the lamp of the creature
> over my barren chest.'

You renounced the warmth,
and dimissed the butterflies of the roses . . .[128]

Clearly, Palestinian resentment of Israeli oppression is both real and intense. The experience of the Palestinians is not unique in the annals of history. Jews themselves have had similar experiences at the hands of the Nazis. One can hope, therefore, that the Jewish experience will move Jews everywhere, especially American Jews, to address the suffering of the Palestinians.

The Role Jews Can Play

In recent years, Jews have played leading roles in social movements aimed at rectifying injustices throughout the world. In the United States in particular, they have been sensitive to civil liberties and human rights. They have supported the constitutional imperative of the separation between church and state. Yet the majority of them, for one reason or another, have closed an eye to the Palestinians' struggle for civil liberties and human rights.[129]

In a recent article in *Foreign Affairs*, for example, Amos Perlmutter,[130] a scholar, appears to want Israel to return the occupied territories because they contain "an alien population." This is his reasoning:

> It should be obvious that the Palestinian problem is the most pressing issue facing Israel. It is not just an Arab problem, not just an international problem, but rather Israel's major strategic, political and territorial problem. . . . Israel must end its rule over the Palestinians and deploy its political and diplomatic efforts to help establish some form of political autonomy for an *alien population*. . . .[131] (Emphasis added)

Professor Perlmutter is not alone in his thinking. Professor Yehoshue Arieli, "a liberal Israeli scholar,"[132] wrote an article in the *Jerusalem Post* advocating the return of the occupied territories because:

> The Jewish state has by its very nature a very limited capacity to absorb non-Jews as fully integrated citizens who would be capable of identifying themselves with the purposes of the state. Possessing as its *raison d'etre* a transcending purpose which goes beyond the concept of citizen-state towards the whole of the Jewish people, Israel cannot, unlike other modern secular states, absorb and integrate large minority groups. Its very nature as a national state

par excellence requires that it should honor the national aspirations of other groups and nations. The integration of such a large minority of Arabs as citizens would therefore mean the suicide of the idea and practice of the Jewish state or the repression of the minority.[133]

If some Jewish scholars, as well as Israeli citizens and politicians, would accept either implicitly or explicitly, that the ultimate purpose of Zionism precludes any possibility of Israel's absorbing its large Arab minority, would it not be morally more acceptable that a "suicide of the idea and practice of the Jewish state" take place, rather than "the repression of the minority," that is, the native Palestinian inhabitants? Is it not morally more sound to abandon the exclusionary principles of Zionism than to endure the ceaseless battling which their implementation ensures? Is not "the suicide of the idea" of Zionism better for humanity than the subjection of innocent Palestinians to its brutal practices?

More significant, however, is the sad conclusion that the motivation of even the most "dovish" Zionist Jews, in their advocacy of leaving the occupied territories, is not a sense of justice or a humanitarian concern for the rights of the Palestinians, but rather a desire to perpetuate an Israel which is demographically Jewish, so as to minimize the possibility of a state which must be open and just to the non-Jewish Palestinians.

The Palestinians will not always be "the minority."[134] Nor is it likely that they will always be unorganized and weak. The Zionists' recollection of history is selective. They remember ancient history, but they seem to have forgotten that the Crusaders, after seventy years of brutal occupation, were expelled from Palestine through a series of bloody and exhausting religious wars.

This more recent history may repeat itself if Jewish sympathizers of Israel are unwilling to urge Israel to remedy the injustices brought upon the people of Palestine.[135] If they refuse to acknowledge that thousands of Palestinians languish in Israeli prisons, many without charges and without trial;[136] if they defend Israel while it persists in blowing up Palestinian homes;[137] if they finance Israel while it continues to take the Palestinians'land and deprive them of their limited supply of water;[138] if they support Israel while it continues to inflict collective punishment on the Palestinians,[139] there will never be peace in the Middle East.

I believe that, although an abundance of information exists, most of the Jews of the world know very little of these injustices. Historians tell us that most Germans did not know about the Nazi concentration camps.[140] Among those who do know of Israel's conduct, however, there are many who support it and attempt to cover it up.[141]

The Role the Government of the United States Can Play

The government of the United States, regrettably, is among those who are fully aware. It also closes an eye, then rewards Israel with massive military and economic aid,[142] in violation of U.S. laws.[143]

Section 116 of the Foreign Assistance Act prohibits U.S. economic assistance to any country, the government of which:

> engages in consistent pattern of gross violation of internationally recognized human rights. . . .[144]

Also, under section 701 of the International Financial Institutions Act, U.S. Executive Directors must:

> oppose any loan, any extension of financial assistance or any technical assistance to any country. . . .[145]

engaged in gross human rights violations.

In justifying $3.35 billion of economic and military assistance appropriated by Congress to Israel in 1985,[146] and in thereby qualifying her for more such assistance in 1986, the United States Department of State certified that:

> Israel is a parliamentary democracy which guarantees by law and reflects in practice the civil, political, and religious rights of its citizens.[147]

Yet the very contents of the State Department's report contradict that certification.[148] Several gross human rights violations by the Government of Israel against its Arab citizens were cited in the report.[149] The most flagrant of these violations was related to the use of the land:

> where title to 93 percent of the land is claimed by the state or by quasi public organizations in trust for the Jewish people. . . .[150]

thus excluding the non-Jewish Israeli-Arabs from its use.[151]

Through its economic and military assistance to Israel, the United States government has become an active accomplice in these human rights violations. When Israel tortures and murders its Israeli-Arab citizens and the Palestinians in the occupied territories,[152] the United States must share responsibility.[153]

For decades, United States policy regarding the Middle East has been one of crisis diplomacy. Whenever a crisis erupts there, U.S. diplomats at home and abroad become frantically engrossed with its immediate demands. When the crisis has passed, however, these diplomats go back to their daily routine. Meanwhile, the architects of U.S. foreign policy seem not to recognize the urgency of developing a broader and deeper understanding of the underlying problems in the region. The U.S. attitude is one of reacting to individual crises without the perspective of an appropriate long-term plan. Hence, those seeking a just and lasting peaceful settlement of the Palestinian-Israeli conflict must deal with human rights violations as one of the underlying conditions perpetuating that conflict, rather than limiting themselves to fighting the fires that continually erupt from it. The vicious cycle of violence involving the hijacking of TWA Flight 847, the Israeli raid on Tunisia, the killing of Israeli civilians in the Sinai, the hijacking of an Italian cruise ship with more than 400 people aboard followed by interception of an Egyptian civilian aircraft by the American Air Force, the bombing of Libya by the United States Navy, the violence involving the hijacking of Pan American Flight 73, and the recent demonstrations rocking the West Bank and Gaza have not been exceptions to the tragic rule of crisis diplomacy.

Dealing in this manner with a region of the world vital not only to U.S. interests but to the interests and security of its Western allies, and undoubtedly to the interests and security of the entire world, is shortsighted and inherently dangerous. Yet the United States has done this for nearly four decades, tending to seek the diffusion of tensions as they occurred, while haphazardly attempting to minimize Soviet influence in the area. It has had no comprehensive plan to deal with the underlying causes of chronically recurring crises, merely a determination to exclude the Soviet Union from the Arab-Israeli peace diplomacy. This bankrupt policy was initiated by Henry Kissinger after turning Egypt from a Soviet ally into an anti-Soviet American ally.[154]

Furthermore, although the peace treaty between Israel and Egypt entered into during the Carter administration may have been well-intentioned, that fragile treaty has failed to deal comprehensively with the basic conflict. It only raised premature hopes that a solution to the Arab-Israeli conflict might finally be found. But Israel's conflict with the Arab world in general and the Palestinians in particular continues as Israel persists in building Jewish settlements in the occupied West Bank with U.S. financial backing, and continues to consider both occupied Arab East Jerusalem and the Golan Heights as part of Israel. Furthermore, one effect of that treaty was to encourage Israel to launch its ill-fated invasion of Lebanon on June 6, 1982, thus rendering peace with the Arab world more elusive than ever before. The U.S. found itself, wittingly or unwittingly, the principal underwriter of that disastrous adventure. This should have been a clear indication that partial or imagined solutions which do not have the backing of both superpowers are not likely to endure.

Although there are various complex problems which continually threaten the security of the Middle East, Israel's conflict with the Arab world is related to most of these problems, directly or indirectly. In addition to the complex economic and political problems evolving from the displacement of hundreds of thousands of Palestinians in 1947 and 1967, the creation of a Jewish state in the Middle East has reinforced and expanded the influence of fundamentalist religious movements throughout the region. In effect, it has awakened and activated a sleeping giant. Although Moslem and Christian fundamentalism in the Middle East is older than the Zionist movement, frustrations over the Palestinian problem continue to be a contributing factor in the lively revival of these fundamentalist movements, as they exploit the political and military failures of the conventional political institutions of the region. The rise of Islamic fundamentalist movements in Iran, Egypt, Lebanon and now Gaza and the West Bank and other parts of the Middle East, as well as Christian fundamentalist movements in Egypt, Lebanon and elsewhere, were thus nourished by the establishment of a Jewish state in Palestine. The failure of U.S. policy makers to give this basic fact full recognition, and their attempt to skirt it, does not alter its vital importance. When the United States condemns certain fundamentalist religious movements, as it has done repeatedly in Iran and in Lebanon, but supports another, as it has done in Israel, the U.S. sends confusing signals. The U.S. also opens itself to the charge of racism and religious prejudice. A nation whose constitution mandates a strict separation between church and state should not fall into this trap.

United States policy concerning the Arab world's conflict with Israel has always been one-sided and uninformed. It has been one-sided because the United States, for domestic reasons, tends to support Israel, right or wrong. It has spent billions of dollars to help build Israel's military strength. The United States pours about $14 million dollars every day into Israel's weak economy. This massive bolstering of a marginally viable state has rendered the U.S. role as neutral mediator suspect. There are about three million Israeli Jews in Israel. The United States government has given them more than one-third of all the aid it has given to the whole world.[155] The rest of the Middle East and most of Africa, whose countries are badly underdeveloped and whose populations number in the hundreds of millions, receive barely a fraction of the aid given to Israel.

As justification for this lopsided distribution of U.S. foreign aid, the myth of a U.S.-Israeli "strategic partnership" has been created by Israel and its supporters in the United States. In a recent article refuting this myth, Harry J. Shaw, former chief of the military assistance branch of the Office of Management and Budget during the Johnson, Nixon, Ford and Carter administrations, wrote in *Foreign Policy*:

> Exaggerated claims of Israel's capabilities and willingness to act as a strategic surrogate for America in the Middle East . . . to justify U.S. military and economic aid to Israel . . . distort the differences in the two countries' interests, responsibilities and capabilities. . . . It also encourages mistaken public and congressional impressions that the United States must support extra Israeli military capabilities. . . . In 1986, the $3 billion total U.S. military and economic aid package to Israel approaches 30% of U.S. worldwide security assistance. . . . Already the justification for Israel's extraordinary share of U.S. foreign aid is being questioned privately by government officials and members of Congress. . . . Israel, in fact, is a small client state that could not survive militarily or economically without U.S. assistance. . . . Americans need to know what they can reasonably expect from Israel's military forces . . . what can Israel do for the United States with respect to the Soviet threat . . . ? First . . . few Israelis regard it as the task of the Israel Defense Forces . . . to engage Soviet Forces. . . . Israel simply lacks the personnel to sacrifice on costly military adventures beyond its immediate neighborhood. . . .[156]

United States policy with respect to this conflict has been uninformed in that it does not properly assess the role religion plays in the conflict. The U.S. ignores the impact of implanting a Jewish state in a predominantly Moslem region. This implantation has led inexorably to the displacement of Christian and Moslem Palestinians and the violation of their human rights through Israel's employment of exclusivist religious criteria to determine full citizenship. Ignoring or attempting to de-emphasize the prejudices, hatreds and self-defeating patterns of behavior stemming from this implantation is not likely to make them go away.[157] They are as much in evidence today as they were in 1948, and they must be dealt with openly and objectively.

Those who are aware of the importance of human rights in American foreign policy should be concerned about the violations of these rights by *any* country. The seemingly contradictory policy followed by the government of the United States in ignoring Israel's gross violations of the human rights of Israeli-Arabs and of Palestinians in the occupied territories should shock the American conscience. Decent people everywhere, especially in the United States, should be sensitive to any act against humanity, regardless of the perpetrator.

A concerted effort by the people of the United States, as well as its government, to encourage Israel to accept the Palestinian Arabs as equals, and to grant them full political and human rights, thereby rendering the state of Israel more secular than religious, would go a long way toward a just and lasting settlement. In the long run, such an effort may well bring more security to the region than all the wars which have been undertaken and may still be undertaken.

Conclusion

The resolution of this tragic conflict, believed by many to be the most complicated social problem of this century, must perhaps begin with the simple principle of equal rights to Israel's Arab citizens.

If Jews, especially American Jews, would insist that the use of the land within Israel, title to 93 percent of which is claimed by the state or by quasi public organizations "in trust" only for the Jewish people, should be opened to all the citizens of Israel, Jews and non-Jews, without any reservation, the seeds of an equitable and lasting solution would be sown.

If Jews, especially American Jews, would assert that they would deny Israel any support unless it adhered scrupulously to the principle of human rights for all its citizens, Jews and non-Jews, a non-violent solution could emerge, and the problem of the West Bank and Gaza could also be addressed.

However, as long as Israeli-Arabs are denied the use of the land, as long as they live under martial law and their movement is restricted, as long as their representation in the Knesset is but symbolic, as long as their right to freedom of expression is denied, as long as their villages are isolated, and their schools are inequitably funded, as long as they are denied the basic necessities for a decent living because they are not Jews, as long as they are forced to live in anxiety, humiliation and despair, as long as these inequities are inflicted by the state which claims them as citizens, and to which, as citizens, they have the right to look for protection of their civil rights, a just and lasting peace will remain a dream.

As long as the Palestinians of the territories live in poverty and want, as long as their land and water are usurped, as long as they are tortured, harassed and murdered, as long as they continue under a ruthless, repressive rule, as long as their agonies do not disturb the human conscience everywhere, violence and counterviolence will continue to pose threats in many spheres to nations around the world.

NOTES

1. George Antonius, *The Arab Awakening: The Story of the Arab National Movement*, Hamish Hamilton, London, 1938, printed in Great Britain by Jarrold and Sons Ltd.,Norwich, pp.79-100.
2. *Ibid.*,p.42
3. J.C. Hurewitz, Editor, *Documents of Near East Diplomatic History*, Near and Middle East Studies, School of International Affairs, Columbia University, New York, 1951, p. 198.
4. *Ibid.*, p. 198.
5. The Covenant of the League of Nations was incorporated into the Treaty of Versailles on April 28, 1919. (See the text of the Covenant in Carnegie Endowment for International Peace, *The Treaties of Peace 1919-1923*, New York, 1924, Vol. 1, pp.10-23.) Article 22 of the Covenant provided:

   To those colonies and territories which as a consequence of the late war have ceased to be under the sovereignty of the states which formerly governed them and which are inhabited by peoples not yet able to stand by themselves under the strenuous conditions of the modern world, there shall be applied the principle that the well-being and development of such peoples *form a sacred trust of civilization and that securities for the performance of this trust should be embodied in this covenant.*

   The best method of giving practical effect to this principle is that the tutelage of such peoples should be *entrusted* to advanced nations who by reason of their resources, their experience or their geographical position can best undertake this responsibility, and who are willing to accept it, and that this tutelage should be exercised by them as mandatories on behalf of the League. . . . *The wishes of these communities must be a principal consideration in the selection of the mandatory.* (Emphasis supplied)
6. This text is taken from Antonius, *op.cit.*, pp. 440-442.
7. *Ibid.*, pp.416 - 427.
8. *Ibid.*, pp.414 - 415.
9. *Ibid.*, pp.415 - 416.
10. *Ibid.*, pp.416 - 427.
11. *Ibid.*, p. 424.
12. See note 15
13. Antonius, *op.cit.*, p.426.
14. *Ibid.*, p.427.
15. The Sykes-Picot Agreement was concluded in London on May 16, 1916, in the form of diplomatic notes exchanged between the governments of three powers - Great Britain, France, and Russia. These notes defined British, French and Russian shares of portions of the Ottoman Empire, in what had been pledged to be an Independent Arab state. The exchange of notes took place between April 26 and May 16 of 1916. The Sykes-Picot Agreement is a classic example of greed coupled with double dealing. It dividedthe Arab part of the Ottoman Empire in such a manner as to make a unified independent Arab state an impossibility. See Antonius, *op.cit.*, pp. 243-275. Also, the Balfour Declaration, made by the Government of Great Britain on No-

vember 2, 1917, favoring "the establishment in Palestine of a national home for the Jewish people," while providing that "nothing shall be done which may prejudice the civil and religious rights" of the Palestinians, is in direct conflict with Great Britain's pledges to the Arabs. See Hurewitz, *op.cit.*, pp. 179-180.

16. During a secret meeting of the Supreme Council of the Allied Powers, held on March 20, 1919 in Paris, President Wilson proposed setting an Inter-Allied Commission to investigate the wishes of the population in the territories earmarked to be mandated regions of the Ottoman Empire. See Baker, Ray Stannard, *Woodrow Wilson and World Settlement*, New York, 1922, Vol. 111, pp. 1-19. The Commission arrived in Jaffa, Palestine, on June 10, 1919. Its presence encouraged the Syrians to convene a "General Syrian Congress" in Damascus. Delegates from all parts of Syria participated, including Lebanon and Palestine. On July 2, 1919, they adopted a resolution framing a statement of their position, which they submitted on the same day to the Commission. (See Antonius, *op.cit.*, pp. 440-442).

17. The above quotations were taken from the full text of the Commission's report as stated in *Editor and Publisher*, (New York), Vol. 55, issue dated December 2, 1922, Section two, pp. IV-XXVI.

18. See the U.N. General Assembly Reports of the Second Sessions, *Official Records: Resolutions*, Lake Success, 1948, pp.131-150.

19. See *Parliamentary Papers*, 1939, Cmd. 6019.

20. See Anglo-American Committee of Inquiry, *Report to the United States Government and His Majesty's Government in the United Kingdom*, (Washington, 1946), Department of State Publication No. 2536, pp. 1-12, which was part of a 91-page report.

21. See United Nations Document A/286.

22. See Resolution 106 (S-111).

23. See note 20.

24. See the official statistics of the Jewish Agency as reproduced and tabulated in Appendices III and IV of Israel Cohen, *A Short History of Zionism*, London, Muller, 1951, pp. 254-261.

25. See the statistics of the British Government of Palestine. Within Israel's own boundaries, as earmarked by the Partition Plan of May 15, 1948, Palestinian property amounted to 7,481,967 dunums, while Jewish property was 1,475,766 dunums. In West Jerusalem, which was held by Israel before the 1967 War, the Palestinians owned 5,478 dunums while the Jews owned 4,885 dunums. Totals: Palestinians - 7,487,445 dunums; Jews - 1,480,651 dunums. (Sami Hadawi, *Facts and Statistics*, Ramallah, August, 1951, (In Arabic) pp. 8-9). Mr. Hadawi was a former land officer for the government of Palestine during the British Mandate.

26. For a discussion of the support the Zionists received during the U.N.'s consideration of the question of Palestine, see Jorge Garcia Granados, *The Birth of Israel: The Drama as I Saw It*, New York: Alfred A. Knopf, 1948.

27. Pearlman, Lt. Col. Moshe, *The Army of Israel*, New York, Philosophical Library, 1950, p.12.

28. *Ibid.*, p. 23.

29. *Ibid.*, p.9.

30. *Ibid.*, p.9.

31. See *The Political History of Palestine Under British Administration; A Memorandum*

by His Britannic Majesty's Government, presented in July 1947 to the United Nations Special Committee on Palestine, Jerusalem, 1947, p. 31.

32. For a graphic description of how the Palestinian farmers were "badly mauled" by the well-equipped, well-trained forces of the Haganah and other Zionist para-military organizations between December 1947 and May 15, 1948, see Public Record Office (London)(PRO), Colonial Office (CO) 537-3855, CID Summary of Events, January 23, 1948, Appendix, entry for January 22, 1948; see also PRO, CO537-3853, "Fortnightly Report 16-31 January 1948," District Commissioner, Gaza, February 3, 1948, and "Fortnightly Report . . . 1-16 February 1948," District Commissioner's Office, Gaza, February 16, 1948; see also David Ben-Gurion (DBG) *Yoman Hamilchama* (the 1947-1949 war diaries) Tel Aviv: Defense Military Press, 1982) Volume I, p. 291, entry for March 10, 1948; see also PRO, War Office 275-90, CRAFORCE to 17/21 L, 1 para Bn, etc. March 6, 1948, which cites Jewish attack on al Samiriya, in the Beit Shean Valley, as an indication that "Jews are preventing villagers from working on the lands" and CO 537-3856, CID Summary of Events, March 3, 1948, Appendix "B", entry for March 2, 1948, which cites Jewish attack on farmers from the village of Qabba and southwest of Kibbutz Ayelet Hashaachar; see also CO 5337-3853,"Fortnightly Report for the period ended the 29th February, 1948," District Commissioner's Office, Galilee District, Nazareth. (All the above were cited by Benny Morris,"The Harvest of 1948 and the Creation of the Palestinian Refugee Problem," *The Middle East Journal* Vol. 40, No. 4, Autumn 1986, pp. 672-673.)

33. See *The New York Times*, April 12, 1948; see also Larry Collins and Dominique LaPierre, *O Jerusalem*, (New York: Simon and Schuster, 1972), p. 272; see also Harry Levin, *Jerusalem Embattled* (London: Victor Gollancz, 1950), p. 57.

34. The massacre of Deir Yassein took place on April 9, 1948, more than two months before the neighboring Arab states invaded Palestine. Hugging a rocky section west of Jerusalem, Deir Yassein had been "quiet since the beginnings of disturbances," according to David Shaltial, a Haganah commander. The village "had done nothing to provoke this attack and had lived peaceably in a sort of agreement with the Jewish suburbs that surround it."*The New York Times*, April 12, 1948.

35. See Menachem M. Begin, *The Revolt: Story of the Irgun*, New York, Henry Schuman, 1951, p. 164, note 1.

36. See James G. McDonald, *My Mission in Israel*, New York, Simon and Schuster, 1951, p. 176.

37. See Hal Lehman, "The Arabs of Israel," *Commentary* (American Jewish Committee, New York), Vol. VII, No.6, December 1949, pp. 529-530.

38. "Ben Gurion Scores U.S. Zionist Chiefs," *The New York Times*, December 13, 1951.

39. The leaflet warned the Iraqi Jewish community of the dangers of remaining in Iraq. It urged them to return to "their natural homeland, Israel." The leaflet exhorted: "O sons of Zion, inhabitants of Babylon, free yourselves . . . O brother Jews, Israel is calling you." See Abbas Shiblak, *The Lure of Zion: The Case of the Iraqi Jews*, Al-Saqi Books, 26 Westbourne Grove, London W2 1986, p. 121.

40. For an extensive study of the exodus of Iraqi Jews, see Shiblak, *Ibid.*, pp.

119-129. See also P.A. Rhodes for the FO to Sir Anthony Nutting, 31 December, 1951; FO371/48767, EQ 1571/2; FO to Baghdad, 29 September 1952; FO 371/98767, EQ 1571/24; Baghdad to FO, 6 June 1950; FO 371/82482, EQ 1571/28; Baghdad to FO, 13 April 1950, FO 371/82480, EQ 1571/17; Baghdad to FO, 1 April 1950, FO 371/8249, EQ 1571/16; Baghdad to FO, 26 May 1950; FO 371/8248, EQ 1571/21, 371/82482, EQ 1571/28.

41. See Shiblak, *Ibid.*, p. 123, where he writes:
    . . . there is reason to believe that the bombings could not have been carried out without a decision taken at high level in Tel-Aviv, and without the personal knowledge of two Israeli leaders: Yigal Allon and David Ben-Gurion. Allon was in charge of the external operations of Mossad and was in constant touch with Zionist activists in Baghdad, giving them instructions and supplying them with arms (Allon, 1970, pp.233-4). Ben-Gurion, who fostered Ben-Porat's political career,showed personal interest in similar acts of violence. This was proved two years later in July 1954, when Mossad agents launched a series of bomb attacks against American and British property in Egypt in what came to be known as the 'Lavon Affair', which forced Ben-Gurion's resignation as prime minister.
    The Israeli defence minister, commenting on the 'Lavon Affair', indirectly admitted the involvement of the Israeli government in the bombing in Iraq: 'This method of operation was not invented for Egypt. It was first tried in Iraq'. . . . Such anti-Jewish acts by Zionists in an attempt to force the emigration of Jewish communities to Israel has been termed 'cruel Zionism' . . .

42. See Wilbur Crane Eveland, *Ropes of Sand: America's Failure in the Middle East* (New York: Norton, 1980), pp. 48-49.

43. See the United States Embassy in Baghdad's views on the emigration of the Iraqi Jewish community in response to questions posed by the State Department's Circular Airgram, dated February 7, 1949, FO 371/75182, E 397/1571/93. In response to the question:
    What attitude would be adopted by the Iraqi government towards the emigration of the Jewish community?
    The U.S. Embassy responded:
    . . . any government which Iraq is likely to have in the foreseeable future would be reluctant to permit the emigration of the Jewish community. Responsible leaders recognize the fact that a mass exodus of the Jews, who play such a prominent role in financial and business circles in Iraq, would seriously disrupt the economy of the country, further endangering its precarious stability.
    In response to the question:
    What would be the general attitude of the Jewish community towards the possibility of emigration?
    The U.S. Embassy responded:
    . . . . the desire of the Jewish community to emigrate will in great part be induced or limited by the amount of aggressiveness and recalcitrance which Israel may display in the future. . . . If Israel . . . displays a policy of moderation . . . not more than a small proportion of Iraq's Jewish community would want to emigrate to Palestine.
    See also Wilbur Crane Eveland, *op.cit.*

44. See Elmer Berger, *Who Knows Better Must Say So*, The Institute of Palestine Studies, Beirut, 1955, pp. 30-38. Cited in David Hirst, *The Gun and the Olive*

Branch: The Roots of Violence in the Middle East, Harcourt, Brace, Jovanovich, New York, 1977, pp. 162-163. See also Elias Chacour with David Hazard, *Blood Brothers: A Palestinian Struggles for Reconciliation in the Middle East*, Chosen Books, Grand Rapids, Michigan, 1984, pp. 124-127.

45. Moshe Dayan stated openly: "We came to this country which was already populated by Arabs, and we are establishing a Hebrew, that is a Jewish state here. . . . Jewish villages were built in the place of Arab villages. . . . There is not one place built in this country that did not have a former Arab population." (See *Haaretz*, April 4, 1969; see also Roberta Strauss Feuerlicht, *The Fate of the Jews: A People Torn Between Israeli Power and Jewish Ethics*, Times Books, The New York Times Book Co., Inc. (New York, Toronto, 1983) p.245.

46. See two recent articles in *The New York Times*, one by David K. Shipler, dated July 6, 1987, on pp. Al, A4, and one by Robert Pear with Richard L. Berke, dated July 7, 1987, on p. A8.

47. See notes 51-55

48. See the *Manchester Guardian Weekly*, March 23, 1986, Vol. 134, No. 12.

49. *The Middle East Journal*, Autumn 1986, Vol. 40, No. 4, pp. 671-672, entitled, Harvest of 1948 and The Creation of the Palestinian Refugee problem."

    See also Livia Rokach, *Israel's Sacred Terrorism; A Study Based on Moshe Sharett's Personal Diary and Other Documents*, AAUG Information Paper Series: No. 23, Belmont, Massachusetts, Third Edition, 1986.

    In a forward to Rokach, MIT professor Noam Chomsky writes:

    The United States . . . is surely one of the least repressive societies of past or present history with respect to freedom of inquiry and expression. Yet only rarely will an analysis of crucial historical events reach a wide audience unless it conforms to certain doctrines of faith . . . the scholarly professions and the media . . . will refuse to submit to critical analysis the doctrines of the faith . . . Moshe Sharett's diary . . . remains outside of 'official history' . . . His diaries give a very revealing picture . . . and offer an illuminating insight into the early history of the state of Israel, with ramifications that reach to the present and beyond . . . (pp. IX-XI).

50. See Erskine Childers, "The Other Exodus," *The Spectator* (London) May 12, 1961. Childers asserts that there is no evidence to support Israel's contention that the Palestinians left voluntarily or as a result of Arab broadcasts urging them to leave.

51. See David Gilmour,"The 1948 Arab Exodus: Laying the Myths to Rest," *Middle East International*, No. 286, October 24, 1986.

52. *Ibid.*, p. 13.

53. *Ibid.*, p. 13.

54. *Ibid.*, p. 13.

55. *Ibid.*, p. 13. Samuel Katz was Minister of External Information under Begin.

56. *Ibid.*, p.13. In referring to the Deir Yassein massacre, however, Jon Kimche referred to that crime as "the darkest stain on the Jewish record throughout the fighting." He continued: The terrorist justified the massacre of Deir Yassein because it led to the panic flight of the remaining Arabs in the Jewish state area." See Jon Kimche, *Seven Fallen Pillars* (New York: Praeger, 1953), p. 228.

57. Begin, *op. cit.*, p. 164, note 1. Don Peretz, a Jewish writer, referred to the

outcome of Deir Yassein as a "mass fear psychosis which grasped the whole Arab community." See Don Peretz, *Israel and the Palestine Arabs* (Washington, D.C.: The Middle East Institute, 1958) p.6. Another writer stated that this "bloodbath . . . was the psychologically decisive factor in the spectacular exodus of Arab refugees." See Arthur Koestler, *Promise and Fulfillment, Palestine 1917-1949* (London:Macmillan, 1949), p.160.

58. See U.N. Document A/648, Progress Report of the United Nations Mediator on Palestine, *General Assembly: Official Records: Third Session: Supplement No. 11*, p. 14, paragraphs 6 and 7.

59. See David Gilmour, *op.cit.*, p.14.

60. *Ibid.*, p. 14.

61. *Ibid.*, p. 14.

62. Contemporary Palestinian poems dealing with civil liberties and human rights center on the injustice perpetrated against the Palestinians by the world community, as creator of the state of Israel and of Zionism in particular, whose role it has been to uproot the Palestinians from their homes and lands. See for example the following:

   1. *A Lover From Palestine and Other Poems*, Abdul Wahab Al-Messiri, Editor, Palestine Information Office, Washington, 1980.

   2. *Ahmad Zaatar*: A poem by Mahmoud Darwish, Translated by Rana Kabbani, Free Palestine Press, Washington, 1976.

   3. *The Wind-Driven Reed and Other Poems*, by Fouzi El-Asmar, Three Continents Press, Inc., Washington, D.C. 1979.

   4. *Enemy of the Sun: Poetry of Palestinian Resistance*, Naseer Aruri and Edmund Ghareeb, Editors, Drum and Spear Press, Washington: Dar Es Salaam, 1970.

63. This quotation is taken from Yehoshafat Harkabi, Elizabeth Monroe, Fayez A. Sayegh, John Coventry Smith, *Time Bomb in the Middle East*, New York: Friendship Press, 1969, pp. 69-70. See also Y.A. Sayegh, "Palestinian Peace: A Joint Venture into a New Society," *Middle East Newsletter*, IV, Nos. 4-5, (July 1970). pp. 2-12.

64. A recent poll which was conducted by a Palestinian researcher at an-Najah University in the West Bank, in cooperation with *al Fajr*, a Palestinian newspaper in the West Bank, the Australian Broadcasting Company and *Newsday*, a U.S. daily newspaper "based on a sample of 11,000 respondents from all over the occupied West Bank and Gaza Strip . . . show that 93% of Palestinians support the PLO, 71% Yasser Arafat, but only 3% King Hussein." See *Middle East International*, No. 283, September 12, 1986, pp. 14-15.

65. In discussing the leadership of Yasser Arafat, a prominent Palestinian-American scholar, Edward W. Said, wrote:

   There are two more factors to be mentioned, neither of which has received as much discussion as it deserves.The first is the generally successful shepherding and husbanding of Palestinian resources by the main leaders, chief among them Yasser Arafat, a much misunderstood and maligned political personality. It would not, I think, be impertinent to say about Arafat that he is the first Palestinian leader to do two completely essential things: (1) maintain a really intelligent grasp of all major factors affecting the Palestinians everywhere . . . (2) hold an equally astonishing *sway* over the detail of Palestinian life. . . .

See Edward W. Said, *The Question of Palestine*, Vintage Books, A Division of Random House, New York, 1980, pp. 165-166.

66. The text was taken from Walter Laqueur and Barry Rubin, Editors, *The Israeli Arab Reader, A Documentary History of the Middle East Conflict*, Penguin Books, 1984, pp. 504-518.

67. In lamenting the sad fact that very few Americans heard or read Yasser Arafat's address to the U.N. General Assembly, a prominent Jewish American wrote:

    How many Americans have been allowed to listen to Yasser Arafat? How many really read what he said when he finally had a chance to address the U.N. General Assembly on November 11, 1974? Many remembered the holster he wore - what media follower was allowed to forget this? But never heard or read one vital word he uttered.

    See Alfred M. Lilienthal, *The Zionist Connection II: What Price Peace*, North American, Inc., P.O. Box 65, New Brunswick, New Jersey, 08903, U.S.A., 1982.

68. Although Arafat has often been portrayed in the United States as an unsavory character, the United States government has apparently sought his help many times, as it did in the Iranian hostage crisis. He is reported to have given his assistance.

    Once more Arafat cooperated. He successfully arranged the release of the first eleven hostages. . . . For this, the Carter Administration thanked Arafat privately—very privately. Publicly, Carter spokesmen did nothing to discourage the unfounded speculation that the PLO has actually conspired with Iran to seize the hostages. . . . Just before he left office, Secretary of State Vance told me that he was in 'almost daily' communication with Arafat . . . enlisting PLO help during the protracted Iranian hostage ordeal, but he never said so in public. . . . On several occasions during off-the-record meetings at the White House, I pleaded with the President to acknowledge publicly the moderate cooperative course chosen by Arafat. . . . Carter listened but never followed my advice. . . .

    See Paul Findley, *They Dare to Speak Out*, Lawrence Hill & Co., Westport, Ct, 1985, pp. 14-15. (Former Congressman Paul Findley served for twenty-two years as a representative from Illinois.)

69. See the Book of Deuteronomy, 16:20.

70. The late William Hugh Brownlee was Professor Emeritus at Claremont Graduate School. He authored *The Lion That Ravages Palestine*, which was his first public statement on the plight of the Palestinians. In it, he discussed some of his personal experiences during the seven months he spent in Jerusalem in 1947-1948. That was one of the most critical periods in the Palestinian-Israeli conflict. (See William Hugh Brownlee, *The Lion That Ravages Palestine*, published by Americans for Middle East Understanding Inc., Room 771, 475 Riverside Dr., N.Y.,N.Y. 10115, 1983.) 71. William Hugh Brownlee, *The Rights of the Palestinians*, published by Americans for Middle East Understanding Inc., Room 771, 475 Riverside Dr. N.Y., N.Y. 10115, 1983, p.18.

72. Nahum Goldmann, *The Autobiography of Nahum Goldmann*, New York: Holt, Rinehart & Winston, 1969, p. 285.

73. Michael Selzer, Ed., *Zionism Reconsidered*, New York: Macmillan, 1970, pp. 191, 192.

74. *Ibid.*, p. 191.
75. Weizmann said, after the Palestinians were expelled from their homes and lands in 1947-1948:
    I am certain that the world will judge the Jewish state by what it will do with the Arabs.
    See Chaim Weizmann, *Trial and Error*, New York, Harper Brothers, 1949, p. 462. Later, however, Weizmann called the Palestinian exodus "a miraculous simplification of Israel's tasks." Lustick, *op.cit.*, p. 28.
76. Hannah Arendt, *The Jew As Pariah*, Ed., Ron H. Feldman, New York, Grove Press, 1978, p. 131.
77. *Ibid.*, pp. 186, 187.
78. *Enemy of the Sun, op. cit.*, p. 89.
79. *Country Reports on Human Rights Practices for 1985*: Submitted to the Committee on Foreign Affairs House of Representatives and the Committee on Foreign Relations U.S. Senate by the Department of State, In Accordance with Sections 116 (d) and 502 (b) of the Foreign Assistance Act of 1961, as Amended, February 1986, pp. 1264-1277.
80. Ian Lustick, *Arabs in the Jewish State*, Austin University of Texas Press, 1986, pp. 172-176.
81. *Ibid.*, pp. 31-32.
82. *Ibid.*, pp. 59-60, 175.
83. *Ibid.*, pp. 171-176.
84. Strauss Feuerlicht, *op.cit.*, pp. 245—247.
85. *Enemy of the Sun, op.cit.*, p. 65.
86. Ian Lustick, *op.cit.*, pp. 74-75.
87. See Raja Shehadah, *Occupier's Law: Israel and the West Bank*, Institute for Palestine Studies, 1985.
88. Israel Shahak, "An Apartheid System of Law," *Middle East International*, No. 282, August 22, 1986, p. 14. Shahak writes that there are "facts . . . among many which show conclusively that there exists a discriminatory separation between Jews and Arabs living in the same territory and under the same authority. It is, in fact, an apartheid system of law. . . ."
89. The Jewish ethic provides: "One law and one ordinance shall be both for you and for the stranger that sojourneth with you." The Book of Numbers, 15:16.
90. Ian Lustick, *op.cit.*, p. 141; Strauss Feuerlicht, *op.cit.*, p. 247.
91. *Country Reports on Human Rights Practices for 1985, op.cit.*, pp. 1260-1261; Ian Lustick *op.cit.*, p. 141.
92. *Ibid.*, p. 157.
93. Strauss Feuerlicht, *op.cit.*, pp. 245-247. See also this poem cited in note 85, *supra*.
    We wash dishes in the hotels And serve drinks to the masters. We mop the floors in the dark kitchens To extract a piece of bread From your blue teeth For the little ones. . . .
94. *Country Reports on Human Rights Practices for 1985, op. cit.*, p. 1266. See Noam Chomsky, *The Fateful Triangle*, South End Press, Boston, MA., 1983, p. 10 note; see also Mohamed El-Khawas and Samir Abed Rabbo, *American Aid to Israel: Nature and Impact*, Amana Books, Brattleboro, Vermont, 1984.
95. See Mohamed El-Khawas and Samir Abed Rabbo, *op.cit.*, pp.1-15.
96. See Roselle Tekiner,"Jewish Nationality Status as the Basis For Institu-

tionalized Racial Discrimination in Israel," *American Arab Affairs*, Summer 1986, Number 17, p.88. See also W.T.Mallison, Jr., "The Legal Problems Concerning the Juridical Status and Political Activities of the Zionist Organization/Jewish Agency: A Study in International and United States Law," *William and Mary Law Review*, Vol. 9, Number 3, 1968, pp.556-629. Mallison writes:

The characterization of the ... Jewish National Fund ... and ... the United Israel Appeal ... as 'institutions of the Zionist Organization' is of considerable legal significance. It means that the conclusions of this study concerning the juridical status of the Zionist Organization apply equally to the Jewish National Fund and the United Israel Appeal. Each of these engage in supposed 'charitable' solicitations in the United States. The contributions which are made to them by United States citizens through the United Jewish Appeal are interpreted as tax deductible charitable contributions for income tax purposes by the United States Government. The apparent assumption is that these institutions are voluntary American private associations. The Covenant indicates, however, that they are integral parts of the Zionist Organization. (pp.593-594).97.

97. Strauss Feuerlicht, *op.cit.*, p. 248. See also *Country Reports on Human Rights Practices for 1985, op.cit.*, pp.1265-1266.
98. *Ibid.*, p.248.
99. Lustick, *op.cit.*, p. 169.
100. *Enemy of the Sun, op.cit.*, p. 21.
101. Strauss Feuerlicht, *op.cit.*, p.251. See also *Country Reports on Human Rights Practices for 1985*, op.cit., pp.1257-1277.
102. Fouzi El-Asmar, *The Wind Driven Reed*, Three Continents Press, Inc., Washington, 1979, p.81. Fouzi El-Asmar, a Palestinian born in Haifa, remained in Israel after its creation in 1948. He was a member of the editorial board of the literary monthly magazine, *al Fajr*. In 1969, he was arrested by the Israeli authorities and remained in prison for fifteen months without any charges having been made against him. He was then exiled without a trial in 1972.
103. *Ibid.*, p. 55.
104. Lustick, *op.cit.*, pp. 255-256. The Koenig document was published in *Al-Hamishmar*, one of Israel's major daily newspapers, on September 7, 1976. See the full text, as translated by Dr. Israel Shahak, with notes, in a special pamphlet dated December 13, 1976, entitled, *Places of Injustice*, published by American Jewish Alternatives to Zionism and Americans for Middle East Understanding.
105. Said, *op. cit.*, pp. 107-110. Said writes: But from time to time there have been inadvertent insights into government for Arabs in Israel given to watchful observers. The most unguarded example was a secret report by Israel Koenig, northern district (Galilee) Commission of the ministry, written for then Prime Minister, Yitzhak Rabin on 'Handling the Arabs in Israel.' (The full text was subsequently leaked to *Al-Hamishmar* on September 7, 1976.) Its contents make chilling reading, but they fulfill the assumptions of Zionism toward its victims, the non-Jews. Koenig frankly admits that Arabs present a demographic problem since unlike Jews, whose natural increase is 1.5 percent annually, the Arabs increase at a yearly rate

of 5.9 percent. Moreover, he assumes that it is national policy for the Arabs to be kept inferior. . . . Therefore he suggested that it is necessary to expand and deepen Jewish settlement . . . where . . . Arab population is . . . more than the Jewish population. . . . The approach and exigency . . . have to deviate from the routine . . . concurrently, the state law has to be enforced so as to limit 'breaking of new ground' by Arab settlements in various areas of the country.

106. See Michael Fischbach, "Galilee's Health Divide," *Middle East International*, No. 286, October 24, 1986, p.15.
107. *Ibid.*, p. 16.
108. *Ha'aretz*, October 23, 1981. See also *The Shahak Papers*, No. 41, pp. 98-105. Dr. Israel Shahak is a professor at the Hebrew University in Jerusalem. He is active in the Israeli League for Human and Civil Rights. Professor Shahak translates from Hebrew to English articles and editorials from Israeli newspapers and other publications which are available only in Israel. These are known as "The Shahak Papers." Amnesty International is one of the human rights organizations which accepts Professor Shahak's credibility. See Strauss Feuerlicht, *op.cit.*, p. 296, note 32.
109. *A Lover From Palestine and Other Poems, op. cit.*, p.57.
110. *Country Reports on Human Rights Practices for 1985, op.cit.*,pp. 1267-1277.
111. See Articles 42-56 of The Hague Land Regulations, as reported in *Treaties and Other International Agreements of the United States of America, 1776-1949*, compiled by Charles I. Bevans, Assistant Legal Adviser, Department of State, Vol.I (1776-1917), Department of State Publication, pp. 651-653.
112. *Ibid.*, p.653. Article 55 of The Hague Land War Regulations provides: The occupying state shall be regarded only as administrator and usufructuary of public buildings, real estate, forest, and agricultural citates belonging to the hostile state, and situated in the occupied country. It must safeguard the capital of these properties, and administer them in accordance with the rules of usufruct.
Also, it has been declared that any occupying power holds a position somewhat similar to that of a trustee. (*In re von Leeb and Others*, (High Command Case)) II T.W.C. 524, 547.
113. *Ibid.*, p. 652. Article 50 of The Hague Land War Regulations provides: No general penalty, pecuniary or otherwise, shall be inflicted upon the population on account of the acts of individuals for which they cannot be regarded as jointly and severally responsible.
114. *Ibid.*
115. *The New York Times*, April 14, 1984.
116. *Shahak Papers*, No. 32, p.5.
117. *The Country Reports on Human Rights Practices for 1985, op.cit.*, p.1277.
118. *The Shahak Papers*, No. 32, p.7.
119. *Ibid.*
120. *Report and Recommended Actions of an Amnesty International Mission to the Government of the State of Israel*, 3-7 June 1979, Amnesty International, 1980, p.5.
121. *Ibid.*, pp. 5-21, 13.
122. *Ibid.*, p. 13.
123. Strauss Feuerlicht, *op.cit.*, p. 260.
124. *Ibid.*, pp. 260-261.

125. *Palestinian Human Rights Bulletin*, Winter 1981-82, as cited in Strauss Feuer-
     licht, *op.cit.*,p. 261.
126. *The Shahak Papers*, No. 41, p.34.
127. Strauss Feuerlicht, *op.cit.*, p. 265.
128. Fouzi El-Asmar, *op.cit.*, p.9.
129. See Elmer Berger, *Who Knows Better Must Say So!* The Institute for Palestine
     Studies, 1955, Reprinted Copy, 1970. Rabbi Berger wrote in 1955:
     I can only hope - humbly - that on the complex problem with which
     these letters treat they may truly help others a little to 'know better' and
     then, knowing better, that they may also feel the moral compulsion to use
     their precious American right to 'say so'.
     Quote is from the first page of the book, which is not numbered.
130. Amos Perlmutter is Professor of Political Science and Sociology at American
     University. He is also Editor of the *Journal of Strategic Studies*. See *Foreign
     Affairs*, Vol. 64, No. 1, 1985, p. 141.
131. See Amos Perlmutter, "Unilateral Withdrawal: Israel's Security Option,"
     Foreign Affairs, Vol. No.1, 1985, p.152.
132. Brownlee, *The Rights of the Palestinians, op.cit.*, p.13.
133. See the *Jerusalem Post*, June 7, 1968.
134. See Mark A. Heller, *A Palestinian State: The Implications for Israel*, Harvard
     University Press, Cambridge, Massachusetts, and London, England, 1983,
     pp. 84-85; see also Edward W. Said, Ibrahim Abu Lughod, Janet L. Abu
     Lughod, Muhammed Hallaj, Elia Zureik, *A Profile of the Palestinian People*,
     printed by the Palestine Human Rights Campaign, 20 East Jackson #1004,
     Chicago, Illinois, 60604, 1986, p.25; see also Said, *The Question of Palestine*,
     op.cit., p.108, where Said writes:
     Koenig frankly admits that Arabs present a demographic problem since
     unlike Jews, whose natural increase is 1.5 percent annually, the Arabs
     increase at a yearly rate of 5.9 percent. . . .
135. See Jan Abu Shakra, "The Making of a Non-Person," *The Link*, published
     by Americans for Middle East Understanding, Inc., Vol. 19, No.2, May/
     June 1986.
136. See *Country Reports on Human Rights Practices for 1985, op.cit.*, pp. 1267-
     1277; see also Strauss Feuerlicht, *op.cit.*, pp. 219-288.
137. See Joost R. Hiltermann, "Israel's Rule by Bulldozer," *Middle East Inter-
     national*, No. 282, August 22, 1986, pp. 15-16.
138. See *Country Reports on Human Rights Practices for 1985, op.cit.*, p. 1277.
139. *Ibid.*,p. 1267.
140. Brownlee, *The Rights of the Palestinians, op.cit.*, p.14.
141. In September of 1986, Amnesty International called upon Israel to co-
     operate in a full investigation of reports that it has been engaged in torture
     in the occupied territories. Israel, however, has refused to allow an inde-
     pendent investigation of its conduct in these territories, and has in fact
     often covered up its violations. In a recent article in Middle East Inter-
     national, David McDowall wrote:
     Amnesty has had a long standing interest in Israel's treatment of de-
     tainees, and this is reported almost annually in the Amnesty International
     Annual Report. . . . The Israeli authorities told Amnesty then that they
     'conduct an ongoing review of the treatment of security detainees, and
     there is no need for the committee of inquiry you recommend.' We are

no doubt supposed to dismiss as wholly without foundation the stream of reports emanating from such internationally respected bodies as Law in the Service of Man, which over the past two years alone has reported on the use of gas and other physical abuse on prisoners. . . . [The] U.S. National Lawyers Guild 'concludes substantial evidence exists that torture has been used in numerous instances against Palestinians' . . . These violations are part and parcel of the wider system of oppression designed to deprive them as a people of what they still have and claim in their homeland. . . .
David McDowall, "Israeli Torture," *Middle East International*, No. 284, September 26, 1986, p.10.

142. See Noam Chomsky, *The Fateful Triangle, op.cit.*, p.10 (note).

    United States economic and military aid to the State of Israel since 1949 is believed to be in the neighborhood of $55 billion. This does not include tax deductible "charitable contributions" or the sale of state of Israel Bonds, exempted by special legislation from the Interest Equalization Tax. See also *Middle East Terror: The Double Standard*, an address of Dr. Alfred M. Lilienthal to Phi Beta Kappa Association of Washington, D.C., on October 16, 1985. The 30th Anniversary Fund, P.O. Box 57177, Washington, D.C., 20037.

143. The United States government recognizes that Israel's presence in the occupied territories is governed by The Hague Regulations of 1907, and the 1949 Fourth Geneva Convention, both of which are ratified U.S. treaties. They are thus "the supreme Law of the Land." (See Article VI of the United States Constitution). By financing Israel's violations of these conventions, the United States violates not only its laws, it violates its own Constitution in becoming a partner in Israel's gross human rights violations.

144. See 22 U.S.C. Section 2151 n(a) (1979).

145. See 22 U.S.C. Section 262 (d) (d) (1979).

146. *Country Reports on Human Rights Practices for 1985, op.cit.*, p. 1266.

147. *Ibid.*, p. 1257.

148. It is difficult to find a plausible explanation for the State Department's seemingly unjustified certification. (See Findley, *op.cit.*, pp. 157-158). Yet a forthright declaration by the State Department that Israel is guilty of gross human rights violations would probably stop the phenomenal flow of U.S. aid to Israel. Israel's human rights violations would probably also "stop if the United States turned off the tap . . . in anger at some excessive lunacy." See the *Manchester Guardian Weekly* of September 12, 1982.

149. *Ibid.*, pp. 1257-1277.

150. *Country Reports on Human Rights Practices for 1985, op.cit.*, p. 1264.

151. Sameeh Al-Qassem,
You may take the last strip of our land
Feed my youth to prison cells
You may plunder my heritage,
You may burn my books, my poems
Or feed my flesh to the dogs
You may spread a web of terror
On the roofs of my village
O enemy of the sun,
But,
I shall not compromise

And, to the last pulse in my veins
I shall resist
See *Enemy of the Sun, op.cit.*, p. XV.
152. Mahmoud Darweesh,
Record!
I am an Arab
You have stolen the orchards
of my ancestors
and the land
which I cultivated
Along with my children
And you left us with those rocks
So will the state take them
as it has been said. . . .
Therefore
Record on top of the first page
I do not hate man
Nor do I encroach
But if I become hungry
The usurper's flesh will be my food
Beware . . . beware
of my hunger . . . and my anger
Ibid., pp. XXXVIII-XXXIX.
153. Salem Jubran,
Flowers on the graves, America,
And dancing and songs on the remains —
There is nothing left but films
films that make you laugh and cry
My dead brothers, it is funny and tearful.
The farms of the colonists stretch across the prairie
Large, green, and fertile.
The noisy factories of the colonists heirs destroy the earth
And pollute the sky —
What shall I say brother?
Alas for your history!
And death for a civilization that lives
on destruction — and blood.
Ibid.,p. III.
Also: Sameeh Al-Qassem,
In which God will you seek shelter?
Which God will bless your napalm?
Who will sell you a writ of absolution?
You, the stooge of colonialism
The agent of skyscrapers
And guardian of petroleum.
Ibid., p. XLIII
154. See Raymond L. Garthoff, *Detente and Confrontation: American Soviet Relations from Nixon to Reagan*, (The Brookings Institution, Washington, D.C., 1985), pp. 360-408: See also Henry Kissinger, *Years of Upheaval*, (Boston, Massachusetts: Little, Brown, 1982), pp. 450-613.

155. "For fiscal years 1978 through 1982, Israel received 40% of all U.S. military aid and 35% of U.S. economic aid, worldwide." See Chomsky, *The Fateful Triangle, op.cit.*, p.10.

156. See Harry J. Shaw, "Strategic Dissensus," *Foreign Policy*, No. 61, Winter 1985-86, pp. 125-130.

157. David Ben-Gurion, Israel's first prime minister, is quoted by Nahum Goldmann, a former president of both the World Jewish Congress and the World Zionist Organization, as having said:

Why should the Arabs make peace? If I was an Arab leader, I would never make terms with Israel. That is natural: we have taken their country. Sure, God promised it to us, but what does that matter to them? Our God is not theirs. We come from Israel, it's true, but two thousand years ago, and what is that to them? There has been anti-Semitism, the Nazis, Hitler, Auschwitz, but was that their faults? They only see one thing: we came here and stole their country. Why should they accept that?

See Nahum Goldmann, *The Jewish Paradox* (New York: Grosset & Dunlap, 1978), p.99.

5

SEPARATISM AT THE WRONG TIME IN HISTORY

BENJAMIN M. JOSEPH

> Israel and South Africa have one thing above
> all else in common: they are both situated in
> a predominantly hostile world inhabited by
> dark peoples.
>
> *Official Yearbook of the Republic of South Africa,*
> 1977 ed.,p.61.

The Israeli-South African embrace in recent decades, a political and military alliance which has been amply documented by now,[1] does not, in itself, tell us a great deal about the countries involved or the ideologies to which they are committed. All governments are there to pursue better military, economic and political standing. It is fair to say that moral considerations and principles are not what international politics is about. States do not often pass up profitable transactions solely because of the political character of their partners; even embargoes might not prove more than a minor inconvenience. And, some anti-Zionist writings not-

Based on material from Benjamin M. Joseph, *Besieged Bedfellows: Israel and the Land of Apartheid* (Greenwood Press, Inc., Westport, CT. 1988) chapters 10 and 11. Copyright (©) 1988 by Benjamin M. Joseph. By permission of the publisher.

withstanding, there is no a priori reason why this should be different in the case of Israel and South Africa.

If alliances in themselves tell us little in a world where politics can make strange bedfellows, how are we to know whether Israeli ties with South Africa are all that different from, say, its extensive dealings with Iran, especially in the 1970's? Commentators friendly to Israel might argue (after minimizing the extent of the alliance with South Africa and pointing out that "everybody does it") that these are simply two relatively isolated states with few alternatives, practicing *realpolitik*. In other words, the harsh realities of this world have required Israel to make a painful sacrifice and reluctantly deal with the white minority government. Critics of Israel, by contrast, often point to the similarities between the treatment of Blacks in South Africa and Palestinians in Greater Israel, as well as to similarities in the history of the colonization of Southern Africa and the Middle East. But even the existence of similarities is not sufficient to establish that the alliance is a departure from *realpolitik* conduct.

In reality, the Israeli alliance with South Africa *is* unique in today's world. One way to highlight this is to look at the attitudes and perceptions, the sense of kinship that has reinforced this partnership. The discussion will then proceed to focus on the consanguinity of Zionism and apartheid, while omitting or touching only briefly on aspects that readers of this *Festschrift* are already likely to be familiar with, such as the history of Zionism, Israeli Zionist legislation and life under Israeli occupation.

White South Africans have never regarded Israel as just another business and military partner for vital transactions. They closely identify with Israel (not necessarily with Jews) and have missed few opportunities to show their admiration and empathy. Numerous establishment Israelis, as the examples below indicate, have likewise shown empathy, understanding and amity towards the besieged white minority. Manifestations such as red carpet receptions for South African officials, Knesset members establishing a friendship league with South Africa or attending ceremonies for bantustan leaders, twin city agreements and the like are not what we would expect between indifferent partners cooperating only because they have no alternative.

Afrikaners have long noticed that their struggle for survival at the foot of Africa parallels that of another "white" country near the head of the continent:

With the partition of Palestine and the establishment of Israel, an apartheid was at the same time carried into effect which had the result that hundreds of thousands of Arab refugees from the Jewish area languished in neighbouring Arab states and formed an insoluble international problem. We say this with no reproach. But Israel owes its existence to the refusal of its Jewish citizens to accept integration and equality with an Arab majority in one state. The apartheid policy is based on the same attitude by European South Africans toward the non-European majority.[2]

Since the countries were seen as sharing a common lot, "their community of interests had better be utilized than denied", as the South African newspaper *Die Burger*, organ of the ruling National Party in Cape Province, pointed out after the 1967 war.[3] South Africa supported Israel in all its wars, and the Israeli victories were a source of inspiration. Among those who felt aroused was General H. van den Berghe, former head of the South African Bureau of State Security (BOSS): "I went to Israel recently and enjoyed every moment there. I told the Prime Minister when I got back that as long as Israel exists we have hope".[4] Excitement about Israel is not limited to the South African leadership: In one Markinor survey respondents ranked their favorite countries and Israel was at the top.[5] There are also numerous "Christian Action for Israel" groups.

Invasions and destabilization of neighboring countries to combat "terrorism" ring a familiar bell in South Africa and are often equated with similar Israeli actions which were met with more understanding in the West. After a trip to South Africa, *New York Times* columnist Flora Lewis observed that "comparison with Israel has become an insistent theme in South Africa when people there discuss their country's action". Thus, "after the murderous South African raid on Lesotho recently, an American correspondent asked the Foreign Ministry how it explained talks with Angola one day and an armed attack on a neighbor next. The answer was simply that Israel invaded Lebanon while negotiating with Egypt and this has been accepted." The African National Congress was regularly equated with the PLO; some in South Africa spoke of "Menachem Botha" and "Magnus Sharon".[6]

The pattern is different in Israel: leaders and the mass media do not regularly equate Israel's history and present problems with those of South Africa. Few Israelis would agree or appreciate hearing that their country is in the same boat as South Africa, although some of those concerned about birth rates and revolt on the occupied West Bank and Gaza fear "another South Africa". But while it is true that there has been little outspoken support and admiration for Pretoria in Israel, it is also true that when it comes to showing amity and cordiality towards South African representatives Israel has often gone well beyond other countries, Western and non-Western. Consider P.W. Botha's tour of Western Europe in the summer of 1984. In Germany,

> A large upholstered sofa was removed from West German Chancellor Helmut Kohl's office last week minutes before South Africa's Prime Minister P.W. Botha came to call. The Chancellor typically sits on the sofa with his foreign guests as photographers snap. This time, Mr. Kohl stared unsmilingly and stiff next to a relaxed-looking Mr. Botha. The Chancellor declined to re-enact a handshake for the cameramen, who did, however immortalize the departing piece of furniture. [7]

In London, Botha's presence "detonated a huge demonstration" and "photographs of her (Margaret Thatcher) glowering countenance in pictures with Mr. Botha were meant to convey Britain's disapproval of apartheid".

Israeli leaders, by contrast, believe that that is no way to treat a white guest from South Africa. Several months later, in November, Foreign Minister Roelof Botha came to Jerusalem. Israeli Foreign Minister Shamir had to have a state-level reception and "went to Ben-Gurion Airport, rolled a red carpet in front of the guest, received him according to all the rules of protocol and even invited reporters to photograph his meeting with Botha at the Foreign Ministry".[8] (An Associated Press photo showed Botha and Shamir beaming and shaking hands). Botha also met with Defense Minister Rabin, was driven in an official limousine and served a state dinner. *Maariv* Columnist Amnon Abramowitz observed that other countries in the West may do business with South Africa "quietly under the table," but Israel's approach is reminiscent of the Jew who not only eats pork but also drips grease for everyone to see.

The above was not an aberration. Recall the way Vorster was received in 1976 by a Labor government. Or, the treatment extended to South African Treasury Minister Owen Horwood by Prime Minister Begin and other officials in December of 1980. The guest was invited to a reception in Yeshiva attended by Chief Rabbi Ovadia Yosef and Jerusalem Mayor Teddy Kollek; Rabbi Yosef wished the South African "may all the Torah's blessings come true for you".[9] Igal Horowitz, his Israeli counterpart, praised the "deep ties" between Israel and South Africa without even the most perfunctory condemnation of apartheid. The South African journal *Beeld* reported that the Hebrew University in Jerusalem awarded him an honorary doctorate in philosophy.[10] "This is not part of a normal relationship which we have to have," complained Knesset Member Amnon Rubinstein who does favor "normal" relations with South Africa. "This is blatant disregard for the basic sensitivity we must have as Jews and Israelis". As soon as you arrive in South Africa, Rubinstein went on, you are reminded of the ghetto, the Pale, stamps in identity cards, places which are off-limits, the absence of the most elementary rights and suppression of dissent. The Knesset critic also noted that by Pretoria's standards most of today's Israelis might be classified as non-whites. Some Israelis have in fact been "mistakenly" abused or removed from "white" buses.[11]

None of this stopped General Nathan Nir, chairman of the Israeli Association for the Welfare of Soldiers, from visiting South Africa the following year "on a mission to help give soldiers the feeling that they are needed and appreciated." Naturally, he also met —"privately"— with several high-ranking military officers and praised the raid into Angola as the only way to deal with terrorists who must be "attacked at their bases. In this way they would never feel safe".[12]

It is not uncommon for Israelis or the Israeli media to refer to those who resist apartheid as "terrorists" with which South Africa, like Israel, is plagued. Similarly, Pretoria's perspective on events in South Africa has been adopted by Israeli state and private media at least some of the time: Israeli television viewers were treated by the state-run network to a South African program celebrating the "new state of Transkei"; resistance in Soweto was explained as "criminal violence" perpetrated by "Communist elements and outside agitators"; and some newspapers described American diplomatic initiatives in South Africa as a "sellout" of the kind that Israel might expect.[13]

Looking at the Knesset record in the 1970's and early to mid-1980's, one finds that the legislative body has had very little to say about Israel's "second most important ally after the United States," as South Africa was characterized by senior columnist Yoel Marcus of *Ha'aretz*, Israel's equivalent of the *New York Times*, in an October 1, 1982 article. The topic came up for debate perhaps once or twice in all those years. What protest there has been in the Knesset or the media was less likely to focus on being an ally of South Africa than on the failure to avoid gratuitous visibility and public relations headaches. Thus Shlomo Avineri, former director-general of the Ministry of Foreign Affairs who is considered a critic of government policy towards South Africa, would like Israel to "do business with it (SA) when it is in our interest but take care not to appear as condoning by overt acts the policies of the government."[14]

The great majority of the Israeli public has shown no measurable concern or opposition. Ties with South Africa burgeoned while being a non-issue for most Israelis. In general, steps taken by the government for the sake of "security" are rarely questioned. Other than a small number of individuals committed to leftist causes, such as "Israelis

Against Apartheid," there is no record of demonstrations or sit-ins demanding that ties be cut off. (There are also sporadic reports about small groups forming on the right to press for *warmer* ties with Pretoria, e.g., the *Jerusalem Post*, August 28, 1985.)

Developments which would be met with vehement protests and boycotts in the United States or Western Europe often pass without notice in Israel; financial considerations have prevailed in situations where most other Western governments or even private companies would likely have drawn the line. Thus it is impossible to imagine New York City's Bloomingdale's department store holding, as did the Shalom department store in Tel Aviv, a promotional "South Africa Week." The event was organized by the South African Department of Commerce with "contributions by the Department of Information in cooperation with the management of Shalom stores." Shoppers were offered "information" about South Africa as a bonus.[15] A similar "South Africa Week" was held by Supersol, the largest Israeli supermarket chain.[16] Such promotions are common. ("It is sufficient to enter an Israeli supermarket," Naomi Chazan noted in *African Affairs* in 1983, "to see the extent of South African goods.") In Israel, a "made in South Africa" label does not cause too many eyebrows to rise.

South Africa was reportedly the first country to open a state-run tourist office in Israel, in 1979.[17] Four years later Israeli Minister of Tourism Sharir awarded South African Airways the title of "Most Favoured Tourist Undertaking for 1983" for its contribution to the promotion of tourism in Israel.[18] South Africa has been a popular vacation spot for Israelis; small Israel is now South Africa's fourth largest source of tourists, topped only by England, Germany and the U.S.. Israel was also the only country from which tourism to South Africa rose in 1986. By January 21, 1987, when these facts were reported in the *Jerusalem Post*, all flights to South Africa for the Passover holiday in mid-April were booked solid on both El Al and South African Airways.

Even in early 1987, amid all the talk about sanctions, South African officials saw room for growth: In January South African master chef William Gallagher came to Israel to promote "South Africa Food and Culture Week," scheduled for August and sponsored by the South African Tourism Board, El Al and a leading Israeli hotel group. Jean-Paul Rebischung, marketing manager for Europe of the South African Southern Sun Hotel chain, was also in Israel in January to help plan "South Africa Week."

Events such as these are barely newsworthy in Israel. They cause no more excitement and controversy than did, for instance, the 1976 declaration of Cape Town and Haifa as twin cities, the latter a city with a

Zionist Socialist reputation.[19] Similar agreements were signed by Simonstown and Akko as well as by Durban and Eilat. And in November 1984 the West Bank colony of Ariel signed a twin city agreement with Bisho, the capital of the bantustan of Ciskei. The agreement called for cultural, scientific, industrial and tourist exchanges, whatever these mean with regard to Bisho and Ariel. "President" Lennox Sebe, who came for the ceremony, was exhilarated: The occasion, he said, was "almost too precious to be scarred by words . . . almost too glorious for ordinary men." Perhaps it was the presence of Knesset members that rendered him nearly speechless. The Israeli legislators "spoke in terms of Israeli-Ciskeian brotherhood and a common struggle against a cruel world of double standards."[20] The *Rand Daily Mail* reported that for Sebe the ceremony and the heavy police escorts which the Israeli authorities sent to protect him were unmistakable signs of the dawning of international recognition. This "shows respect for us from the international community. There are none so blind as those who would not see. . . ."[21] In November 1983 those not blind might also have seen a reception for Sebe at Ben-Gurion airport which included dances by bare-breasted African women. In Ciskei proper, Sebe's personal safety has been assured with the help of retired Israeli senior officers (*Maariv*, August 1, 1985 and elsewhere).

The involvement of establishment Israelis in the bantustans has deepened despite the displeasure of Foreign Ministry officials whose job is to be concerned with Israel's image and diplomatic prospects in Africa and elsewhere. Nechemia Strassler reported in *Ha'aretz* that in Ciskei "money talks" and former Finance Minister Yoram Aridor, now a member of the Knesset, is a "most popular personality" and nearly "a member of the family". In April 1985 Aridor and other Knesset members were expected to attend the opening ceremony of the Ciskeian Parliament and watch a military parade of units trained by Israeli officers. Eventually, after heavy pressure from Foreign Ministry officials, only three members of the original delegation left. The *Ha'aretz* article pointed out that it would be unthinkable for any other politician in the world to visit Ciskei or any other bantustan.[22] (It does seem impossible to imagine a United States senator who is a regular visitor and investor in a South African "homeland".) Among the other Israeli dignitaries who have regularly visited Ciskei are Former Deputy Finance Minister Yehezkel Flomin, Tel Aviv Deputy Mayor David Griffel and Ruth Dayan, Moshe Dayan's widow.

Turning to academic contacts, some Israeli professors have readily accepted invitations to tour and lecture in South Africa—as guests of the Pretoria government. The all-expense-paid trip would often include the academics' spouses.[23] Dr. Benjamin Beit-Hallahmi of Haifa University added in a private conversation that more Israeli academics are finding South Africa an acceptable destination for their sabbaticals, another practice which would be difficult to find in universities elsewhere. The number of Israeli scholars who have chosen to investigate the ties with their country's "second most important ally after the United States" can easily be counted on the fingers of one hand.

The Israeli government has repeatedly said it opposes apartheid. In most cases it has also scrupulously avoided condemning the Pretoria government. Upon closer examination, many of the "anti-apartheid" statements appear to be fairly ambiguous, and not all even mention South Africa, e.g."we cannot be anything but critical of a policy which causes humiliation to others . . . "[24] Other Israeli statements did not require any reading between the lines to notice a degree of understanding and empathy for South African whites even as apartheid was termed unacceptable. Thus former Israeli Ambassador I. Unna was asked by the editors of *The Jewish Press* (New York) whether Jewish communities in the United States and elsewhere ought to look favorably upon South Africa because of the "special relationship" between Pretoria and Jerusalem. The interview took place in South Africa and was published the week the Soweto shootings began. Without mentioning apartheid at any point, Unna replied,

> I would take my guide line from what the Minister of Tourism Mr. Marais Steyn said to you last night. South Africa is not a Utopia, in fact very few countries are, even Israel is not a Utopia, we all have our shortcomings. Nobody doubts, including the South Africans, that South Africa has its shortcomings, but I do believe that such a visit as yours here, as the guests of the South African Tourist Organization and Pan Am, will enable you to have an honest look at South Arica. You will be able to, I think, divorce hostile propaganda from the reality of the situation, which, I believe, is far more sanguine than the propaganda, the anti- South African propaganda slant tends to make out . . .[25]

In another instance, an address on the "impressive relationship" between Israel and South Africa, the Ambassador went beyond portraying apartheid as a "shortcoming" and "not a Utopia," but even as he did so he described South Africa in terms which are not likely to cross the minds of many other foreign diplomats:

> Now it must be clear that, in spite of the good relationship which exists between South Africa and Israel, there can be for us no

acceptance of your domestic structure. . . . If we do not join the symphony of nations who constantly breathe down South Africa's neck, it is not because we are not critical of the domestic structure of South Africa, but because we are people who are surrounded ourselves by hordes of counselors. . . . If our voice is not as shrill and as persistent as some would like it to be in the chorus of criticism of South Africa, it is because we have faith in the sincerity of South Africa to tackle these problems and to seek and establish a society which will move away from social injustices. . . .

I would like to say in conclusion that there is one thing I believe South Africa and Israel really share in common and that is a desire to establish a society based on the vision of the prophet Isaiah, a vision of universal peace and the vision of prophets Amos and Micah, the visions of universal justice.[26]

It is not difficult to imagine the reactions if an ambassador from any other country which considers itself free and democratic said that his country and South Africa shared the same universal ideals of peace and justice expressed by the great prophets. As it turns out, the countries in question and the ideologies to which they are committed do share the same ideals, but those are the type of ideals that could not possibly have crossed the mind of any prophet. These "ideals" and their accompanying features, to which we now turn, are distinct enough to set the two countries apart from the rest of today's world; they occupy a unique position in contemporary history.

In southern Africa, the first permanent European settlement was established in Cape Town in 1652, an era of outward European expansion. As the settlers moved toward the interior of what is today South Africa, they had to overcome the resistance of the local population which had been there since the beginning of recorded history. The Khoi-San were the first casualties: Some were driven further north, others died in combat and still others were assimilated into the racial group known today as "Coloreds". By the 1770's, the forefathers of today's Afrikaners reached far enough north to clash with the Bantu-speaking people, whose colonization, subjugation and exploitation make up a substantial part of South African history. Today, five million whites are in control of a country in which the Africans number more than 24 million.

Had the South African whites been luckier, or smarter, they would have followed the Israeli example of 1948. How much easier it would be to be a South African white today if the indigenous population had been made to flee their bantustans and never allowed to return; Pretoria's leaders would have been as delighted as was Israel's first president Chaim Weizmann after the 1948 war which, he said, accomplished a "miraculous cleaning of the land; the miraculous simplification of Israel's task".[27] But maintaining supremacy without such a miraculous simplification, that is, when you do not have the above luxury of native flight and are vastly outnumbered, requires quite different methods and legislation. With them come more severe public relations problems. One way or the other, there are no other examples in today's world of embattled Western-oriented outposts facing a hostile Third World population within and without their borders. The last such countries were French Algiers and Rhodesia.

> There is no a priori reason why in any one state men of different races and creeds should not be ardent citizens living in peace and harmony with each other. The trend of modern thought, in spite of backwaters and counter currents, is surely in that direction. A Russia which must be purely Slav and of the Orthodox Greek church strikes us as an anachronistic effort. . . .[28]

Zionism and apartheid, the two most striking examples of the anachronisms C.G. Montefiore was writing about at the turn of the century, are today bound by an extensive web of military, economic and political ties.

In South Africa, although biological features have been the determinants of power and privilege for centuries, it was not until 1948, when the National Party took office, that apartheid became official and systematic policy. The Population Registration Act, 1950, is widely seen as the linchpin of apartheid: It classified South Africans as either white, Black, Asian or Coloured, and the latter were subdivided further. The Act, as amended in 1962, defined a white person as someone who

> (a) in appearance obviously is a white person and who is not generally accepted as a Coloured person; or (b) is generally accepted as a white person and is not in appearance obviously not a white person but does not include any person who for the purposes of his classification under this Act, freely and voluntarily admits that he is by descent a native or a Coloured person unless it is proved that the admission is not based on fact.[29]

Classification is subject to change. The Group Areas Act, also passed in 1950, designated the areas where each race may live.[30] Until 1985 when they were abolished, the Pass Laws blocked freedom of movement for Africans, who could legally live only in homelands or townships. Every African over the age of 16—and only Africans—required a pass in order to enter the white man's city. Failure to produce the pass at the demand of a police officer was a criminal offense. The Immorality Act (1927 as amended in 1950 and 1957) and the Prohibition of Mixed Marriages Act (1949), also abolished, prohibited marriage or sex between Europeans and non-Europeans. The legislation allowed police to enter bedrooms to gather evidence. (Even now, however, should an African marry a white woman—in itself never the focus of Black struggle in South Africa—it remains unclear where they can legally live and where their children can attend school. Housing and education remain segregated.)

The Reservation of Separate Amenities Act (1953) and the Liquor Act (1977), in conjunction with the Group Areas Act are the basis for what has come to be known as "petty apartheid." This legislation determines which parks, buses, rest rooms and other facilities are the white man's exclusive domain. Under earlier laws, such as the Native Land Act of 1913 and the Native Trust and Land Act of 1936, the African majority of nearly 74% is limited to owning less than one seventh of South Africa's area, mostly eroded although potentially fertile land. Today, each of the ethnic groups which comprise the African majority is assigned to a "homeland" or bantustan, the only places where they may exercise political rights under the "grand apartheid" scheme. Four of the bantustans are now nominally independent. In November 1983 P.W. Botha received overwhelming white approval for the "new constitution" which provided for a tricameral parliament for white, Coloureds and Indians but excluded the African majority. No other country in the world practices such official and comprehensive discrimination on the basis of biological factors.

In recent years South African leaders have professed to oppose discrimination and apartheid, an "outmoded system," in favor of "power sharing." At the same time they do not leave the slightest doubt that majority rule is unthinkable and that the cities, classrooms and entire way of life must remain racially segregated. This brand of white supremacy seems to be driven less by feelings of racial superiority, as was the case in the Verwoerd era, than by the refusal to yield power and privileges.

Israel, by contrast, found itself with only about 17% of the population non-Jewish, excluding about 1.4 million Arabs in the territories occupied in 1967. The latter, unlike the Jewish settlers in their midst, are denied political and civil rights. Workers from the West Bank and Gaza commute to Israel daily as inexpensive guest workers. They typically fill construction and janitorial openings and may not stay overnight in pre-1967 Israel. Emergency regulations left over from the British mandate period, comparable to those in effect in South Africa at this writing, are enforced against "terrorists" and their families. Among the measures employed by the authorities have been deportations of leaders and intellectuals without trials, severe censorship and bombing of houses as collective punishment. A new generation of Israelis and Palestinians has grown under the dual system of politics and law, and all Israeli governments have opposed total withdrawal. The 1967 boundaries have been erased in every sense, including from official Israeli maps.

Naturally, the above features of life under occupation have invited comparisons with South Africa and the bantustans, but Israeli spokesmen can counter that Israel has not formally annexed the West Bank and is still searching for "authentic" Palestinians (Shimon Peres' term) to negotiate with, etc. In fact, one need not go to the West Bank and Gaza in order to study Israel and Zionism. There is plenty to be learned from pre-1967 Israel.

In the Israeli Declaration of Independence we find an internal contradiction which seems highly suggestive. It states that "by virtue of our natural and historic right and on the strength of the resolution of the United Nations General Assembly (we) hereby declare the establishment of a *Jewish state* in Eretz Israel." The Jewish settlers, having brought "the blessings of progress to all the country's inhabitants" now have a state which "will be open for Jewish immigration and for the Ingathering of the Exiles." But then, in the same paragraph it is stated that the Jewish state will "ensure social and political rights to all its inhabitants *irrespective of religion, race or sex.*"[31] (Emphasis added.) A state established by Jews for Jews promised equality to those who were not Jewish. The equality would be as individuals; national rights are a different matter.

Other than the Law of Return (1950), the Nationality Law (1952) and the World Zionist Organization-Jewish Agency (Status) Law (1952), Israeli laws do not distinguish between Jews and non-Jews. The Law of Return allows virtually any person in the world whose mother is Jewish or who properly converted to Judaism to become an Israeli citizen upon arrival. The Nationality Law is in fact two laws, one for Jews and the other for non-Jews.[32] The Status Law regulates the status of the World Zionist Organization in Israel and its relationship with the state.

It is the latter law that goes a long way to ensure that no matter how "non-discriminatory "and "nationality blind" the rest of Israeli legislation may seem, vastly superior resources and benefits are channeled to Israeli Jews while "lawfully" excluding non-Jews. By granting quasi-governmental status and assigning responsibility for development and settlement to "national institutions" which have received state funds (the World Zionist Organization, the Jewish Agency and the Jewish National

Fund), the state can blatantly discriminate and still allow the government "plausible deniability." The Jewish Agency, for instance, has played a key role in developing the infrastructure and housing in Jewish areas. If new Jewish settlements have roads and electricity while older and larger Arab villages don't, no one can point to a discriminatory Israeli law or cabinet resolution that is directly responsible. As Ian Lustick explains,

> Because they are not formally part of the Israeli government apparatus, they do not serve a constituency of Israeli citizens. . . . They therefore constitute efficient conduits for channeling resources to the Jewish population only, resources which are converted into capital-intensive economic development projects, educational vocational training, social services, land acquisition, etc. In the implementation of such programs, officials of these institutions see themselves ideologically as well as legally justified in ignoring the needs of Arab Israelis and the impact of their activities on the Arab sector.[33]

Not only is there no appearance of "separate development" formally originating from the government, the government may point out, as it does regularly, that Israeli Arabs are materially better off than those in surrounding countries. Still, government spending in the Arab sector is far lower than in the Jewish sector. All in all, the gap between Arab and Jewish settlements is striking, whether one compares housing, employment opportunities, health services, education or numerous other indicators.

Although no state law explicitly denies access to Israeli Arabs, "public" lands—also known as "state" lands—have been effectively reserved for Jewish use with legal mechanisms such as the Jewish National Fund, the Custodian of Absentee Property, the Land Administration and the Jewish Agency Settlement Department. Non-Jewish citizens of Israel have been excluded from long-term leasing or development of approximately 92% of the lands in the pre-1967 borders. Technically, what the JNF charter calls for is not legally binding on the state, but one could hardly tell this from the experience of Palestinians in Israel.

There is, of course, much more to be said about the status and lives of Palestinians in Greater Israel, but even the above outline allows certain significant conclusions to be drawn. Is Zionism a form of racism as the UN General Assembly stated in 1975? People will perhaps never cease to quibble over the meaning of racism and Zionism, but one thing is clear: in a land with growing numbers of non-Jews, policies of "separate development" in some form or another are inevitable if Zionist ideology is to be implemented. Such policies need not be, and at present cannot be found in the letter of most Israeli laws. Yet the more complex and less visible mechanisms have managed to "serve the ideological ends of Zionism while reaping propaganda benefits among liberal circles abroad," as Lustick observed in his book. The avowed character of the state is, of course, a significant departure from contemporary Western notions of secular citizenship rights and political pluralism. And it is at best misleading to describe Israel as "Jewish" in the same sense that France is French: The latter does not officially strive to be the country of one ethnic group or race. Arabs living in the French state are French, but Arabs living in the Jewish state are not Jewish.

It is worth noting that the above ethnic and religious exclusivism does override differences in skin color, as the acceptance of Ethiopian Jews demonstrates, and as defenders of Zionism against charges of racism triumphantly point out. Predictably, the main problem they presented was whether they were genuine Jews, that is, biologically descended from an ancient Jewish tribe. Most rabbis ultimately ruled they were, though in order to be on the safe side the immigrants were requested to "renew" their Jewishness by immersing themselves in the "mikvah" ritual baths and to obtain a document certifying their status as Jews. Black Hebrews from the United States, by contrast, were not recognized as genuine Jews. Many have been deported and denied employment. "Suspect" American Blacks who attempted to visit Israel were often subjected to humiliating interrogations, required to deposit their passports and to post bonds worth thousands of dollars, to ensure that they do not stay too long in the Jewish state.

At the root of apartheid is the definition of nationality in monoracial and unicultural terms. For the purpose of preserving a "white" South Africa, apartheid has designated special homogeneous homelands for each group, a practice also known as "micro-segregation." As noted, other legislation regulates smaller scale segregation at the local level, e.g. the Group Areas Act, the Bantu Education Act and the now-abolished Prohibition of Mixed Marriages Act.

No Israeli equivalent can be found for the latter type of official segregation, or "micro-segregation." Yet the anti-pluralist, exclusivist tendencies of Zionism do converge with the central tenet of micro-segregation. The concept of one-person-one-vote in a pluralistic state shared by the settlers and the indigenous population these settlers found, is as unthinkable under Zionism as it is under apartheid. In both cases the original population is treated as if they were aliens, while those who came from elsewhere and their immediate descendants have assumed the role of natives. In Israel, for instance, a Jewish American is granted upon arrival rights vastly superior to those of any Israeli citizen who is an Arab and whose family has lived there for generations. The notion that the native population should enjoy the same status and rights as the settlers is beyond the bounds of "civilized" discussion in Israel, in fact even more so than in South Africa.

If similar anachronistic concepts of citizenship were applied to the United States, it would be juridically and demographically an Anglo-Saxon Christian America, just as the Soviet Union would be a purely Slav Russia. Such approaches parallel tribal kinship concepts as well as German nationalistic *Volk* thought.[34]

South Africa and Israel do go beyond most modern democratic polities in their anti-pluralistic character. Thus while it is not uncommon for modern democratic nations to be open to some outsiders and closed to others, the legal criteria for admission and benefits are not normally racial, religious or cultural. Yet Zionist Israel and white South Africa can only be what they are now: Secular citizenship rights cannot be granted because *that would mean the end of the polity* as currently constituted. The world was more hospitable to such political systems a century or two or three ago; towards the end of the 20th century and in this post-colonial era Zionism and apartheid do encounter their share of public relations problems. It is the struggle to preserve this type of *Herrenvolk* democracy at what is evidently an inauspicious time in history that, above all else, makes South Africa and Israel natural bedfellows.

The dream of apartheid calls for a white South Africa with autonomous black bantustans; the implementation of Zionism calls for a predominantly Jewish Israel with safeguards against a radical change in the demographic balance. The Likud Party favors annexation and, as a solution for the Palestinian "problem", autonomy under "moderate leadership" within Greater Israel (with more limitations than the South African bantustans—internal security, Jewish settlements, water rights, "state" lands, etc.) The Labor Party prefers "territorial compromise" for areas densely populated with Arabs; it may accept a Palestinian-Jordanian "homeland" of sorts, provided it is not a sovereign state.

Heribert Adam explained in the *Journal of Asian and African Studies* why polities such as Israel and South Africa must be seen as fundamentally different from the many other states where discrimination can be found:

In most hierarchically organized systems certain ethnic segments have a politically inferior status. They are not merely excluded from the spoils of political power as in many divided peripheries, but the state itself is defined in terms of the myths and symbols of the ruling group as its exclusive domain. In these ethnic states the ruling group ideology is enshrined in law or custom at the expense of secular citizenship rights. There are second-class citizens, almost outside the polity who are perceived as untrustworthy by birth.[35]

The collapse of white rule in South Africa would be bad news for Jerusalem not only because of the loss of the important relationship but also because it is understood that more Third World and United Nations heat may then be turned on Israel. As A. Schweitzer explained in *Ha'aretz* in the summer of 1985, "the Third World, with Soviet guidance and Arab financing, has for years been on the offensive against two states which are linked with the West: Israel and South Africa. . . . It should be clear to anyone who has eyes in his head that the fall of either of these states will accelerate the assault on the other. We would therefore not be doing ourselves a favor if we rush to mourn South Africa or speed up her decline by diplomatic or other action."[36]

Zionism has so far escaped the kind of worldwide revulsion and condemnation to which apartheid has been subjected. Yet there is every reason why abhorrence of apartheid should lead one to an identical attitude towards Zionism. A world in which there is no room for apartheid is really a world in which there should be no room for Zionism. This is so not only because they oppress and discriminate; numerous other ruling ideologies, regimes and economic systems have that distinction; it is also because these two ugly anachronisms have become bedmates in their conflict with humanity and history.

NOTES

1. See for instance Benjamin Beit-Hallahmi's *The Israeli Connection: Who Israel Arms and Why* (New York: Pantheon, 1987), and my own *Besieged Bedfellows: Israel and the Land of Apartheid* (Westport, CT: Greenwood Press, 1988).
2. *Die Burger* in 1952 quoted by Gideon Shimoni in *Jews and Zionism: The South African Experience 1910- 1967* (Cape Town: Oxford University Press, 1980), p.221.
3. *Die Burger*, May 29, 1968, in Richard Stevens and A.M. Elmessiri, *Israel and South Africa: The Progression of a Relationship* (New York: New World Press, 1976), p. 196.
4. Zdenek Cervenka and Barbara Rogers, *The Nuclear Axis: Secret Collaboration Between West Germany and South Africa* (New York: Times Books, 1978), p.311.
5. *The Sunday Times* (SA), August 11, 1981.
6. Flora Lewis, "Pretoria's Israel Mask", *The New York Times*, January 28, 1983.
7. James Markham, "Europeans Give Botha a Frosty Reception", *The New York Times*, June 10, 1984.
8. Amnon Abramowitz in *Maariv*, November 9, 1984.
9. Amnon Rubinstein in *Ha'aretz*, December 12, 1980.
10. *Beeld*, December 10, 1980 in *Jewish Affairs* (SA), January 1981.

11. Amnon Rubinstein in *Ha'aretz*, December 12, 1980.
12. The *Rand Daily Mail*, September 5, 1981.
13. Benjamin Beit-Hallahmi, "South Africa and Israel's Strategy of Survival," *New Outlook: Middle East Monthly*, April-May 1977, pp. 56-57.
14. *The Jerusalem Post*, November 15, 1985.
15. *Oogenblad*, July 30, 1977, in *Jewish Affairs* (SA), September 1977.
16. The *Financial Mail* (SA) September 14, 1979, p.18.
17. Rosalynde Ainslee, "Israel and South Africa: An Unlikely Alliance?", United Nations Department of Political and Security Affairs, 1981, # 81-18876, p.25.
18. *Die Transvaler*, July 27, 1983, in *Jewish Affairs*, September 1983.
19. F.R. Metrowich, *South Africa's New Frontiers* (Sandton:Valiant, 1977), p. 137.
20. Roy Isacowitz, "Twinning with a Tyrant," The *Jerusalem Post Magazine*, November 9, 1984.
21. The *Rand Daily Mail*, November 15, 1984, in *Jewish Affairs*, January 1985.
22. Nechemia Strassler, "Aridor's Blacks," *Ha'aretz*, April 11, 1985; *Maariv* weekly overseas edition, April 11, 1985, p. 6.
23. Naomi Chazan, "The Fallacies of Pragmatism: Israeli Foreign Policy Towards South Africa", *African Affairs*, April 1983, p. 183.
24. See for instance a collection of nine Israeli statements, some official, since 1978 in Kenneth Bandler, and George Gruen, "Israel and South Africa," A Special Report of the International Relations Department, The American Jewish Committee, New York, 1985, pp. 12-14.
25. *The Jewish Press*, June 18, 1976.
26. I. Unna, "Israel and South Africa: An Impressive Relationship," *The Zionist Record and South African Jewish Chronicle*, May 20, 1976.
27. Quoted by Ian Lustick, *Arabs in the Jewish State: Israel's Control of a National Minority* (Austin and London: University of Texas Press, 1980), p. 28.
28. C.G. Montefiore as quoted by Ali A. Mazrui, "Zionism and Apartheid: Stange Bedfellows or Natural Allies"? *Alternatives*, No. 9, 1983, p.77.
29. Monica Wilson and Leonard Thompson, *The Oxford History of South Africa* (New York: Oxford University Press, 1971), p. 403.
30. For fuller details see Leo Marquard, *The Peoples and Policies of South Africa* (New York: Oxford University Press, 1969), especially pp. 129-135.
31. Text in *Encyclopaedia Judaica*, (Jerusalem: Keter Publishers, 1972), V.5, col. 1453-1454.
32. On occasion, questions arise about the authenticity of a prospective immigrant or his parents' "Jewishness." "Additional documentation" is then required, and the ordeal that often results is fit to print in the daily newspapers. For the story of one such couple see Shaul Hon, "Playing with the Law of Return," *Maariv*, May 17, 1985.
33. Lustick, *Arabs in the Jewish State*, p. 106.
34. Mazrui, "Zionism and Apartheid," p.75.
35. Heribert Adam, "Ethnic Politics and Crisis Management: Comparing South Africa and Israel," *Journal of Asian and African Studies*, V. 18, #1-2, 1983.
36. A. Schweitzer, "Madua Drom Africa" (Why South Africa), *Ha'aretz*, August 6, 1985.

6

ZIONISM, FREEDOM OF INFORMATION, AND THE LAW

SALLY V. MALLISON and W. THOMAS MALLISON

Events in the United States during 1987, and particularly the United States government's attempt as a result of Zionist[1] pressure to close the Palestine Information Office (PIO) and the Palestine Liberation Organization (PLO) diplomatic mission at the United Nations, have raised fundamental questions under United States statutory and constitutional law as well as under international law. The present study emphasizes the domestic law issues. The most important question is whether or not the constitutional principle of freedom of information, mandated by the First Amendment to the Constitution, entitles the American public to be informed of Palestinian perspectives on the Israel-Palestine conflict situation from Palestinian sources. The American public, of course, is entitled to hear Zionist perspectives on this issue, and no attempt has been or is being made to shut off such perspectives. The fundamental question concerning the presentation of Palestinian perspectives has been raised by the persistent Zionist efforts to dominate the entire media of public information and to exclude anything which is inconsistent with that viewpoint. Before considering the basic statutory and constitutional issues involved, a comparison of the international public body status of

Zionist nationalism and Palestinian nationalism, as well as the accuracy of the registration of each under the U.S. Foreign Agents Registration Act, must be examined.

I. Public Bodies as Subjects of International Law

The Secretary-General of the United Nations recognized in 1949 that the subjects of international law are no longer limited to states. In his legal opinion: "Practice has abandoned the doctrine that States are the exclusive subjects of international rights and duties."[2] Among the subjects of international law other than states, international public bodies or organizations are of particular importance. Public bodies are usually constituted as subjects of international law through the explicit multi-lateral agreement of states (conventional law),[3] and there is no authority for a particular state to constitute an international public body unilaterally. Professor Lauterpacht has provided these succinct criteria for ascertaining the establishment of a public body:

> (I)n each particular case the question whether a person or a body is a subject of international law must be answered in a pragmatic manner by reference to actual experience and to the reason of the law as distinguished from a preconceived notion as to who can be subjects of international law.[4]

The International Court of Justice, in its advisory opinion concerning *Reparation for Injuries Suffered in the Service of the United Nations*, stated:

> (T)he development of international law has been influenced by the requirements of international life, and the progressive increase in the collective activity of States has already given rise to instances of action upon the international plane by certain entities which are not states.[5]

A. Status of the World Zionist Organization as a Public Body

The second point of the Basle Program set forth by the First Zionist Congress in 1897 made it clear that in Zionist conception the Zionist Organization was claimed to be a public body representing all Jews from its inception.[6] Such a claim standing alone is, however, not the equivalent of authoritative international decision. The Balfour Declaration of October 31, 1917,[7] which manifested the British view that the Organization had the juridical status to receive the precatory clause concerning a Jewish national home as well as to be subjected to the safeguards of Palestinian and Jewish rights, was a significant step toward the according of public body status by the community of states and allowed the Organization to participate in the Paris Peace Conference of 1919.[8] This was a tentative multilateral recognition and enabled it to take part in the drafting of the League of Nations Mandate for Palestine.[9] Article 4 of the Mandate is the most important provision concerning the Zionist Organization. It provides for "a Jewish agency" to work with the British government in matters regarding "the establishment of the Jewish national home" and recognizes the Zionist Organization as that agency. Thereby the world community, through the League of Nations, constituted the Zionist Organization/Jewish Agency as a public body subject of international law with certain powers and specific limitations on those powers.

The determination of public body status was made conclusively by the Permanent Court of International Justice in the Mavrommatis Palestine Concessions Cases. The decision in the first of these cases removed any possible doubt concerning the public body status of the Organization. The Court stated:

> This clause [article 4 of the Mandate] shows that the Jewish agency is in reality a public body, closely connected with the Palestine Administration and that its task is to co-operate with that Administration and under its control, in the development of the country.[10]

There is nothing in the dissenting opinions inconsistent with this holding, and it is further strengthened by statements in the second[11] and third[12] cases.

For a short time the Organization/Agency implemented its public body status within Palestine by cooperating with the British Mandatory Government in accordance with the Palestine Mandate and the limitations specifically put upon it by the Churchill White Paper of July 1, 1922[13] but as its political and military power increased, it violated these limitations whenever the political objectives of Zionist nationalism and its claimed constituency of "the Jewish people" made this desirable.[14] Outside of Palestine, in the international forum, it cooperated with the British government only so long as it was dependent on that government.[15] Thereafter, it used its public body status and powers without regard for the legal limitations imposed by the Balfour Declaration and the Palestine Mandate.

In 1947 and 1948 the Zionist Organization transferred its political pressure activities to the United Nations under the "Jewish Agency" name until it was formally replaced by the name of the State of Israel. It also conducted its public body activities within national states including the United Kingdom where its basic objective was to impose upon the British government the principle that the basic legal obligation of that government under the Mandate was to "the Jewish people" rather than to the indigenous inhabitants of Palestine.[16] In the early part of the Second World War the principal focus of the public body activities shifted to the United States where it has continued ever since.

The end of the British Mandate and the establishment of the State of Israel on May 14, 1948 terminated the legal authority for the public body status of the Zionist Organization/Jewish Agency.[17] No action taken by the United Nations provided a continuing juridical basis for the Organization. However, although a number of functions previously performed by it were taken over by the government of Israel, it continued its activities concerning the recruitment of Jewish immigrants into Israel and its fund-raising efforts. It is clear that the functions performed by the Organization and the working relationships between it and the government constituted a *de facto* status for the Organization and a juridical relation between it and the government. By 1951 a "Co-ordinating Board," containing Organization and government representation, existed and was concerned, *inter alia*, with "defining relationships between the two bodies." This series of working relationships were later formalized in Zionist-Israel public law by the Status Law.[18]

B. Status of the Palestine Liberation Organization as a Public Body

Prior to the creation of the Palestine Liberation Organization (PLO), there were two predecessor representatives of the people of Palestine.[19] The first was the Arab Executive Committee which was created by the Palestine Arab Congress. After some hesitation, the British Mandatory Government of Palestine recognized it as the representative of the Palestinian people. At the outset of the Palestine revolt of 1936-1939, the Arab Higher Committee was established by the consensus of Palestinian political parties as the representative entity to replace the Arab Executive Committee. It conducted both political and military operations during the revolt and was subsequently asked by the United Nations Special Committee on Palestine to present the views of the Palestinian people. On May 7, 1947, the United Nations General Assembly adopted resolution 105 which stated that "the decision of the First Committee to grant a hearing to the Arab Higher Committee gives a correct interpretation of the Assembly's intention." The Arab states initially extended *de facto* recognition of the public body status of the Arab Higher Committee. Subsequently, they acted through the Council of the League of Arab States and extended the *de jure* recognition of its public body status on July 12, 1946, agreeing that this Committee was "the one representing all of the Arabs of Palestine and speaking in their name. . . ." After the adoption of the Palestine Partition Resolution 181 (November 29, 1947) which provided for two national self-determinations, the Arab Higher Committee continued in existence until it was replaced by the PLO.

The PLO was established unilaterally on May 24, 1964 by the first meeting of the Palestine National Council which was composed of representative Palestinians as well as the various resistance groups.[20] It was recognized that same year by most of the Arab states individually and by the Arab League as the authentic representative of all Palestinians. Subsequent to this regional recognition of public body status, the United Nations in General Assembly resolution 3210 (October 14, 1974) characterized the PLO as "the representative of the Palestinian people" and invited it to participate in plenary meetings of the General Assembly concerning Palestine. Resolution 3237 (November 22, 1974) invited the PLO "to participate in the sessions and the work of the General Assembly in the capacity of observer." The same resolution also invited the PLO to participate as an observer in all international conferences convened under the auspices of the General Assembly or other organs of the United Nations. The juridical result of these resolutions adopted by the majority of the community of states acting through the United Nations is multilateral *de jure* recognition of the public body status and sole representative capacity of the PLO.

In 1975 the Security Council initiated the practice of inviting the PLO to participate in all of its meetings which concern Palestine.[21] This invitation was extended to the PLO under rule 37 of the Council's Provisional Rules of Procedure which applies to "(a)ny Member of the United Nations which is not a member of the Security Council." The Security Council has thereby used its procedural authority (not subject to a negative vote by one of the five permanent members) to confer a high degree of public body status upon the PLO by inviting it in the same way that a state is invited.

In addition to the multilateral recognition of the PLO by its regional public body and by the United Nations, it has received bilateral recognition as the representative public body of the people of Palestine by more than one hundred states.[22] The result of both bilateral and multilateral recognition by the great majority of the community of states is the undoubted international public body status of the PLO.

C. Conclusions Concerning Status

Upon the termination of the League of Nations Mandate for Palestine in 1947, the World Zionist Organization/Jewish Agency (WZO/JA) was deprived of the international public body status which had been accorded to it by article 4 of the Mandate. When the state of Israel was established in 1948, the WZO/JA was constituted as either a dependent public body or an integral part of the government under Israeli domestic law. In contrast, the PLO has continued its status as an independent public body under international law. This status has been enhanced by its increasing recognition as such by the majority of the states in the world community.

II. The United States Foreign Agents Registration Act

The purpose of the Foreign Agents Registration Act (FARA) [23] is to record a complete description of the identity and characteristics of the foreign principal for which the non-diplomatic agents of foreign governments and public bodies act and their particular activities. It is not designed to prevent their activities, including propaganda, but rather to enhance the knowledge of the American people by accurately identifying the source of the information. Such agents are required to register with the Department of Justice, to provide detailed information, and to file supplementary registration information every six months. The majority opinion of the Supreme Court in *Meese v. Keene*,[24] quotes with approval Justice Black's dissenting opinion in *Viereck v. U.S.*[25] in which he stated the underlying purpose of the FARA:

> Resting on the fundamental principle that our people, adequately informed, may be trusted to distinguish between the true and the false, [FARA] is intended to label information so that hearers and readers may not be deceived by the belief that the information comes from a disinterested source. Such legislation implements rather than detracts from the prized freedoms guaranteed by the First Amendment.

A. Compliance of the World Zionist Organization with the FARA
1. Relationship between the State of Israel and the Zionist Registrant

The state of Israel has no constitution as such, but its "basic laws" possess some constitutional characteristics including having considerably more importance than routine legislation.[26] Such "basic" laws include the statutes which implement Zionist ideology and those which establish the government structure. One such law is the Status Law, which was enacted on November 24, 1952 and went into effect the following December 2.[27] According to then Israeli Prime Minister Ben Gurion, the purpose of the legislation was not to make substantive changes, but rather was to accord *de jure* status to the World Zionist Organization which had been operating on a *de facto* basis. He also stated that while the state is limited in its authority to deal on a political level with Jewish communities beyond its borders, the Organization is not so limited, and that it complements the state in advancing the interests of "the Jewish people."[28] The statute provides that the Zionist Organization "takes care as before of immigration" and that the words "Zionist Organization" (ZO) and "Jewish Agency" (JA) are different names for the same institution. It is further provided that the Executive of the ZO/JA is a juristic body and that it "and its funds and other institutions" shall be exempt from taxes in the state of Israel. In addition to promoting immigration of Jews, the ZO/JA is the designated entity to achieve the "political unity" of Jews outside of Israel to further Zionist objectives.

Section 7 of the Status Law authorizes the Organization to enter into a "covenant" or agreement with the state to arrange the more specific details of the status of the Organization "and the juridical form of its cooperation with the Government." Without this enabling legislation the Organization would not have the authority to make a formal agreement with the state. The question which is raised is to what extent an agreement in which one of the two parties participates by authorization of the other amounts to an actual negotiated agreement as opposed to a unilateral government of Israel public law allocation of functions within a single sovereignty. Whether it is a *bona fide* agreement or merely a unilateral allocation of functions is not important to its effectiveness as Israeli domestic law. This may, however, have some juridical significance concerning the operations of the Organization outside Israel. If the Covenant[29] is not a *bona fide* agreement, the Organization is apparently a part of the government. If the Covenant is *bona fide*, the Organization is apparently a public body which is closely linked in law to the Government.

Annex A appended to the Covenant consists of a note from the government to the Zionist Executive which states in its first paragraph that the Executive "and its institutions" are to be treated as parts of the government of Israel in terms of administrative orders concerning "investigations, searches and detentions in government offices." The note limits investigative and judicial activities of the Executive to those in cooperation with the Attorney General of Israel and consistent with government policies. Zionist Executive acquiescence to the legal limitations imposed on the Organization by Annex A is set forth in the note which appears as Annex C to the Covenant. In Annex B the government establishes an "order of precedence at official ceremonies" which includes both Zionist Organization and government officials, demonstrating that the Zionist Organization officials are recognized in the most direct manner as being a functional part of the structure of the government of Israel.

Section 11 of the Covenant provides, directly and by further "special arrangement" to be added to the Covenant as another annex, for the Zionist Organization or "any of its institutions" to have the benefit of governmental status in tax law, and hence tax exemption, within the state of Israel. In significant contrast, the same Zionist institutions, including the United Israel Appeal and its subsidiary, the United Jewish Appeal, are treated as private charitable funds for tax purposes in the United States. The result is substantial tax benefits to these institutions in both cases but upon opposite juridical bases. It must be doubted that the same fund-raising institutions can be public and governmental in Israel and private and philanthropic in the United States.[30] The tax annex to the Covenant, entitled "Appendix to the Covenant Between the Government and the Executive of the Jewish Agency," was dated July 19, 1957. Its first section provides in full:

> In this Appendix - "The Executive" - includes the Jewish National Fund and Keren Hayesod-United Jewish Appeal.

The balance of the Tax Appendix provides comprehensive tax immunity for "The Executive" and for the funds on the premise that they are an integral part of the Zionist Organization/Jewish Agency.

The Covenant also formalized the Coordinating Board which had been in existence since 1951 and which is composed of cabinet ministers of the government and members of the policy-making Executive of the Organization. This Board effectively controls all aspects of immigration to the State and is a further indication of the integral relationship between the government and the Organization. The purpose of the Covenant was to give the appearance of distinction between the two, but the inter-relationship is clear and is particularly important in evaluating the compliance of the Organization/Agency registration under the United States Foreign Agents Registration Act (FARA).

2. The FARA Registration of the WZO/JA

Section 2(a) (2) of the FARA[31] requires each registrant to provide, *inter alia*:

(A) A true and complete copy of its charter, articles of incorporation, association, constitution, and bylaws, and amendments thereto; a copy of every other instrument or document and a statement of the terms and conditions of every oral agreement relating to its organization, powers, and purposes; and a statement of its ownership and control.

Until 1971, the Zionist registrant under the FARA was the "American Section of the Jewish Agency for Israel," Registrant No. 208. Its initial and supplementary registration statements did not include the Status Law or the Covenant, and therefore did not meet the requirements of section 2 (a) (2). During the period 1968-1970, administrative proceedings were instituted before the Department of Justice to compel compliance, initially on behalf of the American Council for Judaism (then the principal anti-Zionist Jewish organization in the United States) and subsequently on behalf of American Jewish Alternatives to Zionism.[32] In spite of the strenuous Zionist opposing arguments, Registrant No. 208 was compelled to file both the Status Law and the Covenant on August 28, 1969. These two constitutive documents demonstrated that the agent was not the voluntary private organization which it claimed to be.

On June 9, 1970 the Department of Justice also required the filing of the Tax Appendix to the Covenant. Subsequent actions of the Zionist Organization/Jewish Agency demonstrated its concern over these developments. In 1971 there was a "reorganization" of the Jewish Agency which resulted in changing its name, for at least some purposes, to the "Reconstituted Jewish Agency."[33] The apparent purpose was to give the appearance of equal control by the Zionist political and the non-Zionist philanthropic operations of the disposition of funds raised by the Jewish Agency and its subordinate institutions. During that same year, the American Section of the Jewish Agency, Registrant No. 208, de-registered under the FARA on the alleged grounds that it was no longer engaged in political activities. Following that action, the Zionist Organization/Jewish Agency registered under the name, "World Zionist Organization-American Section, Inc." as Registrant No. 2278. Registrant No. 208 had consistently listed its foreign principal as "The Executive of the Jewish Agency for Israel, Jerusalem, Israel," whereas Registrant No. 2278 has consistently listed its foreign principal as "The Executive of the World Zionist Organization, Jerusalem, Israel". In short, the foreign principal of the past and present registrants is identical although the wording is different. The important change in the new registration is that neither the Status Law nor the Covenant, nor the Tax Appendix has been filed initially or subsequently although the foreign principal is the same as that of the prior registrant and the specifics of the registration statements of the past and present registrants provide persuasive evidence that the foreign agents (the registrants) are the same or substantially the same.

In 1975 the Israeli Knesset enacted a law [34] which prescribed certain amendments to the Status Law. It contained a new section 2A which provides in full:

> The Jewish Agency for Israel is an independent voluntary association consisting of the World Zionist Organization and other organizations and bodies. It operates in the State of Israel in fields chosen by it with the consent of the Government.[35]

The juridical effect of this declaration amounts to no change at all in the existing basic government of Israel control of the single Zionist Organization/Jewish Agency which is emphasized by the provision that the Jewish Agency contains the Zionist Organization within it.

Section 3 of the Status Law, which stressed the identity of the Jewish Agency and the Zionist Organization, is replaced by an amendment which states that they (identified separately) "take care of immigration as before." The original wording which was replaced read that the single organization "takes care as before of immigration." A new section 4 of the amendment changes section 4 of the original law by making each of the separately named bodies "authorised agencies" for operation within the state of Israel by authority of its government. This too is not a change in substance since the added section 2A making the Zionist Organization part of the Jewish Agency remains in effect.

The significant section 6 provides for continuing control of the Jewish Agency (and its stated sub-division, the Zionist Organization) by "the laws of the State," and this is a specific enactment resulting in no change in the prior constitutive authority and documents of the Organization/ Agency. Sections 7 through 10 provide some appearance of a separation between Organization and Agency but without change in meaning.

In many ways the most interesting part of the 1975 amendments is section 12,[36] which states that the amendments shall be effective *ex post facto* from June 21, 1971, which is the date when the Jewish Agency was "reconstituted." As Israeli domestic law, the 1975 amendments are designed to give a semblance of reality to the alleged changes made by the "reconstitution," and certainly also to lend credibility to the de-registration under FARA of a Zionist agent and the registration of an allegedly different Zionist agent in 1971. There is no lawful method by which an Israeli law can be given *ex post facto* effect on events in the United States, but even if it could do so it would be without legal significance because of the lack of substantive changes in it.

Because the initial and supplementary registration statements of the World Zionist Organization-American Section, Inc., Registrant No. 2278, do not include the filing of the 1952 Status Law, the Covenant of 1954, and its annexes including the Tax Appendix of 1957 as well as the 1975 amendments, or of the two "covenants" (one with the Agency and another with the Organization) provided for in section 5 of the Israeli amendments, there is a violation of Section 2 (a) (2) of the FARA which requires the filing of these documents. Thus far, the Department of Justice has not compelled compliance with this section. In addition, there is violation of section 2 (a) (3) which requires, *inter alia*, full information concerning:

> the extent, if any, to which each such foreign principal is supervised, directed, owned, controlled, financed, or subsidized, in whole or in part, by any government of a foreign country or foreign political party, or by any other foreign principal.

It is clear that the Zionist Organization/Jewish Agency and its fund raising institutions in the United States, including the Jewish National Fund, the United Israel Appeal, and its subsidiary, the United Jewish Appeal, are either parts of the government of Israel or they comprise a public body created and controlled by that government. The central question which must be asked is why has the government of Israel and its Zionist Organization/Jewish Agency component made such an effort to obscure, and indeed to falsify, the identity of the foreign principal of the registered agent. While it is well known that the government of Israel and its foreign and domestic components frequently apply direct political pressure on the Executive and Legislative Branches of the U.S. government,[37] it is essential from the Zionist perspective that the legal record made by registration under the FARA not reveal the accurate governmental identity of the foreign principal and its registered agent. Since Registrant No. 208 had been compelled to file the constitutive documents which revealed the true relationship, it was essential to remove these damaging documents and to employ the subterfuge of an allegedly new registrant with a claimed non-governmental foreign principal.

In addition, the fund-raising components of the Organization/Agency do not exercise effective domestic control over the allocation and use of funds raised in the United States and cannot do so under the constitutive authority which controls them. Such funds are disbursed under the direct control of the government of Israel or under its equally effective indirect control through the Organization/Agency, resulting in the min-gling of the supposed philanthropic contributions with the other finan-cial resources of the government.[38] Consequently, they do not meet the requirements of United States law for private charitable status and for tax deductibility of contributions made to them.[39] This is not a novel conclusion and has been stated unequivocally by the authoritative Zionist, Professor Nadav Safran:

> Moreover, the American government never seriously attempted to question the classification of the billion dollars of donations made by American Jews as tax-exempt "charity," though this money went, in effect, into the general development budget of Israel.[40]

B. Compliance of the Palestine Information Office with the FARA
1. Relationship between the Palestine Liberation Organization (PLO) and the Palestine Information Office (PIO)

The General Assembly of the United Nations in resolution 3237 of November 22, 1974 provided for the Palestine Liberation Organization (PLO) to have permanent observer status at the United Nations and in all international conferences held under the auspices of the United Na-tions. Under the authority of this resolution, the PLO established an office accredited to the United Nations. This office has diplomatic status consistent with the terms of the United States-United Nations Head-quarters Agreement.[41]

It was not until 1978 that the Palestine Information Office (PIO) was established in Washington, D.C. under the very different legal authority of the FARA. The purpose of this office is to distribute and disseminate information about the Palestinian people and the Palestine Liberation Organization. The PIO and its director and other personnel have no diplomatic status. The personnel of this office comprise United States citizens and aliens with permanent residence status. The office itself is paid for by the Palestine National Fund, which receives its funds from Palestinian and other individuals as well as from Arab governments. The director's salary is paid directly by the League of Arab States, a public body which also has permanent observer status with the United Nations. The activities of the PIO are limited to the distribution of information concerning the Palestinian cause including lectures, radio and television appearances, interviews, correspondence, letters to the editor, and the distribution of various brochures and information, much of which is produced within the United States and includes material from non-Palestinian sources. The office and its staff do not engage in the lobbying of Congress or the Executive Branch of the U.S. Government. The PLO does not participate actively in either the administration or the activities of this office, although the function of the office is the informing of the American public concerning the Palestinian people, of whom the PLO is both the *de jure* and the *de facto* representative, and the PLO is registered as the foreign principal of which the PIO is the agent.

2. The FARA Registration of the PIO

The FARA registration statements of the PIO, Registrant No. 2891, reveal clearly its relationship with the PLO. The statements also fully disclose the sources of its financial support and the activities in which it engages. The initial registration statement of April 17, 1978, as well as the subsequent supplementary statements, filed at six-month intervals, identifies the foreign principal as the PLO public body. The PLO is further identified as the sole legitimate representative of the Palestinian people and as an independent entity which is not controlled by any foreign government. The supplementary statements have consistently revealed the same basic information. A careful examination of all of the statements of Registrant No. 2891 reveals full compliance with all of the requirements of the FARA. There are no relevant internal documents of the PLO which relate to its relationship with the PIO and which would be analogous to the Israeli Status Law, Covenant, Tax Appendix and other documents.

In *Meese v. Keene*,[42] the Supreme Court upheld a provision of the FARA that requires informational materials distributed in the United States on behalf of a foreign principal to be labeled as "political propaganda." The Court noted that the labeling requirement produced more, rather than less, information and did not prohibit, edit, or restrain the distribution of such materials. The PIO has consistently complied with this requirement.

It is not necessary to rely only upon the present analysis to demonstrate the complete compliance of the PIO with the FARA. In a letter of May 13, 1987 from the Department of State to Mr. Robert Clarke, an officer of the National Association of Arab-Americans, it was stated that, "The PLO Information Office in Washington neither reflects nor requires the approval of the United States Government." The letter added:

The Department of Justice has informed us that so long as that office regularly files reports with the Department of Justice on its activities as an agent of a foreign organization, complies with all other relevant U.S. laws, and is staffed by Americans or legal resident aliens, it is entitled to operate under the protection provided by the First Amendment of the Constitution.

The reference to compliance "with all other relevant U.S. laws" should normally be understood to reflect compliance with federal and local criminal laws which apply, of course, to all U.S. citizens and legal resident aliens. There has not been even a suggestion of the violation of criminal laws, or the threat of such violation, by any of the personnel of the PIO. If such a suggestion were to be made, there is not a scintilla of evidence to support it.

C. Conclusions Concerning FARA Compliance

The conclusions which follow from the foregoing analyses are that the existence of the World Zionist Organization, Registrant No. 2278, which is in violation of the FARA, is not under attack. In contrast, existence of the PIO, Registrant No. 2891, which is in full compliance with the FARA, is under attack. A further and necessary conclusion is that the Department of Justice is in violation of its obligations, specified by Section 8 of the FARA, either to compel the WZO registrant to comply with the law or to invoke the appropriate injunctive enforcement provisions or criminal penalties against the registrant.

III. The Zionist Political Pressures to Delegitimize the PLO and to Prevent Informational Activities of the PIO
A. Factual Situation

One of the major Zionist objectives is to control public opinion through domination of the news and information sources in the United States. Through the PIO public information efforts, however small, there has existed a direct source of information on Palestinian and Middle East events which is not subject to this control. There is Zionist concern whenever the views of the Palestinian people are expressed to Americans. Therefore, Zionist pressure groups in the United States have made a consistent effort to close the PIO office in Washington, D.C. In addition, the same groups have sought for at least three years to close the PLO

Permanent Observer Mission at the United Nations.[43] Because the PIO has consistently adhered to all the requirements of the FARA and there has not been even an allegation of violation of this law or of the criminal laws of the United States, alternative methods had to be developed. A two-prong approach through the State Department and the Congress has been utilized.

1. Action Through the State Department

The plan to use the State Department as an instrument for this purpose was developed by stages. The Foreign Missions Act, [44] enacted by Congress in 1982 "to address a serious and growing imbalance between the treatment accorded in many countries to official missions of the United States, and that made available to foreign government missions in the United States" [45] was the vehicle used. The Act, in relevant part, defines a "foreign mission" as:

> any mission to or agency or entity in the United States which is involved in the diplomatic, consular, or other activities of, or which is substantially owned or effectively controlled by —
> (A) a foreign government, or
> (B) an organization . . . representing a territory or political entity which has been granted diplomatic or other official privileges and immunities under the laws of the United States or which engages in some aspect of the conduct of the international affairs of such territory or political entity. . . .[46]

The current version of the statute quoted above includes the word "entity" which was added in 1986.[47] On September 15, 1987 the PIO was informed by undated letter from the State Department that it had been designated as a "foreign mission" under the Foreign Missions Act. In an accompanying document entitled "Designation of Palestine Information Office as a Foreign Mission," dated September 15, 1987 and signed by John C. Whitehead, Deputy Secretary of State, the grounds of the designation were stated to be:

> —it is an entity
> —it is substantially owned and/or effectively owned and/or effectively controlled by the PLO.

The document further states that the PIO conducts its activities on behalf of the PLO which has received "certain privileges and immunities by virtue of its status as an observer to the United Nations" and that it (the PLO) clearly engages in "some aspect of the conduct of international affairs." This appears to reflect the view of the United States government, contrary to the actual facts, that the PIO in Washington should be dealt with as if it had the same diplomatic status as the PLO Permanent Observer Mission at the United Nations. The Observer Mission has diplomatic status under the authority of the United Nations and consistent with the United States-United Nations Headquarters Agreement in which the United States government has undertaken to honor the authority of the United Nations including necessarily its power to establish observer missions with diplomatic status. The PLO has no diplomatic status with, nor indeed is it even given *de jure* recognition by, the U.S. government. The United States, consistent with its alleged security interests, has imposed certain limitations on some diplomatic missions, including the PLO personnel, by prohibiting their travel beyond the New York City metropolitan area. The PIO has no authority or status whatsoever from the United Nations, nor does it have the accompanying limitations. It has no international affairs competence conferred upon it by the PLO. If the PLO attempted to confer such authority upon the PIO, it would be a nullity because the PIO is only an information office under the authority of the FARA. It is clear that the attempt of the U.S. government to treat information provided to Americans as "the conduct of international affairs" is inconsistent with the facts and with the different legal regimes which govern the Observer Mission in New York and the Information Office in Washington.

A second accompanying document of September 15, 1987, entitled "Determination and Designation of Benefits", also signed by the Deputy Secretary of State, stated:

> [I]t is reasonably necessary to protect the interests of the United States to require that the Palestine Information Office cease operation as a mission representing the Palestine Liberation Organization . . . because of U.S. concern over terrorism committed and supported by individuals and organizations affiliated with the PLO, and as an expression of our overall policy condemning terrorism.

The remainder of this document required the PIO to divest itself of all services (including telephones and other communication equipment) as well as all properties, both real and personal.

In contrast to the State Department's official action and justification, the facts show that while the PIO is an entity, it is neither owned nor effectively controlled by the PLO. Both the PLO and the League of Arab States provide financial support for the PIO, but the property of the

PIO has been in the name of its director, a United States citizen, who has complete discretion as to the substance and manner in which he and the office present information concerning Palestine and the Israel-Palestine conflict to the American people. It is clear that the PIO presents no threat to United States national security or other legitimate interests. An overriding interest of the United States, as specified in the First Amendment of the Constitution, is to promote the flow of diverse information on controversial topics to Americans. The action of the State Department is obviously a suppression of this interest as well as a preemptive capitulation to the threat of impending legislation being pushed in the Congress by Zionist interests.[48] In addition, in view of the non-factual and over-broad interpretation of the Foreign Missions Act by the Department of State, it is clear that, if its legality were to be upheld, the same type of maneuver could be used to terminate any other registrant under the FARA.

It should be emphasized that while the Foreign Missions Act is ill-suited to fit the facts of the PIO, the FARA, with which the PIO is in full compliance, fits them precisely. The designation of the PIO as a foreign mission is a transparent attempt to create the fiction that it fits the requirements of the Foreign Missions Act in spite of contrary factual reality. The Department has not even attempted to show that the PIO has any of the factual attributes of a foreign mission in terms of its having any authority to conduct any type of foreign relations activity because it is impossible to do so. In the real world, in contrast to the Department's fiction, the PIO has never had foreign affairs authority or capacity. It is clear that it has had nothing but informational authority under the FARA.

2. Action Through Legislation

Concurrently with State Department action to close the PIO, the Zionist lobby has succeeded in having three bills introduced in Congress seeking either to limit or to prevent informational activities by representatives of the Palestine Liberation Organization in the United States. One bill, by Congressman Jack Kemp of New York, would make it a criminal offense for anyone to provide support of any kind to the PLO. Another, introduced by Senators Robert Dole of Kansas and Charles Grassley of Iowa, would close any office of the PLO. This bill also would make it a criminal act to receive anything of value from, or to expend funds from the PLO. The third bill, identical to the Dole-Grassley bill in the Senate, is the second one introduced by Jack Kemp in the House of Representatives. This proposed legislation would go further than the action of the State Department in attempting to close the PIO in Washington and would affect the PLO Permanent Observer Mission at the United Nations in New York which is protected by the United States-United Nations Headquarters Agreement,[49] a binding international obligation of the United States. According to a spokesman for the American Jewish Congress, that organization played a role in drafting the proposed legislation.[50] The sponsors of these bills and many of the co-sponsors are members of the extreme right wing of the Republican Party, who along with some "liberal" Democrats, are seeking and have received substantial contributions from pro-Israel Political Action Committees (PACs).[51]

Because there were differences between the bills passed by the Senate and House, the matter went to the conference committee of the two houses which agreed to the Senate version. The result was the "Grassley Amendment" which now appears as Title X—Anti-Terrorism Act of 1987 of the Foreign Relations Authorization Act for the Fiscal Years 1988 and 1989.[52] It was signed into law by President Reagan on December 22, 1987 and it provided that Title X become effective 90 days after its enactment. Title X expresses the findings of fact by the Congress that the PLO and its constituent groups have been involved in various acts of terrorism and that Attorney General Meese has stated that, "Various elements of the Palestine Liberation Organization and its allies and affiliates are in the thick of international terror." Therefore, the Congress determined that:

> [T]he PLO and its affiliates are a terrorist organization and a threat
> to the interests of the United States, it (sic) allies, and to interna-
> tional law and should not benefit from operating in the United
> States.

The Act then makes it unlawful for anyone, for the purpose of furthering the interests of the PLO, to receive anything of value, except information, from the PLO; to spend funds provided by the PLO; and to establish or maintain an office within the jurisdiction of the United States at the behest or direction of, or with funds provided by, the PLO. The Attorney General is required to enforce these provisions in U.S. District Courts.

When the so-called Grassley Amendment was being considered on the floor of the Senate, Senator Bingaman of New Mexico pointed out that the Amendment which, in his view, raised "very serious issues of constitutional rights," had neither had hearings nor been considered in any committee of the Senate.[53] He stated that it was a limitation on the right of free speech and the freedom of association of those American citizens who want to consult with or coordinate their activities with the PLO, and that the criteria which it was proposed to apply to the PLO could also be applied, on the same reasoning, to the African National Congress, the Nicaraguan Contras, or, in the situation existing 45 years ago, to the World Zionist Organization because of the activities of the Irgun.[54] He further said that the proposed legislation adds "if it comes out of an office which American citizens run with the advice, consultation, and some kind of direction of one particular organization—the PLO" and is contrary to the traditional constitutional standard of only making free speech illegal if it incites "imminent lawless action."[55]

Senator Lautenberg of Minnesota stated:
> [T]he Director General of the Israeli Foreign Ministry has been quoted as saying that people attached to PLO offices in Europe were preparing a support structure for terrorist operations. . . . With such questions about the PLO offices in Europe, can the PLO office in Washington or New York be so different?[56]

Because there is no evidence to support this statement emanating from the Israeli Government, none was offered. However, this is an interesting example of the influence of Zionist ideology on the United States Congress.

B. Reaction to these Attacks on the Right of Americans to be Exposed to the Palestinian Point of View

One of the most revealing descriptions of the Zionist lobby perspective appeared in the *Washington Jewish Week*, on September 17, 1987, under the headline "Jewish Groups Hail PLO Office Shut-Down" (Zionist groups frequently identify themselves as "Jewish"):

> Jewish activists were jubilant over the administration's decision this week to close the Washington office of the PLO. . . .

> Jewish efforts to convince the administration to shut it down date back some three years. . . .

> Jewish groups were claiming the office's closure as an official PLO operation as a crucial symbolic victory in their campaign to delegitimize the PLO in the Mideast equation.[57]

Jewish perspectives, as opposed to Zionist ones, were in striking contrast. Representatives of Jewish organizations[58] participated in a meeting of a group of thirteen other individuals who were retired United States ambassadors, area specialists, and lawyers, with Assistant Secretary of State Richard W. Murphy on August 21, 1987 to explain to the State Department the adverse effects on public information and the prospects for Israeli-Palestinian peace of the Department's possible action in closing the PIO. This perspective is illustrated by a press release of the New Jewish Agenda dated September 16, 1987 which stated, *inter alia*:

> The U.S. should be using its influence to encourage communication and diplomacy. By stifling the dialogue between Israel and the PLO we increase the likelihood that people on all sides will further dehumanize their enemies and resort to military terror to accomplish their goals. At a time when Israelis and representatives of the PLO are meeting [in violation of Israeli domestic law] to discuss the prospects of peace it is ironic that the Reagan Administration is attempting to close avenues of dialogue.

A number of newspapers throughout the United States have expressed editorial opposition to the closing of the PIO and have recognized that this action is a direct attack on the First Amendment. Among these, the *Des Moines Register* of Friday, September 25, 1987 stated on page 16A:

> But even if one accepts the argument that the PLO is a terrorist organization, will Congress and the State Department also shut down lobbies espousing the causes of other terrorists: Basques, Sikhs, Irish Republicans and Tamils?
>
> The free flow of information—even unpopular information—does not endanger American citizens. Undermining the First Amendment does.

The Milwaukee Journal of Tuesday, October 8, 1987 stated on page 4A:

> Bombs surely have been thrown in the name of the PLO; but bombs have also been thrown by US-backed "freedom fighters" in Nicaragua and Afghanistan, and by opponents of abortion.
>
> Are the free-speech rights of people committed to those causes to be abridged, too? These are the nagging, crucial questions raised by the PLO case. The ACLU [American Civil Liberties Union] is reminding everyone that if the PLO can be successfully intimidated by the government today, the PLO's critics can be the targets of intimidation tomorrow.

On September 17, 1987 the *Los Angeles Times* printed the following on page 24:

The basic issue is the right of Americans to express and to have unhindered access to diverse views, however unpopular some of them may be. No one has accused the information office of committing any crime. Indeed, the only violation of legal rights in this case comes from those who would arrogantly try to deny others the fundamental freedom of political expression.

The *San Jose Mercury News* of Friday, September 18, 1987 stated on page 8B:

Denying the PLO an official voice in the United States has been a longstanding goal of the American Israel Public Affairs Committee, a lobbying group with considerable money to spend—and thus considerable clout—on Capitol Hill. Not surprisingly, AIPAC's agenda found its way into legislation sponsored by presidential hopefuls Sen. Robert Dole, R-Kan., and Rep. Jack Kemp, R-N.Y....

Yes, the PLO has been guilty of terrorism—though its past was far bloodier than its present—and, yes, it embraces within its broad coalition groups that still advocate terrorism. But the organization also is recognized both by Palestinians and others, as the representative of the Palestinian people. As such, it always will be a key player in the Middle East peace process.

The Reagan administration knows this just as it also must know that by striking at the PLO, it is dealing a blow to the prospect for peace. Rather than capitulating, the White House should have taken its case for a balanced Middle East policy directly to the American people.

The Washington Post stated editorially on December 2, 1987, on page A24:

Contrary to the claim of its sponsors, this legislation is not directed at terrorism—every form of which is already illegal—but at speech. . . . (I)t is not criminal in this country to publish and disseminate unpopular views, to challenge decisions of the legislature and the foreign policy establishment or to criticize good friends of the United States. . . .

It is really disgraceful that liberal senators in particular, who usually champion the First Amendment rights of the unpopular, have supported this legislation and the State Department's action.

A final example from many others is from *The New York Times* of September 17, 1987 on page A34:

Closing down information offices is a gesture suitable to closed societies. . . . Yet mindlessly, some American Jewish spokesmen believe this empty gesture strikes a blow against terrorism.

Critics of United States foreign and domestic policy concerning the Middle East have referred to its domination by the Zionist lobby and its ensuing "Israelization."[59] It is significant that the State Department's action in attempting to close the PIO in Washington and the bills introduced in Congress with the same and sometimes a broader objective which includes the PLO Permanent Observer Mission with diplomatic status are reflective of Israeli law which now prohibits any contact with the PLO. By an amendment to the Prevention of Terrorism Ordinance,[60] adopted on August 5, 1986 which refers to the identification of the PLO as a terrorist organization in the *Israeli Official Gazette*, any contact by "a citizen or resident of Israel" with an administrative officer or agent of the PLO is made illegal and is subjected to criminal penalties. Four Israelis are currently being prosecuted under this law.[61]

It must be asked whether the interests of the United States and the present Israeli government are the same or different on this issue. If it is postulated that the interests of the United States include peace in the Middle East, it is clear that the interests are divergent[62] and that United States government actions consistent with the current Israeli law inhibit the information and understanding that are necessary to achieve such a peace. The examples of opinions quoted above show plainly that widespread views in the United States, including those of Jewish groups, are far ahead of the government in its approach to the primacy of the American national interest in peace in Israel-Palestine.

IV. The Basic United States Constitutional Issues

The First and Fifth Amendments to the United States Constitution embody preeminent principles of law and policy to govern the actions of the U.S. government. These Amendments were historically necessary to provide reassurance that the powers accorded to the government were adequately restrained and they continue to do so today.

A. The First Amendment

The First Amendment to the Constitution provides:

Congress shall make no law respecting an establishment of religion, or prohibiting the free exercise thereof; or abridging the freedom of speech, or of the press; or the right of the people peaceably to assemble and to petition the Government for a redress of grievances.

In addition to the clause concerning religion, the Amendment provides for both the freedom of speech (including the right to information) and the freedom of association (including the right of assembly) for all of the purposes for which freedom of speech is guaranteed. The entire process of communication is indisputably protected by this Amendment. This encompasses the right of the American public to information as well as the individual rights of freedom of speech and association. It is clear that because Congress is restrained from the abrogation of these rights, the same restriction necessarily applies to both the Executive and Judicial Branches of the government.

In the U.S. Supreme Court case of *New York Times v. United States*,[63] the concurring opinion of Justices Stewart and White stated:

In the absence of the governmental checks and balances present in other areas of our national life, the only effective restraint upon executive policy and power in the affairs of national defense and international affairs may lie in an enlightened citizenry—in an informed and critical public opinion which alone can here protect the values of democratic government.

The "paternalistic" approach of the government's censorship of information, analogous to the device of closing the PIO office in order to register its symbolic displeasure with the activities of some groups affiliated with the PLO, and thereby attempting to extinguish the First Amendment right to information of the American people, was refuted in *Virginia Board of Pharmacy v. Virginia Citizens Consumer Council*[64] in which the opinion of the Supreme Court included the statement that:

[P]eople will perceive their own best interests if only they are well enough informed, and the best means to that end is to open the channels of communication rather than to close them.

The point was made earlier in *DeJong v. Oregon*[65] where Chief Justice Hughes, speaking for the Court, stated:

The greater the importance of safeguarding the community from incitements to the overthrow of our institutions by force and violence, the more imperative is the need to preserve inviolate the constitutional rights of free speech, free press, and free assembly in order to maintain the opportunity for free political discussion. . . .

The Supreme Court observed in *Red Lion Broadcasting Co. v. FCC*:[66]

It is the purpose of the First Amendment to preserve an uninhibited marketplace of ideas in which truth will ultimately prevail. . . . It is the right of the public to receive suitable access to social, political, esthetic, moral and other ideas and experiences which is crucial here. That right may not constitutionally be abridged.

In addition to the cases reflecting freedoms of information and speech, the Supreme Court has emphasized that the First Amendment necessarily includes the freedom of association. In 1965 the U.S. Supreme Court stated the broad scope of the Amendment in *Griswold v. Connecticut*:[67]

The right of association, like the right of belief, is more than the right to attend a meeting and includes the right to express one's attitudes or philosophies, by membership in a group or by affiliation with it or by other lawful means.

In *Runyon v. McCrary*,[68] the Court quoted with approval the opinion in *NAACP v. Alabama*,[69] in which the relationship between association and speech was stated:

Effective advocacy of both public and private points of view, particularly controversial ones, is undeniably enhanced by group association, as this Court has more than once recognized by remarking upon the close nexus between the freedoms of speech and assembly.

The principal basis claimed by the State Department in attempting to close down the PIO in Washington is that the U.S. government is protesting the alleged terroristic actions of some groups associated with the PLO. That makes the PIO situation very similar to the one considered in *Healy v. James*,[70] in which a unanimous Supreme Court held that a local chapter of Students for a Democratic Society (SDS) could not be lawfully denied university privileges, including access to meeting rooms and bulletin boards, because the university administration was concerned about the allegedly violent tendencies of the national organization. While admitting that the PIO has never engaged in anything other than informational activities protected by the First Amendment, the Department has maintained that the PIO may nevertheless be closed because of alleged terrorism by others. This amounts to nothing more than an attempt, consistent with Zionist tactics and objectives, to invoke the discredited concept of guilt by association which has been invariably rejected by the Supreme Court.[71] Without any evidence of a specific intent by the PIO to carry out acts of terrorism, the State Department has attempted to extinguish or limit the First Amendment rights of the PIO and its director because of alleged terrorist activities by others in another country. This is exactly the sort of governmental conduct which the First Amendment prohibits. The Supreme Court has recently reiterated the controlling legal principle in *NAACP v. Claiborne Hardware*:[72]

> The right to associate does not lose all constitutional protection merely because some members of the group may have participated in conduct or advocated doctrine that itself is not protected.

B. The Fifth Amendment

The Fifth Amendment of the Constitution is designed, *inter alia*, to protect both substantive (basic considerations of fairness) and procedural (frequently requiring due notice and an impartial hearing) due process of law. It provides the basis of the civil and criminal legal systems in the United States. The relevant wording is that no person shall "be deprived of life, liberty, or property, without due process of law." The requirements of due process apply throughout the entire law and are of particular importance in any issues involving First Amendment rights.

The basic requirements of fairness mandate that laws must contain a reasonable degree of precision. In *Grayned v. City of Rockford*,[73] the Supreme Court held:

> [B]ecause we assume that man is free to steer between lawful and unlawful conduct, we insist that laws give the person of ordinary intelligence a reasonable opportunity to know what is prohibited, so that he may act accordingly.

In the situation of the closing of the PIO, there was no way for the PIO and its director to know that the apparently irrelevant Foreign Missions Act would be applied to them since they were in full compliance with the FARA. The PIO was informed by the State Department that it had been designated as a foreign mission because it fell within the specifications contained in the Foreign Missions Act, and that the government's authority to issue a closure order was thereby established. The Department stated that its action was in part based upon the prior public information activities of the PIO, and the PIO was informed simultaneously that the government's actions did not limit or restrict the First Amendment rights of its director. The Department did not refer to the important Fifth Amendment issue concerning the director's property interest in his employment or in the office property which was in his name. The extreme ambiguity, and apparent contradiction, in the Department's interpretation and application of the Foreign Missions Act indicates that the PIO and its director have been given no clear guidance as to what is permitted and what is prohibited. This violates one of the most fundamental principles of due process of law as enunciated in the *Grayned Case*.[74]

The State Department has made no pretense of providing procedural due process in terms of adequate notice and a fair hearing, and this is a clear violation of the Fifth Amendment. The actual facts show that the PIO, engaged in disseminating political information in the United States, has never had authority to act as a foreign mission conducting diplomatic activities. It has no such authority under FARA and, when designated as a foreign mission, it had such authority for at most a fleeting moment without any opportunity to exercise it because of the simultaneous closing order. Consequently, in spite of the State Department's attempt to create a fiction, the PIO never had foreign mission authority in any practical sense. The discrepancy between the actual facts and the State Department's fiction demands an impartial hearing to separate reality from fabrication.

The questions of the legality of the designation of the PIO as a foreign mission and of the closing order are crucial legal issues which must be examined impartially by United States courts. Since, by their actions, both the Executive and Legislative Branches of the government have failed to honor the First and Fifth Amendments, it is urgent that the Judicial Branch undertake this responsibility. Another crucial issue which must be raised is whether or not the Zionist attack on the Permanent Observer Mission of the PLO at the United Nations will succeed.[75] This issue will have to be resolved under the criteria of both international law and United States constitutional law.

V. Conclusion

The "Determination and Designation of Benefits" which was signed by Deputy Secretary of State John C. Whitehead on September 15, 1987 stated that the PIO was being closed "because of U.S. concern over terrorism."[76] While making this symbolic gesture concerning terrorism, with the accompanying frustration of constitutional rights, the United States government has missed practical opportunities to disassociate itself from state terrorism. For example, when the government of Israel named Major General Amos Yaron as the Israeli Defense Attache to the governments of Canada and the United States, the Canadian government refused to accredit him diplomatically while the U.S. government accepted him without hesitation. The report of the Israeli Judicial Commission of Inquiry[77] concerning the massacre of Palestinian civilians at Sabra and Shatila stated the facts concerning General Yaron's active role in those events. It identified him as the general officer commanding the Israeli military occupation forces in the area of Beirut, Lebanon, which included the Sabra and Shatila refugee camps. The Commission detailed General Yaron's participation, which included direct assistance to the murderous activities of the so-called Christian Phalange in sending them into the camps as the agents of the Israeli Army[78] and providing them with logistical support and illumination to further their activities. These same facts should have required the Commission to find General Yaron directly responsible for the "grave breaches" specified in the Geneva Civilians Convention of 1949.[79] Instead the Commission evaded its responsibility by declaring him "indirectly responsible."[80] The Department of State apparently seized upon the Israeli Commission's egregious error of law rather than applying the conclusions of law required by the Civilians Convention. The U.S. government, by accepting General Yaron, has given substance and credence to the charge that the United States practices a double standard on international terrorism.

There is considerable doubt as to the genuine interest of either the Israeli government or the United States government in peace in Israel-Palestine, with as much justice as possible in this imperfect world for both Israelis and Palestinians. The reason for this is the apparent commitment, if not always in words, of both governments to the perpetuation of the present "peace" through the military power of the government of Israel supported in every practical way by the U.S. government and its acceptance of Zionist pressures and objectives. This so-called "peace" is an imposed military solution outside of any considerations of law or morality. As long as the Executive and Legislative branches of the U.S. government allow themselves to be dominated by Zionist interests, including the subsidizing of elections through campaign contributions by Political Action Committees (PACs) and thereby achieving political control, this situation will continue. The only possible solution to this frustration of legitimate American national interests would be a well-informed electorate where the American people's sense of fairness and justice would be a counter-pressure; and it is apparent from the U.S. government responses to Zionist pressures to eliminate Palestinian views by closing the PIO as well as by removing the PLO diplomatic representation at the United Nations in New York, that the government has thus far cooperated with the Zionists to prevent this counter-pressure from materializing. As long as the United States continues its present Zionist policies, the efforts of the world community acting through the United Nations to achieve peace in Israel-Palestine through the two-state solution will continue to be frustrated.[81] This solution for peace in Israel-Palestine is supported by virtually the entire world community with Israel, South Africa, and the United States being the only significant exceptions.

It is necessary that the United States government face the realities that exist in the Israel-Palestine situation.[82] Among these, one which it has consistently neglected is recognition of the importance of the peace forces within Israel as well as those emerging among Jews in the United States. A prominent member of the Israeli Knesset (legislature), Major General (res.) Matti Peled, wrote recently to each member of the U.S. Congress about the then pending legislation concerning the PIO and the PLO, and expressed the Jewish interest in peace in opposition to the Zionist views. His letter stated in part:

> Passage of the bill closing the PLO offices in the U.S. would, in my view, constitute a grave setback for the Middle East peace process. It would mean total abdication by the U.S. of any role as a mediator in the Middle East conflict. . . . Far from "stopping terrorism," as it is supposed to do, this bill would further escalate the cycle of bloodshed and violence in the Middle East. . . . [T]he rejection of this bill will be compatible with the long-term interests of the State of Israel and will be seen as such by a substantial number of Israel's citizens.[83]

It is a regrettable conclusion to this study to report that Congress rejected this Jewish view and adhered to the Zionist position, thereby contributing to the escalating violence in Israel-Palestine. However, there is continuing reason for optimism because the Judicial branch of the United States government has independent constitutional status apart from

Congress and the president, and the authority to decide the constitutionality of the actions of the other branches.

NOTES

1. The term "Zionist" refers to a member or supporter of the modern political movement of Zionism. For a comprehensive definition of this and related terms see W. Thomas Mallison and Sally V. Mallison, *The Palestine Problem in International Law and World Order* (Longman Group, London, 1986) (hereafter *Palestine Problem*), Introduction at 1-17. The fundamental value distinctions between the religion of Judaism and Zionism are set forth in the symposium entitled *Judaism or Zionism: What Difference for the Middle East?* (Zed Books, London, 1986) which was sponsored by the International Organization for the Elimination of All Forms of Racial Discrimination (EAFORD) and American Jewish Alternatives to Zionism (AJAZ).

2. Memorandum of the Secretary General of the United Nations, *Survey of International Law in Relation to the Work of Codification of the International Law Commission*, A/cn.4/Rev.1, p.19 (Feb. 10, 1949).

3. See American Law Institute, *Restatement of the Foreign Relations Law of the United States* (1965), Sec. 5 (a) which defines an international organization as created by an international agreement.

4. *International Law and Human Rights* 12 (1950).

5. [1949] I.C.J. Reps. 174.

6. First Zionist Congress Address of Aug. 29, 1897 by T. Herzl in Hertzberg, *The Zionist Idea: A Historical Analysis and Reader* 226 (1966).

7. For an analysis of the negotiations leading to the Balfour Declaration by the government of Great Britain and the opposite objectives of Zionists and Jews, see Stein, *The Balfour Declaration* (1961).

8. *Palestine Problem*, *supra* n. 1, at 91 describes the Zionist Organization at the Paris Peace Conference.

9. 2 UNSCOP, *Report to the General Assembly*, 2 *U.N. GAOR*, Supp. 11, pp.18-22, U.N. Doc. A/364 Add. 1 (9 Sept. 1947).

10. *Greece v. Great Britain* [1924] P.C.I.J. Ser. A, No. 2, at p. 21.

11. [1925] P.C.I.J. Ser. A, No. 5.

12. [1927] P.C.I.J. Ser. A, No.11.

13. Jewish Agency for Palestine, *Book of Documents Submitted to the General Assembly of the United Nations Relating to the Establishment of the National Home for the Jewish People*, 28, 29 (Tulin ed., 1947).

14. Anglo-American Committee of Inquiry, *Report to the United States Government and His Majesty's Government in the United Kingdom* 20 (1946).

15. *Id.* at 39.

16. *Palestine Problem*, *supra* n. 1, at 101-02.

17. The textual paragraph is based upon *id.* at 103-05.

18. 7 Israel Laws 3 (1952)

19. This section of text is based upon Kassim, "The Palestine Liberation Organization's Claim to Status: A Juridical Analysis Under International Law," 9 *Denver J. Int'l L. & Policy* 1 at 15-18 (1980).

20. *Id.* at 18, 20.

21. *Id.* at 20-21.

22. 2 *Palestine Y.B. Int'l L.* 189-90 (Al Shaybani Society of International Law, Cyprus, 1985).
23. 52 U.S. Stat. 63 (1938) as amended; 22 U.S. Code Sec. 611-21 (1964).
24. 481 U.S.——, 95 L. Ed. 2d 415 (1987). [The complete official U.S. Supreme Court citation (referred to as "U.S.") is not yet available.
25. 318 U.S. 236 at 251 (1943).
26. See generally Baker, *The Legal System of Israel* 14 *passim* (1961). See also *Fundamental Laws of the State of Israel* 3-5 (Badi ed., 1961).
27. 7 Israel Laws 3 (1952).
28. Information Dep't of the Jewish Agency and World Zionist Organization, *The Jewish Agency's Digest of Press and Events* 1060, 1061 (May 16, 1952).
29. The text of the Covenant and its Annexes A, B, and C appear in Organization Dept. of the Zionist Executive, *Session of the Zionist General Council* 106-09 (July 21-29, 1954).
30. See *e.g.*, Mallison, "The Legal Problems Concerning the Juridical Status and Political Activities of the Zionist Organization/Jewish Agency: A Study in International and United States Law," 9 *William & Mary L. Rev.* 554 at 600 (1968). 31. *Supra* n. 23.
32. A charitable organization dedicated to maintaining Judaism as a religion of universal moral values and exposing the basic inconsistency beteen Judaism and Zionism.
33. A comprehensive description and analysis of the "reorganization" is in the semi-official *Jerusalem Post*, "Special Supplement-Founding Assembly: The Reconstituted Jewish Agency," June 21, 1971.
34. World Zionist Organisation-Jewish Agency for Israel (Status) (Amendment) Law, 30 Israel Laws 43 (1975).
35. *Id.* at 44.
36. *Id.* at 45.
37. See *infra* notes 50 and 51.
38. An article by Glenn Frankel in the Washington Post of Dec. 13, 1987, p. A1, cols. 1-4, cont. on p. A44, cols. 1-6, states the position of American Jews at a mid-December 1987 meeting in Jerusalem of the 31st World Zionist Congress as being "frustrated with Israel's tradition of using charitable contributions to feed and lubricate its partisan political machines. . . ."
39. Internal Revenue Code, 26 U.S. Code, Secs. 1-9, 601 and particularly Sec. 301 concerning the requirements for charitable organizations to receive tax deductible funds.
40. *The United States and Israel* 278 (Harvard, 1963).
41. 61 U.S. Stat. 3416, TIAS No. 1676; U.N. Treaty Series 11 (June 26, 1947). There have been four supplementary agreements which define changes in the area of the Headquarters District: 17 U.S. Treaties 74 (Feb. 9, 1966); *Id.* at 2319 (Dec. 8, 1966); 20 U.S. Treaties 2810 (Aug. 28, 1969); 32 U.S. Treaties 4414 (Dec. 10, 1980).
42. *Supra* note 24.
43. *Washington Jewish Week*, Sept. 17, 1987, quoted in *infra* Sec. IIIB.
44. 22 U.S. Code, Secs. 4301-4314 (1982).
45. S. Rep. No. 329, 97th Cong., 2d Sess. 1 (1982).
46. *Supra* note 44 at Sec. 4302(a)(4).
47. S. Rep. No. 307, 99th Cong., 2d Sess.
48. See text at note 50 *infra*. 49. *Supra* note 41.

50. *Christian Sci. Monitor*, Sept. 17, 1987, p. 3; *Middle East International* 16 (London, June 27, 1987).
51. For a comprehensive description of the political activities of the America-Israel Public Affairs Committee (AIPAC) see E. Tivnan, *The Lobby: Jewish Political Power and American Foreign Policy* (1987). See also *Middle East International, supra* note 50 concerning amounts contributed to sponsors of the Dole bill by the PACs, and the quotation from the *San Jose Mercury News* in Sec. IIIB *infra*.
52. H.R. 1777. See the full text of the Act in 133 Cong. Rec. S13851 (daily ed. Oct. 8, 1987).
53. Cong. Rec. *supra* note 52 at S13852.
54. *Id.* at S13853.
55. *Id.*
56. *Id.* at S13854.
57. P. 3, cont. on p. 50.
58. The organizations were: American Jewish Alternatives to Zionism; Washington Area Jews for Israeli-Palestinian Peace; and New Jewish Agenda.
59. Axelgard, "The 'Israelization' of U.S. Middle East Policy," *Middle East International* 10 (London, Jan. 23, 1987). For a comprehensive analysis of the subject see C. A. Rubenberg, *Israel and the American National Interest* (1986).
60. 1 Israel Laws 76 (1948) amended by the statute of Aug. 5, 1986 which is not yet printed in Israel Laws. There is also an earlier amendment concerning "support for a terrorist organization" by flying its flag, displaying its emblem, or singing its anthem in a public place: 34 Israel Laws 211 (1980).
61. MERIP Middle East Research & Information Project, *Middle East Report* 28 (Jan.-Feb.,1988).
62. C. A. Rubenberg, *supra* note 59, documents a succession of instances in which by following the Israeli line the U.S. Government has severely damaged important United States interests.
63. 403 U.S. 713 at 728 (1971). (This citation and ensuing ones are the official ones to United States Supreme Court reports.)
64. 425 U.S. 748 at 770 (1976).
65. 299 U.S. 353 at 365 (1937).
66. 395 U.S. 367 at 390 (1969).
67. 381 U.S. 479 at 483 (1965).
68. 427 U.S. 160 at 175 (1976).
69. 357 U.S. 449 at 460 (1958).
70. 408 U.S. 169 (1972).
71. See: *United States v. Robel*, 389 U.S. 258 (1967); *Elfbrandt v. Russell*, 384 U.S. 11 (1966); *Noto v. United States*, 367 U.S. 290 (1961); *Scales v. United States*, 367 U.S. 203 (1961).
72. 458 U.S. 886 at 908 (1982)
73. 408 U.S. 104 at 108 (1972).
74. *Id.*
75. See the Grassley Amendment in the text accompanying *supra* notes 52-56.
76. See the detailed text in *supra* Sec. IIIA1.
77. Known informally as the Kahan Commission Report. The official English language text, on which this textual paragraph is based, was supplied to the authors by an Israeli friend.

78. Art.29 of the Geneva Convention IV Relative to the Protection of Civilian Persons in Time of War of August 12, 1949 (6 U.S. Treaties 3516; TIAS No. 365; 75 U.N. Treaties 287) provides in full: The Party to the conflict in whose hands protected persons may be, is responsible for the treatment accorded to them by its agents, irrespective of any individual responsibility which may be incurred.
79. *Id.* at arts. 146-149.
80. A comprehensive and objective analysis of the facts and law in the Kahan Commission Report is in L. A. Malone, "The Kahan Report, Ariel Sharon and the Sabra-Shatilla Massacres in Lebanon: Responsibility Under International Law for Massacres," 1985 *Utah Law Review* 373-433.
81. See *Palestine Problem, supra* note 1, and especially Chap.8, entitled "The Solution of the Palestine Problem Within the World Legal Order," and Chap.3, entitled "The United Nations and the Palestine Partition Resolution."
82. One of the grim realities appears in U.N. Doc. S/19443 of Jan. 21, 1988 entitled "Report Submitted to the Security Council by the Secretary-General in Accordance with Resolution 605 (1987)." The report is based upon the fact-finding trip of Mr. Marrack Goulding, Under-Secretary-General for Special Political Affairs, to the occupied territories of the West Bank and Gaza in 1988 and describes the killings of Palestinians and the related brutal activities of the Israeli Army along with the specific violation of many articles of the Geneva Civilians Convention (cited in *supra* note 78) which have been committed.
83. General Peled's letter is reproduced in full in the Appendix to this study.

APPENDIX

23th July 1987
Dear Member of Congress:
I am writing to you concerning the bill known as "The Anti-Terrorism Act of 1987," which is aimed at closing down the PLO offices in the United States. This is being presented as a "pro-Israel" bill, and for that reason U.S. senators and representatives who consider themselves friends of Israel are being urged to support it.

As a member of the Israeli Knesset (Parliament), I would like to dispute that view. I believe that achieving peace is a prime requirement for Israel's long-term survival and prosperity. There can be no peace without negotiations between the Israeli government, representing the Israeli people, and the representatives of the Palestinian people. Such representatives can only be chosen by the Palestinians themselves, and on each occasion that the Palestinians were asked for their opinion, they unequivocally expressed their support for the Palestinian Liberation Organization, the PLO. Such for example, was the result of the 1976 municipal elections on the West Bank, which were the last free elections to be held there. Similar results were the outcome of a public opinion poll, held in the Occupied Territories in August 1986. Indeed, The

Government of Israel itself, in refusing to permit new municipal elections on the West Bank, admits that in its view such elections would be won by supporters of the PLO.

Together with many of my fellow-citizens of Israel, I have been urging the Israeli government to reconsider its policies and to agree to negotiate with the PLO in the context of an international peace conference. Recently this idea has been spreading; not only opposition members such as myself, but also Ezer Weitzmann, member of the Israeli Cabinet, as well as several Knesset Members from the Israeli Labor Party, have publicly voiced their support for Israeli negotiations with the PLO.

Passage of the bill closing the PLO offices in the U.S. would, in my view, constitute a grave setback for the Middle East peace process. It would mean total abdication by the U.S. of any role as a mediator in the Middle East conflict. Hardliners in the Israeli Cabinet would be encouraged to persist in their intransigent position and their refusal to talk with the PLO. Far from "stopping terrorism," as it is supposed to do, this bill would further escalate the cycle of bloodshed and violence in the Middle East.

Therefore, as an Israeli concerned with the wellbeing of my country and my people, I urge you to voice your opposition to this so-called "Anti-Terrorism Act." By so doing, you will not be taking an "anti-Israel" stand; on the contrary, the rejection of this bill will be compatible with the long-term interests of the State of Israel and will be seen as such by a substantial number of Israel's citizens.

> Yours Sincerely,
> (signed) Matti Peled
> Major General(res.)Matti Peled Member of Knesset

7

AMERICAN EFFORTS FOR PEACE IN THE MIDDLE EAST: 1919-1986

CHERYL A. RUBENBERG

Introduction
Zionism and Israel on the Questions
Central to Peace in the Middle East

The history of Palestine in the twentieth century has been one of almost continuous conflict and violence, although the root causes of the conflict are little comprehended in the United States. This lack of understanding is primarily the result of social engineering—the rewriting of history by the victorious to distort and obfuscate reality in a highly successful Orwellian construction. Reduced to its essentials the conflict may be accurately described as the confrontation between Zionism, with its objective of establishing an exclusive Jewish state in Palestine, and the interests and aspirations of the indigenous Palestinians for a normal national existence in their native homeland. However, in spite of the obscurantism that Zionist scholars and analysts have practiced in their attempt to legitimize Israel, it is possible to ascertain the true nature and meaning of Zionism from the recent work of several Zionist writers. The following brief insights provide a framework for comprehending the persistent failures of American efforts for peace in the Middle East.

The Zionist goal of creating a Jewish state in Palestine of necessity involved force. No rational individual could have expected Palestinians to willingly acquiesce in the transformation of their country to a nationalist entity that by definition excluded them. Yet a myth has long existed about the desires of the Zionist settler-colonists for peaceful co-existence with the Arab inhabitants of Palestine, and their grave despair on realizing that such fraternity would not be forthcoming. Contradicting this perspective, Shabtai Teveth, the biographer of David Ben-Gurion, Israel's founding father and first prime minister, writes:

> A careful comparison of Ben-Gurion's public and private positions leads inexorably to the conclusion that this twenty-year denial of the conflict [between Zionists and Palestinians] was a calculated tactic . . . The idea that Jews and Arabs could reconcile . . . was a delaying tactic. Once the Yishuv had gained strength, Ben-Gurion abandoned it. The belief in a compromise solution . . . was also a tactic, designed to win continued British support for Zionism. The only genuine convictions that underlay Ben-Gurion's approach to the Arab question were two: that the support of the power that ruled Palestine was more important to Zionism than any agreement with the Arabs, and that the Arabs would reconcile themselves to the Jewish presence only after they conceded their inability to destroy it.[1]

Teveth adds that Ben-Gurion believed at least as early as 1935 that "the tragedy of the Jews outweighed the minor dispossession of the Arabs. . . . immigration still came before peace."[2] This assessment predates the Holocaust, thus to understand the mentality that considered dispossessing Palestinians "minor" and viewed Jewish immigration as more important than peace with the indigenous population, one must look to the roots of Zionist thought. The "political Zionism" of Leo Pinsker, Theodor Herzl, and Vladimir Jabotinsky which evolved into "revisionist Zionism" has long been recognized for its militaristic nature and objective of statehood. On the other hand, the "cultural Zionism" of Achad Haam which evolved into the "labor Zionism" of David Ben-Gurion, has typically been presented as intending only to create a Hebrew cultural renaissance or "spiritual center" in Palestine that would radiate to Jews living in other parts of the world. But listen to Achad Haam in 1898:

> This Jewish settlement, which will grow gradually, will become in the course of time the center of a nation. . . . And when our national culture in Palestine has attained that level . . . we may be sure that it will produce men . . . who . . . will be able to establish a state which will be a *Jewish* state, and not merely a state of the Jews. . . . [In

addition, it would be necessary for Jews to become] . . . a majority of the population, own most of the land, and control the institutions shaping the culture of the country.[3] (Emphasis in original)

Moreover, as scholar Bernard Avishai notes: "According to Achad Haam, Jews were such promising candidates for the moral sentiments of modernity that he simply . . . pronounced the Jews a 'superpeople'— as it were, a secularized version of the biblical notion of the chosen people."[4] Perhaps such "modern" "chosen" people felt it unnecessary to consider the fate of those they were displacing? Teveth provides further insight into Zionist attitudes toward Palestinians: "Ben-Gurion must have known that the Arabs would never consent [to the Zionist project] . . . for he himself had asked 'what Arab cannot do his math and understand that immigration at the rate of 60,000 a year means a Jewish state in all of Palestine?' "[5] What then was to be the fate of the Palestinians? According to Avishai "the culturalists had no more respect for Arab or Moslem religious culture than for Jewish Orthodoxy . . . [but] no culturalist seriously considered—as did Herzl—transferring the Arab population across the Jordan River."[6] Yet Teveth relates that Ben-Gurion saw the solution to Palestinian opposition to the Zionist enterprise in the forcible expulsion of the Palestinians: "The compulsory transfer of the Arabs from the valleys of the proposed Jewish state . . . could give us something which we never had, even when we stood on our own during the days of the First and Second Temples [i.e., an Israel free of non-Jews] . . . a real Jewish state. . . ."[7]

Dr. Benny Morris, an Israeli scholar, has laid bare several of the Zionist tactics that were used to rid Palestine of its indigenous population. For instance, based on Israeli Defense Forces (IDF) Intelligence Branch documents, Morris demonstrates that of the 400,000 Palestinians who fled the country between November 29, 1947 and June 1, 1948, 70 percent fled because of Jewish military action including 55 percent who left because of direct, hostile, Haganah (Zionist regular army) operations against Arab settlements.[8] In addition, Morris details the forcible expulsion of the Arab populations of Lydda and Ramle (towns that had been allocated in the November 1947 U.N. partition resolution to the Palestinian state) by the IDF on July 12-13 (and thereafter) in 1948 which resulted in the creation of some 70,000 more Palestinian refugees.[9] Morris also reveals methods other than force employed by Zionists:

Through the summer, autumn and winter of 1948, the Israeli security forces prevented Arab cultivation of abandoned fields. . . and the cultivation of 'unabandoned' lands (those whose owners had stayed in Israel). The policy and measures designed to prevent

Arab cultivation . . . served to consolidate the separation of the exiles from their lands, driving home the message that there would be no return.[10]

While the official IDF policies described by Morris were for decades buried in Zionist archives, the terrorist campaign waged against Palestinian civilians by the "dissident" Irgun and Stern groups has long been recognized as one cause of the Palestinian exodus. Of the deliberate massacre by the Irgun, which involved mutilation, rape and disembowelment of 250 old men, women and children at Deir Yassin in April 1948, the leader of the Irgun and later prime minister of Israel, Menachem Begin, wrote: "[Palestinians throughout the country] were seized with limitless panic and started to flee for their lives. This mass flight soon turned into a mad, uncontrollable stampede. Of the about 800,000 Arabs who lived on the present territory of the State of Israel, only some 165,000 are still living there. The political and economic significance of this development can hardly be overestimated."[11]

Dr. Tom Segev, another Israeli scholar, discussing a statement made by Ben-Gurion in March 1949, further illuminates the Zionist attitude toward Palestinians: "Ben-Gurion tended to ignore the human tragedy of the Palestinian Arabs. . . . 'Land with Arabs on it and land without Arabs on it are two very different types of land,' he told his party's central committee as if he were a real estate agent discussing a business."[12] Similarly, Israel's first foreign minister, Moshe Sharett—considered a "dove" within the Labor Party—wrote: "The most spectacular event in the contemporary history of Palestine, in a way more spectacular than the creation of the Jewish state, is the wholesale evacuation of its Arab population. . . . The opportunities opened up by the present reality for a lasting and radical solution of the most vexing problem of the Jewish state, are so far-reaching, as to take one's breath away. The reversion to the *status quo ante* is unthinkable."[13] And, in fact, Israel has rejected all efforts to repatriate Palestinians.

Uri Avnery, an Israeli who has made great personal contributions toward realizing an Israeli-Palestinian peace based on the original partition resolution, recounted a speech given by Moshe Dayan, a former minister of defense, on the grave of a friend killed on the Gaza border in 1956. Dayan's remarks provide an especially searing, and honest, depiction of the meaning of Zionism for Palestinians:

Let us not today fling accusations at the murderers. Who are we that we should argue against their hatred? For eight years now, they sit in their refugee camps in Gaza, and before their very eyes we turn into our homestead the land and villages in which they and their forefathers had lived. . . . We are a generation of settlers, and without the steel helmet and the cannon we cannot plant a tree and build a house.

Let us not shrink back when we see the hatred fermenting and filling the lives of hundreds of thousands of Arabs, who sit all around us. Let us not avert our eyes, so that our hand shall not slip. This is the fate of our generation, the choice of our life—to be prepared and armed, strong and tough—or otherwise, the sword will slip from our fist and our life will be snuffed out.[14]

Avnery, writing in 1986, then analyzed why he believed Zionist leaders were so uncompromising with regard to Palestinians:

. . . The early Zionists were convinced, or convinced themselves, that the new Jewish national home would be founded in an empty country. When it became clear that this was not so, and in the face of growing Arab opposition, they still pretended that the Palestinians did not really exist, that the whole Palestinian issue had been invented one way or the other by the enemies of Zionism, that the Palestinian national movement was but a bunch of terrorists. Somewhere in the Israeli mind there is an unconscious feeling of guilt, a feeling that in doing justice to the Jews an injustice has been done to the Palestinians. These feelings are troubling the national soul, creating mental blocks, making even highly intelligent politicians and historians utter the most lamentable nonsense when touching upon the Palestinian issue.[15]

Avnery's analysis of the moral/psychological core of Israel's rejectionism in dealing with Palestinians is undoubtedly close to the mark. Nevertheless, the vast majority of his countrymen remain unmoved by his arguments or his painstaking documentation of PLO efforts to reach accommodation with Israel. The Palestinian situation remains unchanged since 1948.

Another myth about Palestine has centered on the "reasonableness" of Zionists, who "accepted" the partition, and the "irrationality" of Palestinians who did not agree to the dismemberment of their homeland. Yet, as Teveth notes, Ben-Gurion wanted "to include in the establishment [of the Jewish state] all the territory of the biblical Land of Israel, including areas under French mandate"; and, moreover, he "regarded the creation of a Jewish state in part of Palestine as a stage in the longer process toward a Jewish state in all of Palestine."[16] Ben Halpern, another Zionist scholar, described Zionist territorial objectives some years before Teveth: "In order to have resources sufficient to allow it to perform its proper function in solving the Jewish problem, Palestine needed control of the Litani and Jordan waters as well as agricultural land east of the river, short of the Hejaz railway line."[17] These objectives have been borne out in the foreign policy of Israel since its establishment in May 1948—a policy of continuous territorial expansion.

A further myth concerns the "rejectionism" of the Arab states toward the existence of Israel and the persistent quest of Israel for peace with its neighbors. Segev contributes much to the historical record on this issue. On the question of Israel's borders:

> As Israel's Declaration of Independence was being drafted, Felix Rosenbluett [who was soon to change his name to Pinhas Rozen and become the country's new minister of justice] demanded that the document cite the country's borders. Ben-Gurion objected, and the exchange between the two men was recorded as follows:
>
> Rozen: "There's the question of the borders, and it cannot be ignored."
> Ben-Gurion: "Anything is possible. If we decide here that there is to be no mention of borders, then we won't mention them. Nothing is *a priori* [imperative]."
> Rozen: "It's not *a priori*, but it's a legal issue."
> Ben-Gurion: "The law is whatever people determine it to be."[18]

During the armistice negotiations in January 1949,[19] Ben-Gurion told his aides: "As for setting the borders—it's an open-ended matter. In the Bible as well as in our history there are all kinds of definitions of the country's borders, so there's no real limit. No border is absolute. If it's a desert—it could just as well be the other side. If it's a sea, it could also be across the sea. . . ."[20] Forty years later Israel has yet to delineate its boundaries.

Concerning Jordanian-Israeli relations, Segev relates the multiplicity of meetings that took place between various Israelis (including Moshe Dayan, Moshe Sharett, Eliyahu Sasson, Golda Meirson [Meir], and Walter Eitan) and Jordanians (including Abdullah Tall and King Abdullah) in Jerusalem, Paris, London, and Amman in 1947-49. Of the meetings between Israelis and the King, Segev writes: "Abdullah was known for his friendly attitude and good will toward his Israeli guests. . . . Sometimes they read poetry together, sometimes they exchanged gifts. And at least once they raised the possibility that the Israeli air force would help the Jordanians conquer Damascus. . . ."[21] However, Ben-Gurion considered Abdullah "a worthless man."[22] Nevertheless, "by the time they began negotiating [the armistice agreement], Israel and

Jordan had already unofficially agreed that the territory [allocated in the U.N. partition resolution to the independent Palestinian state] would be divided between them, and so would the city of Jerusalem. They had also agreed in principle that the Palestinians would have no say in the matter."[23]

Regarding Syria, Segev relates that in the course of the fighting in 1948 Damascus had managed to seize a small portion of territory beyond the international border set by the partition resolution. Israel demanded that Syria withdraw, while Syria insisted on remaining in that territory. Shortly before the armistice negotiations began, there had been a military coup in Syria and the new ruler was a colonel by the name of Husnei Zaim. "Some time after he seized power, Zaim proposed a meeting with Ben-Gurion with the aim of reaching a peace agreement. Moreover, he stated that he would be willing to give permanent residence to between 300,000 and 350,000 Palestinian refugees in his country. On April 16, Ben-Gurion wrote in his diary: 'The Syrians have offered to make separate peace with Israel. Cooperation and a joint army . . . I instructed . . . that the Syrians be told plainly—first of all, an armistice agreement based on the international border. Then talks about peace. . . .' "[24] Segev continues:

> Thus far, no one in the Israeli administration had given serious thought to Zaim's offer to take in 300,000 refugees. Their attention was riveted on the border problem. . . . The American representative in Syria continued to lavish praise on Zaim, on whom he hung "the last hope," provided Israel was willing to compromise, or at least if Ben-Gurion was willing to meet him. Everyone who has met Zaim, reported the American diplomat, was impressed by his sincerity and his open-mindedness toward Israel. . . . After prolonged hesitations and consultations with Ben-Gurion, Sharett announced that he was willing to go to Syria to meet with Zaim and discuss two subjects with him, armistice and peace, in that order. Once an armistice agreement was achieved, including a Syrian withdrawal to the international border, it would be possible to talk about peace. The Syrians were not interested in such a discussion. Sharett hastened to conclude that the whole thing was a fraud.[25]

In January 1950, the United Nations convened a Conciliation Commission, with the objective of transforming the armistice agreements into formal peace treaties. The Commission was directed by the U.S., France, and Turkey, and met in Lausanne, Switzerland, with the participation of the Arab states, a Palestinian delegation, and Israel. Concerning the Palestinian delegation, Avnery relates:

There appeared before it [the Conciliation Commission] a delegation officially representing the Palestinian refugees but which was actually a kind of unofficial Palestinian negotiating team. This group, which included the Ramallah lawyer Aziz Shihadeh, approached the Israeli delegate, Eliahu Sasson, and told him that the Palestinians were ready to make peace with Israel. After consulting his government, Sasson rebuffed them bluntly. The government of Israel was not interested in dealing with people who did not represent any government. He would deal with the King of Jordan only.[26]

Moreover, according to Segev: "The Arab states agreed to negotiate with Israel on the basis of the UN Partition Resolution of 1947. Israel responded with the demand that Egypt evacuate the Gaza Strip and Jordan the West Bank. . . ."[27] Thus a stalemate ensued. In addition, Abba Eban relates that his main goal at the conference was "to prevent the elaboration of a statute for an international city [for Jerusalem], or if it was formulated, we could seek to prevent it from being put into effect."[28] During the Lausanne Conference the head of the Egyptian delegation and Israeli officials held a lengthy meeting, of which Segev writes: "This was not the first such meeting between Israelis and an Egyptian diplomat; its course, content, and results indicated once again that there was no problem of communication between Israel and the Arab countries. The Arabs 'recognized' Israel and were ready to discuss peace, but Israel did not accept the conditions."[29] Segev adds that most of the American diplomats at Lausanne believed that peace depended on Israel: "Mark Ethridge, the U.S. delegate . . . wrote President Truman that Israel's inclination to base her future on military security, while foregoing the chance for peace, seemed 'unbelievable'. . . ."[30].

But Israel was apparently not interested in peace. On July 28, 1949, Foreign Minister Sharett had told the MAPAI members of the Knesset: "We do not need peace. We are satisfied with the present agreement. Perhaps the Arabs need peace."[31] Prime Minister Ben-Gurion had declared to a correspondent from the London *Times* ten days earlier regarding peace treaties with the Arab states: ". . . . I am in no rush. I can wait ten years. We are under no pressure."[32]

Finally, on the question of Jerusalem, reiterating the stipulations of the 1947 partition resolution, the General Assembly resolved on December 9, 1949, that Jerusalem should be a "separate body" under permanent international authority. Ben-Gurion responded by proposing to the Cabinet that the Israeli government transfer the Knesset from Tel Aviv to Jerusalem, "thereby demonstrating that Jerusalem was inseparable from the State of Israel. . . . We must challenge the U.N.," the prime minister declared.[33] Shortly thereafter the transfer began. Ben-Gurion's reaction established a precedent the Zionist state has followed ever after, "challenging" all United Nations resolutions concerning the Israel/Palestine question, and consistently refusing to comply with the recommendations and norms of the international organization, in spite of the fact that its own legitimacy and existence are directly tied to a resolution passed by that body.

It must be noted that Zionist leaders calculated very carefully the importance of American support to the success of the Zionist enterprise. Teveth writes in this regard: ". . . . Ben-Gurion turned his eyes again toward a world power, the United States, in his quest for a prop to replace Great Britain. As early as 1940, he predicted American ascendance as a great world power, and his cultivating of American public and official opinion yielded fruit. . . "[34] And, to ensure American support, Zionists have undertaken extraordinary measures to construct a social reality that conforms to their interests. In so doing they have attempted to dehumanize Palestinians, and they have distorted and perverted the entire history of the Middle East in this century. That some Zionists are finally coming to terms with their past is helpful in explaining to Americans the nature of Zionism, the causes of the Arab-Palestinian-Israeli conflict, and the failure of all efforts to resolve that conflict.

————

In 1947, the United States government, led by President Harry S Truman, took a position in the Palestine conflict squarely on the side of Zionism and played a singularly significant role in facilitating its success. Subsequent American administrations pursued policies that reinforced and sustained the ability of the Zionist state to maintain itself and its exclusive institutions, and to pursue expansionist and militaristic policies throughout the region. It is not the objective of this paper to discuss the reasons for the continuum of official U.S. support for Israel.[35] Rather this article will analyze American efforts—governmental and private sector—directed toward resolving the Palestine conflict, both before Israel's independence and in the turbulent years thereafter. Space does not permit a discussion of every single effort on behalf of peace but an attempt has been made to consider the most important proposals and plans in some detail, and at least to mention the others.

Some of the American peace efforts were based on a comprehensive approach and addressed the totality of issues in the conflict, as for example the 1970 report prepared by the American Friends Service Committee; others were more narrowly focused on a particular problem that seemed to carry the potential for outright hostilities, such as Eric Johnston's 1953 regional plan for sharing the Jordan River waters. One of the striking aspects of all the various American efforts is the implicit values contained within them, including a belief in democracy as expressed in the concepts of equality of opportunity and equality before the law for all citizens regardless of ethnic identity or religious affiliation; a respect for international norms, principles, and laws; and a commitment to peaceful resolution of disputes based on justice and equity. However, in addition to sharing an underlying value consensus, the common denominator amongst all the American peace efforts is their abysmal failure. And perhaps as important as the tragedy of the failures themselves is the fact that they occurred against the triumph of an ideology and an organization that manifested values antithetical to those described above. Israeli-Zionist society is predicated on a concept of religious/national exclusivity, resting on the distinction between "Jew" and "non-Jew" that is institutionalized into all the formal state structures;[36] and on a concept of democracy as no more than rule by the majority without any protection of the rights of minorities.[37] Israel's approach to conflict resolution is based on the premise that "might makes right," coupled with a complete disregard for internationally recognized standards of state behavior and, as noted, a particularly cavalier disregard for the principles and resolutions of the United Nations.[38]

For those who have understood the reality behind the facade Zionism has attempted to present, most of the American proposals discussed herein will seem woefully inadequate. I believe, however, it is necessary to suspend personal political preferences and attempt to appreciate the genuine good will and humanistic motivations of the majority of the individuals engaged in these efforts. Indeed, compared with the Machiavellian power machinations of persons, such as Henry Kissinger— who gave Israel carte blanche in the Middle East to assure its effectiveness as a "surrogate power" for American interests—or the craven subservience and political expediency of those members of Congress who have wanted the money and votes domestic pro-Israeli forces could deliver, most of the individuals involved in the peacemaking efforts, as well as their proposals, stand out as courageous, innovative, equitable, and constructive.

Pre-State Peace Efforts

In the aftermath of the First World War President Woodrow Wilson took the lead in attempting to forge a post-war order based on principles of self-determination, collective security, open covenants as an end to secret diplomacy, and the dissolution of colonial empires. In the first formal articulation of his post-war vision, Wilson stated that "other nationalities which are now under Turkish rule should be assured an undoubted security of life and an absolutely unmolested opportunity of autonomous development. . . ."[39] Wilson was particularly disturbed by British and French behavior toward the remains of the Ottoman Empire; indeed, both openly flouted the president's principles.

The British were especially duplicitous. As inducement to the Arabs to revolt against their Ottoman overlords in order to assist Britain's war effort, London promised the Arabs it would facilitate the independence of the Arab East after the war. These commitments were contained in the 1915 Hussein-McMahon Correspondence, which included specifications concerning the boundaries of the area designated as the independent Arab state, and explicitly encompassed Palestine.[40] Subsequently, and contradictorily, the British pledged to Zionist leaders their assistance in establishing a Jewish homeland in Palestine. This promise was first given in the 1917 Balfour Declaration which stated in part: "His Majesty's Government view with favor the establishment in Palestine of a National Home for the Jewish people . . . it being clearly understood that nothing shall be done which may prejudice the civil and religious rights of existing non-Jewish communities in Palestine."[41] (The British commitment to the Zionists was structured into the mandate Great Britain assumed for Palestine at the San Remo Peace Conference in May 1920).[42] In addition, London had concluded a secret accord with Paris in 1916—the Sykes-Picot Agreement—in which the two powers carved up the Arab East into spheres of influence.[43] Against this backdrop of deception Wilson dispatched an official American delegation to the Middle East to ascertain the attitudes and desires of the local peoples concerning their future.

Dr. Henry C. King, President of Oberlin College, and Charles Crane, a successful businessman, together with staff, spent approximately forty days in the area. The following are excerpts from the King-Crane Commission Report presented in August 1919:

> We recommend . . . serious modification of the extreme Zionist program for Palestine of unlimited immigration of Jews, looking finally to making Palestine distinctly a Jewish State.
> . . . The Commissioners began their study of Zionism with minds predisposed in its favor, but the actual facts in Palestine . . . have driven them to the recommendation here made.
> . . . If, however, the strict terms of the Balfour statement are adhered to— . . . "it being clearly understood that nothing shall be

done which may prejudice the civil and religious rights of existing non-Jewish communities in Palestine"—it can hardly be doubted that the extreme Zionist program must be greatly modified. For "a national home for the Jewish people" is not equivalent to making Palestine into a Jewish State; nor can the erection of such a Jewish State be accomplished without the gravest trespass upon the "civil and religious rights of existing non-Jewish communities in Palestine." The fact came out repeatedly in the Commission's conference with Jewish representatives, *that the Zionists looked forward to a practically complete dispossession of the present non-Jewish inhabitants of Palestine. . . .* (Emphasis added)

. . . In his address of July 4, 1918, President Wilson laid down the following principle . . ."The settlement of every question, whether of territory, of sovereignty, of economic arrangement, or of political relationship upon the basis of the free acceptance of that settlement by the people immediately concerned, and not upon the basis of the material interest or advantage of any other nation of people which may desire a different settlement. . . ." If that principle is to rule . . . then it is to be remembered that the non-Jewish population—nearly nine-tenths of the whole—are emphatically against the entire Zionist program . . . To subject a people so minded to unlimited Jewish immigration, and to steady financial and social pressure to surrender the land, would be a gross violation of the principle just quoted, and of the peoples' rights. . . .

. . . The fundamental principles laid down by President Wilson . . . impel us to protest most emphatically . . . against any private engagement aiming at the establishment of Zionism in the southern part of Syria. . . . No British officer, consulted by the Commissioners, believed that the Zionist program could be carried out except by force of arms. . . . That of itself is evidence of a strong sense of the injustice of the Zionist program . . . the initial claim, often submitted by Zionist representatives, that they have a "right" to Palestine, based on an occupation of 2000 years ago, can hardly be seriously considered.

. . . Palestine is "the Holy Land" for Jews, Christians and Moslems alike. Millions of Christians and Moslems all over the world are quite as much concerned as the Jews with conditions in Palestine, especially with those conditions which touch upon religious feeling and rights . . . It is simply impossible, under those circumstances, for Moslems and Christians to feel satisfied to have these places in Jewish hands, or under the custody of Jews. . . . It [the extreme Zionist program] would intensify, with a certainty like fate, the anti-

Jewish feeling both in Palestine and in all other portions of the
world which look to Palestine as "the Holy Land."
. . . In view of all these considerations, and with a deep sense of
sympathy for the Jewish cause, the Commissioners feel bound to
recommend . . . that Jewish immigration should be definitely limited, and that the project for making Palestine distinctly a Jewish
commonwealth should be given up.[44]

A variety of circumstances—including Wilson's failure to secure
American congressional approval of the Paris Peace Treaty and the
United States' non-participation in the League of Nations, the president's
declining health, America's temporary retreat into diplomatic isolationism, the geopolitical power of the British and French, the growing international influence of Zionist leaders, and conversely the dearth of
influence that Arabs were able to marshall vis-a-vis the Europeans—
converged to render the recommendations of the King-Crane Commission completely ineffectual. In this context, it is worthy of note that as
a result of its close relations with the British government, the World
Zionist Organization (WZO) was invited to send representatives to appear
before the Supreme Council of the Paris Peace Conference, and subsequently the WZO participated in drafting the mandate for Palestine.[45]
But clearly, neither Britain or France paid any attention to the King-
Crane proposals; nor did Washington even give them serious consideration. Indeed, the United States' inherent antipathy to nationalist
movements anywhere in the Third World and its growing economic
interests in the Middle East (particularly as regards oil) ensured that
Washington would not emerge as a defender of Palestinian rights. Nevertheless, the recommendations stand as an accurate, honest, and prescient
analysis by impartial American observers of the meaning of Zionism.

The United States took little further interest in the Palestine problem
until after the termination of WWII. In 1945 London and Washington
engaged in one attempt at cooperation—the Anglo-American Committee of Enquiry—to resolve the Palestine conflict. On April 20, 1946, the
joint committee made a series of ten recommendations, one of which—
that 100,000 Jews be permitted immediate entry into Palestine—Truman seized on and made the centerpiece of his highly politicized pronouncements on Palestine. However, several of the other
recommendations are of interest, though they received little attention
at the time, and are virtually unknown today. Analysis of them here is
relevant since Americans were equal participants on the Committee, and
because of their substantive content:

. . . Jew shall not dominate Arab and Arab shall not dominate Jew in Palestine. . . . Palestine shall be neither a Jewish state nor an Arab state. . . . Thus Palestine must ultimately become a state which guards the rights and interests of Moslems, Jews, and Christians alike and accords to the inhabitants, as a whole, the fullest measure of self-government, consistent with the . . . paramount principles set forth above.

. . . We have reached the conclusion that the hostility between Jews and Arabs . . . makes it almost certain that, now and for sometime to come, any attempt to establish either an independent Palestinian state or independent Palestinian states would result in civil strife such as might threaten the peace of the world. We therefore recommend . . . the execution of a Trusteeship Agreement under the United Nations.

. . . We recommend that . . . The Trustee should proclaim the principle that Arab economic, educational, and political advancement in Palestine is of equal importance with that of Jews, and should at once prepare measures designed to bridge the gap which now exists and raise the Arab standard of living to that of the Jews. . . .[46]

These recommendations demonstrate that the Anglo-American Committee did not support the Zionist program for the establishment of a Jewish state in Palestine. Had the recommendations been implemented, a secular, democratic Palestinian state would have been the most likely outcome. The idea of a temporary trusteeship until Jewish-Palestinian hostilities were cooled was eminently reasonable; and the recognition of the potentially global nature of conflict originating in Palestine has been borne out in the two near confrontations between the U.S. and the Soviet Union during the 1967 and 1973 wars. Moreover, Israel's present nuclear capability is assuredly one of the most dangerous threats to world peace in the international system.[47]

Also of interest in the Committee's recommendations is the recognition of the imbalance between the indigenous Palestinian Arabs and the European Jewish settlers in the areas of education, economic development, and political experience. It is evident that Palestinians never had the remotest opportunity of having their interests receive an equal hearing with Zionist interests. The European Jews brought with them the culture of the dominant West; enormous advantages in education; skills in industrial, technological, and agricultural affairs; Western diplomatic and political practices; tremendous financial resources; and a world-wide network of Jewish communities with access to the political leaders of their countries. The significance of the latter alone is illustrated in the successful efforts of American Jews in winning the support of President Truman to the Zionist cause. It is impossible to imagine how the largely peasant population of Palestine, for centuries before the Zionist colonization a backwater province of the decaying Ottoman Empire, could have competed with the Jewish settler-colonists. However, had the trusteeship been implemented and the recommendations to provide education, etc., also instituted, perhaps when it came time to work out the details of an independent state, the Palestinians would have been able to compete for their interests from a position of greater equality. It is at least of interest that the members of the Anglo-American Committee recognized the imbalance between the two communities and considered ways of rectifying it.

Zionists were willing to endorse the Committee's suggestion for admitting 100,000 Jews to Palestine, but they reacted with strong antipathy to the report's other recommendations. Zionists in the U.S., Britain, and in the Yishuv (the Zionist administrative structure in Palestine) insisted on nothing less than Jewish statehood. The Jewish Agency made a formal statement on the Committee's recommendations which included the following passage:

> ... Certain other recommendations of the Committee bear the marks of inadequate opportunity for full inquiry, e.g., the suggestion that Jewish education, as to text books and curricula, should be controlled by the Palestine Administration. The most serious flaw in the Committee's conclusions must, however, at once be pointed out ... the Committee fails to provide for their needs [European Jewish victims of the Holocaust beyond the 100,000 stipulated] *or for those Jews in other parts of the world whose position is no less insecure.* ... The terms of reference of the Committee limited its investigations to the Continent of Europe and to Palestine. The central problem of the homeless and stateless Jewish people has been left untouched. ...[48] (Emphasis added)

It is thus apparent that the real concern of Zionism was with the immigration of *all* the world's Jews to the land of Palestine.

British and American officials developed what was termed the Morrison-Grady Plan to implement the recommendations of the Anglo-American Committee. However, intense Zionist political pressure in Washington and London resulted in the rapid demise of the plan.[49]

In 1947 Britain handed the Palestine problem to the United Nations. In November the General Assembly passed Resolution 181 recommending the partition of Palestine into a Jewish state and a Palestinian

Arab state, and stipulating that Jerusalem be maintained as an international zone under permanent U.N. trusteeship. The Palestinians rejected the U.N. recommendation, the Zionists accepted it, and the hostilities in Palestine escalated. By that time British power was seriously reduced by wartime losses, and American influence had become a critical leaven. As a result of domestic political considerations, and against the advice of every senior official in the Department of State, the War Department, and the Joint Chiefs,[50] President Truman emerged as the foremost champion of the Zionist program among the world's leaders.[51] The political nature of the president's decisions was reflected, in one instance, in a comment Truman made to a group of State Department representatives concerned about the direction of U.S. diplomacy: "I am sorry gentlemen, but I have to answer to hundreds of thousands who are anxious for the success of Zionism. I do not have hundreds of thousands of Arabs among my constituents."[52] Truman was able to bring the weight of the U.S. to bear on behalf of Zionism in the international community. And, indeed, without U.S. support the partition resolution would assuredly not have been adopted.

The Truman Administration undertook no serious efforts to resolve the conflict raging in Palestine; in fact, by siding wholeheartedly with Zionism the administration contributed to the imbroglio. The one attempt—a trusteeship proposal—that was made to quell the hostilities was torpedoed by political expediency. That occurred in March 1948 when the U.S. ambassador to the United Nations, Warren Austin, proposed to the Security Council a U.N. trusteeship to replace the partition plan. Although the proposal had originally received the president's approval,[53] after American Zionists made known their outrage Truman adroitly distanced himself from the trusteeship idea, subsequently making "amends" by offering immediate recognition to Israel when it announced its independence on May 14, 1948.

As suggested above, Israel, which owed its legitimacy to U.N. Resolution 181, proceeded, after its birth, to ignore with wanton disregard the provisions of that resolution that did not suit its interests, as well as subsequent resolutions that conflicted with its desires and objectives. For instance, in direct violation of Res. 181, Israel seized the western portions of Jerusalem during the 1948 hostilities and by March 1949 began moving its governmental offices there. (During the June 1967 war it seized the eastern portions of the city and shortly thereafter legislated the "reunification" of Jerusalem as Israel's "eternal" capital.) On December 11, 1948 the General Assembly passed Resolution 194 calling for repatriation of the Palestinian refugees to their homes or for compensation paid to those who chose not to return. Israel did not permit the repatriation of Palestinians and refused to pay any compensation for the lands and properties it seized. While the U.S. voted for both resolutions, the Truman Administration made no effort to implement them beyond facilitating Zionist objectives.

Peace Efforts After the Establishment of Israel

With the establishment of Israel the nature and contours of the conflict over Palestine assumed different dimensions in American diplomacy and political culture. Subsequent peace efforts were directed at mediating a settlement between the new state and the neighboring Arab states. The Palestinians, over half of whom (some 770,000) were dispossessed and forced into exile, acquired the status of "refugees." For the next twenty years the Palestinian "problem" was defined in the context of refugee resettlement—jobs and homes for individual refugees—and not, as was appropriate, in terms of the Palestinians as a national community with interests and aspirations as a collectivity, and the right to self-determination. Moreover, the Palestinian Arab state stipulated in the partition resolution vanished from the political agenda.

By the time the Eisenhower Administration came to office in 1953, Israel was militarily unchallengeable. It had also established a reputation for unbridled aggression with a policy of "massive retaliation" against neighboring Arab states in response to incursions by Palestinians attempting to return to their homes or lands. These as well as numerous other points of conflict characterized the Middle East; but unlike the Truman years, a number of attempts were made during Eisenhower's tenure to find solutions to the various Arab-Israeli discords. Within the administration, Secretary of State John Foster Dulles and Assistant Secretary of State Henry A. Byroade, took the lead in peace-making efforts. Private or semi-official initiatives were undertaken by Eric Johnston, Elmore Jackson, Robert B. Anderson, and Lewis Strauss. However, in the end, despite a more "evenhanded" approach to the Arab-Israeli conflict, the administration's obsession with international communism and the threat it perceived from what was termed "radical Arab nationalism," catalyzed the U.S.-Israeli partnership as a means of dominating the Arab world. Still, the Eisenhower Administration stands in marked contrast to the Truman Administration—and to administrations succeeding it—in its attempts to facilitate peaceful solutions.

Less than four months after entering office, Dulles spent several weeks visiting the Middle East. On his return, in June 1953, the secretary gave a major evaluation of conditions in the area with suggestions for resolving some of the problems:

> . . . Jerusalem is divided into armed camps . . . the atmosphere is heavy with hate. . . . Jerusalem is, above all, the Holy place of the Christian, Moslem and Jewish faiths. This has been repeatedly emphasized by the United Nations . . . the world religious community has claims in Jerusalem which take precedence over the political claims of any particular nation.
>
> . . . Closely huddled around Israel are most of the over 800,000 Arab refugees, who fled from Palestine as the Israelis took over. . . .
>
> . . . Some of these refugees could be settled in the area presently controlled by Israel. . . .
>
> . . . the Arab peoples are afraid that the United States will back the new State of Israel in aggressive expansion. They are more fearful of Zionism than of Communism, and they fear lest the United States become the backer of expansionist Zionism.
>
> . . . the United States joined with Britain and France in a Declaration of May 25, 1950, which stated that "the three Governments, should they find that any of these states of the Near East was preparing to violate frontiers or armistice lines, would, consistent with their obligations as members of the United Nations, immediately take action, both within and outside the United Nations, to prevent such violation." The declaration when made did not reassure the Arabs. It must be made clear that the present U.S. Administration stands fully behind that Declaration.
>
> . . . There is need for peace in the Near East. . . . Israel should become part of the Near East community and cease to look upon itself, or be looked upon by others, as alien to this community. This is possible. To achieve it will require concessions on the part of both sides.[54]

Israel did not like Dulles' analysis of the nature of the problems in the Middle East, and argued contrarily that they arose from an "endemic anti-Westernism" that pervaded the Arab capitals as well as a "tendency for non-identification" (i.e., non-alignment) by the Arab regimes (implying Soviet influence in the context of the Cold War).[55] Israel presented itself as a bastion of Western civilization in a sea of barbarous, infidel Arabs, and as a wholly devoted pro-American state. In addition, Israel engaged in some sordid efforts to undermine America's relations with the Arabs—for example, the 1954 "Lavon Affair," in which an Israeli-led ring of spies and saboteurs operating in Cairo bombed and set fire to a number of American facilities in order to disrupt Egyptian-American friendship and to deter Egypt from joining a U.S.-sponsored Middle Eastern alliance.[56] Israel's persistence and sophistication in presenting its arguments and analysis, coupled with Washington's unwillingness to deal with Arab nationalism on its own terms, ultimately served Israel well. By the end of the Eisenhower Administration, Dulles reversed his initial evaluation, disregarding the fundamentally Western orientation of the Arab states and the possibilities for U.S.-Arab cooperation, and set the United States on a course of interminable hostility with the Arab world. The sole beneficiary of this misdirected U.S. policy was Israel.

Despite Dulles' insightful evaluation of the regional scene in 1953, no comprehensive policy was developed to ameliorate the many problems he identified, although one of the efforts at conflict resolution attempted during the Eisenhower years was a direct result of Dulles' visit to the Middle East. In the early months of 1953 Israel had begun a diversion of the waters from the Jordan River (for the irrigation of its ambitious agricultural schemes and for its development projects in the Negev) in the demilitarized zone north of Lake Tiberias. Its actions earned Israel a cease-and-desist order from the U.N. truce supervisor and a temporary cutoff of U.S. aid until it stopped construction. Lebanon, Syria, Jordan and Egypt objected to the diversion scheme because they feared the development of the Negev would give Israel an increased military advantage, and, more important, the diversion project would deprive Jordan and Syria of much-needed water resources. Dulles took note of the potentially explosive nature of this situation and President Eisenhower appointed Eric Johnston as a special ambassador to work out a technical plan for an equitable sharing of the water.

The main objective of the plan Johnston devised was to establish a Jordan Valley Authority (based on the idea of the Tennessee Valley Authority), composed of Israel, Jordan, and Syria, for the joint exploitation of the resources of the Jordan River. A major goal of the project was also to provide newly irrigated land for the resettlement of a large number of Palestinian refugees. In addition, an underlying motive, shared by Americans and Israelis, was to, in effect, co-opt the Arabs through technical cooperation as a means to eventually drawthem into a political settlement in line with Israel's interests. However, the Arabs were explicitly informed that the Johnston Plan entailed no political strings.[57] It is of particular significance that the Arab states were willing to cooperate in a project that benefited Israel, especially since it was first presented just after Israel's October 1953 attack on the Palestinian town of Qibya (located on the West Bank under Jordanian occupation), in which the village was destroyed and over fifty men, women, and children were murdered by Israeli troops.

The Israelis initially showed interest in the project, but when Johnston presented his proposals, they objected to the details. Some officials insisted that Israel should proceed unilaterally with its diversion plans, using force if necessary, although eventually the government agreed that Israel would "study" the plan and suggest modifications.[58] Syria, Jordan, and Lebanon agreed to consider the plan, and Egypt gave Johnston strong assurances of its support for his efforts. Eventually both Israel and the Arabs presented plans of their own. One prominent analyst said of the Arab proposal:". . . . most encouraging. First and foremost, it provided for the sharing of water with Israel. In effect, the Arabs agreed in principle to cooperative efforts in the field of economic and social development."[59] As to the sharing of water, according to the Johnston Plan, Israel would receive about 35 percent of the water; according to the Arab plan about 20 percent; and according to the Israeli plan about 50 percent. Moreover, Israel insisted on bringing the maximum amount of water south to irrigate the Negev, even though "this meant taking water right away from the river basin . . . [which] was contrary not only to international practice but to the principles of the Johnston Plan."[60] Israel wanted a supervisory body composed of Israelis and Arabs; the Arabs wanted an international supervisory body, possibly the United Nations. Israel objected to U.N. supervision on the ground that "it was an unsatisfactory organization to work with."[61]

Negotiations lasted from 1953 to 1955. By August 1955, all but complete agreement had been reached on a final plan, the Arab states having made the extraordinary concession of agreeing to allow Israel to use its share of the water in the Negev. However, events in August seriously complicated the regional scene. In February, Israel had staged a massive attack on Gaza; in April, Nasser had initiated a secret peace process with Israel; but in August, Israel struck Egypt again with a major raid on Khan Yunis. Thus the Egyptian government no longer saw any basis for peaceful cooperation with Israel. What is more, in an official speech Dulles gave on the Middle East in August, he tied the Jordan Valley Authority to a set of peace proposals which negated Johnston's promise concerning "no political strings." For all these reasons, Arab interest cooled significantly.

The Arab League debated Johnston's plan in October 1955, and while not rejecting it, put it aside pending further study. After the plan was "shelved" Israel went ahead with its extensive diversion scheme, the "National Water Carrier" project, and successfully diverted most of the Jordan's waters for its own use. Subsequently, Jordan and Syria developed independent programs for water usage but they were never implemented. In the mid-1960's, the Arab League attempted to develop a water utilization project; however, Israel employed military force to derail the construction works which was sufficiently strong to permanently discourage Arab interest in the project. After the June 1967 war, Israel terminated the on-going dispute with finality through its occupation of the Golan Heights, putting most of the Jordan's headwaters securely under its own control.[62]

Another proposal dealing with the question of water was put forward by Lewis Strauss, Chairman of the Atomic Energy Commission. In a memorandum he prepared for President Eisenhower, Strauss argued that the two elements which underlay all other problems in the area were water and the displaced Palestinian population. Strauss believed that if sufficient water could be generated to irrigate agriculture in barren areas of Egypt, Jordan, and Israel, the Palestinians would have new lands in which to settle, and the various states would be engaged in productive endeavors, thus decreasing the likelihood of conflict. Strauss proposed construction of three large nuclear plants for desalination and for producing power, two on the Mediterranean coast and one at the northern end of the Gulf of Aqaba. One plant alone would have produced as much fresh water as the entire Jordan River system and the project did not require cooperation between the Arabs and Israel. Eisenhower reportedly liked Strauss's plan but never sought its implementation through congressional financing. (The president held a particularly restrictive view of American "foreign aid.") In the end nothing came of Strauss's ideas.[63]

In April 1954, Assistant Secretary of State Byroade made a public speech calling on both Arabs and Israelis to make an effort for peace:

> . . . To the Israelis I say that you should come to truly look upon yourselves as a Middle Eastern state and see your future in that context rather than as a headquarters, or nucleus so to speak, of worldwide groupings of peoples of a particular religious faith who must have special rights within and obligations to the Israeli state. You should drop the attitude of the conqueror and the conviction that force and a policy of retaliatory killings is the only policy that your neighbors will understand. You should make your deeds correspond to your frequent utterances of the desire for peace.
>
> . . . To the Arabs I say you should accept this state of Israel as an accomplished fact. I say further that you are deliberately attempting to maintain a state of affairs delicately suspended between peace and war, while at present desiring neither. This is a most dangerous policy and one which world opinion will increasingly condemn if

you continue to resist any move to obtain at least a less dangerous *modus vivendi* with your neighbor.[64]

In fact, one year later, in April 1955 (three months after Israel's massive attack on Gaza), Egypt's president, Gamal Abdul Nasser, initiated an effort to reach a peaceful settlement with Israel. Egypt's ambassador to Washington, Dr. Ahmad Husayn, approached the American Friends Service Committee (AFSC) and asked it to play the role of independent mediator between Egypt and Israel. A prominent American Quaker, Elmore Jackson, assumed that position for the AFSC, with the knowledge and approval of the U.S. government. Between April and September 1955 Jackson shuttled between Cairo and Tel Aviv. However, despite Nasser's genuine interest in a settlement, nothing came of Jackson's efforts. That the Egyptian initiative ultimately failed was the result of a number of factors, including Israel's policy of massive retaliatory raids on Egyptian soil, especially the Khan Yunis attack in August 1955; contradictory U.S. government policies toward Egypt; and internal Israeli politics.[65]

Shortly after his April 1954 public speech, Assistant Secretary Byroade delivered an address on May 1, before the American Council of Judaism, in which he called attention to Israel's policy of unlimited immigration and to Arab fears of Israeli expansion, urging that Israel find some way to lay those fears to rest.[66] Israel's reaction to both of Byroade's speeches was extremely negative. Abba Eban, at the time Israel's ambassador to the U.S., termed Byroade's suggestion that Israel integrate itself into the region and become another Middle Eastern state, "grotesque," and records that he made an official protest against the assistant secretary's "frivolous oratory," which, according to the ambassador, "caused a partial retraction from the State Department."[67] Nor were the assistant secretary's insights and recommendations ever translated into policy.

In August 1955, two years after his first statement on the Middle East, Secretary Dulles again addressed the major problems plaguing the region and suggested solutions:

> . . . Three problems remain that conspicuously require to be solved.
> . . . The first is the tragic plight of the 900,000 refugees who formerly lived in the territory that is now occupied by Israel.
> . . . The second is the pall of fear that hangs over the Arab and Israeli people alike. The Arab countries fear that Israel will seek by violent means to expand at their expense. The Israelis fear that the Arabs will gradually marshall superior forces . . . and they suffer from the economic measures now taken against them.

. . . The third is the lack of fixed permanent boundaries between Israel and its Arab neighbors.

. . . Serious as the present situation is, there is a danger that, unless it improves, it will get worse. . . . The United States, as a friend of both Israelis and Arabs, has given the situation deep and anxious thought and has come to certain conclusions. . . .

. . . To end the plight of the 900,000 refugees requires that these uprooted people should, through resettlement and—to such an extent as may be feasible—repatriation, be enabled to resume a life of dignity and self-respect. To this end there is need to create more arable land where refugees can find permanent homes and gain their own livelihood through their own work. . . . All this requires money.

. . . Compensation is due from Israel. . . . If [Israel is unable to pay] there might be an international loan to enable Israel to pay. . . . President Eisenhower would recommend substantial participation by the United States in such a loan for such a purpose. Also he would recommend that the United States contribute to the realization of water development and irrigation projects. . . .

. . . The United States would join in formal treaty engagements to prevent or thwart any effort by either side to alter by force the boundaries between Israel and its Arab neighbors. . . .

. . . If there is to be a guarantee of borders, it would be normal that there should be prior agreement upon what the borders are. . . it is possible to find a way of reconciling the vital interests of all parties. The United States would be willing to help in the search for a solution if the parties to the dispute should desire.

. . . It should also be possible to reach agreement on the status of Jerusalem. The United States would give its support to a United Nations review of this problem. . . .[68]

Again, no comprehensive policy was developed reflecting Dulles' analysis, but in January 1956, Eisenhower sent Robert B. Anderson, a successful Texas business leader and a close friend of the president, on a secret mission to Israel and Egypt. The proposals in Dulles' August speech constituted the basic agenda for the Anderson Mission. Specifically, Anderson was instructed to offer financing for the Aswan High Dam, a U.S. pledge to guarantee the borders between the two countries, and major economic aid to help Israel pay compensation to the Palestinians. However, Israel's prime minister, David Ben-Gurion, was only interested in direct negotiations between himself and Nasser, and in obtaining American arms. Israel's adamant refusal to delineate its boundaries made the offer of American "good offices" to assist in such an endeavor moot, and in turn the offer to provide formal treaty arrangements to guarantee the borders equally ineffectual. Likewise, Israel's persistent refusal to acknowledge its obligation to compensate Palestinians for their expropriated lands and properties was not altered by Washington's offer to arrange international financing for such compensation. At the same time, while Nasser was interested in American support for the Aswan Dam, he was also increasingly sensitive to Egyptian and Arab public opinion, which was quite inflamed over a massive Israeli attack on Kinnereth, Syria in December 1955, in which more than seventy Syrians were killed. Nasser was far more wary of negotiations with Israel at this point than when he initiated the opening in April 1955, and wanted to talk seriously about peace only if the U.S. could tell him in advance what the boundary adjustments would be. Anderson's shuttle thus ended in failure. A second Anderson mission at the end of February was no more successful than the first.[69]

After the tripartite aggression against Egypt by Israel, France and Britain in November 1956, the Eisenhower Administration evidenced no further interest in seeking peaceful solutions to the Middle East's problems. Instead, fearing that in the wake of the Sinai/Suez war Nasser might turn to the Soviet Union for protection of Egypt's national security, and angry over the Egyptian president's persistent independence, Washington announced the "Eisenhower Doctrine."[70] The doctrine was allegedly concerned with Communist penetration of the Middle East but was in reality directed at Nasser and Arab nationalism—a fact that did not escape the Egyptian president or his fellow Arab nationalists. In effect, it told the Arab states to fall into line with American interests or be considered Soviet clients. At the same time, Washington denied Egypt food aid, froze Egyptian assets in the U.S., and attempted to promote King Ibn Saud of Saudi Arabia as a rival to Nasser's leadership in the Arab world.[71] Indeed, without minimizing the sincerity of the various efforts of Eisenhower, Dulles, and Byroade to resolve some of the problems associated with the Arab-Israeli conflict, their contribution to its perpetuation and intensification cannot be ignored either.

Eisenhower and Dulles considered Nasser's position on pan-Arab nationalism and non-alignment an obstacle to the American design for dominance of the Middle East. (His domestic economic policies were also highly suspect.) The administration's treatment of the Egyptian president was full of contradictions. It attempted to persuade Nasser to join the Baghdad Pact, but when he refused, Eisenhower and Dulles built up Iraq against him; after the devastating Israeli raid on Gaza in February 1955, Dulles offered to sell Nasser arms, but the offer was later withdrawn without explanation (leading to Nasser's purchase of weapons from the Soviet Union—the so-called "Czech arms deal"); Eisenhower invited Nasser to Washington, then failed to follow through on the invitation; Dulles pledged to construct the Aswan High Dam, but reneged when Egypt accorded China diplomatic recognition; and so on. Finally, the inability to induce Nasser to follow Washington's directives led to the conviction within policy-making circles that his tenure had to be ended. "Nasserism" was deemed as great a threat to American interests in the Middle East as Communism in Southeast Asia. (In fact, both involved nationalist challenges to U.S. global hegemony—something Washington was not prepared to tolerate in any form.) Moreover, this attitude in turn precipitated consideration of an alignment between the U.S. and Israel as a means of unseating Nasser and projecting American power in the region. This idea, which came to be known as the "strategic asset thesis," gradually gained acceptance in Washington, and after the June 1967 war became the cornerstone on which the dominant trends in U.S. Middle East policy were based.

President John F. Kennedy made several efforts to establish better relations with the Arab states but his administration undertook nothing that could be considered a peace initiative. President Lyndon B. Johnson was not even interested in the Middle East—his attention was focused on Vietnam; moreover, he was an unabashed Israeli partisan. However, an important and carefully researched plan was put before the American government in 1963 by Dr. Joseph E. Johnson, president of the Carnegie Endowment for International Peace. Dr. Johnson had been asked by the Palestine Conciliation Commission in 1961 to develop a proposal for resolving the problem of the Palestinian refugees. His plan contained five basic elements: (1) each Palestinian would be given an opportunity, free from all external pressures, to express whether he/she preferred repatriation or resettlement;(2) Israel's legitimate security interests would be safeguarded by allowing it, subject to U.N. review, to reject individual Palestinians as security risks; (3) both repatriation and resettlement would be handled on a gradual, step-by-step process and would be undertaken simultaneously; (4) a special fund, to which Israel would be expected to make a substantial contribution, would be set up to pay compensation for Palestinian properties expropriated by Israel, as well as to provide financial help to assist the resettled Palestinians to become self-supporting; and (5) the United States would play a vital role in supervising all aspects and stages of the program.[72] Dr. Johnson had assumed that when presented with a practical, detailed proposal, the Israelis would soften their position regarding the Palestinians; they did not, and rejected the plan out of hand. In the United States, Israel's

American advocates pressed President Johnson to ignore the plan, which he did, and nothing ever came of it.

In the aftermath of the June 1967 war President Johnson put forward a set of five proposals for peace in the Middle East; however, as a basis for a just and lasting settlement, the president's ideas were so flawed that they do not warrant discussion here.[73] They may be more properly understood as a statement of solidarity with Israel—the heralding of U.S.-Israeli "strategic cooperation."

In November 1967, the U.N. Security Council passed Resolution 242.[74] (After the 1973 war the Security Council passed Resolution 338, which was essentially a restatement of 242).[75] Res. 242 was predicated on the principle of the inadmissibility of the acquisition of territory by force and the concept of exchanging territory for peace. Israel was asked to withdraw from the territories it conquered in the war in return for peace treaties with the Arab states. The resolution also created the mandate for a special representative (Gunnar Jarring received the appointment) to mediate peace among the parties. The major flaw in the U.N. declaration was its failure to address the Palestinians as a party to the conflict. Indeed, the only reference to Palestinians in Res. 242 is an indirect comment on the "refugee problem." That the PLO and the Palestinian people have found Res. 242 (and Res. 338) by themselves, insufficient bases for a Middle East peace is understandable. However, the U.S. "requirement" for talking with the PLO has been its unconditional acceptance of 242 and 338—obviously intended to preclude peace with the Palestinians rather than promote it.

Subsequent to its adoption, Res. 242 became the official basis of U.S. policy with regard to the Arab-Israeli conflict. Egypt and Jordan immediately accepted it. Israel made no formal mention of the resolution until May 1970, when it finally tendered its consent. However, Israel's "reunification" of Jerusalem in June 1967 and the colonization and settlement of the West Bank it initiated in September of that year were *de facto* negations of the resolution. In 1980, Israel formally "annexed" Jerusalem, and in 1981 it "annexed" the Golan Heights, rendering Res. 242 totally meaningless. The United States provided the financial wherewithal that made the settlements possible, and imposed no sanctions on Israel for its other violations of the Security Council declaration—further illustrating the specious nature of American policy on this issue.

In the autumn of 1968, President Lyndon Johnson's secretary of state, Dean Rusk, developed a set of proposals designed to move Israel and Egypt toward a bilateral peace settlement. The proposals have not been published, but reportedly they were based on the idea that the U.S. would back a full withdrawal of Israeli forces from Sinai and a restoration of Egyptian sovereignty in exchange for a formal, signed peace agreement.[76] Egypt showed some interest, Israel less. Egypt insisted on complete Israeli withdrawal, Israel demanded negotiations for new boundaries. The initiative, coming at the end of the Johnson Administration, is significant mainly in that it laid the groundwork for the Nixon-Kissinger approach, brought to fruition by Jimmy Carter, of a separate, bilateral Egyptian-Israeli agreement. Such an approach must be understood, however, as the antithesis of a just and lasting peace in the Arab-Palestinian-Israeli conflict.

In 1968, shortly before his inauguration, the newly-elected president, Richard M. Nixon, sent former Pennsylvania Governor William Scranton on a fact-finding tour of the Middle East. When he returned, Scranton stated in a news conference:"America would do well to have a more evenhanded policy. . . . We are interested, very interested, in Israel and its security, and we should be. But it is important to point out in the Middle East and to people around the world that we are interested in other countries in the area and have friends among them."[77] On February 6, 1969, President Nixon made a statement that seemed to indicate he was serious about facilitating a peace process in the Middle East:

> . . . We're going to continue to give our all-out support to the Jarring mission; we are going to have bilateral talks at the United Nations preparatory to the talks between the four powers; we shall have four-power talks at the United Nations; we shall also have talks with the countries in the area, with the Israelis and their neighbors; and in addition we want to go forward on some of the long range plans, the Eisenhower-Strauss plan for relieving some of the very grave economic problems in that area.[78]

It is impossible to judge the sincerity of Nixon's original intentions as regards a Middle East settlement; however, he was soon persuaded by his national security advisor, Henry Kissinger, that pursuing peace in the Middle East was far less important than arming and strengthening Israel as a regional military surrogate.

In fact, the Nixon Administration is marked by two divergent approaches to the Middle East taken by different sectors of the bureaucracy. One approach, generally outlined in the above comment by the president, was centered in the State Department with William Rogers as secretary of state. It focused on the indigenous nature of the regional conflict and was aimed at facilitating a Middle East peace process based on Res. 242. The second approach was directed by Kissinger and was located in the White House. It viewed events in the Middle East as nothing more than reflections of Soviet-American super power rivalry and was predicated on the thesis that the status quo in the Middle East was the most favorable situation for both American and Israeli interests. This notion was buttressed by the belief that Israel could act as a "strategic asset" or "surrogate power" for the U.S. in containing Soviet Communism and maintaining regional stability if it was provided an unlimited supply of armaments and economic aid, and allowed a free hand to pursue its own interests. Kissinger oversaw the transfer of vast amounts of weapons and aid to Israel, and was confident that the area was stable and secure under the Zionist state's awesome might. Rogers and his colleagues at State understood the fundamentally unstable nature of the regional equation and sought to resolve some of the local issues. The State Department initiated "Two Power" talks between the U.S. and the Soviet Union and "Four Power" talks among the U.S., the U.S.S.R., France, and Britain. Both sets of discussions were grounded in Resolution 242 but were focused on an Egyptian-Israeli settlement.[79]

Israel strenuously opposed these American initiatives. For instance, in response to a meeting among the four powers in April 1969, Israel released a communique stating: "Israel rejects from the outset any trend to convene representatives of states outside the Middle East to work out recommendations on affairs of this region. . . . Israel is not and will not be the object of the policy of a great power or great powers, and will not accept any recommendations that contradicts its vital interests, rights, and security."[80] Kissinger too objected to the State Department initiatives and worked in a variety of ways to undermine them. Thus despite an auspicious beginning, by the end of 1969 the two sets of informal discussions had collapsed. Secretary Rogers felt that the demise of the talks seriously diminished U.S. credibility among the Arabs and he believed it was necessary to clarify American policy in a formal statement of U.S. interests and objectives.

On December 9, 1969, Rogers delivered a speech, subsequently known as the "Rogers Plan," that contained the following points:

. . . We have friendly ties with both Arabs and Israelis. To call for Israeli withdrawal as envisaged in the U.N. resolution without achieving agreement on peace would be partisan toward the Arabs. To call on the Arabs to accept peace without Israeli withdrawal would be partisan toward Israel. Therefore, our policy is to encourage the Arabs to accept a permanent peace based on a binding agreement and to urge the Israelis to withdraw from occupied territory when their territorial integrity is assured as envisaged by the Security Council resolution.

. . . We believe the conditions and obligations of peace must be defined in specific terms. For example, navigation rights in the

Suez Canal and in the Strait of Tiran should be spelled out. Respect for sovereignty and obligations of the parties to each other must be made specific.

. . . There should be demilitarized zones and related security arrangements more reliable than those which existed in the area in the past. The parties themselves, with Ambassador Jarring's help, are in the best position to work out the nature and the details of such security arrangements.

. . . The Security Council resolution endorses the principle of the nonacquisition of territory by war and calls for withdrawal of Israeli armed forces from territories occupied in the 1967 war. We support this part of the resolution, including withdrawal, just as we do its other elements.

. . . We believe that while recognized political boundaries must be established and agreed upon by the parties, any changes in the pre-existing lines should not reflect the weight of conquest and should be confined to insubstantial alterations required for mutual security.

. . . There can be no lasting peace without a just settlement of the problem of those Palestinians whom the wars of 1948 and 1967 have made homeless. . . . We are prepared to contribute generously along with others to solve this problem. We believe its just settlement must take into account the desires and aspirations of the refugees and the legitimate concerns of the governments in the area.

. . . The problem posed by the refugees will become increasingly serious if their future is not resolved. There is a new consciousness among the young Palestinians who have grown up since 1948 which needs to be channelled away from bitterness and frustration toward hope and justice.

. . . The question of the future status of Jerusalem, because it touches deep emotional, historical, and religious wellsprings is particularly complicated. We have made clear repeatedly in the past two and a half years that we cannot accept unilateral actions by any party to decide the final status of the city. We believe its status can be determined only through the agreement of the parties concerned, which in practical terms means primarily the Governments of Israel and Jordan, taking into account the interests of other countries in the area and the international community.[81]

Israel rejected the Rogers Plan out of hand, arguing that it took no account of Israel's need for secure boundaries, and that by advocating a withdrawal to the pre-1967 lines with only minor changes, it prejudiced Israel's bargaining position. Israel was especially angry about the statements on Jerusalem and the Palestinians, and retorted that it would never accept a redivision of sovereignty over the city while alleging that the proposals concerning the Palestinians were a threat to the continuation of Israel's character as a Jewish state. Kissinger was equally opposed to the Rogers Plan and he persuaded Nixon to "distance" the presidency from it. And, with remarkable rapidity this major American policy initiative faded from the political scene as if it had never been uttered. Nor was it ever resurrected.

In June 1970 Secretary Rogers undertook an initiative to end the fighting between Egypt and Israel in what had come to be known as the "War of Attrition" along the Suez Canal. In this effort, which is often referred to as "Rogers Plan II" or the "Second Rogers Plan," the Secretary proposed that Israel, Egypt and Jordan (who was not a participant in the fighting but who was host to the growing PLO, which Rogers hoped to pressure King Hussein to rein in) agree to a cease-fire, affirm their commitment to Res. 242, and participate in discussions under the auspices of Ambassador Jarring. Israel was not pleased with Rogers' initiative and the U.S. had to make a number of concessions to persuade it to participate. Abba Eban commented:

> Her [Prime Minister Golda Meir's] first response . . . had been negative. But in the ensuing weeks President Nixon deepened his commitment to Israel's security in several ways. He let us understand that his undertaking to me about the Phantoms should be taken seriously, and he gave assurance that Israel would not be expected to withdraw a single soldier from any of the cease-fire lines except in the context of a contractual peace agreement which Israel would regard as satisfactory for its security. There was also an undertaking to use the American veto in the Security Council to resist resolutions calling for a complete withdrawal to the pre-1967 lines.[82]

Eventually all three countries consented to Rogers' proposals which went into effect August 7;[83] however, Israel claimed the following day that Egypt had violated the agreement by moving missiles into the standstill zone. Egypt asserted that the missiles were moved into the zone before the agreement was operative. Since there had been no American U-2 reconnaissance the truth could not be ascertained. Nevertheless, two weeks later the American government issued a statement charging that Egypt was at fault. Israel was "compensated" by receiving additional weapons and being relieved of the requirement to participate in the talks with Jarring (to which it had objected from the outset). Rogers' initiative also led directly to King Hussein's crushing of the PLO in September 1970 (the "Black September" crisis) which included the massacre of thousands of Palestinians (estimates range from 20,000 to 40,000) and the expulsion of the PLO from Jordan.

No further American governmental efforts at Middle East peace-making occurred until 1973 in the aftermath of the joint Egyptian-Syrian military endeavor to retake the territories occupied by Israel in 1967. In the meantime, in February 1971, the new Egyptian president, Anwar Sadat, offered Israel a full peace treaty with security guarantees, based on Israel's return to the pre-June 1967 borders. Israel ignored the offer. In February 1973 Jordan's King Hussein offered to negotiate directly with Israel over the future of the West Bank, allowing that there could be some border changes to meet Israel's security needs as well as Israeli military outposts along the Jordan River and some Israeli settlements.[84] With regard to the Jordanian offer Henry Kissinger commented: "Wryly the King said that all these proposals had already been made directly to Israel and had been rejected . . . On March 1 she [Meir] proclaimed that 'we never had it so good' and insisted that a stalemate was safe because the Arabs had no military options."[85] The Nixon Administration accepted this Israeli rejectionism and perpetuated the myth of the intransigent Arabs.

Perhaps because of the dearth of governmental efforts at peace-making, the initiative to find a Middle East settlement shifted to the private sector. In 1970 the American Friends Service Committee (AFSC) published a remarkable book analyzing the causes of the Middle East conflict and recommending solutions to end it. This represents the first major, entirely private peace initiative, and it is all the more impressive for the solidity of its analysis and for its insistence on self-determination for the Palestinian people—something virtually no one else was then discussing. The following are the major proposals put forward in *Search for Peace in the Middle East.*

> . . . the Israeli government must give forthright assurances on eventual withdrawal from occupied territories as part of an overall peace settlement and should attempt to refute accusations of further expansionist aims. Second, the Arab governments must declare their acceptance of the fact of Israel's existence as a sovereign state and must make clear their willingness to live in a condition of true peace with Israel. Third, the Big Four should declare their readiness to underwrite a peace settlement agreed upon by Israel, Jordan and Egypt and negotiated in consultation with the Palestinian Arabs. . .
> . . . a most urgent issue in the area and before the United Nations

and the Big Four is finding the means to reduce and, it is hoped, to halt the violence. . . .

[The AFSC recommended peace-keeping forces, buffer zones, U.N. supervision of cease-fire lines with one purpose being accurate record keeping of all acts of terrorism by all parties, reducing the flow of arms to the area, and making it a nuclear free zone.]

. . . the creation of a political settlement (along the following) fundamental guidelines. . . :

a) The right of existence for all states in the Middle East must be accepted by all other states in the area.

b) All claims and acts of belligerency of one Middle Eastern state against another must be ended.

c) Israeli claims to the acquisition of territory by conquest in the June War of 1967 must be abandoned and Israel must make firm commitments for withdrawal from territories occupied after June 5, 1967, it being understood that other provisions of the U.N. Resolution will be faithfully implemented.

d) The right of self-determination for the Palestinian Arabs must be recognized by all parties to the conflict and appropriate United Nations arrangements should be set up to determine the will of the Palestinians. Pending such a determination, a temporary United Nations Trusteeship or some comparable type of international administration should replace Israeli military occupation for Gaza and the West Bank.

e) During the necessary interval before the establishment of peace in the area, some form of temporary international authority must be established in the demilitarized Sinai and in the Golan Heights.

f) Jerusalem is unique, and a solution to the problem of Jerusalem will have to be unique. The story of the last two decades is a denial as much of the uniqueness of Jerusalem as of its holiness. . . . the most satisfactory arrangement would seem to be separate Jewish and Arab boroughs, with certain shared municipal services, under some coordinating United Nations agency. That the city should be undivided and demilitarized is obvious common sense. That it should be united under exclusive Israeli control seems unlikely ever to be acceptable to most Muslims and Christians of Palestine. Jerusalem must not again become a divided zone of conflict as it was for twenty years. It cannot peacefully become the sole possession of one religion or one national state.

g) The shipping of all nations must be guaranteed and the right of free and innocent passage through the Gulf of Aqaba and the Suez Canal.

h) The Palestine Arabs who became refugees after the passage of the 1947 U.N. partition resolution have the right, in accordance with repeated U.N. declarations, to one of two forms of compensation. Within some agreed annual maximum, Israel should agree to receive within its 1967 borders a number of returning refugees, who are willing to live at peace with their Jewish neighbors and who will receive compensatory assistance in their reestablishment within Israel.

For most refugees, this course will be neither feasible nor desired. These should receive compensation for the loss of their property, including appropriate payment for the years of non-use of lands, houses and other properties left in Israeli hands. They should receive generous assistance in re-establishing themselves.

. . . Many acts of support will be required on the part of the international community for such enterprises of reconciliation to succeed. . . .

. . . A greater role should be envisioned for international economic aid, and it should be calculated more in human terms and less in international political terms. . . .

. . . A Middle East Bank for Development should be created. . . .

. . . A Middle East Human Resources Institute should be established. . . .[86]

The AFSC's report was received with hysteria in the American Zionist community. The Anti-Defamation League of the B'nai B'rith labeled it a "pro-Arab document masquerading under repeated claims of objectivity in a rewrite of history."[87] Israel's position was complete rejectionism. Indeed, with regard to the Palestinians, Prime Minister Golda Meir, reflecting the Labor Party position, had stated flatly in 1969: "It was not as though there was a Palestinian people in Palestine considering itself as a Palestinian people and we came and threw them out and took their country away from them. They did not exist."[88] As a result of the reaction from American and Israeli Zionists, the report was ignored by the media and others in the mainstream establishment. Nor does it appear to have received any official attention within the U.S. government, although it was widely distributed. However, that those in powerful elite circles— in the public sector, the media and elsewhere—chose to ignore this courageous and important document should not obscure its significance. It stands as the most comprehensive and thoughtful analysis of the Arab-Palestinian-Israeli conflict by Americans to this time. While not without its shortcomings, it is a beacon of integrity and humanity.

After the October 1973 war between Israel and allied Syrian-Egyptian forces, the United States, in the person of Henry Kissinger—then secretary of state as well as national security advisor (and in light of the Watergate crisis, *de facto* head of state)—initiated a flurry of diplomacy in the Middle East with the stated purpose of facilitating a "peace" process. In fact, Kissinger specifically opposed a comprehensive peace settlement, and even the means he employed—the so-called "step-by-step approach"—was designed to obstruct a comprehensive solution. The real objectives of the diplomatic initiative were to: (1) end the oil embargo imposed by Arab members of OPEC during the fighting; (2) facilitate a separate Egyptian-Israeli settlement; (3) exclude the PLO and the Palestinian issue from the political agenda; (4) preclude Soviet cooperation in a settlement; and (5) maintain and strengthen the U.S.-Israeli relationship so as to further the "strategic partnership."

Kissinger succeeded in each of his goals, the most visible results being three disengagement agreements—two between Israel and Egypt (the Sinai I and Sinai II accords), and one between Israel and Syria. The second Sinai accord, concluded in September 1975, is as significant for its American linkages as for its role in the Egyptian-Israeli modus vivendi. It included a Memorandum of Agreement from the U.S. to Israel, that among a host of other American concessions, provided the Zionist state a veto over American relations with the PLO.[89]

The two Egyptian-Israeli agreements laid the foundation for the initiative undertaken by Anwar Sadat in 1977 that led to the Camp David accords in 1978 and culminated in a 1979 Egyptian-Israeli peace treaty.[90] These were but illusions of peace, however.

Given the ascendancy of the PLO after 1967 including: its unanimous designation in 1974 at the Rabat Arab Summit Conference as the sole, legitimate representative of the Palestinian people; Chairman Arafat's invitation to speak before the U.N. General Assembly in 1974—a decision approved by 105 countries (only the U.S., Israel, Bolivia and the Dominican Republic voted against it); the legitimacy the PLO was accorded by virtually every Palestinian—evidenced in one instance by the fact that all but one of the municipal leaders elected in 1976 in the West Bank (in the last elections Israel permitted in the occupied territories) campaigned as "pro-PLO" candidates; and considering the on-going and desperate situation of the Palestinian people who remained dispersed, dispossessed, stateless, and homeless (the majority confined to squalid refugee camps in Lebanon, Syria, Jordan and elsewhere) plus the 1.4 million Palestinians under Israel's military occupation after June 1967— no rational person could continue to deny the centrality of the Palestinian question to Middle East peace. And, indeed there were attempts both within the American government and outside of it to fashion a more realistic settlement than Kissinger envisioned. Some of the efforts were more serious than others—none, however, succeeded in derailing the forces that insisted on excluding the Palestinians.

The first such effort was governmental. The occasion was hearings on "The Palestine Issue in the Middle East Peace Effort" held by the House Foreign Affairs Subcommittee on the Middle East in November 1975. Harold H. Saunders, Deputy Assistant Secretary of State for Near Eastern and South Asian Affairs, delivered a prepared statement that included the following comments:

> . . . the legitimate interests of the Palestinian Arabs must be taken into account in the negotiation of an Arab- Israeli peace . . . the Palestinian dimension of the Arab- Israeli conflict is the heart of that conflict.
>
> . . . in addition to meeting the human needs and responding to legitimate personal claims of the refugees, there is another interest that must be taken into account. It is a fact that many of the three million or so people who call themselves Palestinians today increasingly regard themselves as having their own identity as a people and desire a voice in determining their political status. . . . The Palestinians collectively are a political factor which must be dealt with if there is to be a peace between Israel and its neighbors.
>
> . . . what is needed as a first step is a diplomatic process which will bring forth a reasonable definition of Palestinian interests—a position from which negotiations on a solution of the Palestinian aspects of the problem might begin. The issue is not whether Palestinian interests should be expressed in a final settlement, but how. There will be no peace unless an answer is found.
>
> . . . the major problem that must be resolved in establishing a framework for bringing major issues of concern to the Palestinians into negotiations therefore is to find a common basis for the negotiation that Palestinians and Israelis can both accept. This could be achieved by common acceptance of the above-mentioned Security Council resolutions [242 and 338], although they do not deal with the political aspect of the Palestinian problem.
>
> . . . a particularly difficult aspect of the problem is the question of who negotiates for the Palestinians. It has been our belief that Jordan would be a logical negotiator for the Palestinian-related issues. The Rabat Summit, however, recognized the Palestine Liberation Organization as the "sole legitimate representative of the Palestinian people. . . ."[91]

To be sure, Saunders hedged on the PLO, noting its use of "terrorism" and its refusal to recognize Israel. Yet he also pointed out the representational and popular character of the PLO and specifically mentioned its welfare apparatus for widows and orphans. Most important, Saunders' statement testified to the fact that the American government was aware of the significance of the Palestine issue in the Middle East conflict. However, reaction to Saunders' testimony from pro-Zionist forces in the U.S. and from Israel was severely negative. In an attempt to placate Israel and its supporters, Secretary of State Henry Kissinger called Saunders' statement an "academic exercise explaining in a purely theoretical manner several aspects of the Palestine problem."[92] Kissinger's hypocrisy was revealed by William Quandt, at the time on the National Security Council staff, who wrote that Kissinger had gone over the statement with extreme care before the Assistant Secretary presented it.[93] In addition, Ford and Kissinger made "amends" to the Zionists in January 1976 by using the U.S. veto in the Security Council to kill a resolution that called for the establishment of an independent Palestinian state, Israeli withdrawal from the territories occupied in 1967, and guarantees for the security and territorial integrity of all Middle Eastern states. The Saunders statement may be understood as a "trial balloon," put out by the State Department, but quickly defused when the Zionist reaction was negative. The U.S. government was clearly not to be in the forefront of peace-making.

The first private effort for peace in the post-1973 period involved a study group at the Brookings Institution that published a report in December 1975 entitled *Toward Peace in the Middle East.* The Brookings Institution is one of the key "policy planning groups" in the foreign policy-making network. These groups bring together people at the top of the corporate and financial institutions, the universities, the foundations, the mass media, select intellectuals, and influential figures in government. They review relevant research on topics of national significance and attempt to reach a consensus about what actions should be taken. Their goal is to develop action recommendations—explicit policies or programs designed to resolve or ameliorate domestic or foreign problems which are passed on to the government for adoption and implementation. In addition, through such avenues as books, journals, policy statements, press releases, and speakers these groups influence the climate of opinion both in Washington and the country at large.[94] It is of interest to note that while policy planning groups determine policy on virtually every foreign and domestic issue, on the question of the Arab-Palestinian-Israeli conflict they have been completely unsuccessful. The explanation for this resides in the ways in which Zionist forces intersect the domestic political processes in the U.S. and disrupt the usual elite consensus.

The Brookings report spoke of the need for a "comprehensive settlement" and attested to the necessity of a multilateral forum for negotiations. The report addressed issues of security as well as the nature of genuine peace agreements. On the question of boundaries the report stated: "Israel undertakes to withdraw by agreed stages to the June 5, 1967 lines with only such modifications as are mutually accepted. Boundaries will probably need to be safeguarded by demilitarized zones supervised by UN forces." And, on Palestine:

> There should be provisions for Palestinian self-determination, subject to Palestinian acceptance of the sovereignty and integrity of Israel within agreed boundaries. This might take the form either of an independent Palestinian state accepting the obligations and commitments of the peace agreements or of a Palestine entity voluntarily federated with Jordan but exercising extensive political autonomy.[95]

The report was equivocal about the PLO noting that "its claim [to represent the Palestinians] is not unchallenged." Significantly, however, Zbigniew Brzezinski, who was part of the Brookings study group, became President Jimmy Carter's national security advisor in 1977, and several of Carter's positions on the Middle East appear to have been drawn from this study. Of note too is the fact that behind the scenes, Israel's Ambassador to the U.S., Simcha Dinitz, vigorously fought the Brookings recommendations.[96]

President Carter came to office committed to pursuing a Middle East peace process. His initial objectives included a comprehensive settlement involving a normalization of relations between Israel and its neighbors— that is, exchange of ambassadors, trade, open borders, and tourism; secure and recognized borders with a U.S.-Israeli defense pact as part of an overall settlement; a fresh U.S. position on the Palestine question involving the concept of a "homeland" for the refugees; and a commitment to reconvening the Geneva Conference as a genuine forum for negotiations.[97] (Kissinger had originally organized a meeting at Geneva in December 1973 as mandated by Res. 338 but it was a mere charade.)

The Carter Administration's approach differed from Kissinger's in its emphasis on the need for a multilateral framework for negotiations and on the desirability of a comprehensive settlement. It was initially less wedded to the concept of Israel as an outpost of American power and was willing to bring the Palestinian issue onto the political agenda.

However, the Carter Administration remained faithful to the post-1967 rejectionist "no's" that had become institutionalized in official American political dogma—no recognition of the PLO, no independent Palestinian state, no internationalization of Jerusalem, and no use of American financial or military leverage vis-a-vis Israel to induce concessions in a diplomatic process. And, in the end, despite seemingly better intentions, Carter agreed to a settlement that was entirely congruent with Kissinger's perspective rather than his own stated principles.

Carter's first comments about the need for a Palestinian homeland came on March 15, 1977 at a town meeting in Clinton, Massachusetts.[98] Within the U.S. the president's remarks had an immediate effect—no American leader had ever made such forthright statements about the Palestinians. However, pro-Zionist forces reacted with an overwhelmingly negative response, and the president was forced to back down.[99] Thus, shortly after the Clinton remarks, Carter "clarified" his position: "The exact definition of what that homeland might be, the degree of independence of the Palestinian entity, its relations with Jordan, or perhaps Syria and others, the geographical boundaries of it, all have to be worked out by the parties involved."[100] The "parties" of course included Israel. By January of 1978, as a result of domestic Zionist pressure and Israeli government opposition, the president circumscribed even further the limits of the Palestine question. Palestinians, Carter stated, must be permitted to "participate in the determination of their own future."[101] That "others" would have more determinant roles in deciding that future was implicit. In the Camp David Accords, presided over by Carter in September 1978, the president gave Israel a veto over the disposition of the occupied territories, and relegated the limits of Palestinian political life to "autonomy"—a concept left undefined and in Israel's hands.[102]

On the question of reconvening the Geneva Conference, Carter worked quite hard during his first ten months in office to bring such a meeting to fruition. Israel, however, was very displeased by the prospect of what it, incorrectly, perceived as the portent of an "imposed settlement," and was extremely unenthusiastic about a Geneva Conference. Nevertheless, Carter persisted even to the extent of participating with Moscow in a joint statement on the Middle East as a prelude to convening the conference. A Soviet-American communique, issued on October 1, 1977, called for: (1) Israeli withdrawal from occupied Arab lands; (2) resolution of the Palestinian question, including insuring the legitimate rights of the Palestinian people; (3) termination of the state of war between Israel and the Arabs with the establishment of normal, peaceful relations among the countries on the basis of mutual recognition, territorial integrity, and political independence; (4) international guarantees (in which both the U.S. and the Soviet Union would participate) to ensure compliance with the terms of the settlement; and (5) reconvening the Geneva Conference as the appropriate vehicle for negotiations.[103] The statement was also significant for what it did not say: it did not mention the PLO; it said nothing about a Palestinian state; and Israel was not asked to return to the pre-1967 war borders or to abandon East Jerusalem.

The Israeli government and pro-Israeli forces in the United States reacted to the communique with outrage and hysteria. Typical was the statement of Rabbi Alexander M. Schindler, Chairman of the Conference of Presidents of Major American Jewish Organizations, who said of the joint statement: "On its face, it represents an abandonment of America's historic commitment to the security and survival of Israel."[104] To emphasize its disapproval, Israel dispatched Foreign Minister Moshe Dayan to the U.S. to "consult" with President Carter. After a lengthy session at a New York hotel, a U.S.-Israeli "joint working paper" was issued in which the president agreed that the U.S.-Soviet declaration was "not a pre-requisite for the reconvening and conduct of the Geneva Conference," and promised never to use military or economic sanctions to pressure Israel to make concessions in a negotiating process. Carter thus negated the statement in which he had just participated with Moscow and forswore all American leverage (economic and military aid) to mitigate Israeli inflexibility.

On November 19, 1977 President Sadat made his historic trip to Israel. This initiative, in combination with Israel's opposition to Carter's substantive and methodological approach, led to the demise of the president's previously stated objectives, i.e., convening the Geneva Conference, a comprehensive Middle East settlement, and a resolution of the Palestinian issue. More disheartening still is the fact that the end result of the bilateral Egyptian-Israeli "peace" was a serious deterioration in the Palestinian situation. This occurred because Israel used the 1979 treaty with Egypt as cover and legitimation for: (1) an aggressive extension of its settlement and colonization program on the West Bank and Gaza; (2) the tightening of its repressive military rule in the occupied territories; and (3) a savage invasion of Lebanon in 1982 which included destruction of the Palestinian refugee camps in South Lebanon and the rendering homeless of more than 200,000 persons, the bombardment and siege of West Beirut for ten weeks, some 20,000 civilian deaths, overseeing the massacre of hundreds of Palestinian civilians by its Lebanese allies in Sabra and Shatila, and driving the PLO from the country.

Significantly, even before the 1982 war numerous individuals recognized the inherent dangers in the separate Cairo-Tel Aviv entente, and several efforts were made to devise a peace process that was more genuinely comprehensive in nature. All of these came from the private sector; official Washington did not involve itself in the search for peace until after the devastation of Israel's war in Lebanon. The private initiatives were products of the International Peace Academy, the Seven Springs Center, the American Enterprise Institute, and the American Friends Service Committee. All of these groups, except the AFSC, are part of the policy planning network, although the American Enterprise Institute is by far the most influential. The proposals of each are examined below.

John Edwin Mroz prepared a major study of the Middle East conflict, analyzing its causes, and suggesting alternative solutions, as a member of the Middle East Task Force of the International Peace Academy.[105] In *Beyond Security*, published in 1980, Mroz argued that the *private* views of Arabs, Palestinians and Israelis were far more conciliatory, and demonstrated a greater willingness to experiment with new options than the *public* positions articulated by the *same* people; that the main stumbling block to progress toward peaceful solutions was the negative perceptions each group held about threats to its security; and that the key to peacemaking in the Middle East lay in bringing the protagonists' perceptions about security issues closer to the factual reality (which Mroz viewed as involving more security for each actor than the actors themselves perceived).[106] Mroz's main thesis was that:". . . security for people and territory remains the cornerstone which must support any settlement."[107] It was Mroz's sensitivity to the security concerns of each party that gave this work its strength and uniqueness.

The International Peace Academy was also attentive to the substantive issues in the Middle East conflict, as evidenced by the comments of the president of the Academy in the introduction:

> Only a solution of the Palestinian question will prevent the disintegration of Lebanon and decide the future of the West Bank, as well as Jerusalem and the Gaza. Only then will the security of Israelis and Arabs be assured, peace between Israel and its neighboring Arab states become possible, and comprehensive settlement be achieved in the Middle East.[108]

Of the Palestinians, Mroz wrote:

> The Palestinians recognize the Israelis' ability to maintain control over the occupied territories for the foreseeable future. They see a reversal of U.S. policy as the key to influencing the Israelis, believing that the Israelis will never choose to leave the West Bank

and Gaza. Palestinians believe that although most of the world community has condemned the occupation and the expanding settlements and has called for a return to the 1967 borders, the rhetorical support has not been translated into practical support, such as pressure on Israel to make concessions. The Israeli experience since 1948 was regularly cited as one continuous example of how the Israelis have worked to deny the Palestinians the right to self-determination and their homeland. . . .

The Palestinians argue that Israel is attempting to alter the very character of the occupied territories through its policies of establishing Jewish settlements; deporting Arabs; restricting the development of the economy by discouraging outside investment in industry and placing severe restrictions on everything from export of foodstuff to Israel and other countries to drilling for water on Arab lands; discouraging creation of jobs which would keep young educated Palestinians in the territories; and other practices which harass and complicate the daily life of the Arab people in the occupied territories. . . .

Most Palestinians agree with a PLO official who said, "The policies are deliberate and clear: to destroy all vestiges of the Palestinian character of the land and build a Jewish structure to become part of Israel. . . . "

In the meantime the PLO continues to build its infrastructure, which today includes dozens of factories in Lebanon, modern hospitals, nursing and other schools, an extensive pension system for families of those who have died in the conflict, a computer center for statistical and financial information, a scholarship program for university students, a tax collection system including five percent of the wages of Palestinians working in the Gulf and other states, and a large, democratically elected Palestine National Council (301 members). "It becomes evident," argues a retired Jordanian Cabinet member, "that the PLO is in fact a government in exile—and a government with a track record that is more impressive than perhaps 75 member states in the United Nations, in term of its services, efficiency, and, I would even say, democracy."[109]

Mroz's characterization of the Israeli occupation, though couched in terms of "Palestinian perceptions" is clear and accurate; his description of the social and political aspects of the PLO is factual and evidences more knowledge than most "experts"—scholarly or other—possessed about the organization.

Moreover, despite his emphasis on security and perceptions of threat, Mroz was also concerned about questions of substance. He analyzed in detail two possible compromise options for resolving the Palestinian issue (though he was careful not to advocate either): (1) a neutral Palestinian state on the model of Austria or Switzerland; and (2) a confederation of a Palestinian entity or state with Jordan. He analyzed the juridical and political meanings of neutrality and confederation; the advantages and disadvantages to Palestinians, the Arab states, and Israel of each option; and discussed the security assurances that both would entail. Mroz also recognized the importance of a comprehensive settlement, and addressed the issues of the Golan Heights and Syrian-Israeli security as well as the future status of Jerusalem and the internal reintegration of Lebanon. Mroz emphasized that Israel will have to withdraw from the Golan, and suggested several possible security arrangements. Mroz considered Jerusalem the most difficult issue and admitted that the majority of Israelis, even in private, are not willing to compromise over the city. Yet he also acknowledged that the Muslim attachment to Jerusalem is equally as strong as the Jewish attachment. He suggested three possible compromise solutions, though I think none would be acceptable to Muslims. On this issue, more than any other, the author seemed to feel that Israeli domination, at least *de facto*, was unlikely to change. Finally, Mroz stated with an unusual clarity of vision: "Until the Palestinian question is resolved, there can be no peace for the Lebanese people."[110]

In sum Mroz argued that a comprehensive and lasting peace must be predicated on three things:(1) "Basic security has to be grounded in normal relations between neighboring states." (2) "Beyond the search for security lies the search for a trust which is based on the confidence that the ultimate intention of each disputant is not a desire to defeat others or affect their religion, ideology, or territory." And, (3) "The political will to transform the words into policy" is the key to success.[111] Mroz's concluding words provide a telling insight:

Whether the desire by the people in the region for an end to violence and the achievement of a final peace can be translated into political realities in the 1980's depends in great measure upon the future actions of the region's leadership. These actions can either build confidence that mutual security can be achieved or continue to fuel particular security fears of one or more parties. Their choice will determine whether the decade of the 1980s will witness another war or the achievement of peace and an end to a costly and protracted conflict.[112]

It is of no small consequence that subsequent to the publication of this study, Israeli leaders chose to undertake some of the most boldly aggressive acts in Zionist history, i.e., the formal "annexation" of Jerusalem in 1980; the bombardment in 1981 of a nearly completed French-built nuclear reactor in the outskirts of Baghdad; the bombing of a residential sector of Beirut in July 1981 in which 300 civilians were killed and hundreds more wounded; the "annexation" of the Golan Heights in November 1981; the invasion and occupation of Lebanon in 1982 which broke a cease-fire agreement between Israel and the PLO that the PLO had scrupulously observed for its eleven-month duration; and the massive colonization and settlement program in the West Bank and Gaza. Could any Arab or Palestinian view the Zionist/Israeli entity as anything other than a threat to their security?

In 1981, the American Enterprise Institute (AEI), a highly influential policy planning group, published a study it had commissioned of the Arab-Israeli conflict. In *The Middle East Problem in the 1980s*, Harold Saunders (at the time a resident fellow of the Institute), analyzed the issues in the context of the global significance of regional problems and American national interests, and made a series of recommendations concerning what policies would best serve the interests of the United States in the Middle East.[113] Saunders began with a clear set of assumptions:

> More globally critical issues and issues important to the position of the United States in the world come together in the Middle East in the early 1980s than any other part of the developing world.
> . . . Judgments of the abilities of the United States to play its role as a world power in the 1990's will be shaped heavily by the way we handle those issues in the Middle East in the 1980s.
> . . . Apart from the independent development of U.S. and Soviet military capabilities and barring significant political realignments in Eastern Europe, this volatile area could well be critical in shaping the global balance of power in the 1990s.
> . . . New relations between the emerging nations and the great powers in a rapidly changing world in which power is becoming even more diffused will evolve and will be severely tested in the Middle East as in other areas of the nonaligned world.[114]

In his analysis of the issues surrounding an Arab-Israeli peace, Saunders wrote: "The U.S. commitment to the security of Israel has been reaffirmed without qualification by eight presidents. At the same time, the Arab world is becoming even more disillusioned by what it regards as an unquestioning support of Israeli policies directed at control of all the former Palestine Mandate west of the Jordan River."[115] Saunders further commented:

> ... since the disintegration of the Ottoman Empire, the Arabs have sought the right to work out their own destiny in homelands of their own—the right of self- determination in the full meaning of the term. They have suffered foreign occupation in this area for centuries, most recently within the Turkish Empire. Many of them have seen the Zionist settlement of Palestine and the establishment of Israel as another form of Western colonialism in land they regard as their own. Their understanding of historic agreements relating to the establishment of a Jewish homeland is that this was to be achieved without prejudice to the Arab inhabitants of the land. Today they see Palestine divided and a Jewish state established, but they see nothing on the Arab side of the equation. The goal of those [Palestinians] who accept the division of the land between Arabs and Jews is to exercise the right of self-determination in an Arab portion of a partitioned Palestine. Any negotiating process in which this right does not seem to them to be recognized cannot succeed.
>
> ... Americans should reflect long and hard on the fact that the apparent rejection by the United States of the principle of self-determination is a prime factor in the erosion of the credibility of the United States in the Middle East.[116]

Unfortunately, Saunders significantly qualified the meaning of self-determination and seriously weakened his own analysis of the Palestinian situation: "An independent state is not necessarily the only outcome of an act of self-determination. . . . There are many instruments through which an act of self-determination can take place, including consultation, mediation, negotiation, elections, and referendums . . . the issue is to achieve agreement on a process that allows the exercise of that principle [self-determination] in a practical and politically feasible way."[117]

Saunders was equally unavailing on the PLO, presenting no more than Israel's definition of the organization:

> Israel has refused to negotiate with the Palestine Liberation Organization (PLO), in part because its charter does not accept the existence of the Jewish state and because there is no authoritative, unequivocal, and convincing statement from the Palestinian movement on behalf of a majority of Palestinians that they are prepared to live at peace with Israel. I hasten to add that Israeli authorities

also say they will not talk to the PLO because of its terrorist actions.[118]

Saunders appeared to have retreated significantly from his 1975 testimony before the House Foreign Affairs Subcommittee; and moreover, he chose to ignore all the statements from the PLO—dating at least from the 1977 PNC meeting—regarding Palestinian willingness to accept a two-state solution and live in peace with Israel. Undoubtedly he was bruised by the domestic Zionist outcry in 1975 as well as by Henry Kissinger's rapid *volte-face* at that time. Indeed, Saunders demonstrated his sensitivity to Zionist pressure four paragraphs later: "The difficult questions arise over whether the United States can break the Arab-Israeli impasse and, if so, whether the United States can invest the political capital that would be required. . . . The fundamental strategy for a president is whether he is prepared to pay a high political price in efforts to achieve peace. . . . Whatever is done will produce substantial opposition—perhaps unprecedented pressure from supporters of Israel. . . ."[119]

Saunders' concluding section, "Towards a National Policy," revealed the fundamental dilemma of American foreign policy in the Middle East—the contradiction between the maximization of American national interests and the limitations imposed on the formation of policy by Zionist forces. One is struck by the fact that Saunders (and by implication other members of the policy-making elite) understands wherein American interests lie but are constrained from articulating policies that would serve those interests—or discussing the interests forthrightly—by virtue of Zionist influence. Of note too, is the delicate language employed by Saunders—language that only infers, but never directly addresses, the nature and extent of Zionism's hold on the American government. The following rather lengthy passage is presented because it so clearly illustrates the dilemma that Zionism has posed for American efforts for peace in the Middle East:

> . . . the work of making policy at its best progresses through several stages. In the *first* stage, there must be a thoughtful analysis of what our interests are, what the trade-offs are between them, and what choices the decision-makers have. In this stage, professionals in and out of government have an obligation to examine all sides of a situation. . . . They would be negligent if they left out any important point[sic].
>
> In the *second* stage, a process of narrowing and focusing the choices takes place. The question of what is politically feasible is introduced

because there can be no viable foreign policy in a democracy without popular support. . . .

The *third* stage centers on taking this exchange to the president . . . the predominant figures are the president's close political advisors. He may also consult with members of Congress. . . .

The *fourth* stage involves presenting the course of action that has been decided upon to the electorate and to its representatives in Congress. . . .

The *fifth* stage begins as individuals, press, and interest groups in the United States react to an administration's presentation of policy. . . ..

If our analysis of the nation's interests leads to the conclusion that an active policy in the Middle East is justified, the next question is that of devising an approach for carrying out that policy. . . . How do we approach an area in which our interests are as complex—and sometimes conflicting—as in the Middle East? . . . Today in the United States there is no broad agreement on the way we should pursue our interests in the Middle East. Often there is not even a common view of what the main problems are. . . .

. . . The United States cannot deal with the Middle East problem piecemeal in the 1980's when there are so many aspects of our interests in flux at the same time. . . . We cannot afford the luxury of addressing one part of the Middle East problem at a time. And we cannot deal with each interest separately, despite our wish to avoid specific linkages among them. . . .

If we try to pursue a strategy that encompasses the full range of our interests in the Middle East, it is necessary to find some integrating concept and to inject some sense of priority. . . .

From one quarter after another, we hear the affirmation that peacemaking is not just the act of establishing greater military power to enforce peace or ending war or preventing violent conflict—that *peacemaking must be rooted in removal of the causes of the conflict and even in addressing the basic questions of human security and survival.* . . . (Emphasis added)

An integrated political-military strategy toward this area might begin with the proposition that the United States in the last two decades of the century needs to give at least as much attention to the strength of its peacemaking arsenal as it does to its military power and its economic strength. . . .

The Soviets thrive on conditions of conflict. They do not thrive where nationalism is strong and offers possibilities for pursuing national growth in an orderly way. . . .

Suggesting that the United States conduct an active and complex strategy toward the Middle East immediately raises the question whether we have the structure or the political base within our political . . . system for the conduct of such a policy.

In the executive branch there are two essential requirements:

The critical one is the full personal involvement of the president and the secretary of state in establishing a strategy and following it through. . . .

The second . . . is an organizational structure to coordinate among the departments and agencies involved in the complex strands of bureaucratic perspective and interest that inevitably find lives and connections of their own when so many separate American interests are involved. . . .

. . . *in the Congress and in our polling booths, consider how often judgments are reached about the Middle East on the basis of a tug-of-war between interest groups rather than on the basis of a bipartisan understanding of our interests in the Middle East and a strategy for pursuing them.* Since that is the way the U.S. political system works, heavy responsibility falls on a president and his key advisors for explaining to the American people what is at stake, for laying out our choices and their consequences clearly, and for setting a clear national policy. We have heard many foreign policy speeches through the years, but rarely have we heard a searching discussion—apart from moments of crisis—from the highest levels of our government of what is at stake for the United States in the Middle East. . . . (Emphasis added)

. . . The Arab-Israeli conflict not only involves the U.S. commitment to the security and future of Israel but also engages the interests of countries throughout the Middle East. The Palestinian cause has even become an important symbol in North-South relations. Active U.S. diplomacy in reducing the causes of conflict and moving the conflict toward resolution is critical to the pursuit of U.S. interests throughout the Middle East and can also enhance the capacity of the United States to deal with conflict elsewhere in the developing world. . . .[120]

It is only necessary to reiterate how clearly this passage illustrates the extent to which the adherents of Zionism have constrained American thinking, talking, and acting in the pursuit of peace in the Middle East.[121]

Saunders assigned responsibility for breaking Zionism's hold over the American government to the president, who he argued, must take the initiative in clearly and compellingly articulating the totality of American interests; in formulating policies that will serve those interests; and in mobilizing public opinion to support pursuit of such policies. It was a hopeful vision but one that political expediency and substantive misperception in the Reagan Administration completely negated. Moreover, after Carter's deeply disappointing performance in this regard, one wonders if Saunders grounded his analysis in the basic realities of American political culture.

A third effort was sponsored by the Seven Springs Center. That organization sent a four-member private study group to the Middle East in August 1981 and issued a report in October entitled *The Path to Peace: Arab-Israeli Peace and the United States*.[122] The report analyzed the readiness to negotiate peace on the part of Israel, the Palestinians, Saudi Arabia, Jordan, Syria, and Egypt, and presented a set of five general conclusions including:

1. Hopes for a negotiated peace between Israel and its eastern neighbors are fading . . . our judgment is that it is essential to reestablish the momentum in negotiation. We reject the thesis that the United States can only assume leadership in the pursuit of peace when it is driven by tragic events.

2. Hopes for a negotiated peace are fading just at a moment when acceptance of Palestinian national identity in the Arab world and beyond and growing Arab willingness to accept the Israeli state have created the best possibility of an Arab-Palestinian-Israeli negotiation since Israel was established. . . . *Arab leaders everywhere we visited expressed acceptance of Israel within defined and secure borders. That was also the position of all Palestinian Arabs to whom we spoke, even those under military occupation. . . . Palestinians to whom we spoke are prepared to make peace if Israel withdraws and they have the opportunity to exercise the right of self-determination in the land Israel leaves.* They believe this would result in an independent Palestinian state in the West Bank and Gaza. . . . We do not believe it is appropriate for the United States now to express its views in favor of a Palestinian state, but we do believe it is inconsistent with the principle of a freely negotiated settlement to rule out a sovereign Palestinian state before the negotiations have taken place. . . . (Emphasis added)

3. Palestinian nationalism and the Palestinian desire for a state— whatever their roots and their status may have been when Resolution 242 was written in 1967—must be fairly faced and dealt with in negotiations in ways consistent with the rights and security of

their neighbors, or the prospect for peace will be radically diminished. . . . Arab leaders whom we met were virtually unanimous in volunteering that Israel's security—as well as that of Israel's Arab neighbors—must be guaranteed in a settlement to assure each side's right to determine its own future in peace and security. . . . *Palestinians in the West Bank and elsewhere as well as other Arabs regard the Palestine Liberation Organization both as the legitimate representative of the Palestinian people and as the expression of Palestinian nationalism. It is a fact—not a policy statement—that no peace will be possible without the PLO being involved in the process in some way.* . . . In our view there can only be a durable peace with a negotiated settlement and there can only be a negotiated settlement if there is a fair compromise between Israelis and Palestinians. A winner-take-all solution favoring the more powerful party will perpetuate conflict. (Emphasis added)

4. If a fair settlement is to be negotiated, a basis for negotiation between Israel and its eastern neighbors—the Palestinians, Jordan, and Syria—will have to be developed. It will have to acknowledge but transcend what was achieved under the Camp David accords and go on to define practical steps toward the peace envisaged in these conclusions. . . . Negotiations could become possible if each side believed the other's position could lead to a fair negotiated settlement. The status of Jerusalem . . . is still challenged and must be part of an overall settlement. . . . Jerusalem should never again be divided by barbed wire or access to the holy places be denied. Peace for Jerusalem must assure free access to the holy places to followers of all religions, and both Israeli and Arab roles in the city's government, reflecting the city's ethnic, religious and political diversity. . . . In our view, however, the next breakthrough on the path to peace is not most likely to come in the autonomy talks but in the evolution of an eastern Arab negotiating front that will present Israel an offer of peace Israel cannot easily dismiss. . . . We believe the U.S. role should be an active one. We also believe that the PLO will have to become involved in some way in negotiations but we recognize the tactics governing their involvement would have to be carefully managed by the authorities involved.

5. There is widespread conviction in the Middle East that only the United States can effectively help to achieve peace, but there is deep doubt that the U.S. is prepared to play a role as a just mediator and to work actively for a negotiated peace. . . . We believe that the U.S. must, in the words of one Mid-Easterner, "wed military and diplomatic strength" in a coherent strategy.[123]

The Seven Springs report clearly went beyond the AEI document in grappling with the issues involved in the conflict over Palestine, but it remained attached to certain notions that in themselves are obstacles to peace. For example, the report avoided calling for an independent Palestinian state though it said the U.S. should not rule out such a possibility at the start of a negotiation. Was that to be understood as a tactical position in the sense that Palestinians were to be lured into negotiations by the absence of a U.S. declaration against a sovereign state, but in the end would be denied such a possibility? Or, was it to have been understood as leaving the question of an independent state as an issue for negotiation? It is not possible to ascertain what the writers actually thought—undoubtedly the ambiguity was intentional. The report recognized the PLO as the legitimate representative of the Palestinians but said only that it must be "involved in negotiations in some way." The phrasing suggests that the writers, while acknowledging the centrality and credibility of the PLO, favored dealing with it indirectly, rather than as a full and equal party to the conflict. This would appear to be contradictory. However, if Zionist influence is factored into the calculation of policy options—which this report did *not* do, even by inference—the constraints on the writers, and the contradiction in the recommendation, is explained. On the question of Jerusalem, the authors assumed continued Israeli sovereignty over an undivided city with some "local" power-sharing. It is striking that in discussing options for resolving the Palestine/Israel conflict, analysts (these and others) ignored the 1947 partition resolution—Res. 181—which remains as valid today as when it was passed, and contains the juridical and political bases for an independent Palestinian state as well as for the internationalization of Jerusalem.

The issue of Israeli occupation of Syria's Golan Heights was not addressed, except tangentially, by the Seven Springs report—surely an unwise omission in the calculation of a just and lasting peace. Moreover, the report placed the onus on the Arabs and Palestinians to offer Israel a peace that it "cannot refuse." Why, it may be asked, must the victims be required to recognize and legitimate those who victimized them when no similar requirement is made of the Zionists? The Seven Springs report shared the AEI document's conviction that the U.S. should play an active role in Middle East peace-making and suggested, similarly, that the American approach should involve a "coherent strategy." Yet, by declining to deal with Syrian concerns, not challenging Israeli sovereignty over Jerusalem, avoiding the issue of an independent Palestinian state, and skirting the need to negotiate directly with the PLO, the writers ensured that their approach would not lead to a comprehensive settlement in the Middle East. Moreover, American policy, as outlined here, was surely not "coherent." Nevertheless, this report must be credited with significantly expanding the parameters of the discussion concerning Palestine. Given the influence of pro-Zionist forces in the domestic scene at this time, the Reagan policy of unqualified support for Israel's most outrageous aggressions, and the fanatically right-wing Likud party in power in Israel, this was a very courageous document.

A fourth private effort for peace, undertaken by the American Friends Service Committee, was completed in December 1981. The conclusions were published in 1982, entitled *A Compassionate Peace: A Future for the Middle East.*[124] As with its 1970 report, the AFSC was far ahead of its countrymen in analyzing the Middle East conflict and recommending solutions. However, this AFSC report was more cautious than the original, undoubtedly reflecting the organization's sensitivity to the hostile reaction the first document elicited. The language here was decidedly softer and the recommendations more carefully framed.

In its chapter on Israel, the AFSC noted: ". . . Zionism. . . was very much a political event, reaffirming the land of Palestine as the Jewish homeland. . . . What did not enter deeply enough into the consciousness of the early twentieth-century settlers was the extent to which their national aspirations conflicted with legitimate Arab claims to the same land."[125] The report devoted a full chapter to the realities of Israel's occupation practices in the West Bank and Gaza, severely criticizing Israeli claims that the territories are governed according to the "rule of law"; illustrating the systematic destruction of native agriculture, proletarianization of the peasants, usurpation of water, and control of electricity; describing the vigilantism of the Jewish settlers; and exposing occupation practices related to control of education, deportation, collective punishment, and other such policies.[126]

In its chapter on the Palestinians, the AFSC wrote: "There are two recent distinct Palestinian experiences that are critical in every Palestinian's consciousness: occupation and dispersion."[127] The PLO was presented in a realistic light, and the report argued that while "for Israel and for the U.S. the PLO was declared an organization with which neither power would deal, for most Palestinians it is *the* representative of their nationalist activities. . . . It is an illusion to believe that some other group exists that can speak on behalf of the Palestinians or engage in any serious negotiations for Palestinians without PLO involvement and endorsement."[128] The report carefully documented the PLO's legitimacy at all levels of Palestinian society, as well as in the Arab world, and in the international system, illustrating that only Israel and the U.S. remain outside the international consensus on this issue. It also documented the transition in PLO objectives from the goal of a democratic secular state of Palestine to an independent Palestinian state alongside Israel. A statement by PLO Chairman Yasser Arafat, made during the 1977 PNC debates, in defense of his aide Dr. Issam Sartawi's meetings with Israelis, was revealing in this regard:

> Are you willing to live together with the Jews? If not, you are using false slogans, since the day the Palestinian state will be created, we shall have to live with the Jews side by side and in peace.[129]

The AFSC correctly apportioned blame for the ongoing conflict: ". . . if the trajectory of Palestinian policy has led it steadily toward limiting its claims and the acceptance of an independent state alongside Israel, the Israeli government policy, especially since 1977, has hardened appreciably, now claiming permanent sovereignty in the West Bank and the Gaza Strip."[130]

How can the Israeli/Palestine conflict be resolved? Again the AFSC demonstrated its courage and foresight. First,"To begin to move toward a peaceful solution to the Palestinian problem, the United States should enter into a dialogue with the PLO."[131] Further, since

> Israeli settlement policies may fast be foreclosing options for peaceful resolution with Palestinians. . . funds [U.S.] given to Israel should be under regular scrutiny so that they are not diverted to building settlements in the occupied territories. The U.S. could reduce U.S. aid in proportion to Israeli expenditures for West Bank settlements as a strong symbolic representation of U.S. disapproval of Israel's claim to full sovereignty in the West Bank and Gaza. U.S. policies in relation to Israel and the Palestinians should reflect a true intent to achieve peace based on a secure Israel and self-determination for the Palestinians. . . . Israel's current policy of sovereignty over the occupied lands seems to foreclose any solution to the Palestinian problem. If Israel wishes a solution, it should halt any further West Bank-Gaza settlements and the creation of an elaborate Israeli infrastructure. Israel could indicate the terms on which it would meet with the PLO in a process leading ultimately to negotiations. . . . Israel could take up the negotiating proposals of the Arab states, with their implied recognition of Israel, and use them to fashion an agenda for further exchange. . . .[132]

Significantly, however, Israel's position on dealing with the PLO was reiterated by Yitzhak Rabin, former Labor Party prime minister, speaking for Prime Minister Menachem Begin, in 1982. The PLO, he said, could not be a partner to any negotiations, "even if it accepts all of the conditions of negotiations on the basis of the Camp David agreements [in addition to Resolutions 242 and 338], because the essence of the willingness to speak with the PLO is the willingness to speak about a Palestinian state, which must be opposed."[133]

The AFSC report discussed the question of security and stated unequivocally: "Terrorism and violence, whether conducted by small guerrilla groups or by the military arm of a state, are inexcusable and morally unacceptable."[134] The report presented the arguments of Israelis (and others) from a variety of political perspectives, including the military, to demonstrate that Israel's security will be best maximized through a political resolution with the Palestinians. An Israeli analyst, Simcha Flapan, was thus quoted: "In the long run, the eradication of terrorism is possible only by eliminating the condition that breeds it. Palestinian terrorism is a result of statelessness and a refugee existence. Only a political solution that offers the prospects of statehood, of a normal economy and a productive life for the Palestinians might put an end to terrorism."[135]

The AFSC report also discussed various options and proposals for resolving the Israeli/Palestinian conflict including autonomy, autonomy plan variants, the Jordanian option, the Eban proposal, and an independent Palestinian state. Clearly the authors favored the latter. Additionally, they presented a series of practical proposals (some already discussed herein) that would facilitate a transition to a Palestinian state. The final comment in this section was left to General Yehoshafat Harkabi, former chief of Israeli intelligence, "a man with a hawkish reputation," who stated: "I am for finalizing the conflict, and you cannot do that without recognizing that the Palestinians, like any other human group, deserve self-determination. . . . Israel will have to get out of the West Bank."[136]

On Jerusalem the AFSC stated: "When Israeli security is ensured and Palestinian statehood assured, Jerusalem may be discussed with new confidence and mutual trust."[137] It did not offer a final solution but presented four assumptions upon which it believed any final peace over Jerusalem must be based:

—there is to be free movement about the entire city;
—for the Israelis, this freedom is not at the sufferance of an Arab authority;
—Arab residents of East Jerusalem are under Arab, not Israeli, rule; and
—Jerusalem is to be the capital of both Israel and the West Bank Arab state.[138]

As regards Lebanon the AFSC declared: "A full internal Lebanese solution will not be possible until the Israeli-Palestinian conflict is resolved and the Palestinians have achieved a political entity of their own."[139] Syria was not dealt with independently in the AFSC study; however, its comments on the November 1981 Israeli annexation of the Golan Heights clearly indicate the group's position:

> the move . . . has the broader effect of directly abrogating the terms of U.N. Security Council Resolution 242. Except for the annexation of Jerusalem and some surrounding West Bank land, this is the most serious move Israel has taken to make explicit its intention to maintain sovereignty over territories occupied in the 1967 war. It further strains the already frail peace process, and again brings Israel into sharp contest with international opinion. . . . It will cause even deeper isolation of Israel. . . .[140]

Despite the good intentions and serious efforts of the various Americans involved in the preparation of the four peace proposals discussed above, not only was there no progress made in the peace process, but in 1982 the Zionist state undertook its most aggressive project to date, the invasion and occupation of Lebanon—supposedly the final attack on the Palestinians, intended to destroy all the PLO institutions in Lebanon, drive the Palestinian population out of Lebanon, and eradicate the spirit and idea of Palestinian nationalism in order to facilitate the extension of Israeli sovereignty over the West Bank and Gaza.

In the aftermath of the war's devastation, the American government temporarily reversed its permissive attitude toward Israel and proposed an official initiative for peace. President Reagan sent Prime Minister Begin a letter on August 31, 1982 outlining the U.S. plan. The president asked for a freeze on Jewish settlements in the West Bank and the Gaza Strip, and suggested that these territories ultimately be linked in a confederation with Jordan. Israel was asked not to annex the areas, and the proposals were placed in the context of a comprehensive plan for the next phase of negotiations under the Camp David formula. The president also pointedly reiterated U.S. opposition to an independent Palestinian state or a negotiating role for the PLO. Israel's reaction to Reagan's letter was immediate and absolutely negative. Thus the president appeared on American television on September 1 to explain the proposals to the American public, hoping to counter Zionist opposition.

In his speech, the president stated that the war in Lebanon had demonstrated that "the military losses of the PLO have not diminished the yearnings of the Palestinian people for a just solution of their claims. . . . Palestinians feel strongly that their cause is more than a question of refugees. I agree . . . [reconciling] Israel's legitimate security concerns with the legitimate rights of the Palestinians can only come at the negotiating table."[141] The president then outlined the American position on a settlement. He retained the Camp David concept of a five-year transitional period of Palestinian "autonomy," and in this context declared that he would "not support the use of additional land for the purpose of settlements" during that time. "Indeed," Reagan said, "the immediate adoption of a settlement freeze by Israel, more than any other action, could create the confidence needed for wider participation in the talks." In addition the president stated:

> Beyond the transition period, as we look to the future of the West Bank and Gaza, it is clear that peace cannot be achieved by the formation of an independent Palestinian state in these territories. Nor is it achievable on the basis of Israeli sovereignty or permanent control over the West Bank and Gaza.
> . . . So the United States will not support the establishment of an independent Palestinian state in the West Bank and Gaza, and we will not support annexation or permanent control by Israel.
> . . . There is, however, another way to peace. The final status of these lands must, of course, be reached through the give-and-take of negotiations. But it is the firm view of the United States that self-government by the Palestinians of the West Bank and Gaza in association with Jordan offers the best chance for a durable, just and lasting peace.[142]

The president also made clear that he would not support a full return to the 1967 borders, remarking that under the pre-1967 lines "the bulk of Israel's nation lived within artillery range of hostile Arab armies. . . . I am not about to ask Israel to live that way again."

One is struck by the consistency of the official American position as expressed in the Reagan Plan: rejection of the PLO as a negotiating partner, rejection of the Palestinian right to self-determination, and rejection of an independent Palestinian state. Nevertheless, the Israeli government totally repudiated it. Begin called the president's proposals "suicidal" and "a betrayal of the Camp David agreements." The Israeli Cabinet voted to reject the plan and to "continue a vigorous program of establishing Jewish settlements on the West Bank in order to consolidate Israel's hold on the area." It announced that forty-two new settlements would be established in the West Bank within five years, with 100,000 new Jewish settlers. In addition, the Cabinet reaffirmed Israel's "right" to sovereignty over the territories.[143] The Reagan Administration ruled out using any form of pressure on Israel to halt the settlement campaign; in fact, the administration's annual subsidy to the Zionist state was increased for the next fiscal year, and Congress then added on an additional sum. Israel thus proceeded to rapidly construct new settlements, and the Reagan Plan faded from the American scene, much as the Rogers Plan had vanished thirteen years earlier.

There were no further public or private efforts for peace in the Middle East save Secretary of State George Shultz's abortive May 1983 Lebanese-Israeli accord.[144] (Lebanon abrogated that agreement in March 1984.) Israel remained in occupation of Lebanon until the summer of 1985, when Lebanese resistance groups managed to inflict substantial enough damages on the IDF to catalyze an Israeli withdrawal. However, the occupation triggered renewed civil war in Lebanon and resulted in ongoing massacres of Palestinians by various Lebanese groups.

In 1985 the American Enterprise Institute published a book by Harold Saunders entitled *The Other Walls: The Politics of the Arab-Israeli Peace Process*.[145] While the book appeared, as Henry Kissinger's terse comment on the cover noted, to be "a reflection of his own perspective and experience," it was nevertheless important that it came from AEI, indicating the concern in elite policy-making circles over the unresolved question of Palestine. Indeed, while the period from 1980 to 1985 was a high watermark in the U.S.-Israeli relationship and in Zionist influence in American political culture, it was also the period in which the Arab-Palestinian-Israeli conflict deteriorated most seriously. Thoughtful observers were obviously troubled by the implications of the convergence of these two factors.

In his book, Saunders focused upon the human or psychological obstacles that obstruct the peace process. Of this approach Saunders wrote:

> This book is less concerned than the Brookings Report of 1975 or the Seven Springs Report of 1981 with describing a possible settlement. Like the agreement at Camp David, it seeks to define a way of looking at the problem and a process that will lead us toward a settlement. Specifically, we need to know how to shape a political environment in which negotiation can take place and agreements can be fashioned and implemented. My aim is more to refocus perspectives and discussion than to define specific steps or solutions.[146]

Saunders employed psychology, theology, and concepts of affirmation and reconciliation to develop a theory of negotiation. He considered the experiences of victimization of Israelis and Palestinians, and examined ways in which those experiences skewed perceptions. He stressed the concept of national identity, and the importance of both Palestinians and Israelis recognizing each other's identity and humanity as a means of promoting substantive negotiations. Of the Palestinians, Saunders wrote:

> . . . the main elements in the PLO leadership are prepared to see Palestinians living at peace with Israel in a partitioned Palestine. In early 1985, the real debate among the PLO leaders about the shape of a settlement began at this point. The real issues had become pragmatic ones. . . .[147]

Yet in mid-1987, as the present article is written, the Palestinian condition remains unchanged, and the Zionist/Israeli entity continues to reject even recognition of the Palestinians as a people.

Conclusion

The repeated attempts by Americans in both the public and private sectors to find a solution to the conflict between Zionists and the Arab/ Palestinian people illustrates not so much the flaws in the American proposals—though they were many—but rather Zionism's absolute rejectionism on all issues concerning fundamental Palestinian rights, as well as its approach to conflict resolution, which is based on the premise that "might makes right" and is buttressed by an aggressive militarism, made even more threatening by Israel's nuclear arsenal.[148] Since its establishment Israel has behaved as an outlaw state in the international system, making a mockery of international law and world order. Indeed, Israel has refused to abide by the laws, norms, and principles that exist to govern the conduct of states in the international system. Moreover, in spite of owing its legitimacy to the United Nations, Israel has demonstrated utter disregard for the principles and resolutions of the world organization.

After nearly a century of conflict between Zionists and Palestinians, it is clear that there will no peace or stability in the Middle East without a just resolution of the Palestinian issue. Forty years after the establishment of Israel, Palestinians remain stateless, homeless, exiles. There are approximately 4.65 million Palestinians in the world, 57.5 percent (2.65 million) of whom live in diaspora, prohibited by Israel from returning to their homeland. The majority of these reside in squalid refugee camps in Lebanon, Jordan, and Syria in conditions of utter deprivation. Palestinians comprise 15 percent of Israel's approximately 3.86 million people though they are at best "third-class" citizens. In addition, there are an estimated 1.4 million Palestinians who exist as subjects of Israel's occupation authority in the West Bank and Gaza.[149] While Israel is committed to maintaining a Zionist state *and* the extension of Israeli sovereignty over all of Palestine; Palestinians, repressed and brutalized in virtually every country wherein they have been scattered as "refugees" since 1948, are more determined than ever to secure a state of their own in which they can possess and exercise their right of national self-determination. In the collision between the Palestinian quest for survival and the Israeli determination to deny it resides the core of Middle Eastern instability and the potential for a cataclysm that may engulf not only the Near East but in this nuclear era could endanger the entire globe.

A formula for the settlement of the Palestine-Israel conflict exists in international law and United Nations resolutions, and involves the division of Palestine into two states, one Jewish and one Palestinian Arab. The two-state solution has been accepted by the PLO as well as by the entire international community. Only Israel and the U.S. reject it. The two-state concept is the basis of the General Assembly resolution—Res. 181—adopted in November 1947, that originally recommended the partition of Palestine and (with stipulated qualifications) legitimized the establishment of Israel. Moreover, a two-state resolution is grounded in fundamental legal norms that have remained constant over time.[150] While many Palestinians as well as other individuals with universal, humanistic values (including this writer) would prefer to see a democratic, secular state in Palestine where all people, regardless of religion or ethnic affiliation, could live as equal citizens with full access to civil, human, and political rights, it does not appear at this historic juncture that such an outcome is viable. Thus not only is the two-state formula grounded in international law and world order principles but it is the most *practical* solution for the present.

The United Nations has been consistent in its attempt to mediate and resolve the Palestine/Israel conflict. Since 1947, the General Assembly has passed a series of additional resolutions reaffirming Res. 181 and defining Palestinian rights.[151] (Israel, backed by the United States and relying on military coercion, has ignored each resolution.) The Security Council too, has contributed to the effort to find a settlement. Res. 242, passed in the aftermath of the June 1967 war, requires Israel to withdraw from the territories it occupied during the hostilities, calls for the "termination of all claims or states of belligerency," and for the establishment of peace based on territorial integrity and political independence. While Res. 242 is flawed by its failure to treat the Palestinians as anything but refugees, it does provide the basis for Israeli withdrawal from the West Bank and Gaza, and Israel's compliance would create the space for the establishment of an independent Palestinian state. The Security Council reaffirmed the basic principles of Res. 242 in the aftermath of the October 1973 war, in Res. 338. (As with the General Assembly resolutions, Israel has rejected all efforts to secure its withdrawal from the West Bank and Gaza derived from Security Council declarations.) A further Security Council effort involved a draft resolution that was placed before the Council in January 1976, supported by Egypt, Syria, Jordan, the PLO, and the Soviet Union, calling for a Middle East settlement based on the 1967 borders, with "appropriate arrangements . . . to guarantee . . . the sovereignty, territorial integrity, and political independence of all states in the area [including Israel and a new Palestinian state] and their right to live in peace within secure and recognized boundaries."[152] (At Israel's urging, the United States used its veto to kill the resolution.)[153]

As discussed in the text, Res. 242 has been the "official" basis of American policy toward the Arab-Israeli conflict since 1967, though U.S. tolerance and facilitation of Israel's annulment of the resolution is indicative of the real American position. Nevertheless, the U.S. has made the PLO's *unconditional* acceptance of Res. 242 a prerequisite for American recognition and negotiation with the PLO. (Israel, as noted above in Yitzhak Rabin's statement, insists that it will never recognize or negotiate with the PLO even if it accepts all the conditions of negotiations on the basis of the Camp David agreements and Resolutions 242 and 338.)[154] However, since Res. 242 treats Palestinians as "refugees" rather than as a national community, it is an unacceptable basis, by itself, for a settlement of the Palestine question. Were Palestinians to accept it unipartite, that would mean a unilateral Palestinian recognition of Israel and a negation of the Palestinian right to self-determination. It would also lend credence to Jordan's illegitimate claim to the West Bank.

But the PLO has said that it will accept Res. 242 together with *all* U.N. resolutions dealing with the Palestinian question in the context of mutual recognition between the PLO and Israel. At the 13th Palestine National Council (PNC) meeting in March 1977, the PLO formally declared its willingness to enter into an international peace process and replaced its previous policy of a democratic secular state *of* Palestine with acceptance of an independent national state in part of Palestine.[155] Agreeing to the two-state formula represented an enormous compromise by Palestinians though it was unremarked upon by Israel or the United States.

In one demonstration of its ongoing efforts since 1977 to seek a peaceful solution, the PLO submitted to American officials three proposals on February 5, 1986, clarifying its position on a peace settlement. Statements from the proposals include the following:

... The PLO would agree to participate in this conference [an international conference under the auspices of the Security Council—based on Res. 38/58—see below] on an equal footing within a joint Jordanian-Palestinian delegation and on the basis of securing the legitimate rights of the Palestinian people, including their right to self-determination within a confederation with the Hashemite Kingdom of Jordan, as stipulated in the Jordanian-Palestinian accord signed in February 1985 and on the basis of implementing UN and Security Council resolutions pertinent to the Palestine question, including Resolutions 242 and 338.

In this context, the PLO reaffirms its condemnation of terrorism as confirmed in the Cairo Declaration...

... The PLO expresses its readiness to negotiate within the framework of an international conference attended by the permanent members of the Security Council with all the concerned parties, including Israel, on the basis of the Jordanian-Palestinian accord ... and on the basis of UN resolutions pertaining to the Palestine question, including Security Council Resolutions 242 and 338.[156]

Israel and the United States rejected these PLO proposals.[157]

The most recent initiative undertaken by the General Assembly to facilitate a solution to the Palestine-Israel conflict is Resolution 38/58, passed on December 13, 1983 (referred to in the above PLO proposals). This resolution calls for an international conference under the auspices of the Security Council with the U.S., the U.S.S.R., Israel, the PLO, Syria, Lebanon, Jordan, and Egypt participating on an equal footing, in conformity with the following principles:

a) the attainment by the Palestinian people of its legitimate inalienable rights, including the right to return, the right to self-determination and the right to establish its own independent state in Palestine;

b) the right of the Palestine Liberation Organization, the representative of the Palestinian people, to participate on an equal footing with other parties in all efforts, deliberations and conferences on the Middle East;

c) the need to put an end to Israel's occupation of the Arab territories, in accordance with the principle of the inadmissibility of the acquisition of territory by force, and, consequently, the need to secure Israeli withdrawal from the territories occupied since 1967, including Jerusalem;

d) the need to oppose and reject such Israeli policies and practices in the occupied territories, including Jerusalem, and any *de facto* situation created by Israel as are contrary to international law and relevant United Nations resolutions, particularly the establishment of settlements, as these policies and practices constitute major obstacles to the achievement of peace in the Middle East;

e) the need to reaffirm as null and void all legislative and administrative measures and actions taken by Israel, the Occupying Power, which have altered or purported to alter the character and status of the Holy City of Jerusalem, including the expropriation of land and property situated thereon, and in particular the so-called "Basic Law" on Jerusalem and the proclamation of Jerusalem as the capital of Israel;

f) . . . the right of all states in the region to exist within secure and internationally recognized boundaries, with justice and security for all the people, the *sine qua non* of which is the recognition and attainment of the legitimate, inalienable rights of the Palestinian people. . . .[158]

Following the passage of this resolution, the U.N. Secretary General addressed letters to all the parties directly concerned to ascertain their views on the organization and convening of an international conference. Israel and the United States categorically rejected the resolution and stated they would never participate in such a conference. The Soviet Union, Syria, Jordan, Egypt, the PLO, and Lebanon agreed to participate. Israeli rejectionism, backed by its American patron, was again notable. Subsequently, however, Israel's Labor Party leader, Shimon Peres, gained considerable diplomatic recognition for advocating an "international conference." But Peres' concept of such a conference was the direct opposite of the intention of Res. 38/58.[159]

Nevertheless, the soundest, most equitable means of resolving the Palestine-Israel conflict resides in the concept of an international conference based on the procedural and substantive principles outlined by Res. 38/58. In the words of two international legal authorities: "The alternative to enforcement of the law is to accept an international system based upon the use of military power outside the law. Such a system is the antithesis of a just and stable peace and requires the entire world community to live under the cloud of impending nuclear catastrophe."[160] It is to be hoped that at some point the collective will of the global community will transcend Israel's rejectionism and militarism, supported by U.S. acquiescence, and impose a settlement consonant with the principles, laws, and norms that form the basis of the international commonwealth of nations and that provide the only genuine guidelines for the peaceful resolution of international disputes.

NOTES

1. Shabtai Teveth, *Ben-Gurion and the Palestinian Arabs: From Peace to War*, New York, Oxford University Press, 1985, pp.198-99.
2. *Ibid.*, p. 159.
3. Quotation in Bernard Avishai, *The Tragedy of Zionism: Revolution and Democracy in the Land of Israel*, New York, Farrar Straus Giroux, 1985, p. 50, and pp. 57-58.
4. *Ibid.* p. 54.
5. Teveth, *Ben-Gurion*, pp. 171-72.
6. Avishai, *The Tragedy of Zionism*, p. 49.
7. Teveth, *Ben-Gurion*, p. 181.
8. Benny Morris, "The Causes and Character of the Arab Exodus from Palestine: The Israeli Defense Forces Intelligence Branch Analysis of June 1948," *Middle Eastern Studies* (London), January 1986.
9. Benny Morris, "Operation Dani and the Palestine Exodus from Lydda and Ramle in 1948," *The Middle East Journal*, Vol. 40, no. 1, Winter 1986, pp. 82-109. Also: Benny Morris, "Haifa's Arabs: Displacement and Concentration, July 1948," *The Middle East Journal*, Vol. 42, no. 2, Spring 1988, pp. 241-259.
10. Benny Morris, "The Harvest of 1948 and the Creation of the Palestinian Refugee Problem," *The Middle East Journal*, Vol. 40, no. 4, Autumn 1986, pp. 671-85.
11. Menachem Begin, *The Revolt*, London, W.H. Allen, 1951, quoted in I.F. Stone, "The Other Zionism," in *Underground to Palestine: And Reflections Thirty Years Later*, New York, Pantheon Books, 1978, pp. 258-59.
12. Tom Segev, *1949: The First Israelis*, New York, The Free Press, 1986, p. 28. Of course, non-Zionist scholars and analysts have been saying for decades what Segev, Teveth, and Morris are only now addressing. See for example: Ibrahim Abu-Lughod, ed., *The Transformation of Palestine: Essays on the Origin and Development of the Arab-Israeli Conflict*, Evanston, Ill., Northwestern University Press, 1971; Sabri Jiryis, *The Arabs in Israel*, New York, Monthly Review Press, 1976; and others.
13. Segev, *1949*, p. 29.
14. Uri Avnery, *My Friend, the Enemy*, Westport, Conn., Lawrence Hill & Co., 1986, p.86.
15. *Ibid.*, p. 86.
16. Teveth, *Ben-Gurion*, pp. 161-63; 187.
17. Ben Halpern, *The Idea of the Jewish State*, second edition, Cambridge, Harvard University Press, 1969, p. 296. Also see p. 304 for more details of the areas "required."
18. Segev, *1949*, p. xviii.
19. For the texts of the armistice agreements see: "General Armistice Agreement between Israel and Egypt, February 24, 1949:" "General Armistice Agreement between Israel and Lebanon, March 23, 1949;" "General Armistice Agreement between Israel and Jordan, April 3, 1949;" and "General Armistice Agreement between Israel and Syria, July 20, 1949" in John Norton

Moore, editor, *The Arab-Israeli Conflict III: Documents* (American Society of International Law), Princeton, New Jersey, Princeton University Press, pp. 380-414.

20. Segev, *1949*, p. 6.
21. *Ibid.*, p. 13.
22. *Ibid.*, p. 20.
23. *Ibid.*, p. 14. For an excellent analysis and documentation of Jordanian and Zionist collusion to negate Palestinian interests see Avi Shalaim, *Collusion Across the Jordan: King Abdullah, The Zionist Movement, and the Partition of Palestine*, London, Oxford University Press, 1988. Also see: Michael J. Cohen, *Palestine and the Great Powers 1945-1948*, Princeton, New Jersey, Princeton University Press, 1982. And: Dan Raviv and Yossi Melman, "Hussein's Secret Talks with Israel," *Miami Herald*, May 10, 1987, who detailed the many meetings between Jordan's King Hussein and Israeli leaders over the years.
24. Segev, *1949*, p. 16.
25. *Ibid.*, pp. 16-17.
26. Avnery, *My Friend*, p. 58.
27. Segev, *1949*, p. 23.
28. Abba Eban, *Abba Eban: An Autobiography*, New York, Random House, 1977, p. 149. For an analysis of the juridical status of Jerusalem see: W. Thomas Mallison and Sally V. Mallison, *The Palestine Problem in International Law and World Order*, London, Longman Group Limited, 1986, pp. 207-239.
29. Segev, *1949*, p. 23.
30. *Ibid.*, p. 35.
31. *Ibid.*, p. 40.
32. *Ibid.*, p. 40.
33. *Ibid.*, pp. 41-42.
34. Teveth, *Ben-Gurion*, p. 200.
35. For an analysis of that issue see Cheryl A. Rubenberg, *Israel and the American National Interest: A Critical Examination*, Champaign, University of Illinois Press, 1986.
36. See for example Uri Davis, *Israel: An Apartheid State*, London, Zed books, 1987.
37. The central thesis of Avishai's *The Tragedy of Zionism*, is the absence of a meaningful concept or practice of democracy in Israel.
38. Mallison and Mallison, *The Palestine Problem*, provide a superb analysis of Israel's persistent violations of international law and disregard of United Nations resolutions.
39. "United States War Aims: President Wilson's XIV Points Speech to Congress (excerpts), January 8, 1918," in Ralph H. Magnus, editor, *Documents on the Middle East*, Washington, D.C., American Enterprise Institute for Public Policy Research, 1969, p. 27.
40. The promises to the Arabs were contained in a series of letters between Sir Henry McMahon, the British High Commissioner for Egypt, and Sharif Hussein of Mecca (and the Hejaz), between July 14 and December 13, 1915, known as "The Hussein-McMahon Correspondence." For a full text of these letters see George Antonius, *The Arab Awakening*, New York, G.P. Putnam & Sons, 1946, pp. 413-27.
41. The Balfour Declaration was a letter dated November 2, 1917 from Lord

Arthur James Balfour, the British Foreign Secretary, to Lord Rothschild. For the full text see Moore, *Documents*, pp. 31-32. Also see Mallison and Mallison, *The Palestine Problem*, who argue convincingly that the Balfour Declaration *protected* Palestinian rights; and, moreover, that the protection clause supersedes in international law the clause which states that the "government view with favor. . . "

42. For the provisions of the Mandate see: "The Mandate for Palestine Confirmed by the Council of the League of Nations on July 24, 1922. . . " in Moore, *Documents*, pp. 74-84.

43. "The Sykes-Picot Agreement, May 16, 1916," in Moore, *Documents*, pp. 24-28.

44. "Excerpt from the Report of the American Section of the International Commission on Mandates in Turkey (The King-Crane Commission), August 28, 1919," in Moore, *Documents*, pp. 51-63.

45. Mallison & Mallison, *The Palestine Problem*, p. 91.

46. "Excerpt from the Report of the Anglo-American Committee of Enquiry Regarding the Problems of European Jewry and Palestine, April 20, 1946," in Moore, *Documents*, pp. 244-53.

47. On Israel's present nuclear capability see "Revealed: the Secrets of Israel's Nuclear Arsenal," *The Sunday Times* (London), October 5, 1986. The information obtained by the *Times* was provided by an Israeli nuclear technician, Mordechai Vanunu. For an article analyzing the suppression of this critical information in the American media see Nabeel Abraham, "Covering Israel's Bomb in America," *Mideast Monitor*, Vol. 4, no. 1, April 1987.

48. "Statement of the Jewish Agency Concerning the Report of the Anglo-American Committee of Enquiry, May 1, 1946," in Moore, *Documents*, p. 256.

49. For an allusion by a Zionist to the pressure tactics used by Zionists see Halpern, *The Idea of the Jewish State*, p. 364.

50. There is much information to support this assertion in the government's own documents. See *Foreign Relations of the United States, 1947, Vol.5, The Near East, South Asia and Africa*, Washington, D.C., U.S. Government Printing Office, 1975, pp. 1166-70 (especially 1153-59), 1248, 1281-82, 1290, 1291, 1305-9 and others.

51. The best analysis of the domestic political factors affecting Truman's decisions on Palestine is John Snetsinger, *Truman, the Jewish Vote, and the Creation of Israel*, Stanford, Cal., Hoover Institution Press, 1974.

52. William Eddy, *F.D.R. Meets Ibn Saud*, New York, American Friends of the Middle East, 1954, pp. 36-7.

53. *Foreign Relations of the United States, 1948, Vol. 5, The Near East, South Asia, and Africa* (in two parts), Part 2, "Israel," Washington, D.C., U.S. Government Printing Office, 1976, pp. 637, 745, 746, 749-50, 759-60.

54. "Report on the Near and Middle East by Secretary of State John Foster Dulles, 1 June 1953," in J.C. Hurewitz, editor, *Diplomacy in the Near and Middle East: A Documentary Record 1914-1956*, Volume II, Princeton, New Jersey, D. Van Nostrand and Co., Inc., 1956, pp. 337-42. With regard to the May 25, 1950 joint communique, commonly referred to as the "Tripartite Declaration," it must be noted that in direct violation of that agreement France sold Israel a continuing supply of heavy arms including aircraft and tanks, and Britain (together with Canada) sold it a variety of major arms—

all with U.S. blessing and dollars, while Washington itself sold Israel small armaments.

55. See for example the comments by Eban, *Abba Eban*, p. 181.
56. On the Lavon affair see Stephen Green, *Taking Sides: America's Secret Relations with a Militant Israel*, New York, William Morrow, 1984, pp. 107-14, and Avishai, *The Tragedy of Zionism*, pp. 197-200, 219-25.
57. Earl Berger, *The Covenant and the Sword: Arab-Israeli Relations 1948-56*, London, Routledge & Kegan Paul, 1965, p. 136.
58. *Ibid.*, p. 137.
59. *Ibid.*, pp. 138-39.
60. *Ibid.*, p. 141.
61. *Ibid.*, pp. 140-41.
62. For additional analysis of this issue see: Georgiana G. Stevens, *Jordan River Partition*, Stanford, Cal., Hoover Institution, 1965; Kathryn B. Doherty, "Jordan Waters Conflict," *International Conciliation*, No. 553, May 1965; John C. Campbell, "American Efforts for Peace," in *The Elusive Peace in the Middle East*, edited by Malcolm Kerr, Albany, State University of New York Press, 1975, p. 278; and U.S. Department of State, *Department of State Bulletin*, 5 September 1955, pp. 378-380.
63. Campbell, "American Efforts for Peace," p. 279. Also see U.S. Congress, 90th Congress, 1st Session, Senate Committee on Foreign Relations, *Hearings Before the Committee on Foreign Relations on S. Res. 155*, Washington, D.C., U.S. Government Printing Office, 1967, pp. 60-61.
64. "A Direct Appeal to the Israelis and Arabs: Speech by Assistant Secretary of State Byroade, April 9, 1954," (excerpt) in Magnus, *Documents*, pp. 167. See *Department of State Bulletin*, April 26, 1954, pp. 628-33 for a complete transcript of the speech.
65. For an account of this Egyptian-American initiative see Elmore Jackson, *Middle East Mission: The Story of a Major Bid for Peace in the Time of Nasser and Ben-Gurion*, New York, W.W. Norton & Co., 1983.
66. A transcript of the speech may be found in the *Department of State Bulletin*, May 10, 1954, pp. 708-711.
67. Eban, *Abba Eban*, pp. 175 and 181.
68. "Proposals by Secretary of State Dulles for a Settlement in the Arab-Israeli Zone, 26 August 1955," in Hurewitz, *Diplomacy*, pp. 395-98.
69. Jackson, *Middle East Mission*, pp. 91-92.
70. "The Eisenhower Doctrine: Special Message to the Congress on the Situation in the Middle East, January 5, 1957," in Committee on Foreign Relations, United States Senate, *A Select Chronology and Background Documents Relating to the Middle East*, First Revised Edition, Washington, D.C., U.S. Government Printing Office, 1969, pp. 144-50.
71. See Campbell, "American Efforts for Peace," p. 274.
72. Joseph E. Johnson, "Arab vs. Israeli: A Persistent Challenge," address given before the American Assembly, Arden House, Harriman, N.Y., October 24, 1963, text in *The Middle East Journal*, Winter 1964, pp. 1-13. Also see Fred J. Khouri, *The Arab-Israeli Dilemma*, second edition, Syracuse, N.Y., Syracuse University Press, 1976, p. 146. Johnson's complete official report to the CCP was never published.
73. "President Lyndon B. Johnson, Five Principles for Peace in the Middle East, (excerpts), June 19, 1967," in *The Search for Peace in the Middle East: Documents*

and Statements, 1967-79, Report prepared for the Subcommittee on Europe and the Middle East of the Committee on Foreign Affairs, U.S. House of Representatives, by the Foreign Affairs and National Defense Division Congressional Research Service, Washington, D.C., U.S. Government Printing Office, 1979, pp. 286-89.

74. "Security Council Resolution 242 for a Just and Lasting Peace, November 22, 1967," in *The Search for Peace in the Middle East: Documents and Statements 1967-79*, p. 93.

75. "Security Council Resolutions 338 and 339 on Cease Fire, October 22-23, 1973," in *Ibid.*, p. 97.

76. Campbell, "American Efforts for Peace," pp. 286-88.

77. "A More Even-Handed Policy, Governor Scranton's News Conference Statement December 13, 1968 (excerpts)," Magnus, *Documents*, p. 223.

78. "President Richard M. Nixon, News Conference (excerpts), February 6, 1969," in *The Search for Peace in the Middle East: Documents and Statements 1967-79*, p. 291.

79. See for example "Four Power Discussions, Joint Communique, April 5, 1969" in *The Search for Peace in the Middle East: Documents and Statements, 1967-79*, p. 140.

80. "Israel: Cabinet Communique Issued March 30, 1969," in *A Select Chronology and Background Documents*, p. 286.

81. "Secretary of State William P. Rogers, Statement on Peace in the Middle East (excerpts), December 9, 1969," in *The Search for Peace in the Middle East Documents: and Statements, 1967-79*, pp. 292-300.

82. Eban, *Abba Eban*, p. 467.

83. See:"Israel's Acceptance of the Rogers' Initiative, August 4, 1970"; "Reply from the Jordanian Foreign Minister Antun Atallah to Secretary Rogers' Initiative, August 5, 1970;" "Reply from United Arab Republic Foreign Minister Mahmoud Riad to Secretary Rogers' Letter of June 19, August 7, 1970;" "Cease-fire Standstill Agreement between Israel and the United Arab Republic Effective August 7, 1970;" in Moore, *Documents*, pp. 1048-65.

84. Henry Kissinger, *Years of Upheaval*, Boston, Little Brown, 1982, pp. 219-20. Also see Noam Chomsky, *The Fateful Triangle: The United States, Israel and the Palestinians*, Boston, South End Press, 1983, pp. 64-65.

85. Kissinger, *Years of Upheaval*, pp. 219-20.

86. A Report Prepared for the American Friends Service Committee, *Search for Peace in the Middle East*, Revised Edition, New York, Hill and Wang, 1970, 126 pages, citation from pp. 94-104. Members of the working party who researched and wrote the AFSC report included: Landrum R. Bolling, William E. Barton, Colin W. Bell, Alan W. Horton, Paul and Jean Johnson, Frances Neely, Hanna Newcombe, and Don Peretz.

87. Quoted in Alfred M. Lilienthal, *The Zionist Connection II: What Price Peace?*, New Brunswick, New Jersey, North American, 1978, p. 452.

88. *The Sunday Times* (London), June 15, 1969, quoted in Chomsky, *The Fateful Triangle*, p. 51.

89. "Sinai Disengagement Agreement, Egypt and Israel, January 18, 1974," in *The Search for Peace in the Middle East: Documents and Statements, 1967-79*, p. 1; "Golan Heights Disengagement Agreement, Israel and Syria, May 31, 1974," *Ibid*, p. 2; "Second Sinai Disengagement Agreement, Egypt and Israel,

September 1, 1975," with secret U.S. Memoranda of Agreement and assurances given to Israel, *Ibid.*, pp. 3-19. On the veto Israel was given over U.S. relations with the PLO, the wording was: "The United States will continue to adhere to its present policy with respect to the Palestine Liberation Organization, whereby it will not recognize or negotiate with the Palestine Liberation Organization so long as the [PLO] does not recognize Israel's right to exist and does not accept Security Council Resolutions 242 and 338. The United States Government will consult fully and seek to concert its position and strategy at the Geneva Peace Conference on this issue with the Government of Israel. Similarly, the United States will consult fully and seek to concert its position and strategy with Israel with regard to the participation of any other additional states. It is understood that the participation at a subsequent phase of the Conference of any possible additional state, group, or organization will require the agreement of all the initial participants." *Ibid.*, p. 15.

90. The prelude to the Egyptian-Israeli peace treaty was the Camp David Accords. See "Framework for Peace in the Middle East" and "Framework for a Peace Treaty between Egypt and Israel, September 17, 1978," in *The Search for Peace in the Middle East: Documents and Statements, 1967-79*, pp. 20-29. Then see "Egyptian -Israeli Peace Treaty, March 26, 1979" (with annexes and letters, and private memoranda of agreement, assurances, and commitments given by the U.S. to Israel) in *Ibid.*, pp. 30-90.

91. "Deputy Assistant Secretary of State for Near Eastern and South Asian Affairs, Harold H. Saunders, Statement on the Palestinians Before House Foreign Affairs Subcommittee on the Middle East, November 12, 1975," in *The Search for Peace in the Middle East: Documents and Statements, 1967-79*, pp. 305-07.

92. *New York Times*, December 31, 1975 cited in Marwan R. Buheiry, "The Saunders Document," *Journal of Palestine Studies*, Vol. 8, no. 1, Autumn 1978, p.35.

93. See William Quandt, *Decade of Decision: American Policy Toward the Arab-Israeli Conflict, 1967-1976*, Berkeley, University of California Press, 1977, pp. 278-79, cited in Buheiry, "The Saunders Document," pp. 39-40. Quandt was a Middle East staff person to the National Security Council.

94. For an analysis of the policy planning groups (or the policy planning network) in domestic and foreign policy decision-making, see for example: G. William Domhoff, *Who Rules America Now? A View for the '80's*, Englewood Cliffs, New Jersey, Prentice Hall, 1983, pp. 82-112 and Thomas R. Dye, *Who's Running America? The Carter Years*, Englewood Cliffs, New Jersey, Prentice Hall, 1979, pp. 211-215.

95. Report of a Study Group, *Toward Peace in the Middle East*, Washington D.C., The Brookings Institution, 1975, 23 pages, quotes from p. 2. Participants in the study group included: Monroe Berger, Robert R. Bowie, Zbigniew Brzezinski, John C. Campbell, Najeeb Halaby, Rita Hauser, Roger W. Heyns, Alan Horton, Malcolm Kerr, Fred Khouri, Philip Klutznick, William Quandt, Nadav Safran, Stephen Spiegel, A.L. Udovitch, and Charles W. Yost.

96. Lilienthal, *The Zionist Connection*, p. 680.

97. William W. Quandt, *Camp David: Peacemaking and Politics*, Washington, The Brookings Institution, 1986, pp. 558-60. For a detailed analysis of why

Carter undertook an apparently "fresh" approach to the Middle East, as well as why he ended up adopting Kissinger's perspective on virtually every count, see Cheryl A. Rubenberg, "U.S. Policy Toward the Palestinians: A Twenty Year Assessment," *Arab Studies Quarterly*, Vol. 10, no. 1, Winter 1988, pp. 1-43.

98. "President Jimmy Carter, Response to Questions on Middle East Peace, Town Meeting, Clinton, Mass., March 16, 1977," in *The Search for Peace in the Middle East: Documents and Statements*, 1967-79, p. 311.

99. See Rubenberg, *Israel and the American National Interest*, pp. 210-211.

100. *Weekly Compilation of Presidential Documents*, March 21, 1977, p. 361.

101. "Text of Statements by Sadat and Carter Following Meeting Aswan," *New York Times*, January 5, 1978.

102. See footnote # 90.

103. "U.S.-U.S.S.R. Joint Communique, October 1, 1977," in *The Search for Peace in the Middle East: Documents and Statements*, 1967-79, pp. 159-60.

104. "Mideast Peace Initiative Provokes Criticism in the United States," *New York Times*, October 3, 1977.

105. The International Peace Academy is a non-governmental, educational institute devoted to the skills of peacekeeping, mediation, and negotiation. It engages in research, education, and publication—a book previously produced for the institute was Malcolm H. Kerr's *The Elusive Peace in the Middle East* (Albany, SUNY Press, 1975). The Academy's president is Major General (Ret.) Indar Jit Rikhye. The task force that did the research for the volume *Beyond Security* included John Edwin Mroz, Lt. General Wilhelm Kuntner (Commandant, Austrian National Defense Academy), and Major General Rikhye. Most of the information concerning the perceptions of the Arabs and Israelis that forms the basis of the study was collected by the task force from interviews during 1978-79 with 175 governmental and non-governmental leaders in Egypt, Jordan, Israel, Lebanon, and Syria as well as with Palestinians including the PLO.

106. John Edwin Mroz, *Beyond Security: Private Perceptions Among Arabs and Israelis*, New York, Pergamon Press, 1980.

107. *Ibid.*, p. 189.

108. *Ibid.*, p. 18.

109. *Ibid.*, pp. 91-97.

110. *Ibid.*, p. 181. See pp. 136-83 for an analysis of all the points.

111. *Ibid.*, pp. 188-89.

112. *Ibid.*, pp. 189.

113. Harold H. Saunders, *The Middle East Problem in the 1980s*, Washington, American Enterprise Institute for Public Policy Research, 1981, 83 pages. It is stated in the volume that "This analysis was prepared for the American Enterprise Institute project on American Vital Interests in Regions of Conflict: U.S. Foreign Policy Alternatives."

114. *Ibid.*, p.75. Also see pp. 1-5.

115. *Ibid.*, p. 37.

116. *Ibid.*, p. 44.

117. *Ibid.*, p. 45.

118. *Ibid.*, p. 39.

119. *Ibid.*, p. 45-46.

120. *Ibid.*, pp. 74-82.

121. See Rubenberg, *Israel and the American National Interest*, Chapters 1-7 for an analysis of the ways in which the U.S.-Israeli relationship has contradicted U.S. national interests. See Chapter 8 for a detailed discussion of how pro-Israeli forces operate in the domestic political system. For two other pieces that challenge the thesis of Israel as a strategic asset see: Harry J. Shaw, "Strategic Dissensus," *Foreign Policy*, no. 61, Winter 1985-86, pp. 125-41 and Stephen Green, "Strategic Asset, Soviet Opportunity," *American-Arab Affairs*, no. 9, Summer 1984, pp. 46-54. For two important books on the ways in which pro-Israeli forces affect American Middle East policy-making see: Paul Findley, *They Dare to Speak Out: People and Institutions Confront Israel's Lobby*, Westport, Ct, Lawrence Hill & Co., 1985 and Edward Tivnan, *The Lobby: Jewish Political Power and American Foreign Policy*, New York, Simon & Schuster, 1987.

122. The Seven Springs Center is located in Mount Kisco, New York. It says of itself: "Seven Springs Center's aim is to promote scholarship, creativity, and understanding in matters of major intellectual, cultural and public significance. In sponsoring this report, the Center does not embrace any particular view of the issues—or their resolution. It does, however, take responsibility for providing an opportunity for their illumination." In the introduction it is stated that the Center has held six symposia over the past five years directed at an effort to identify issues blocking peace between Israel and its neighbors. Twenty-seven individuals are listed on the board of directors. The members of the study mission included Joseph N. Green, Jr. president of the Center and a former foreign service officer; Philip M. Klutznick, former president of the World Jewish Congress and of the International B'nai B'rith; Harold H. Saunders; and Merle Thorpe, Jr., a practicing attorney in Washington, D.C. and president of the Foundation for Middle East Peace. The report is fully cited as: Joseph N. Green, Jr., et.al., *The Path to Peace: Arab-Israeli Peace and the United States: Report of a Study Mission to the Middle East*, Mount Kisco, New York, Seven Springs Center, 1981, 50 pages.

123. *Ibid.*, pp. v-xii.

124. A Report Prepared for the American Friends Service Committee, *A Compassionate Peace: A Future for the Middle East*, New York, Hill and Wang, 1982, 226 pages with bibliography and appendixes. The working party that prepared the report was appointed by the board of directors of the AFSC and included: Everett Mendelsohn, Professor of the History of Science at Harvard University; Arthur Day, former U.S. diplomat; Joseph Elder, Professor of Sociology and South Asian Studies, University of Wisconsin; Marcia Sfeir-Cormie, former AFSC Middle East staff person; Gail Pressberg, Director, Middle East Programs, AFSC. The working group acknowledged the help of the following people in preparing the book: James Fine, Max Holland, Jonathan Gans, Ann Mosely Lesch, Catherine Essoyan, Charles Kimball, and others for editorial assistance.

125. AFSC, *A Compassionate Peace*, pp. 10-11.

126. *Ibid.*, pp. 25-38.

127. *Ibid.*, p. 39.

128. *Ibid.*, pp. 42-43.

129. *Ibid.*, p. 52. For a detailed analysis of the transformations in PLO policy, strategy and tactics see Cheryl A. Rubenberg, "The Structural and Political

Context of the PLO's Changing Objectives in the post-1967 Period," in *The Arab-Israeli Conflict: Twenty Years After the Six Day War*, editors, Yehuda Lukacs and Abdalla Battah, Boulder, CO, Westview Press, 1988.

130. AFSC, *A Compassionate Peace*, p. 54.
131. *Ibid.*, p. 56.
132. *Ibid.*, pp. 56-57.
133. *Davar* (Israel), November 11, 1982, cited in Chomsky, *The Fateful Triangle*, p. 112.
134. AFSC, *A Compassionate Peace*, p. 65.
135. *Ibid.*, p. 67.
136. *Ibid.*, p. 87. For a full and very important analysis by Harkabi see Yehoshafat Harkabi, *The Fateful Choices Before Israel*, Essays on Strategy and Diplomacy, Number Seven, the Keck Center for International Strategic Studies, Claremont, CA, College Press, 1987.
137. AFSC, *A Compassionate Peace*, p. 87.
138. *Ibid.*, p. 91.
139. *Ibid.*, p. 100.
140. *Ibid.*, p. 24.
141. *New York Times*, September 2, 1982.
142. *Ibid.*
143. *New York Times*, September 3, 1982 and *Miami Herald*, September 3, 1982.
144. For a text of the Lebanese-Israeli agreement see the *New York Times*, May 17, 1983.
145. Harold H. Saunders, *The Other Walls: The Politics of the Arab-Israeli Peace Process*, Washington, D.C., The American Enterprise Institute, 1985, pp. 179.
146. *Ibid.*, pp. 18-19.
147. *Ibid.*, p. 63.
148. For an analysis of Israel's approach to conflict resolution, an apology for the actions of the Israeli state to be sure, but nevertheless revealing, see Avner Yaniv, *Dilemmas of Security: Politics, Strategy, and the Israeli Experience in Lebanon*, New York, Oxford University Press, 1987. On Israel's nuclear capability see *The Sunday Times* (London), October 5, 1986 and October 12, 1986.
149. Statistics from Janet Abu Lughod, "The Demographic War for Palestine," *The Link*, Vol. 19, no. 5, December 1986.
150. Mallison and Mallison, *The Palestine Problem*, pp. 407-24. Also see pp. 142-73 for an analysis of Res. 181 and its foundation in international law.
151. The most important other resolution in this regard is Res. 194 (1949) which calls for the repatriation of Palestinians to their homes or for compensation to those who choose not to return, establishing the *right of return* for Palestinians who are living in exile. Other significant General Assembly resolutions include: 2535 (December 10, 1969), 2649 (November 30, 1970), 2672 (December 8, 1970), 2787 (December 6, 1971), 2792 (December 6, 1971) which recognize the status of the Palestinian people as a colonized people entitled to independence and possessing inalienable rights; Resolution 3210 (October 14, 1974) recognizing the PLO as the representative of the Palestinian people; and Resolution 3236 (November 22, 1974) reaffirming the rights of the Palestinians to self-determination, national independence, and sovereignty.
152. For a text of the resolution see *Approaches for the Practical Attainment of the*

Inalienable Rights of the Palestinian People, prepared for, and under the guidance of, the Committee on the Exercise of the Inalienable Rights of the Palestinian People, New York, United Nations, 1986, pp. 6-7.

153. For an analysis of the resolution and Israel's response see Noam Chomsky, *Towards A New Cold War: Essays on the Current Crisis and How We Got There*, New York, Pantheon Books, 1982, pp. 267, 300, 461 and Chomsky, *The Fateful Triangle*, p. 67.

154. Quotation by Rabin cited in *Davar* (Israel), November 11, 1982, quoted in Chomsky, *The Fateful Triangle*, p. 112.

155. See Alain Gresh, *The PLO: The Struggle Within: Towards an Independent Palestinian State*, London, Zed Press, 1985, p. 206.

156. This document may be found in the *Journal of Palestine Studies*, Vol. 15, no. 4, Summer 1986, pp. 241-43. In February 1985 the PLO and Jordan signed an accord on the basis of an independent Palestinian state to be followed by a Jordanian-Palestinian confederation, and a joint Palestinian-Jordanian negotiating delegation to engage in the diplomatic process. See "Text of the Jordanian-PLO Accord Released February 23, 1985," *Journal of Palestine Studies*, Vol. 14, no. 3, Spring 1985, p. 206. This agreement was signed in the context of a serious split within the PLO, and Fateh undertook the initiative unilaterally. However, after Israel and the U.S. rejected the PLO proposals (parts of which are in the text), Jordan, an American client state, abrogated the Jordanian-PLO Accord on February 19, 1986. For a transcript of Hussein's statement abrogating the Jordanian-PLO agreement, see *Journal of Palestine Studies*, Vol. 15, no. 4, Summer 1986, pp. 206-32. Jordan then made an unsuccessful attempt to undercut the PLO on the West Bank, to strike a separate accord with Israel, and to reassert its illegitimate authority over the area. However, at the 18th session of the Palestine National Council in April 1987, the PLO re-united all its disparate elements and from a position of unity reiterated the Palestinian right to national self-determination and an independent state in Palestine as well as reaffirming its endorsement of an international conference as specified by Res. 38/58. Moreover, the Jordanian-PLO Accord (which in effect negated the Palestinian right to self-determination in an independent state and negated the status of the PLO as the sole, legitimate representative of the Palestinian people) was abrogated by the PLO at the Algiers' PNC.

157. For the U.S. rejection of the PLO's proposals see the letter from Acting Assistant Secretary of State James W. Dyer to Representative Lee H. Hamilton, Chairman of the Subcommittee on Europe and the Middle East, House Committee on Foreign Affairs, in response to an inquiry from Hamilton to Secretary of State Shultz, in *Journal of Palestine Studies*, Vol. 16, no. 1, Autumn 1986, pp. 236-38.

158. *Approaches for the Practicable Attainment of the Inalienable Rights of the Palestinian People*, pp. 19-20.

159. For an analysis of the reasons for the advocacy by Shimon Peres, prime minister then foreign minister in Israel's "national unity government," during the fall and winter of 1986 and the spring of 1987 of an "international conference" as well as an analysis of the Israeli formula for such a conference see Rubenberg, "U.S. Policy Toward the Palestinians: A Twenty-Year Assessment."

160. Mallison and Mallison, *The Palestine Problem*, p. 424.

8

ISRAEL'S CHRISTIAN COMFORTERS AND CRITICS

RUTH W. MOULY

The Religious Right and Christian Zionism

Millions of American Christians embrace the concept of Zionism and give as unquestioning support to the State of Israel as do the most fervent Jewish Zionists. Other Christians consider the idea that Jews have an exclusive right by divine dispensation to rule in Israel as nonsense; some regard the whole matter with indifference.

We begin with a look at those Christians actively and energetically advancing the Zionist cause. Such believers are found primarily in the most influential segment of the Religious Right—fundamentalists, pentecostals/charismatics and dispensationalists—usually referred to simply as "evangelical fundamentalists." They are all outgrowths of the broader, more venerable and pluralistic evangelical movement. When some evangelicals expressed a willingness to adapt their theology to modern scholarship in the early 20th century, fundamentalism arose as a protest against erosion of the faith by Biblical criticism and modernist ideas.

While pentecostals/charismatics stress emotional religious experiences such as speaking in tongues and faith healing, fundamentalists emphasize doctrine. Dispensationalists are found in large numbers in all the other conservative denominations. They believe God is directing human history through a series of dispensations and have a special interest in Biblical prophecies relating to the Second Coming of Christ. These conservative Christians all share the same basic beliefs that characterize fundamentalism, as summarized by Edward Dobson, editor of *The Fundamentalist*:

> Our faith is deeply rooted in our commitment to the inspired and inerrant word of God—the Bible. We believe that the Scriptures are without error, not only in matters of religion, but also in matters of history, science and the cosmos. As such, they are the authoritative guide for faith and practice. We believe that Jesus Christ is the virgin-born Son of God, the promised Messiah of Old Testament Scripture . . . We believe that faith in Christ is the only way to heaven and we are commanded to preach the gospel around the world. We believe that Jesus Christ is coming back to this planet to establish His kingdom and to reign.[1]

The entire right-wing of evangelicalism can loosely be termed fundamentalism. With respect to Zionism, the dispensationalist contribution to fundamentalism is the most significant. Dispensationalists are heavily involved in the study of final events in the history of the world. They are pre-millennarians convinced that Christ's return will precede the millenium and will indeed usher it in. The millennium is anticipated with the greatest longing because it is expected to be God's kingdom on earth—a 1000-year reign of peace, abundance, brotherhood and bliss. The living will be spared from death and faithful believers already deceased will be resurrected.

In times of great upheaval, economic insecurity, wars, and social unrest, the hope of the second coming and the millennium with its promise of release from sin and pain and death gives believers the determination to persist in the face of personal and collective tragedy. They take special comfort from their belief that they don't have much longer to wait for salvation because the end is rapidly approaching. Their analysis of scripture convinces them that we are in "the homestretch of history."

The Book of Revelation contains a graphic description of a time of Great Tribulations—a seven-year ordeal of wars, famines, floods and earthquakes which precedes the end of days—and dispensationalists are certain that the Tribulation is already upon us or just about to take place. Almost any catastrophe thus becomes a fulfillment of prophecy, as Pat Robertson reminds his followers:

We are not to weep as the people of the world weep when there are certain tragedies or breakups of the government or systems of the world. We are not to wring our hands and say, "Isn't that awful." That isn't awful at all. This is a token, an evident token of our salvation, of where God is taking us.[2]

Dispensationalists don't fear the impending doom in any case because they fully expect, as good Bible-believing Christians, that they will escape the Tribulation by being "raptured" before the worst of the horrors begins—physically snatched up into heaven to be with Christ until he returns to the world, while the rest of humanity struggles on through the new dark age.

To them, there are "signs" which indicate the approach of the second coming. The most crucial of these signs is the return of the Jews to Israel. Christ will not come back until the Jews are regathered in their ancient homeland and restored as a nation. The Old Testament contains numerous references to the eventual return to Israel of the Jewish remnant scattered to the ends of the earth, such as Jeremiah 16:14: "The Lord brought up the children of Israel . . . from all the lands He had driven them, and I will bring them again into their land that I gave to their fathers."

Years before the actual return of the Jews in any number to Palestine, evangelical Zionists (predecessors of Jewish Zionists) were looking for this ingathering to happen. When it actually took place they were jubilant, convinced that Biblical prophecies were being fulfilled and the second coming finally nearing realization. For dispensationalists, the establishment of the state of Israel was of enormous interest and import. "Behold," one writer exclaimed, "we who now live are seeing the most significant event of all the ages—Israel revived." The "prophetic countdown" to Armageddon began on May 14, 1948, the date of the founding of the state of Israel. However, the fact that East Jerusalem remained a part of the Kingdom of Jordan somewhat diminished the enthusiasm of pre-millennarians. When the rest of Jerusalem was occupied as a result of the 1967 War there was no doubt that the prophetic time-clock was indeed ticking away. "What a thrill it is to be alive and to see God fulfill his word before our very eyes"![3] exclaimed one zealot. A writer in the most widely-read evangelical journal in the U.S., *Christianity Today*, wrote:

For the first time in more than 2000 years Jerusalem is now completely in the hands of the Jews. This gives a student of the Bible a thrill and renewed faith in the accuracy and validity of the Bible.[4]

Hal Lindsey, author of the best-selling book popularizing the dispensationalist scenario, explained Israel's biblical fate to millions of readers in *The Late Great Planet Earth*:

> To be specific about Israel's great significance as a sign of the times, there are three things that were to happen. First, the Jewish nation would be reborn in the land of Palestine. Secondly, the Jews would repossess old Jerusalem and the sacred sites. Thirdly, they would rebuild their ancient temple of worship upon its historic site.[5]

The first two conditions have been met, but the third remains—the rebuilding of the temple, on the site of two previous Hebrew temples. The Dome of the Rock, the third holiest place of the Muslim faith, where the Prophet Mohammed is reputed to have taken a night journey to heaven, is located squarely in the middle of what is believed to be the old temple site. But for Lindsey and his cohorts: "Obstacle or no obstacle, it is certain that the temple will be built, prophecy demands it."[6] What dispensationalists are doing about the temple issue will be discussed in a subsequent section of this essay.

During the period of Tribulation Israel will be engaged in numerous wars and social convulsions, killing off large numbers of Jews, but a remnant will survive. Some dispensationalists claim that two-thirds of the Jews will perish; Lindsey predicts that only 144,000 will survive, convert to Christianity and become the most fervent proselytizers for the true Christian faith:

> . . . God is going to reveal himself in a special way to 144,000 physical, literal Jews who are going to believe with a vengeance that Jesus is the Messiah. There are going to be 144,000 Jewish Billy Grahams turned loose on this earth—the earth will never know a period of evangelism like this period.[7]

Conversion of the Jews is an essential element of the divine plan in dispensationalist eschatology, but one that is muted by some fundamentalists in deference to Jewish sensitivities, a practice that occasionally causes acrimonious debates in evangelical circles.

As the end of time approaches, vast armies from all corners of the earth converge at Armageddon (the Valley of Megiddo in Israel). A colossal bloodbath ensues between the forces of good and evil. It is commonly assumed that nuclear weapons will be employed during the final conflict (and possibly in the wars during the Tribulation). This is the "nuclear Armageddon ideology" of the Religious Right, chillingly described in two recent books and numerous articles.[8] Just when total destruction is imminent, Christ appears with the saints who were raptured before the Tribulation, bringing the fighting to an end. As the new millennium dawns, all non-believers accept Christ as the Messiah (including the small numbers of Jews who had not already converted) or are damned for all eternity. Christ takes up his 1000-year benevolent, one-man rule of the earth from the new capital of the world—Jerusalem.

These beliefs are the core of Christian Zionism. But Christian Zionism is by no means confined to those who subscribe to pre-millennial dispensationalist theology; it is accepted by numerous other Christians as well. The notion that the Jews are "God's Chosen People" is another belief underlying Christian Zionism. Christians of this ilk want to solace and console Jews in times of collective grief and trouble, harkening back to the words of Isaiah: "Be comforted, be comforted, my people, saith your God." One of the Christian Zionists' most oft-repeated passages from scripture is Genesis 12:2-3 in which God declared that he would make "Israel's name great and bless them that bless thee and curse them that curse thee." Rev. Jerry Falwell maintains that the reason the U.S. has prospered is because it has supported Jews and Israel:

> If this nation wants her fields to remain white with grain, her scientific achievements to remain notable and her freedom to remain intact, America must continue to stand with Israel. God has blessed America because America has blessed the Jews, His Chosen People.[9]

Mike Evans, a Christian Zionist evangelist, insists that "Israel is America's key to survival." Another evangelist warns, "If we choose to oppose Israel, we are going to be fighting against God." To these believers support for Israel is not just an option but a biblical imperative, America's religious duty. For them, unstinting financial and military aid to Israel is a means of obtaining blessings for the U.S., and the fact that the U.S. contributes more in foreign aid to Israel than to any other country in the world is viewed with deep satisfaction among those Christian Zionists who are aware that this is the case.

There are no more steadfast supporters of incorporation of the occupied Arab West Bank into the Israeli state than Christian Zionists. Their uncompromising position on the Occupied Territories comes from a deeply-rooted conviction that this area—Judea and Samaria—is the heartland of biblical Israel, the patrimony given by God to the Jewish people for all time. This, incidentally, is a view shared by the Jewish *Gush Emunim* in Israel. There are differing and contradictory scriptural promises relating to God's covenants with the ancient Hebrew tribes. In Genesis 17:7 is the promise to the Jewish patriarchs and their descendants: "I will give unto thee and to thy seed . . . all the land of Canaan as an everlasting promise," which is a far different land grant than that promised to Abraham in Genesis 15:18: "Unto thy seed have I given this land, from the river of Egypt to the great river, the river Euphrates." Regardless of which "title deed to Palestine" is accepted, Israel is perceived as the rightful inheritor of the lands under dispute in the Israeli-Palestinian conflict today. For Christian Zionists the claims of the Palestinians have no validity whatsoever.

Christian Zionist Influence

How widespread and influential are Christian Zionist beliefs? It is estimated that approximately 40 million Americans are evangelicals, but this is a cluster of disparate elements, certainly not one huge monolith. The Religious Right, in which *dispensationalism* plays a leading role, is a minority of the evangelical fundamentalist community. A Gallup survey found that 37% of evangelicals classified themselves as "right of center" and a pre-millennarian scholar estimated that a conservative figure for the number of pre-millennarians in the U.S. is about 8 million.[10] Whatever its actual numbers, the group which embraces Christian Zionism is the most vocal, the best known and the most influential sector of contemporary American conservative Christianity. The most popular media personalities in the Christian Right are dispensationalists: Jerry Falwell, Pat Robertson, Jimmy Swaggart, Jim Bakker (until his recent downfall), James Robison, Pat Boone; so are the major evangelists of earlier fame who still command large followings: Billy Graham, Rex Humbart and Oral Roberts.

While the ecumenical churches struggle to keep their members, the fundamentalist, pentecostal, dispensationalist churches are booming. The dispensationalist Assemblies of God is the most rapidly growing church in the U.S. A sizeable minority of the largest Protestant denomination in this country, the Southern Baptist Convention, accepts dispensationalist views. Many of the leading conservative Christian seminaries have a dispensationalist thrust, led by the Dallas Theological Seminary, the fountainhead of American dispensationalism. Preachers and teachers of dispensationalist dogma make sure that their constituencies are well aware of their Zionist agenda. In sermons, Bible classes, prophecy conferences, and in the publications of their denominations, the dispensationalists' Zionism is advanced. Zionist themes, emphasizing Israel's role in the end days and the new millennium, are frequent fare in religious broadcasts which reach millions of viewers who may not be members of any church. The Christian Broadcasting Network, beaming its programs by satellite across the nation and around the world, gives uncritical support to Israel. The 700 Club (until last year, Pat Robertson's program) presents interviews with Israeli visitors and Robertson often "educates" his public on biblical prophecy. During the Israeli invasion of Lebanon in 1982 Robertson devoted several programs of the 700 Club to explaining how Israeli troops were fulfilling the vision of the prophet Ezekiel.

Evangelist Mike Evans, a Jewish convert to fundamentalist Christianity, devotes most of the efforts of his ministry to the Zionist cause. He has produced two lavish television programs—*Israel, Key to America's Survival* and *Jerusalem, D.C. (David's Capital)*. These films depict Israel in the most glowing terms, highlighting its achievements and strengths, and totally omitting any mention of its religious controversies, its economic problems or conflicts with its Palestinian population. Much is made of the biblical prophecies involving the return of the Jews to Israel and the need to support Israel in order to secure blessings for the U.S. Falwell's televised *Old Time Gospel Hour* is another conduit for Zionist propaganda as was Jim and Tammy Bakker's *PTL Club* until its demise. There are also numerous lesser known programs which provide radio and television audiences with daily or weekly reminders of Israel's role in the great drama of the end times.

Christian Zionist preachers often lead tours to the Holy Land, making certain that their flocks not only visit shrines and holy places but also meet with Israeli leaders who give them a warm welcome while reminding them about Israel's vibrant democracy and close ties with the U.S. More than 100,000 Christians a year visit Israel, many of them fundamentalists. In 1983 and 1984 Rev. Falwell led groups of 600-700 people to Israel. Interspersed with visits to Bethlehem, Jericho, and the Mount of Olives were meetings with prominent Israelis, like General Ariel Sharon, and a special session encouraging political action back home. Falwell made clear that no one should be elected to public office who does not wholeheartedly support Israel.[11]

Apocalyptic messages, prominently featuring Israel, pour out in innumerable tracts, pamphlets, books, articles and cassette tapes. The shelves in many religious bookstores are bulging with volumes on biblical prophecy. The most popular book of the whole decade of the 1970's was not a new diet plan or a racy novel, but *The Late Great Planet Earth*, one of five successful dispensationalist-oriented books by Hal Lindsey, which led the *New York Times* to name him the best-selling author of the decade. Material relating to the Second Coming has been the subject of films, stage plays, gospel songs and even bumper stickers.

Over the years, whenever American policy-makers seemed to be encouraging Israel to negotiate an accommodation with its Palestinian population on the West Bank, Christian Zionists placed prominent ads in major American newspapers denouncing these efforts. In the fall of 1977, when there was a proposal to convene a conference, which would have included the Soviet Union, to consider a negotiated settlement of the Israeli-Palestinian conflict, a fundamentalist group ran a full-page ad in the *New York Times*, informing readers that "fundamentalists vote with Israel" because "the covenants made with Abraham, Isaac and Jacob by Almighty God are not myth or legend. These are . . . a land grant and a divine deed from God."[12] Another ad in several leading newspapers hammered home the same basic theme:

> We affirm as evangelicals our belief in the promise of the land to the Jewish people . . . We would view with grave concern any effort to carve out of the historic Jewish homeland another nation or political entity.[13]

In 1982 when President Reagan urged negotiations between Israel and Jordan concerning the West Bank, a group of Christian Zionists sent a petition to the President declaring:

> The Lord gave the land of Israel to the Jewish people and the Bible specifically delineated Israel's borders of which modern Israel has only a portion . . . Israel's right to Judea and Samaria is based both on Biblical and contemporary history. . . [14]

Across the country from Vermont to California, there are lay-led fundamentalist groups working at the grass-roots to heighten public awareness and sympathy for Israel. A *Directory of Pro-Israeli Elements in American Christianity* compiled in 1983 listed the names of 276 individuals and groups who are engaged in advocacy on behalf of Israel.[15] Many of the organizations are minuscule and short-lived. But others conduct regular meetings, issue newsletters, encourage the sale of Israeli bonds and products and write letters on behalf of Israel to members of Congress.

Among the best organized and financed of the groups supporting Israel were the affiliates of the International Christian Embassy, Jerusalem (ICEJ). This organization began its operations in 1980 when several foreign governments moved their embassies from Jerusalem to Tel Aviv in protest against Israel's action in unilaterally incorporating all of Jerusalem into the state and making Jerusalem the capital. The ICEJ wanted to show its devotion to Israel in contrast with the action of the secular powers. A network of ICEJ affiliates was established worldwide to promote conservative Christian support for Israel. At one time there were affiliates in approximately 30 countries but in recent years those in several major countries, including the U.S., have withdrawn their memberships, for reasons not entirely clear. New efforts are underway in the U.S. to organize another nationwide community-based group, Christian Friend of Israel, to take over the work of the ICEJ "consulates."

A number of specialized groups have been formed to appeal to specific constituencies, such as the American Forum for Jewish-Christian Cooperation, created to bring Jewish and Christian Zionists together in support of Israel. In 1984 this organization was influential in arranging a White House briefing for selected members of the conservative Jewish and Christian communities, where they listened to National Security Advisor, Robert McFarlane, and other notables discuss the foreign and domestic policies of the administration.

A group known as the Temple Mount Foundation was the brainchild of a multimillionaire, Terry Risenhoover, who took to heart the dispensationalist injunction about the urgency of rebuilding the temple in Jerusalem. He gathered a group of like-minded temple enthusiasts among the fundamentalists into the Temple Mount Foundation in order to raise the consciousness of the Religious Right about the importance of rebuilding the temple. Risenhoover gave financial assistance to several Israeli organizations also anxious to replace the Muslim shrines on the Temple Mount with a Hebrew temple (some for purely nationalistic reasons; others because they believe the Jewish Messiah will not appear until the temple is built). When 29 Israelis were arrested in 1983 for carrying explosives to the Temple Mount, Risenhoover's organization paid all their legal expenses; the so-called "Temple Mount 29" were acquitted.[16] In recent years Risenhoover suffered serious financial reverses and in April 1987 was sentenced to four years in prison for his role in bilking an estimated 3000 investors out of millions in worthless oil exploration leases.[17] The Temple Mount issue is being carried on by other dispensational fundamentalists who continue to write, preach and raise money on behalf of rebuilding the Temple of Solomon.[18]

Generous financial backing for Christian Zionist activities is provided by others like Risenhoover. Bunker Hunt, who serves on the board of the conservative Religious Roundtable, contributes heavily to Christian Zionist causes. In addition to the tycoons, there are numerous smaller contributors who help swell the coffers of organizations devoted to popularizing Israel in the minds of Americans.

Christian Zionists have undoubtedly furthered the cause of the Israeli state among their own constituencies and in other Christian circles where their print and electronic messages are read and heard. Whether they have had much of an impact on non-conservative Christians or non-religious persons is more open to question. In the political arena the efforts of the Religious Right up to this time have been marginal at best and counter-productive at worst regarding advocacy for Israel. The Religious Right, which contains the most vociferous elements of Christian Zionism, has a full domestic agenda to which it gives first priority and for which it tries hardest to mobilize support. The litmus test for candidates supported by the Religious Right is not their position on Israel but how they stand on abortion, prayer in the schools and homosexuality; in fact, Israel is not even mentioned on the "score card" which some fundamentalist groups distribute to members of Congress. If candidates do not pass muster on the social issues, they are repudiated regardless of how strongly they support Israel. In the 1980 elections the Religious Right was credited with contributing to the defeat of three of the most effective champions of Israel in the U.S. Senate—Jacob Javits, Frank Church and Birch Bayh. A wry comment in the *Jerusalem Post* indicates how some Jews feel:

> . . . By their political works the fundamentalists have let us know their priorities. Obviously it is more important to them to support candidates who will stop unwed teenagers from getting abortions than someone who will provide Israel with the arms it needs to defend itself.[19]

There has been little need, except in a few cases such as those discussed below, for any group to come to Israel's defense politically, since Israel is already the recipient of the most generous diplomatic, financial and military assistance from the U.S. and is regarded as one of our most dependable allies. There are no powerful countervailing forces or fierce political battles over aid to Israel.

The sale of AWAC planes to Saudi Arabia in the fall of 1981 and the war in Lebanon in the summer of 1982 were two instances in which Israel and American Jews were actively seeking support from organized political groups in the U.S. The Reagan administration strongly backed the sale of the AWACs to Saudi Arabia while the Israeli government and American Jewish groups opposed the sale. Several fundamentalist organizations urged their members to contact senators and members of the House of Representatives to defeat the sale, stressing that they should identify themselves as Christians. This writer contacted 30 Congressional offices to determine if the Christian Right was making an impact on the issue and was told that only a minuscule number of communications were received from identifiable Christian sources concerning the matter.

During the Israeli invasion of Lebanon, Israel was criticized in the media and in many other quarters for its bombings of civilians in Beirut.

Christian Zionist leadership, however, applauded the invasion, not only in terms of Israel's military and political interests but, as Pat Robertson and Mike Evans put it, "a dress rehearsal for Armageddon." The rank and file of the fundamentalists, if they agreed with Robertson and Evans, did not let members of Congress know about it. In Israel's most recent embarrassments over the Pollard spy case and its involvement in the Iran arms sales, the Religious Right was mute.

In 1985 the question of moving the American embassy from Tel Aviv to Jerusalem was considered by the Foreign Relations and Foreign Affairs Committees of Congress. Among those who presented testimony in favor of the move were Jerry Falwell, along with the Vice-President of the Moral Majority, and a representative of the International Christian Embassy. Again, there was no grassroots response. Interestingly, a spokesman for the liberal wing of evangelicalism spoke against the moving of the embassy, highlighting the split within the evangelical community on the issue of Israel and the Palestinians.

None of the issues concerning Israel described above involved any real threat to the security of Israel and were not the kind of issues which stir fundamentalists' souls.

Between 1976 and 1981 ten studies compared the political activities and attitudes of evangelicals with those of persons holding other religious views. Without exception, evangelicals were the most politically involved. They conducted mass mailings, leafletted church parking lots, raised money for political causes and lobbied for legislation. A Gallup survey reported that evangelicals registered and voted in larger numbers than non-evangelicals.[20] These activities were carried out on behalf of the domestic program of the fundamentalists, but there is no reason to believe that support could not be mustered for a foreign policy issue as well.

Based on the past activities of Christian Zionists regarding Israel's right to all its land, one might have expected that this group would have come out in strong opposition to the plan of Secretary of State Schulz in February, 1988 for the eventual trading of land for peace, especially since the land involved is Judea and Samaria. The Executive Director of the National Christian Leadership Conference for Israel informed the writer that the group had had a meeting on the subject but that views differed widely and no public statement has been issued (as of March 15, 1988). He thought the reason for the silence on the part of the fundamentalists is due, at least in part, to their preoccupation with the scandals involving two of their media superstars, Swaggart and Bakker.

Up until the middle of March the writer found only one major public declaration of support for Israel since the recent Palestinian Uprising. This was at the 7th Annual Prayer Breakfast for Israel. These Breakfasts are held in conjunction with the National Religious Broadcasters Conventions in Washington, D.C. every February. This year's Breakfast was in honor of the 40th anniversary of "the rebirth of God's chosen land." The 600 persons in attendance heard several evangelical luminaries emphasize the importance of Israel and of American support for that country. The most distinguished non-cleric at the event was Senator Bob Dole. Few references were made to the unrest in the Occupied Territories except to claim that Israel was, once again, being persecuted by outsiders and that newspapers and television reports were "lying" about recent events there. Moshe Arad, Israel's Ambassador to the U.S., made a few comments about the need to restore order and received a standing ovation.

It is not unlikely that the Religious Right will still come out strongly against the Schulz Plan and firmly in support of Israel's policies in the Occupied Territories, considering their belief that setbacks for Israel could delay the Second Coming of Christ and the millennial kingdom.

Non-fundamentalist Christian Zionism

Christian Zionism, with its enthusiasm for Israel, is not an exclusively fundamentalist phenomenon. While most pronounced and fervently advocated among the right wing of the evangelical movement, Christian Zionism has adherents among moderate and liberally-minded Christians as well, though based on non-dispensational premises. A complex of factors accounts for mainstream Christian zeal for Israel. Practicing Christians, from the conservative to the most liberal, are influenced by the role of Israel in scripture—familiarity with people and places in biblical Israel, by religious imagery and the whole weight of the Judeo-Christian heritage, as well as by the widely held secular perception of Israel as a valiant little country surrounded by vicious enemies; a talented people who have suffered the most horrendous persecution in history and deserve a land of their own; the only democracy in the Middle East and a deserving ally of the U.S. in the struggle against Communism.

One student of Christian Zionism, Ronald Stockton, Professor of Political Science at the University of Michigan-Dearborn, believes it is "a mainstream cultural theme linked to American self-identity and to the perception of America as a moral community." He admits that Christian Zionism is "disproportionately associated with the evangelical Christian base from which it historically sprang," but points out that the survey data indicate that it transcends these origins and has support in all religious, ideological and political strata.[21]

Popular approval of Israel has been consistently strong and has shown little fluctuation even during crises in American-Israeli relations, attested to by numerous public opinion polls over many years.[22]

Christian Critics of Israel—Evangelical

There are pockets of resistance to the "Israel can do no wrong" syndrome in this country and a growing number of them are found in the Christian community. We have already noted that the majority of evangelicals are not found in the Religious Right and even those in the right wing are not all pro-Zionist. The Liberty Lobby and its national newspaper, *The Spotlight*, has a fundamentalist orientation but is one of the most vociferously anti-Israeli organizations in the country. Virtually every issue of *The Spotlight* contains horror stories about American Zionists'machinations against the American government and people, or Israeli mistreatment of its Arab population.

There are *religiously conservative* evangelicals who are *politically moderate or liberal*. This is especially true of Black evangelicals. While the Black theologians and clergymen who espouse Liberation Theology come from the non-fundamentalist churches, even those in the most conservative Pentecostal denominations are less than whole-hearted supporters of Israel with its long and close ties to the apartheid regime in South Africa.

On the left-wing of the evangelical movement there are several groups and individuals who reject Christian Zionism. The most outspoken is the Sojourners community and its publication by the same name, a group deeply immersed in evangelical Christianity but which concerns itself with biblical admonitions against militarism, racism, economic exploitation and other forms of injustice rather than with purely personal salvation. This maverick evangelical group is critical of many aspects of American life and finds Israel also guilty of serious moral lapses. One of the contributing editors of Sojourners (Wes Michaelson) pointed out that while Israeli leaders appeal to the Bible in justifying their government's claim to the Occupied Territories, the state of Israel's actions would call forth the wrath of Old Testament prophets. He reminded readers of the parallel between Israel's treatment of Palestinians and the story of Ahab, the king of Samaria who asked Naboth to give him his vineyard. When Naboth refused to surrender the land that he and his ancestors had cultivated for generations, Ahab's wife Jezebel had Naboth stoned to death. As Ahab took possession of Naboth's vineyard, the prophet Elijah was sent to announce the Lord's judgment and condemnation on him. Michaelson explained further why contemporary Israel is not the Promised Land:

> Modern Israel exhibits the dangers of blind, religious nationalism. It grants rights and privileges of citizenship to Jews which are not equally extended to those who are not Jews. And in the name of its right to exist securely, Israel still continues to deny land, livelihood, basic rights and political self-determination to the Palestinians.[23]

Another prominent evangelical, Marvin Wilson, Professor of Old Testament at Gordon Conwell Divinity School, discusses the issues of morality and justice as they apply to Israel in a scholarly article in the *Journal of the Evangelical Theological Society*:

> If one grants the rights of Israel to exist as a nation, that decision must be made on the basis of what is just and moral rather than simply on the grounds that it fulfills prophecy. Humanitarian and altruistic motivations must be of prime consideration . . . The Hebrew scriptures are replete with examples of those who stood under the judgment of God for their unjust actions. The end has never automatically justified the means.
> The Israelis of today have a prophetic mandate. It is to practice justice toward those whom they consider to be "strangers" in the land. This often means the displaced, homeless, and powerless. . . [24]

The connections between the ancient covenants and contemporary Israel are disavowed by Rev. Louis DeCaro, a staunch evangelical:

> Are the modern Palestinian Arabs to be categorized with the ancient Amorites in terms of moral suitability so that the God of Moses and Joshua sanctions their removal from Palestinian territory to make room for modern Israelites? Are modern Israelis more morally and spiritually suited to inhabit that territory than are the Palestinian Arabs? Who would assume this presumptuous judgment and, in New Testament revelation, where is its support?[25]

One of the most influential evangelical publications in the U.S. is *Christianity Today*, representing the center of evangelicalism. This journal has published articles clearly in keeping with the prophetic view of Israel as the fulfillment of prophecy, but it has also on occasion been critical of Israeli policies and sympathetic to the Palestinian cause. The lead article in the April 18, 1986 issue of *Christianity Today* was devoted to the Palestinian people in Israel proper and on the West Bank. One of the journal's staff writers went to Israel and the Occupied Territories to interview Palestinian Christians, who constitute roughly 10 percent of the Palestinian population, in order to better understand the beliefs, and aspirations of Arab Christians. The major concern expressed in the article was with the greatly diminishing Christian-Arab presence in the Holy Land, for which U.S. evangelicals must take part of the blame: "U.S. evangelicals may inadvertently hasten the dismemberment of the Arab-Christian community by offering uncritical support to the state of Israel."[26]

Several years ago *Christianity Today* published an editorial dealing with two sensitive subjects: whether the political state of Israel can be equated with spiritual Israel and whether it is acceptable for Christians to proselytize among Jews. The editor declared:

> Not a few evangelicals confuse the political state of Israel with the spiritual Israel and in so doing lose sight of one important fact: both in Israel and around the world, most Jews do not recognize Jesus Christ as their Messiah. Therefore, the political state of Israel cannot be equated with spiritual Israel. We hope and pray that many Israelis will come to know Jesus as their Messiah.
>
> The same point can be made another way. Evangelicals may love their Jewish friends and support Jewish causes without suggesting that they regard Judaism as a religion sufficient for salvation . . . Jews object strongly when evangelicals "proselytize" among their company. But for evangelicals to refrain from sharing the Good News with all men, including Jews, would be inconsistent with their faith.[27]

Christian Critics of Israel—Mainline Churches

The theology of the mainline Protestant denominations and the Roman Catholic Church leads to a far different perspective on Israel than does that of the fundamentalists. Ecumenical Christians believe that most of the promises and prophecies in the Bible either were fulfilled centuries ago or were allegorical in nature. For members of the major mainline churches the Bible does not provide a blueprint for contemporary foreign policy, nor is it a real-estate manual. The passages from scripture which are most meaningful to them are those dealing not with ancient covenants and predictions but with the moral principles of prophets like Amos, Micah and Isaiah—and preeminently of Christ himself—who condemned oppression, injustice, and tyranny and pleaded for righteousness, compassion, and justice. Liberal Christians—especially, but not exclusively, those who embrace Liberation Theology—have deep concerns for the poor and the powerless, finding inspiration in words like Luke 4:18:"The Lord has anointed me to preach good news to the poor . . . to proclaim release to the captives and to set at liberty those that are oppressed."

These values lead a segment of mainstream Christians who have studied the Israeli-Palestinian problem to view with dismay and disapproval Israel's treatment of its Palestinian population. They see the Palestinians as a people occupying for centuries the land of Palestine, uprooted by another people, the Jews—fleeing indescribable horrors in Europe, which the Arabs had nothing to do with—and believe that both peoples are entitled to separate states of their own. Perceptive non-Zionist Christian observers of the scene note that the Palestinians are denied self-determination and have become the victims of a brutal occupation by the Israeli government. Arab lands, often cultivated for generations by Palestinian families, are illegally confiscated, often turned over to Jewish settlers; the lands left in Arab hands are deprived of water, so that crops dry up. Palestinian leadership is decimated by deporting and imprisoning persons of influence and ability. Arbitrary arrest, administrative detention of up to six months without any formal charges, and torture are commonly resorted to, not only for actual (or suspected) crimes but also for mere membership in proscribed nationalist organizations, or for speech considered a "security threat." Draconian collective punishments are widespread, such as the demolition of approximately 1500 homes since 1967, leaving 10,000 people homeless, often for only suspected crimes by one member of a family. These violations of basic human rights have aroused the Christian conscience and have led the major Protestant denominations and the Roman Catholic Church to pass resolutions and statements indicating their belief that the Palestinians should have a separate, independent state of their own.

The churches which are most sympathetic to the Palestinians are those which have their roots in the Middle East or which have either engaged in active mission or humanitarian work in that part of the world. The most militantly pro-Palestinian denomination is the Antiochian Orthodox Church, whose origins go far back in Middle East history. Its headquarters are in Damascus. The U.S. members of this church (approximately 150,000) are mainly Arab-Americans of the first or second generation, often with non-Arab spouses. Many have family ties in Syria, Lebanon and the West Bank.

The Roman Catholic Church has maintained a presence in the Middle

East since the first years of the Christian era. Beginning with the Crusades, Roman Catholic missions influenced the course of Christianity in the Arab world. A Latin Patriarchate, first created in Jerusalem at the end of the 11th century, was reestablished there in 1847. Missionary orders worked throughout the area, starting with the Franciscans in the 13th century. In 1926 Pope Pius established the Catholic Near East Association in New York City which still serves as the Pope's official mission and relief agency in the Middle East. In the same period a Catholic university was built in Bethlehem with funds donated by the Vatican. The Roman Catholic Church has a natural concern for the welfare of Arab Catholics. The Vatican opposed the establishment of the state of Israel and has not given diplomatic recognition to Israel. However, the Vatican and the American hierarchy now support the continued existence of Israel, while at the same time criticizing certain Israeli policies with regard to the Palestinian population and the status of Jerusalem.[28] The National Conference of Catholic Bishops has advocated the right of Palestinian Arabs to a homeland of their own and to participate in negotiations affecting their destiny.

In spite of the position of the Vatican and the National Conference of Catholic Bishops, there is great ambivalence in the American Catholic community regarding the state of Israel, with views ranging all the way from the fervent Christian Zionism of Father Robert Drinan[29] to the scathing denunciations of Father Daniel Berrigan:

> . . . It is a tragedy beyond calculation that the state of Israel should become the repository, and finally the tomb, of the Jewish soul. That in place of Jewish compassion, Israel should legislate evictions, uprootings, destruction of goods, imprisonment, terrorism. That in place of Jewish peaceableness, Israel should legislate a law of expanding violence. That in place of Jewish prophetic wisdom, Israel should launch an Orwellian nightmare of double talk, racism . . . aimed at proving its racial superiority to the people it has crushed.[30]

American Protestant missionary work in the Middle East began with the dispatch of missionaries from a few of the major denominations in the early 19th century. Though they did not succeed in converting large numbers of Muslims, their influence was significant in other ways. They introduced an Arabic printing press and one of their converts translated the Bible into Arabic. Elementary and secondary schools were established by the missionaries; in 1866 the Presbyterians founded the Syrian Protestant College, later known as the American University of Beirut.

The Protestant missionaries' encouragement of the Arabic language through the use of the print media helped to stimulate a revival of interest in the beauty of the Arabic language and culture. The schools established by the missionaries not only taught Arab students how to read and write but also introduced them to American social and political values. American missionary endeavors became closely bound up with Arab nationalist strivings, especially through the American University of Beirut, which had more influence than any other institution in creating a nationalistic revival among youth from all over the Middle East.

Missionaries were influential in interpreting the Arab world to members of their own churches and to the American public in general. They were one of the best informed sources of information on developments in the Near East (as the Middle East was then called). Their advice on this area was sought by the highest councils of the government and they became an interest group on behalf of the Arab world. The president of the American University of Beirut, Dr. Howard Bliss, exerted a major influence both in the U.S. and at the Paris Peace Conference after World War I. Bliss opposed the Balfour Declaration and tried to forestall the establishment of a Jewish national homeland in Palestine.

For several decades American Protestant missionaries continued to play a role in American policy-making through the State Department. Some of the missionaries themselves went to work for the government and their children and grandchildren have held positions in the foreign service and in the Middle East division of the State Department. Ambassador Talcott Seelye, who served in Syria, is from a missionary family in Lebanon; the former ambassador to Egypt, Dr. John Badeau, was a Reformed Church missionary in Cairo.

In the 20th century the Quakers, through the American Friends Service Committee, have worked in the Middle East for 35 years in various projects involving the Palestinian people, including several well-known schools on the West Bank. The Mennonite Central Committee is also engaged in a number of activities in the Israeli Occupied Territories, as is the Church of the Brethren.

Because of their long associations with Arab peoples and concern about Arab-Christians, as well as their commitment to justice and morality, the leadership of several of the mainstream Christian churches, both in their separate denominations and in the national and international bodies which represent them—the National and World Council of Churches—have taken a keen interest in the basic human rights of the Palestinians and in what they believe to be the unjust policies of the Israeli government. The major publications of the ecumenical churches—*The Christian Century* and *Christianity and Crisis*—have reflected these concerns over many years. Editors and staff writers for these publications have often visited the Middle East and written about their first-hand impressions of the oppression of Palestinians under Israeli rule. Rosemary Reuther is but one of a number of distinguished religious thinkers who have contributed articles to these journals expressing dismay about the violation of Palestinian rights. In the December 8, 1986 issue of *Christianity and Crisis* Reuther confessed:"For me the story of Jesus, born in a stable because there was no room in the inn, merges with that of homeless Palestinians because there is no room for them in their native land."[31]

The leadership, the national bureaucracies and the press of the liberal churches often do not express the views of the grassroots membership. We have already noted that pro-Israeli sentiments are widespread in all sectors of the Christian community, including those in which the leaders and the mission personnel are highly critical of the whole Zionist enterprise. The gap between the leaders and the members in local churches is largely a result of the greater knowledge and understanding of the issue by the people in the national offices who have extensively studied the Arab-Israeli problem, lived and worked in the area or made frequent fact-finding trips to Israel and the West Bank. Local parishioners, on the other hand, are often poorly informed, simply accepting the conventional wisdom, which is favorable to Israel and hostile to the Palestinians, or know so little about the subject that they are merely indifferent to it.

There are special sections in the headquarters of the Presbyterian, Methodist, United Church of Christ and the Mennonite Churches, the American Friends Service Committee and the National Council of Churches devoted entirely or primarily to Middle East issues, headed by able, knowledgeable and deeply dedicated individuals who are trying to educate their memberships about the Arab-Israeli problem. Their efforts are not wholly in vain. Year-long studies of the Middle East have been sponsored by several mainline churches, using materials supplied by the Friendship Press, a publishing house which serves many denominations. In the United Methodist Church, women's groups are especially active in conducting studies and working with others concerned about the Israeli-Palestinian issue, such as the North American Coordinating Committee for Non-Governmental Organizations on the Question of Palestine (affiliated with the UN). A few years ago 75 United Methodist Conference Schools of Christian Missions offered a course on the Middle East during one of their summer schools, attended by approximately 10,000 women, who in turn taught the course in their local churches.

The Presbyterian Church—which has been sending missionaries to the Middle East for more than 150 years and has 50,000 members of its denomination in Arab countries—is in the forefront of efforts to heighten awareness among its members, and the general public, about the tragic situation in the Israeli-occupied West Bank.[32] Presbyterian organizations have brought members of the Israeli peace movement and Palestinians to the U.S. to conduct seminars and classes in their churches. They have devoted many hours to hammering out resolutions on the Middle East to present to their General Assemblies which have been the most comprehensive and carefully drafted statements of any of the Protestant churches on the Middle East in general and the Arab-Israeli conflict in particular.

Dr. Donald Wagner, a Presbyterian minister, is the national director of the Palestine Human Rights Campaign (PHRC), the organization most active in educating churches, the peace movement, human rights groups and academia about the problem of human rights violations in the Occupied Territories, and in bringing pressure to bear on the U.S. and Israel on behalf of Palestinian victims of Israeli occupation policies. Five of the 20 members of the PHRC's board of directors are clergymen or seminary professors. Since 1979 the PHRC has worked with churches and human rights groups to counterbalance what they consider the misinterpretation of the Bible by Christian Zionists. The two La Grange Conferences (held in La Grange, Illinois in 1979 and 1981) and a subsequent conference sponsored by the PHRC produced the first substantial American critiques of Christian Zionist theology.[33] The PHRC has issued a collection of essays, *All in the Name of the Bible*, dealing with Israel, South Africa and Christian fundamentalism. Twice in the past two years the PHRC worked with the U.S. religious leadership in opposing Congressional legislation which would move the U.S. embassy from Tel Aviv to Jerusalem. The group brings prominent Palestinian leaders, such as Father Elias Chacour, to the U.S. to speak in cities across the country about the Israeli-Palestinian problem, and they take delegations of American Protestant and Catholic leaders to the Holy Land. Recently the PHRC established a Religious Task Force, with a speakers bureau, newsletter and action alert network. Another activity of the PHRC is a computerized data-base project on Palestinian human rights, where detailed up-to-date information on the oppression of the Palestinians is stored and made available.

The national heads of several of the Protestant denominations and of the National Council of Churches have connections with persons in policy-making positions in the federal government. An official of the national Presbyterian Church and the former director of the Middle East office of the National Council of Churches both told this writer that they have occasional day-long working conferences with high level State Department personnel, at which the views of their organizations on the Israeli-Palestinian question are given careful consideration.

Among the members of the mainstream churches who have been involved in formulating and popularizing the Middle East resolutions of their churches (and of the National Council of Churches) are prominent men and women who are opinion leaders in their communities— corporation executives, leading clergymen, lawyers, journalists and academics who express their views in the media and in numerous interpersonal contacts. These are people who always vote, keep abreast of current events, know how to articulate their opinions, and have connections with persons of power and influence at all levels of government.

The major denominations maintain Washington offices with lobbyists for their churches' causes; some include the Israeli-Palestinian issue. The Presbyterian Church's Washington office conducts advocacy of its denomination's policies and perspectives on the Arab-Israeli problem among the Presbyterian members of Congress and the administration. Recently the Presbyterian Church's Washington office created a national network to encourage its membership throughout the country to contact government officials and respond to action alerts about the Middle East.

In 1985 a new organization was launched called Churches for Middle East Peace, with eleven faith groups, including the Presbyterian, American Baptist, Methodist, United Church of Christ, Episcopalian, Unitarian-Universalist denominations and the National Council of Churches. It maintains advocacy offices in Washington, D.C. where it communicates to Congress and the Executive branch its concerns about human rights, the peace process, arms transfers and the unique status of Jerusalem.

All these groups contact members of Congress and their staffs and testify before Congressional committees. For example, Paul Quiring of the Mennonite Central Committee, probably one of the most knowledgeable Americans regarding the problem of land and water use in the Occupied Territories, was asked to testify before a sub-committee of the U.S. House of Representatives which was trying to assess the impact of Jewish settlements on the West Bank. Quiring testified about instances of land confiscation and how the Israeli settlements affect the local Arab population.

The Mennonite Central Committee and the American Friends Service Committee, the two church groups with the longest direct involvement on the West Bank, have compiled some of the most compelling first-hand accounts of conditions in Israel's Occupied Territories for distribution to legislators and their staffs. Unfortunately, even the most graphic empirical data about the Palestinian situation in Israel and the West Bank, related by respected and credible men and women, appear to make only a minimal impact on members of Congress, judging by the enormous extent of aid to Israel which is approved on every occasion when foreign aid is voted on.

Many obstacles limit the success of the mainline churches in influencing either public opinion or policy-making vis-a-vis Israel and the Palestinians. It is extremely difficult to challenge the pervasive myths about Israel as a humane democracy administering a "benign occupation." Furthermore, the modest activities of the liberal Christians in presenting the Palestinian case to the American public cannot really compare with the militant zealotry of the Christian Zionist efforts to extol Israel. For fundamentalists, devotion to Israel is a religious concern, tied up with their own salvation and that of all humanity, while for liberal Protestants and Catholics Israeli treatment of Palestinians is a matter of human rights with no greater salience than a host of other issues, such as apartheid in South Africa, world hunger, the arms race, or Central America.

Mainstream Christians concerned about justice for the Palestinians are voices crying in the wilderness, but they just might be the voice of conscience which will ultimately prevail against tortured interpretations of scripture and the fiction of Israel's beneficence.

NOTES

1. Edward Dobson, "Fundamentalism," *Face to Face: An Interreligious Bulletin*, Vol. XIII, Winter, 1987, p.26.
2. Quoted by William Martin, "Waiting for the End," *The Atlantic Monthly*, June, 1982, p.34.
3. Robert Lindsted, *The Foot of Asher*, publication of the S.W. Radio Church, Oklahoma City, OK., 1983. p.7.
4. L. Nelson Bell,"Unfolding Destiny," *Christianity Today*, July 21, 1967, p. 1044.
5. Hal Lindsey, *The Late Great Planet Earth*, N.Y.,: Bantam Books, 1980, p.40.
6. *Ibid.*, p. 47.
7. *Ibid.*, p.33.
8. Grace Halsell, *Prophecy and Politics: Militant Evangelists on the Road to Nuclear War*, 1985; A.G. Mojtabai, *Blessed Assurance—At Home with the Bomb in Amarillo, Texas*, 1986.
9. Jerry Falwell, *Listen, America!* N.Y.: Doubleday, 1980, p.113.
10. Dwight Wilson, *Armageddon Now!* Grand Rapids: Baker House Books, 1977, p.12.
11. An acquaintance who took these trips with Falwell supplied me with this information.
12. *New York Times*, Nov.14, 1977.
13. *New York Times*, Nov. 1, 1977.
14. Petition to Pres. Reagan and members of Congress by American Forum for Jewish-Christian Cooperation, Nov. 11, 1982.
15. Unpublished document by Douglas Krieger, Los Angeles, CA., 1984.

16. Barbara and Michael Ledeen, "The Temple Mount Plot," *The New Republic*, June 18, 1984, p. 20-23.
17. *Los Angeles Times*, April 21, 1987.
18. Robert I. Friedman, "Terror on Sacred Ground - the Battle for the Temple Mount," *Mother Jones*, Aug./Sept., 1987, pp. 37-44.
19. "Fundamentally Flawed," *Jerusalem Post*, Sept. 14, 1984, p.9.
20. Robert Wuthnow, "The Political Rebirth of American Evangelicals" *The New Christian Right*. N.Y.: Aldine P)ub.Co., 1984, p. 168-69.
21. Ronald R. Stockton, "Christian Zionism: Prophecy and Public Opinion," *Middle East Journal*, Vol. 41, No.2, Spring, 1987, p. 251.
22. *Public Opinion* 6 (4), Aug.-Sep., 1983; Connie DeBoer, "The Polls: Attitudes toward the Arab-Israeli Conflict," *Public Opinion Quarterly* 47, 1983, p. 121-131; William Adams, "Middle East Meets West: Surveying American Attitudes," *Public Opinion*, Apr.-May, 1982, p.51-55. A poll reported in *U.S. News and World Report*, Nov. 18, 1987 indicated how favorably Americans view 10 foreign nations. The most favorable response was for Great Britain with 85%; the least favorable, South Africa with 25%. Israel was regarded favorably by 56%. The writer has been unable to find a poll taken since that date regarding attitudes toward Israel.
23. Wes Michaelson, "The Necessities of Peace, *Sojourners*, Oct., 1979, p.5.
24. Marvin R. Wilson, "Zionism as Theology: An Evangelical Approach," *Journal of Evangelical Theological Society*, Mar. 29, 1979, p.43.
25. Louis A. DeCaro, *Evangelical Zionists, Israel and Biblical Prophecy*, unpublished manuscript, p.3.
26. Beth Spring, "Palestinian Christians: Caught in a War of Two Rights," *Christianity Today*, Apr. 18, 1986, p. 16-21.
27. Editorial, "Let's Clear Up the Fuzziness and Still Be Friends," *Christianity Today*, Mar., 1977, p.29.
28. For an excellent analysis of the Vatican and the Arab-Israeli problem see: George E. Irani, *The Papacy and the Middle East—The Role of the Holy See in the Arab-Israeli Conflict*. University of Notre Dame Press, 1986.
29. Robert Drinan, *Honor the Promise: America's Commitment to Israel*, Garden City, N.Y.: Doubleday & Co., 1977. This is a laudatory commentary on Israel and reasons why the U.S. should continue its strong commitment to that country.
30. Daniel Berrigan, *The Great Catholic Debate*, N.Y: Committee on New Alternatives in the Middle East, 1974. p.3.
31. Editorial, Rosemary Reuther, *Christianity and Crisis*, Vol. 46, No.18, Dec. 8, 1986, p. 427.
32. Ari Goldman, "Presbyterians Debate Proposal on Jews," *New York Times*, June 13, 1987, p.6.
33. The conferences were titled: "Palestinian-Israeli Conflict: Responsibilities for the Christian Church," and "Toward Biblical Foundations for a Just Peace in the Holy Land." Scholarly papers of a high calibre were presented by seminary professors, clergymen and notable public figures and were attended by members of many denominations. Two subsequent conferences of a similar nature were held in the past five years.

9

ZIONISM AS A RECIDIVIST MOVEMENT: ORIGIN OF ITS SEPARATIST AIMS

ISRAEL SHAHAK

PART I

A Point of Departure in History

The usual treatments of Zionism, whether by enemies, friends or apologists, are usually vitiated by two interconnected errors. The first is lack of discussion of the related historical background. Although the Jewish situation in the nineteenth century is almost always discussed, especially the second half of that century, the immediately preceding period is usually ignored. This is a great mistake because the 19th century was a time of rapid change for Jews. But during the previous three hundred years, from 1492-1498, when the expulsions from Spain and Portugal took place, until near the end of the eighteenth century, significant developments took place in Jewish history. It was then that all essential aspects of Orthodox Judaism developed—from the rabbinate (which did not exist before) to the very clothes worn by ultra-orthodox Jews. The influences of the Jewish mode of life persisted, together with the beliefs that were created or crystallized during that period. To a greater or lesser extent in the various countries, these influences continue to the present time. In fact, they are increasing and have greatly influenced the Zionist movement.

The second common error in treatments of Zionism is forgetting that *Zionism is a Jewish movement*, the first objective of which was to influence Jews. Other aims, such as expulsion or enslavement of Palestinians and domination of the whole of the Middle East, are basically for a Jewish reason. We are so concerned about the injustice and the daily suffering inflicted on Palestinians, that the Jewish reasons are often forgotten. Zionists ignore them when speaking or writing in languages other than Hebrew. To give but one example, General (reserves) Rehavam Ze'evi was asked recently why he proposed to "transfer" all Palestinians from the occupied territories to Arab countries. The *first* reason he gave was to prevent mixed marriages between Jews and non-Jews.[1] Although most Zionists would agree with him, it is certain that this reason would not be relayed to *The New York Times* or other American media. Abhorrence of marriages between Jews and non-Jews is a predominant Jewish characteristic. It persists not only among Jews who have not been profoundly influenced by Western civilization but also among Zionists who are generally perceived to be westernized. Chaim Weizmann, for example, devoted much effort to preventing marriages between Jews and non-Jews, not only in Palestine but worldwide. In this, as in other matters, Zionism presents a facade of "secular" or "western" values while perpetuating many characteristics of Jewish society of the sixteenth, seventeenth and eighteenth centuries.

Zionism cannot be understood by concentrating only on Zionist actions in Palestine and the whole of the Middle East. Their worldwide purposes have been profoundly influenced by early periods of Jewish history which cannot be ignored. The aim of this essay is to demonstrate that Zionism as a Jewish movement is a reaction against progressive changes in Jewish life starting about 100 to 200 years before Zionism's beginnings. "Reaction" or "recidivist movement" means a movement which, *after* political and social change of essentially a liberating and progressive character, tries "to put the clock back" by attempting to revitalize the pre-change situation.

A first step toward understanding Zionism is an honest description in realistic terms of the essentials of the Jewish situation before the liberating change began. General histories about Jews are mainly unreliable, except for some recent ones written in Hebrew by Israelis. Those written in English tend to be even more misleading or inaccurate than histories of the USSR published under Stalin. Fortunately, many collections of original documents or specialized studies are being published in Hebrew, making it now possible to obtain a fairly good approximation of early

Jewish societies. To have an anchor point in time, I shall describe the years from 1764-1774. I choose this particular decade to describe the pre-change situation of Jews because 1764 is the date when the previously existing central organization of Polish Jews, "The Committee of Four Lands," was dissolved (after a period of decay), with the consequent decentralization of Jewish life. 1774 is the date of the first partition of Poland. Before that time, the overwhelming majority of Jews of the world lived in only two states: the Polish Commonwealth and the Ottoman Empire. The Ottoman Empire of 1774, the Muslim states of Iran, Morocco and Yemen, together with Poland of 1774, account for more than 90% of Jews of that time.

Both Poland and the Ottoman Empire touched the bottom of a long social and political decline at about the same time. A strong movement of enlightenment in Polish society which produced many improvements in all areas of life began only after the shock of the 1774 Partition. The first modernizing movement in the Ottoman Empire, associated with Sultan Selim III, came somewhat later. The first measurable toleration of Jews in a state with a large Jewish population occurred after these dates—in the Austrian Empire under Emperor Joseph II in 1782. The greater part of the Austrian Empire's Jewish population of 1782 came only in 1774 as a consequence of the First Partition of Poland. Before that date the Jewish population of the Austrian Empire was extremely small, mostly in Bohemia. In Vienna, which subsequently became an important Jewish center, the number of Jews was legally limited to a few hundred. There was no Russian Jewry before 1774. The first Jews in Russia were Polish Jews, following Russia's annexation of the Polish territories in 1774. 1774 is therefore a convenient date to start a description of Jewish society before the process of change began, that is, preceding influences of "modernization" or "westernization".

Demography and Geography

The number of the Jews in the world before 1800 is reliably estimated to be only one million. Their great increase to 16.5 million in 1939, before Hitler's extermination of six million, was a nineteenth-century development. It created the present Ashkenazi Jewish majority, for it was only during the nineteenth century that the numbers of Ashkenazim rapidly increased. Indeed their natural increase was even greater than that of the Palestinians in twentieth-century Palestine, and for the same reasons, one of which was a decrease in infant mortality.[2]

In the late seventeenth century the largest Jewish congregation in the world was in the Ottoman capital, Constantinople, followed closely by the two Ottoman cities, Salonika and Izmir. Probably the same situation existed in 1774. In Christian Europe, however, most Jews lived in very small cities or villages. This was particularly true in Poland. In 1774 the largest cities of Europe, with the sole exception of Amsterdam, were closed to most Jews who did not have a special permit (Paris, Vienna). There were other reasons that kept the number of Jews in cities small or even negligible (as in London). Jews were not then an urban people interdependent with the rest of society as they are now in the Western world. They lived in small towns and villages. Unlike peasants, they were largely independent of surrounding populations.

Compared with Great Britain, France, the states of Central Europe (Austria, Prussia and several smaller Germanic states) and the American Colonies (where the number of Jews was very small), the Polish Commonwealth and the Ottoman Empire—the two states where the great majority of Jews lived in 1774—were both very undeveloped. Again using modern terminology, Poland and the Ottoman Empire were decidedly "peripheral" while Western Europe (almost devoid of Jews) was the center of economic and other developments. Under various "enlightened absolute monarchs" they had undergone considerable improvement in most aspects of society. Both Poland and the Ottoman Empire suffered declines in prosperity, power and culture from previous positions. Poland was a much stronger, and a more prosperous, cultured and tolerant country in 1574 than in 1774, and the same is true of the Ottoman Empire. By 1774, some of the ruling classes of the two countries—but by no means all—knew that their countries were in a decline. In other words, two hundred years ago—even a hundred years ago— almost all Jews were living in a decaying periphery under worsening economic and political conditions and not in a center of world development. This situation affected basic attitudes in many ways.

Jews in 1774 Poland

From now on I shall concentrate on Polish Jews of 1774 because the great majority of all contemporary Jews are their descendants or were strongly influenced by them. In Israel, where the so-called "Oriental Jews" form the majority, the Ashkenazi community maintains its dominant position. This continues even though some Sephardi (Oriental) communities have changed and even though many Jews who came to Israel from Spain and many more who came from Iraq constitute exceptions. They are exceptions in that, unlike most "Oriental Jews", they have been able to integrate themselves into Israeli society and move upward. The rich, historical Jewish tradition in Spain during the so-called "Golden Age," and in Iraq, where the Babylonian Talmud and Geonim developed,[3] provided the contextual framework for these exceptions. Perhaps more important, many Iraqi Jews had become extremely rich by the beginning of the 1960's. They had achieved a high level of education and politically were about evenly divided between Labor and Likud.

Although later nineteenth-century developments were very different among the Polish compared with the Ottoman Jews, it should not be overlooked that, in terms of society, culture and religion, all Jews in 1774 constituted and felt themselves to be one people. Influences, ideas, customs, books, etc., moved among them easily and rapidly. Contact was particularly strong between Jews of the Ottoman Empire and Jews of Poland. Before 1774, Mediterranean Jews and Jews of the Ottoman Empire clearly dominated all Jewish culture, literature and religion, while Ashkenazim (those of Poland and the Germanic States) were, and felt themselves to be, parvenus. To give an example, before the eighteenth century very few books of any originality, even in Jewish religious law (Halakha), were written by Ashkenazim. They mostly composed commentaries on original works done elsewhere. All new and innovative Jewish movements before 1774 invariably began outside the Ashkenazi community. This situation did not change until the eighteenth century.

A short characterization of Poland and Polish Jews until 1774 is here in order. For many reasons, development in medieval Poland lagged behind countries like England and France. A strong feudal-type monarchy, without any parliamentary institutions, was established in the 14th century under Casimir the Great (1333-70). Immediately after his death, changes of dynasty and other factors led to a rapid increase, first in the power of the noble magnates and then of the petty nobility. By 1572 the king's power was reduced to that of a figure-head and the exclusion from political power of all other non-noble estates was virtually complete. In the following two hundred years, absence of a strong government resulted in acknowledged anarchy which reached a point where a court decision in a case affecting a nobleman became only a legal license to wage a private war to enforce the verdict. There was no other way to enforce it. Feuds between great noble houses in the 18th century involved private armies numbering tens of thousands, much larger than the inefficient, official army. This process was accompanied by a debasement of the Polish peasants. They had been free in the early Middle Ages but were reduced to the status of abject serfdom, hardly distinguishable from outright slavery and certainly the worst in Europe. The desire of no-

blemen in neighboring countries to enjoy the same kind of power the
Polish "pan" had over his peasants (including the absolute power of life
and death) was instrumental in the territorial expansion of Poland. The
situation in the "eastern" lands of Poland (Byelorussia and the Ukraine),
colonized and settled by newly enserfed peasants, was the worst of all.

Jewish Autonomy

A very small number of Jews in important positions had apparently been
living in Poland since the creation of the Polish state. A significant Jewish
immigration began with the decline in the Jewish position in western
and then in central Europe in the 13th century and increased under
Casimir the Great. Not much is known about Polish Jewry during that
period. But with the decline of the monarchy in the 16th century, particularly under Sigismund I the Elder (1506-48) and his son Sigismund
II Augustus (1548-72), Polish Jewry burst into social and political prominence, accompanied by a much greater degree of autonomy. It was at
this time that Poland's Jews were granted their greatest privileges, cul-
minating in the establishment of the famous "Committee of Four Lands,"
a very effective autonomous institution of Jewish rule and jurisdiction
over all Jews in Poland's four divisions. One of its many important functions was to collect taxes from Jews all over the country, deducting part
of the yield for its own use and for the use of local Jewish communities,
passing the rest on to the state treasury.

With the decline of royal power from the beginning of the 16th century until 1795, the king's usual role in relation to Jews was rapidly
assumed by the nobility, as it was in other countries. This development
had lasting and tragic results both for the Jews themselves and for the
common people of the Polish Republic. All over Poland the nobles used
Jews as their agents to undermine the commercial power of the Royal
Towns, which were weak in any event. Alone among the countries of
western Christendom, a Polish nobleman's property inside a Royal Town
was exempt from the town's laws and guild regulations. Most nobles
settled their Jewish clients in such properties which gave rise to a lasting
conflict. Jews were usually "victorious" in the sense that the towns could
neither subjugate them nor drive them off. In the frequent popular
riots, Jewish lives and Jewish properties were lost. The nobles still acquired the profits. Similar or worse consequences followed from the
frequent employment of Jews as commercial agents of noblemen. This
status won them exemption from most Polish tolls and tariffs, resulting
in loss for the native bourgeoisie.

The most lasting and tragic consequences occurred in the eastern provinces, roughly the area east of the present Soviet border, including almost the whole of the present Ukraine and reaching up to the Great Russian language frontier. (Until 1648 the Polish border was far east of the Dnieper, so that Poltava, for example, was inside Poland). There were hardly any Royal Towns in this great expanse of territory. The towns were established by nobles and belonged to them. They were settled almost exclusively by Jews. Until 1939, the population of many Polish towns east of the river Bug was at least 90 per cent Jewish and this demographic phenomenon was even more pronounced in that area of Tsarist Russia annexed from Poland and known as the "Jewish Pale." Many Polish Jews outside the towns, particularly in the east, were employed as direct supervisors and oppressors of the peasant-serfs, as bailiffs of noble manors (invested with the landlord's full coercive powers) or as lessees of particular feudal monopolies such as the corn mill, the liquor still and public houses (with the right of armed search of peasant houses for illicit stills) or the bakery, and as collectors of customary feudal dues of all kinds. In short, in eastern Poland under the rule of the nobles (and of the feudalised church, composed exclusively of the nobility) Jews were the immediate exploiters of the peasantry and constituted the great majority of the dwellers. In 1779 Jews constituted 10% of the population of Poland. Only 7% of the remaining, non-Jewish 90% of the population lived in urban areas.

Most of the profit extracted from the peasants was passed on to the landlords in one way or another. In turn, the nobles often severely oppressed and subjugated Jews. The historical record tells many a harrowing tale of the hardship and humiliation inflicted by noblemen on "their" Jews. But the peasants suffered even worse at the hands of both landlords and Jews. This situation remained unchanged until the advent of modern states, by which time Poland had been dismembered. Poland was the only big country in western Christendom from which the Jews were never expelled. A new middle class could not rise out of the utterly enslaved peasantry, and the old bourgeoisie was geographically limited, commercially weak and therefore powerless.

Internal conditions within the Jewish community took a similar course. In the period 1500-1795, one of the most superstition-ridden in the history of Judaism, Polish Jewry was the most afflicted with superstition and fanaticism of all existing Jewish communities. The considerable power of Jewish autonomy was increasingly used to stifle all original or innovative thought among Jews, to promote the most shameless exploitation of the Jewish poor by the Jewish rich in alliance with the rabbis and to justify the Jews' role in the service of the nobles for oppression of the peasants. The ancient rule by which rabbis had to earn their own livelihood from their profession, operative in Yemen and in other communities, was changed in Poland. In Poland, rabbis either married the daughters of rich men or they were supported by funds from rich men. These rabbis thus became ex-officio members of the ruling class who both controlled and rejected rights and privileges for much of the population. Here too, there was no way out except by liberation from the outside. In pre-1795 Poland the social role of Jews was more important than in any other classical diaspora and illustrates better than in any other country the spiritual bankruptcy of Judaism before the beginning of the modern period.

It should be emphasized that bad as the situation of Polish Jews was in 1774, the situation of Polish peasants, many of whom were not Polish by nationality was much worse. They were really slaves under the absolute rule and jurisdiction of their noble lord. He was their only judge and could sentence them to death. If a peasant were killed, the usual punishment was compensation to the victim's master. Peasants were bought and sold with and without the land on which they lived. Polish Jews were notably advantaged in every way over about 75% of the population, legally and economically. In many cases they were able to exploit the enslaved peasants who comprised the majority of the population. Attitudes deeply implanted during this period seem to persist among many descendants of those Jews.

No Common Language

The factor of language must also be taken into consideration. Polish Jewry was unique in Jewish history in that for many hundreds of years a great Jewish community did not understand the language of the majority of the population among whom they lived. They spoke a completely different tongue. This linguistic separation was much more extreme in Poland of 1774, than, let us say, among their ultra-Orthodox descendants in New York of 1987 who, while using Yiddish as their primary language, do know English. In Poland, until well into the nineteenth century, there is no record of a single rabbi who knew either Polish or Latin (which in many ways served as the official language of the Polish Commonwealth). Jewish education of that time had totally excluded foreign languages, even in the most elementary form. (Also, Hebrew grammar and style were not taught because they were considered contributors to religious infidelity). Few Jews—even among intellectuals—had a working knowledge even of Yiddish. Few Jews, except perhaps Jewish servants of nobles, were conversant in any tongue but Hebrew. In 1760 in Lvov, for example, all rabbis were ordered to assemble to answer a blood-libel charge, often repeated during the Passover period. None of the assembled rabbis knew either Polish or Latin; hence the discussants had to utilize a Jewish agent of a Pole who knew Polish and a Christian theologian who knew Hebrew. This condition in Poland (or East European Jewry) was exceptional among all known Jewish communities in the long course of Jewish history. All other Jewish communities spoke and wrote a language which was common to their neighbors, even if sometimes in the form of a Jewish dialect.

This was true even in Biblical times, where Hebrew is often called in the Bible itself "The Canaanite language". Ancient inscriptions show that it was basically the language used by Phoenicians, the Moabites and other neighboring peoples. This was true also of the three alternate languages used by Jews: Aramaic, Greek and Arabic. Philo, for example, wrote in Greek; Maimonides wrote in Arabic.[4] Knowledge of the majority's language was also common in other European Jewish communities: Spanish and Portuguese Jews spoke in Spanish and Portuguese, Italian Jews in Italian, and in early medieval times French Jews in French and German Jews spoke and continue to speak German. The Jews of Spain kept their Spanish (or Portuguese) language and until modern times they knew and used the languages of the countries in which they settled. Jews became famous in the Ottoman Empire (and other countries) for their linguistic skills and the profession of translator even became one of their common occupations.

Polish Jewry refused to learn the language of the nation in which it lived. Its leaders were completely ignorant of any spoken language other than Yiddish and used Hebrew in a debased form as their literary language. Even the great works of science or Hebrew literature and poetry of Medieval times, written or translated into Hebrew, were effectively prohibited in Poland from the sixteenth century on. The result was a degree of ignorance, superstition and fanaticism which is difficult for us to realize. The extent of this intellectual aridity may best be illustrated by a few examples of some early efforts, after 1774, still in Hebrew, to elevate the intellectual level of Polish Jews.

In the preface to the first book about the geography of the world, published in 1803, the author solemnly laments the fact that many rabbis and other Jews deny the existence of America (because it is unmentioned in the Talmud). There were great suspicions about mathematics from non-Jewish sources making it necessary to begin (about 1790-1820) by republishing the mathematical and geometric elementary treatises written by Rabbi Abraham Ibn Ezra who died in 1167!! He was a well-known

Bible commentator who enjoyed prestige among the rabbis. This linguistic separatism endured in a lesser form until compulsory elementary education began in the nineteenth or twentieth century, depending upon the country. A well known, true story recounts that in Warsaw, about 1930, the Polish writer Slonimsky heard about the popular Yiddish poet and dramatist Yitzik Manger and wanted to meet him. The meeting was arranged, but Manger did not know enough Polish to speak even one sentence and Slonimsky, of course, did not know Yiddish. They discovered however that both had spent some years in London and therefore could converse (in Warsaw) in English.

This linguistic cultural barrier, almost absolute in 1774, continues even now in Zionist policies. It is apparent in the efforts to revive in Palestine [Israel] a distinctly parochial "Jewish" culture. Reinforced by overwhelming military power, it is effectively antisepticized against serious interaction with any other culture. A notable, political consequence of this parochialism is the predilection of Israeli apologists for many Israeli international policies to claim that normal, negative, international reactions are a matter of "us" against "them." Or, in language more characteristic of Zionist political polemics, that these negative reactions are motivated by "anti-Semitism." It is in this spirit that the United Nations General Assembly is often described as "anti-Semitic."

Cultural Isolation

Many contemporary Jews seem nostalgic for that isolated world, their paradise lost, the comfortable closed society from which they were not so much liberated as "expelled." A significant element in the Zionist movement always wanted to restore it and it appears that this element has gained the upper hand in Israel at the present time. Many motives behind Israeli politics that so often bewilder the superficially informed, confused, western "friends of Israel" are explicable once they are seen as recidivist, or reactionary, in the political sense of this word. They represent a forced return to the earlier, less open or completely "closed" period. Using the language of Karl Popper, Zionism represents a revolt against the entrance of Jews to modern "open society."[5]

It is important to note that many of the supposedly "Jewish characteristics," by which I mean traits that in the West are popularly attributed to "the Jews," are modern characteristics. They were quite unknown during most of Jewish history and appeared only when the totalitarian "Jewish community" began to lose the power to coerce Jews. They were completely unknown in the Judaism of 1774. The Polish Jews of that date would consider these traits heretical and anti-Jewish.

Take, for example, the so-called "Jewish sense of humor." Before the 19th century humor is rare in Hebrew literature. It occurs only during a few periods in a few countries: in Italy between the 14th and 17th centuries and in Muslim Spain, where the Jewish upper-class was relatively free of the rabbinical yoke. Humor and jokes are noticeably absent in traditional Judaism with the exception of some jokes directed against other religions. The *Shulchan Aruch* and other collections of Judaic laws are good examples. Judaism never internalised satire against rabbis and leaders of the community. There were no Jewish comedies, just as there were no comedies in Sparta, and for a similar reason. Or, take the love of learning. Except for purely religious learning, which was itself often in a debased and degenerate state, all forms of Jewish learning were (as noted above) forbidden and even held in contempt.

The critical sense, supposedly characteristic of Jews, was totally absent. Nothing was so feared and forbidden as innovation, however modest, or constructive criticism, however benign. The total lack of any rudimentary historiography about Jews or Judaism among Polish Jews in 1774—(and preceding centuries)—is best illustrated by some specific examples.

Talmudic Judaism had little interest in describing or explaining itself to members of its own community, whether or not educated in Talmudic studies. The writing of Jewish history, even in the driest analytical style, ceased completely from the time of Josephus Flavius (end of first century) until the Renaissance. It was then revived for a short time in Italy and in other countries where Jews were under strong Italian influence. Characteristically, the rabbis feared Jewish history even more than general history. The first "modern" history book published in Hebrew (in the sixteenth century) was entitled *"History of the Kings of France and of the Ottoman Kings"*. It was followed by some histories dealing solely with persecutions of Jews. The first book of Jewish history proper, which dealt with ancient times, was promptly banned—suppressed by the highest rabbinical authorities. It did not reappear until the 19th century.[6] The rabbinical authorities of Eastern Europe furthermore decreed that all non-Talmudic studies be forbidden, even when they contained nothing specific to merit anathema. The reason was that they encroach on time that should be employed either in studying the Talmud or in making money to subsidise Talmudic scholars. The only loophole left was the time that even a pious Jew must perforce spend in the privy. Sacred studies were forbidden in that unclean place but it was permitted to read history provided it was written in Hebrew and was completely secular, meaning devoted exclusively to non-Jewish subjects. (Very likely those few Jews who developed an interest in the history of the French kings— no doubt tempted by Satan—were constantly complaining to their neighbors about the constipation from which they were suffering). As a consequence of these prohibitions, the vast majority of all Jews two hundred years ago—and particularly Jews in Eastern Europe—were completely ignorant of their own history. They were therefore easy prey to myths, superstitions and all manner of deviant thought.

It is small wonder that Jewish society of premodern times was saturated with Jewish chauvinism and extreme racism. Although Jewish chauvinism was present to some extent during all periods of historical Judaism, the widespread acceptance of the mystical, cabalistic beliefs in Judaism after the mid-16th century created a Jewish super-chauvinism of a radically new type. The central theme of this later mysticism was, quite simply, that Jews and God are one entity, while non-Jews are creatures of Satan. This pervasive belief was reinforced by a whole inventory of social customs, many strongly held by Jews in lands from Morocco to Poland. For example, several popular books of morality flatly stated that a Jew, and even more a Jewess, must be wary of four satanic creatures, to wit: a dog, a pig, a donkey, and a non-Jew. If a Jewess were seen by one of those four Satanic creatures after her monthly purification bath, a devil could enter into her. To expel that devil she must purify herself again. This advice appears even now in authoritative books and is actually followed by many in Jerusalem (and, I am sure, by some in London and New York as well).[7] The very few Jews who did not believe this demonology two hundred years ago were considered heretics to be persecuted and perhaps even killed.

A whole regimen of similar customs affecting many aspects of life was established in Judaism and piously followed. Today many rabbis (and also many Israeli military officers under their influence) say that the universe is divided into five parts: the inanimate, the vegetative, the animal, the human (or, as some of them say, the "speaking animal") and the Jew. They are resurrecting and continuing a tradition which prevailed in Judaism in the not so distant past. Although western influence has materially diminished this tradition in recent times it is still very much alive in some places.

Some Consequences in Israeli Society

Another example demonstrates how such beliefs influence much of Israeli society and how little such social facts are known outside Israel.

From the qualitative cleavage assumed to exist between Jews and non-Jews, it follows that those who profess that type of Judaism would regard all other religions and their symbols not only with contempt but even with horror as a source of dangerous demonic influences. The noticeable return of such attitudes in Israeli society is illustrated by changes made in Israeli school books. One may not consciously be aware that the plus sign in arithmetic is a cross, but those who see every cross as a threatening Satanic presence attach grave significance to any cross. In the early 1970's the international plus sign was removed from all elementary textbooks in Israel and replaced by a kind of inverted capital T. Had this been ordered by a Khaddafi or a Khomeini, the world would undoubtedly have been dramatically informed of it. The example demonstrates the extent to which Israel, seen by the world mostly through orchestrated propaganda and a primitive, vestigial form of Judaism, remains a *Terra Incognita*. Despite the considerable attention Israel commands or generates for itself, most of the world knows nothing of such anachronisms.

Clearly, one reason why Jews of the 17th and 18th centuries held the opinions they did about non-Jews, their religions and their cultures, was the general social climate in the countries where most Jews lived. In Poland or the Ottoman Empire two hundred years ago or in Yemen or parts of Morocco forty years ago, Jews were town dwellers (in many areas the only town dwellers). They were socially "above" the great majority of non-Jews who were either serfs or peasants not far removed from serfdom. In comparison, Jews were free, however much they were discriminated against. They had freedom of movement while the peasants were tied to the soil. Another socially important example is that non-Jews were often and still are servants of Jews but hardly ever the reverse.

There are many similar examples of such vestigial holdovers in present Jewish fanaticism. Even some Jews who are far from being extremists consider Jews superior to non-Jews, this belief tempered by various expedient considerations. Ezer Weitzman, the former Israeli Defense Minister, considered a moderate, titled his book about the Israeli Air Force *Thine Are the Heavens, Thine is the Earth*. This is a verse from Psalms praising the Almighty, not the Israeli Army. When he was taken to task by a journalist, Weitzman replied that because Jews and God are one and the same, verses about one can be transferred to the other. In current prevalent Israeli mentality, Weitzman represents the majority and the center while the journalist represents the extremists of the Left. Phrases like "Gentiles kill Gentiles and blame the Jews,"[8] or the supposed superiority of something called "the Jewish mind," more common in the Diaspora than in Israel, all suggest the same mentality.

There are many more examples. We who live in modern societies might ask: Why did individual Jews not try "to break the ranks" and through their own efforts change at least their own situation? The answer is that they were prevented by the power of the Jewish community or the congregation, *legally recognized* by all regimes in 1774. All European or Moslem states (except Britain to some extent) recognized "the Jewish community" as an autonomous entity with enormous powers of coercion without appeal to any higher authority. In Poland of 1774, and in the earlier history of Polish Jews, from the sixteenth century to 1764, it was not individual Jews who paid taxes, but the Jewish community. The supreme committee, the famous "Committee of Four Lands" as it was called, represented all Jewish communities. This institution was abolished in 1764 but the powers of the individual communities remained, particularly in towns of some size. The history of Jews everywhere from the late Roman Empire (if studied in the original documents and not in the more common apologetic "histories"), is full of recorded persecutions inflicted on Jews by other Jews for religious or other reasons. The most horrible punishments were inflicted, including the death penalty.

Only a few years before our chosen vantage point of 1774, during the outburst of the heretical Frankist Movement among the Polish Jews in 1756-1760, Jewish sources record that in Lvov (Lemberg), a city with one of the largest Jewish communities in Poland, a Jew who dared ride a horse on Sabbath on the street where the town rabbi dwelt while smoking a pipe, was put to death by the Jewish community with permission of the Polish authorities. The leading Jewish personages of Poland punished other Jewish heretics with a variety of punishments only a little less horrible. The mob could be incited against them by formally declaring that any Jew can kill such "heretics" with religious impunity. (This was a common declaration before the rise of the modern state and the prohibition of such practices. It is called in Hebrew and Yiddish,"permitting [to shed] blood" of certain Jews. It is "Hatarat Dam" in Hebrew and the expression is also used in Yiddish). There are many recorded cases of the use of this kind of threat. Assassinations were often carried out by the Jewish communities of Poland and subsequently those of Eastern Europe. In the middle of the thirteenth century such sentences were imposed not only on religious heretics, but also on any Jew who "told the Gentiles" ("Goyim") anything detrimental about the Jewish community or about any individual Jew, including those engaged in clearly criminal activities like smuggling. Similar punishment existed in other societies as Sicily and southern Italy or first and second generation Italian emigrants from those areas to the USA. The social situation which made the Sicilian "Mafia" possible is fairly common knowledge. But the

similar situation among Jews of that long-ago is almost completely unknown, although it persists in parts of contemporary Jewish society in
the USA and in Israel and probably in parts of Jewish communities
elsewhere.

Two very recent examples come to mind. Those who followed closely
the case of Jonathan Pollard and Pollard's Jewish supporters, as reported
in the Jewish press, will recognize exactly this sort of "Jewish Mafia"
solidarity which motivated both Pollard and many of his Jewish supporters. Seventy members of the Knesset (out of 120) recommended
that President Reagan pardon Pollard and send him to Israel where the
Israeli authorities would—if necessary—punish him themselves. This
thinking is obviously a throwback to the mentality of the separate, corporate, autonomous "Jewish community" which continued in countries
such as Yemen or Morocco until the mid-twentieth century. Also a throwback was the widespread condemnation of the Israeli government in
those circles and in the Jewish press in general for "denouncing" Pollard
to "Gentiles." A rabbi writing in the self-declared liberal American-Jewish
magazine *Tikkun* reminded his Jewish readers of exactly the fact mentioned above: that Jewish communities once put to death Jews who denounced their fellow Jews to "Gentiles." He condemned the Israeli
government on this basis for their treatment of Pollard.

The second example involves the Mexican Jewish community, particularly that part in Mexico City. In many ways this community preserved
and reproduced the absolute separation between Jews and "Gentiles"
on grounds of Jewish superiority. On average, Mexican Jews are very
rich compared with the general Mexican population. Jewish social life
in Mexico City is concentrated in the exclusive "The Sports Club," from
which all non-Jews, except as servants, are arbitrarily excluded. A few
days after the massacres at Sabra and Shatila in 1982, this community
together with the Israeli ambassador to Mexico, held an official protest
against non-Jews and the media of the whole world. It was attended by
most of the community. The protesters claimed the poor Jews suffering
around Beirut were being maligned. In January and February of 1988,
Mexican Jews were fighting a Jew of Argentina, Teodurv Rukef, who
had immigrated to Israel many years ago. Mexican Jews had known him
from Mexico City in the '70's as the educator of youth in the extreme
"Beitar," the Zionist Revisionists. Rukef later became Israeli correspondent of the Mexican paper *Excelsior* and described the situation in "the
territories" as everyone now sees it. The Mexican-Jewish community
denounced him publicly and officially for "slandering the Jews." They
called on the Israeli authorities to expel him from Israel and recommended that owners and editors of his paper dismiss him.

These attitudes reflect historically ingrained predilections, even among people who have not been subjected to adverse and prejudicial influences. Because such attitudes are less openly expressed it may be assumed that they are not common among Jews in the USA and elsewhere. This is a profound political mistake, a mistake that reflects ignorance of the Jewish past. In that past, Jewish solidarity was so strong that open rebellion of Jews against Jewish social solidarity was probably very rare in 1774. History records that for many reasons, numerous Jewish heretics wanted emancipation from the more restrictive rules of Jewish orthodox behavior. The "community rulers," therefore, found it necessary to inhibit them with such methods as floggings, the pillory and stocks, or other humiliating punishments. In Poland at that time, these were considered a necessary and often-used procedure of every synagogue of any size. The congregation was often encouraged to spit on an offender after prayers. With the rise of Zionism, an inventory of such punishments was made by religious Zionists to serve as a model of original Jewish jurisprudence, although Israeli practice today is based on English common law. The most important study of this phenomenon is a book written by Simha Asaf, who subsequently became one of the first nine Supreme Court Judges of the State of Israel. One of the punishments he solemnly cited as a precedent (although from Germany, not Poland) is the case of a Jew whose eyes were torn out by order of a rabbi for the "crime" of eating on Yom Kippur. Rabbi Shlomo Luria of sixteenth-century Poland, one of the greatest Polish rabbis of all times, debated whether to mutilate a Jewish offender. He considered cutting off hands, feet or tongue, or blinding, but it is not clear whether these were to be administered separately or together, or if it would be better to kill him outright. Rabbi Luria favored the death penalty, the reason being that his learned teacher once ordered a mutilation of a Jewish offender. The mutilated criminal then converted to Christianity, married and had children "and from that time all his family hated Jews very much."

This rather brutal example suggests that the only route of escape open to individual Jews from the absolute rule of the communities and their rabbis was conversion, either to Christianity or Islam. The result, of course, was that those who took this step ceased to be Jews. If they did not elect conversion, they could not ride a horse or smoke a pipe on Sabbath or learn mathematics or geography without the certainty that great punishment would be enforced by the autonomous Jewish communities. In fact, in Central and Eastern Europe and in the Muslim countries, horrible "punishments" were illegally inflicted in a lynch-like manner a long time after they were legally forbidden. In the same town of Lvov, mentioned above, the first Reform rabbi of the town, together with part of his family, was poisoned by the Orthodox Jewish community in 1848. Hebrew and Yiddish literature produced in Central Europe in the mid-nineteenth century (for example the Hebrew novels of P. Smolenskin) is full of well-founded allegations and descriptions of heretical or rebellious Jews being murdered in secret on orders of the rabbis and heads of their community. These persecutions continued despite vigilance of the police who by that time were trying to prevent them.

The "New World" vs. The "Jewish Community"

How then has the situation changed? The USA was the first, and for a long time the only state which treated Jews as individual citizens, enjoying full equality of rights, including, more importantly, protection by the state from the "Jewish community." These gains were the result of the Constitution and Bill of Rights. But during the period covered by this essay, the number of American Jews was very small. On the European continent, emancipation from the tyranny of the Jewish community resulted from two movements. In Western Europe the French Revolution insisted upon including Jews in matters of civil rights, and was followed by the Napoleonic regimes which established for the first time the rights of individual Jews in both France and in countries conquered by Napoleon. In central and Eastern Europe, enlightened but absolute rulers were influenced by the same liberating forces, but with more limited results. One of the principal objectives of Napoleonic rule was destruction of "intermediate authorities," including Jewish autonomous communities. The state's own central institutions were established, such as police forces (which did not exist in the Polish Commonwealth of 1774). Consequently, individual Jews, even in the Tsarist empire, enjoyed a measure of protection as individual subjects that they did not have before. They could no longer be legally punished for smoking on Sabbath or eating on Yom Kippur. Hebrew and Yiddish literature makes it clear that some began to indulge in these pleasures once they could do so without penalties. They also began to learn geography and send their children to non-Jewish schools.

These new opportunities and possibilities produced enormous changes in the whole Jewish situation and character, including even demography, as remarked above. In a relatively short time, from 1774 to the beginning of Zionism (whether we date it formally to 1897 or to a few years before this), the whole scene of Judaism in Europe and to a similar extent in the Ottoman Empire was transformed.[9] It changed from an almost perfectly closed society to one which was now legally quite open in many countries, and in other countries was liberated from many of the suffocating inhibitions of the earlier coercive, closed Jewish societies. Such social transformations can be painful in different ways for many individuals. A romantic tendency often lingers, regretting loss of the old certitudes. A romantically perceived old simplicity is often adorned with sentimental nostalgia to look idyllic—a self-deception or outright falsification. Inability to learn quickly the duties and corresponding rights of full citizenship complicates the transformation. And exaggerated expectations often blind individuals to the fact that transformation is not an instantaneous change but a gradual process. There are also those who suffer the fears that always accompany profound social changes. "The fear of freedom" may be among the most frightening. In the second part of this essay I will show how Zionism was really born from a mixture of all these factors which became its most characteristic and persistent qualities.

Part II

Zionism's Ideological Roots: Impact Upon Jews

Zionism is an ideology. Its political/national form, with which this essay is concerned, is the foundation for the State of Israel's national character. It dictates much of Israel's foreign and domestic conduct. In the state's international policies, Zionism is a major consideration along with the state's militarism in shaping Israel's territorial aspirations. In domestic affairs, the state's "fundamental" or "basic" laws are predicated upon the basic Zionist concept that "the Jewish people" is included in Israel's nationality constituency. In the famous case of Adolph Eichmann, Israel's highest court ruled that "the State of Israel is the sovereign state of the Jewish people." The "Status Law" declares that "the central task of the State of Israel and the Zionist movement" is "the mission of gathering in the exiles," which means Jews who live outside Israel.

This positioning of Jews at the centrality of Israeli concerns leads to a less-than-equal status for Israel's minority of people who are not Jews. Israel's claims to territory beyond June 1967 is based upon Zionism's perceived role as the agency for translating biblical lore into contemporary reality. This has led to conflict with the neighboring Arab states who hold claims to the disputed territory, claims that are widely recognized internationally. In both this domestic and international incorporation of Zionist ideology, powered by Israeli sovereignty, are to be found the root cause of the deprivation of the human and national rights of the displaced Palestinians and the inequities in status of Palestinians living within pre-June 1967 Israel. Both of these conditions have increasingly become matters of international concern because these Zionist-based Israeli policies are considered threats to peace.

The state to which first Zionist ideologues and later Zionist and Israeli statesmen aspired was always to be for "the Jewish people," defined according to rabbinic law in its most restrictive and narrow sense. Qualification as a Jew derived from birth by a Jewish mother or conversion by some ritual acceptable to the Israeli state. People who cannot meet these qualifications are "different" in the eyes of the state and generally in the less formal attitudes of much of the Israeli Jewish population whose lifestyle is naturally influenced profoundly by the governing institutions of the state.

There is another side of the same coin. Destructive and wounding as the impact of Zionist ideology, sovereignized in a powerful state, has been on Arabs, particularly on Palestinians, consequences for many Jews have been hardly less profound. If left to its own devices, it is hardly less threatening for the future of Israeli Jews and even for the greater number of Jews who live in other countries who aspire to acculturation in the lands of their citizenships and loyalties. It is to this Jewish context that I devote the rest of this essay.

Political/national Zionism diligently adhered to the basic Herzlian dogma proclaiming, "We are a people—one people." This means that all Jews, no matter where they live or what their citizenship, constitute a nation. Recognizing that many Jews of western, democratic states found the idea of a separate Jewish nationality unacceptable and even repugnant, Zionism frequently employed euphemisms and coined slogans in attempts to make its nationalist ideology more palatable. Many of the slogans were designed to suggest that the movement was dedicated to ameliorating the degradations imposed upon some Jews in the ethno-centered and/or theocratic regimes of eastern and central Europe. For Jews living in more open and free societies, Zionism offered the promise of relief from the tensions of surviving as Jews in "alien" cultures and societies. One such slogan was,"To live a full Jewish life in freedom, the most hospitable place is in a Jewish state." Another was, "Make Jews a nation like all other nations." Another, referring to Palestine,"A land without people for a people without a land."

Implicit in such simplistic presentations of Zionist ideology and program was a response to a sense of insecurity and/or self-doubt suffered by many Jews over the prevalence and persistence of anti-semitism, real or imagined, virulent or covert, suspected as being ultimately inevitable. During Hitler's domination of Germany, for example, a slogan used in the United States to expand acceptance of Zionism, or at least to minimize opposition, was "If it can happen in Germany it can happen anywhere." This was constantly reiterated despite the glaring differences between German and United States history.

Theological explanations for the disabilities endured by many Jews appealed to some of the intellectual elite. Jews were called "the suffering servants of the Lord," the idea borrowed from the prophecies of the Second Isaiah. Various metaphysical explanations were given for the collective longevity of Jews managing to survive in the world perceived by Herzl to be incurably hostile. But none of them, nor all together, provided satisfying answers to the average Jew. Not surprisingly, most hoped for a normal life like the people among whom they lived. Small wonder then that some Jews advantaged by greater learning and relieved of the debilitating and stultifying anxieties of feeding, clothing and housing their families, began to speculate intellectually with formulas which, at least in theory, seemed to offer some escape for their fellow Jews from frightening historic memories and even contemporary anxieties, and to hold out a promise for living a "normal" life.

A number of such thinkers were precursors of Herzl. One of the more renowned was Leo Pinsker, born in Russian Poland in 1821, the son of a teacher and a scholar who had been well trained in secular knowledge. The son studied law and medicine. Early in life he devoted himself to spreading secular knowledge among Jews. He wrote extensively for Zionist publications, advocating an increase of secular reforms as a way of improving the status of Jews in the countries in which they lived. In the late 1880's, however, a reactionary wave throughout Russia produced repressions and pogroms. Pinsker's faith in this process was shattered. Assailed by doubts and coached by more orthodox Zionists, he was persuaded that Jews could emancipate themselves into normality only in a territory where they could exercise political control by insuring they would constitute a majority. This profound alteration of his thinking led him to author a pamphlet which he titled "Auto-Emancipation." The term survived both as a goal and as substance in mainstream Zionist ideology.

It should be emphasized at this point that Pinsker, and practically all earlier architects of Zionist thought, believed that Jews possess certain secular, cultural, ethnic or extra-religious characteristics which were distinctive products of their history. In modern terminology these might be called "roots." They wanted these preserved because they gave "the Jewish people" intellectual and spiritual qualities different from those of other peoples. But they needed to adapt to changing, modern, secular environments, which Jews could do only in an atmosphere free of stressful "abnormalities" experienced as minorities in generally hostile societies. This intriguing prospect captured the imagination of many—but not all—Jews in the eastern parts of Europe. It had considerably less appeal to those who enjoyed the freedoms of the more liberal and open democracies of the West. But the majority of Jews at the end of the nineteenth and earliest years of the twentieth centuries lived in less liberal nations. For these Jews, Zionism acquired a positive dynamic for its program of persuasion to "go up" (*aliyah*) to Palestine, the future site for the proposed "Jewish state."

These are some of the forces which enabled Herzl to launch his organized movement. It widely advocated international recognition of "the Jewish people" as a "homeless nation" prepared to eliminate its abnormal status by finding "normality" through mass migration to a "Jewish state." And without publicly advertising the precise terminology, "Jewish nationalism" became a factor to be reckoned with in the lexicon of and as substance in international diplomacies pertaining to Palestine and the Middle East.

To understand the significance of Zionism and its impact upon contemporary reality, it is necessary to address *first of all* its design for Jews. This question has been neglected during the last forty years or so because of the emphasis on what may be called "classical Zionism," or the body of doctrine common to *all* Zionists in the first decades following the primacy given to Herzlian Zionism in 1897. In efforts to give the movement more apparent compatibility with democratic principles, those "classical" ideas have been either diluted or disguised by Zionist propaganda employed in the United States and other western countries. But in Israel, "classical Zionism" remained very important as the common ideology of all Zionist parties governing Israel. It also permeates the highly centralized and ideological Israeli system of education, indoctrinating all Israeli children (*and* soldiers!) with considerable success.

I do not deny the politically important fact that within Zionism the various parties are marked by differences, but I strongly emphasize the more important principles on which they agree and which most young Israeli Jews are dogmatically taught. The candid presentation of these principles will come as a surprise to most westerners, and even more to most Arabs. But this simply illustrates how much the Israeli and the general Jewish reality, both past and present, is unknown outside Israel or outside tightly held control of *organized* Jewish circles in other countries.

The fundamental Zionist doctrine holds that Jews in non-Jewish societies are not "normal" either as individual human beings or as "communities." They will become "normal" only when they live in a society which will be absolutely or at least mostly Jewish, meaning that non-Jews will not be more than a small minority. It must be recognized and emphasized that classical Zionism has interpreted "normality" in its broadest sense. It was strongly implied by both Socialist Zionists as well as right-wing Zionists that all Jews living in the diaspora, if not actually mentally ill were at least neurotic or had strong potential tendencies to become so simply because they live as a minority in other countries. Every ideological shading within Zionism added its own peculiar "explanation" to the basic dogma. But all of them—even that advocated by Judah Magnes—accepted as a matter of faith that diaspora Jews suffered some abnormality, or at least serious impediments to attaining the normality of the majority population.

The Socialist Zionists attributed Jewish lack of normality to the predominance of certain professions which they labelled "secondary," such as trade, in contrast to the "primary" professions, such as heavy industry. The principal explanation offered by right-wing Zionists for abnormality was the absence of Jewish militarism. Others explained it by the absence of physical work, mainly agricultural. There have been other explanations, and shortly after the organized establishment of Zionism many "explanations" of the "abnormal" Jewish status were advanced. Each variant in Zionism insisted, and continues to insist, on the primacy of its own particular "explanation." Recently there has been a rather extensive fusion. Zionist militarists continue to believe in the primacy of the military effort, not only to continue oppression of the Palestinians but also to dominate the Middle East. Basically, they argue that militarism will make Jews "normal," but many now add that agricultural settlements serve the same purpose, but less effectively than army service. Correspondingly, those who believe that virtue claimed for agricultural work is the best instrument to make Jews "normal" also believe that the army, particularly if it incorporates agricultural work, can serve as a supporting secondary instrument.

To understand Israel it is necessary to understand this ideological base which is common to the entire Israeli establishment, including the structure and the behavior of its army and its secret services. This does not mean that Zionist ideology actually dominates and determines everything. Actually it is now in decline as pragmatic considerations play a role. Corruption, party interests and other factors operating in every ideological state or movement thwart full realization of ideology. But even with such dilutions, the basic ideological principles cannot be ignored. Israel is established on these principles and continues to make every effort to fortify them in its population and also among its sympathizers, Jews as well as non-Jews, in other countries.

Exporting the Ideology

The dogma of the "normality" of Israeli Jews and "abnormality" of other Jews provides the key to understanding some of the most important aspects of actual Israeli political behavior involving Jews of other countries and also Palestinians. First of all, it explains the strong feelings of superiority of Israeli Jews toward other Jews and the systematic and often quite successful efforts to create a strong inferiority complex among Jews living outside Israel, simply for living where they live. It also accounts for the denigrating Israeli treatment of Israeli Jews who emigrate from Israel. They are officially denounced, and a few years ago Yitzhak Rabin called them "misfits." It is noteworthy that most Israeli Jews who leave Israel to live in the United States willingly accept the stigma of "abnormality." Such is the power of ideological indoctrination. This point was made by Benjamin Beit-Hallahmi.[10] The Hebrew language paper *Yisrael Shelanu* (*Our Israel*), published in the United States for the benefit of Israeli Jews who immigrated to the United States, continually condemns its readers for the "sin" of having become "abnormal" by leaving Israel. Nevertheless its circulation continually increases, presumably for the same masochistic reasons that make some preachers popular when they constantly berate their audiences for being sinners. Sin is also regarded as a departure from normality in addition to being an offense against God.

This Israeli sense of superiority was much stronger thirty or forty years ago when all Jews living outside Israel were described in many Israeli's publications as "human dust." This was a favorite term of Ben-Gurion's, among others. Only a concerted effort by Zionism and the state could turn the "dust" into "real human beings." More liberal Zionist interpretations moderately amended the restorative prescription to claim that the movement and the State would "help" the Jews outside Israel remake themselves. The totalitarian tendencies inherent in all Zionism derive from this dogma. Given the air of Israeli superiority over non-Israeli Jews, no leap of the imagination is required to understand the origins of the near contempt in which many Israelis hold Palestinians and other Arabs. Translated into political/military reality, this attitude is a major factor in the physical suffering of Arabs. It is far more life-damaging than the emotional and psychological distress imposed on susceptible non-Israeli Jews.

As long as non-Israeli Jews either actively or passively accept Israel's political/legal claims to a "Jewish people"-nationality relationship with the Zionist state and acquiesce in the presumption of the superiority of Israeli Jews, there will be no change in the popular perception that all non-Israeli Jews stand in a surrogate relationship to Israeli Jews.

So-called American Jewish "doves" display a proclivity to entertain privately an arms-length distance from Israel. At the same time, many maintain a kind of prudent public silence about much Israeli conduct that is contrary to world consensus. In the American Jewish debate about Israel, there is a widespread tendency to quote extensively the opinions of Israelis as authoritative support for one's own views. It is as if an Israeli "authority" were necessary to defend a position that does not follow an official Israeli "line," even though no similar higher authority is considered necessary to legitimize personal views over U.S. policies or those of any other country—except Israel. This deferential attitude toward Israeli Jews reflects some acceptance of Zionist claims that Israeli Jews possess a more authentic Jewish identity than other Jews, and are therefore entitled to a superior status in something too often called "the Jewish world" or "world Jewry," as if some overall, corporate entity composed entirely of Jews really existed.

Such fabrications may have their roots in old political gerrymandering of vote counting in the World Zionist Organization. Votes of Palestinian Jews were given twice the weight of Zionists in other countries. Or it may be associated with the tribalistic notion that direct contact with "the land" provides Israeli Jews with some mystical qualities not possessed by other Jews. Whatever the explanation, the result demeans the universality of Judaism's basic ethical values and the elementary human values of non-Israeli Jews. In a political sense, the perception that their best spiritual and intellectual talents are, in some measure, at the service of another state rather than to the welfare of the society of which they are an integral part, tarnishes the reputation of citizens of a democracy.

Present Israeli policies or officially proposed future policies toward the Palestinians generally proceed from the central Zionist dogma that Jews become "normal" only in a totally or predominantly Jewish society. It does not matter whether the Zionist party is "hawkish" or "dovish." All of them modify policies in various ways only to meet pragmatic political considerations while all adhere to the same central proposition. There is however, an old, internal Zionist debate on the character of the "Jewish society" that all consider vital for Jewish "normality." Should this Jewish society be based on an exclusively Jewish heritage, usually meaning Jewish religious orthodoxy, or should it be open to western or even Arab cultural influences? There are other internal disputes in the Zionist movement. They include: how many Palestinians can there be in this Jewish society without invalidating its status as a "normal" Jewish society. The fear of an expanding Palestinian population is greater than all the so-called "security considerations" that are presented to the world as justification for Israel's oppression of Palestinians. Another subject of debate is the extent to which Palestinians in the occupied territories constitute "a danger to the Jewish character of the State of Israel," as the conventional Israeli expression puts it.

Regardless of their policy differences, all Zionist parties—from extreme doves to extreme hawks—consider the mere existence of Palestinians *in Palestine* to be potentially a serious threat to the "Jewishness" of the so-called "Jewish state." Two different basic policies are advocated to support this shared ideological parochialism for achieving a "normal" Jewish society. There is certainly a difference in kind and degree between "transfer" (expulsion) of all Palestinians (or perhaps only Palestinians in the occupied territories), and return of the territories to establish an independent Palestinian state, but the motivation is the same. It is the basic ideology which holds that "normality" for Jews is possible only in a society composed preponderantly of Jews.

Put another way, it is important not to continue making the popular mistake of the early sixties which erroneously heralded the end of ideology. Those who reduce their analysis of the actual Israeli policies of expansionism or victimizing Palestinians to pragmatic considerations, are ignoring a very important factor in the enduring dynamics of Zionism's fundamental ideological dogma. In actual practice, Israeli political behavior is always a combination of ideology and pragmatics, never purely pragmatic considerations alone. With few exceptions, Zionist dogma is the very essence of political debate inside Israel. When Shimon Peres argues with Yitzhak Shamir or when "Peace Now" argues with Gush Emunin, the first and most important component of the debate is what constitutes a "normal" Jewish society as defined in historic Zionist ideology. All aspire to "ingather" all Jews into such a society to make them "normal." Each side accuses the policies of the other of militating against this central common goal. It is not possible to understand, much less influence the debate, without insight into the generally recognized terms of reference which govern the debate.

Such powerful beliefs, tenaciously held by so many people for so long a time and contrary to the persuasive evidence that American Jews, for example, are as "normal" as the Israelis and as "normal" as other Americans, do not persist in a social vacuum. Recorded human history is full of examples of strongly held beliefs that are similar to the absurd Zionist dogma concerning Jewish "abnormality" and "normality." The explanations for the longevity of such ideological rigidity may be discovered by examining the history of the societies sustaining the beliefs. There is more than a superficial symbiotic relationship between Zionist dogma about Jewish "abnormality" and the absurd anti-semitic notions about Jews. But it is not so much the origins of such beliefs which warrant continued investigation as their persistence and their injurious successes.

An Effort to Explain

The following explanation of Zionism as first of all a Jewish movement takes into consideration the conditions of the Jews (or most of them), as described in the first part of this essay. This is followed by examination of changes in those conditions, until and after, the rise of Zionism. Finally, the influence of European nationalism and chauvinism in general must be considered, and even more important, the specific influences of various rational movements of the middle to late nineteenth and early twentieth centuries.

The situation described in Part I makes clear that, contrasted to present conditions in all western countries, most Jews were either living in homogeneous Jewish societies or in situations where the life of non-Jews with whom they came into contact was easily ignored. Jews in modern societies cannot do so, nor does much evidence suggest they wish to do so. For example, the educational systems developed by all modern states are open to all citizens. Even expensive private schools that are supported wholly or partially by minority groups are to a great extent influenced by state standards. Most Jews in western countries are educated in public schools as part of a school population composed of other citizens. Any additional Jewish education is mostly marginal.

This is in dramatic contrast to the situation of Jews in Eastern Europe in 1774 when a Jewish child's education was strictly Jewish. All subjects which might have formed a bridge with a non-Jewish child, even as neutral in substance as mathematics or language learning, were systematically excluded from Jewish curricula. Another example, on a different level, is that no adult Jew in the United States can avoid the state tax authorities. His ancestors of two hundred years ago paid taxes exclusively to officials of the Jewish congregation. Part of the taxes were passed on to non-Jewish authorities. Other examples demonstrate that the majority of Jews of Eastern Europe, in 1774, lived in exclusively or predominantly Jewish small towns. Their cultural environment was wholly Jewish, totally isolated from any contact with the oppressed peasant serfs, who were poorer and more oppressed and more culturally deprived than Jews, and with only the most formal contact with the ruling group.

Enter, the Era of Enlightenment

All this began to change with the emergence of the modern state. At the end of the eighteenth century, the era of Enlightenment and the evolution of the nation-state began to transform the situation of the Jews. Individual taxation replaced taxes for a separate, corporate community. Compulsory state-supervised education was introduced. These and many other reforms dramatically increased contacts between Jews and the majority of citizens of the countries in which they lived. Even more important were the individual freedoms introduced by the modern state. They include not only those familiar in the democracies, but also those introduced by enlightened Absolutism and those allowed by even authoritarian systems which are not totalitarian. An example in this category is the right of the individual, under the protection of common law, to change his residence or his occupation and to live where he wants and to do or not do what he wants. In 1774 Poland, the great majority of the population were peasant serfs who were completely restricted to their villages of origin. Jews were forbidden by law to live in many of the larger cities. The Napoleonic era lifted this restriction for a time in the capital, Warsaw, but Jewish residency in the villages was prohibited unless permitted by a generous lord of the village. It requires mind-stretching effort today to imagine how people lived under such conditions, but if we make this effort it becomes clear that one effect was to reduce to a bare minimum contacts between Jews and non-Jews. When Jews have the right to choose where they live, some settle where the influence of the Jewish community structure is greatly reduced. But Jewish and Hebrew literature of the nineteenth century records that, once the non-Jewish peasants were free to move into towns that were formerly Jewish, the distinctive, predominantly Jewish character of the towns diminished, sometimes becoming almost extinct. These examples indicate that the emergence of the enlightened, modern state and its rule of law was accompanied by a progressive decline in Eastern Europe of the exclusively Jewish society which had been decreed in earlier times by whimsical and/or prejudicial ruling classes. Wherever it may still linger in vestigial form and in small pockets, it is less "purely Jewish" than before.

The pervasive and dominant influence of these modern states contributed to and was accompanied by Jewish Enlightenment during the last quarter of the eighteenth century. Many differences existed in this multifaceted movement which took place in different places and cultural environments. However, these are some of its common characteristics: the promotion of secular education which included the teaching of modern European languages and Hebrew and Yiddish in a correct and more useful form; introduction of such subjects as mathematics and sciences in the curricula; cultivation of the arts, such as poetry and appreciation of aesthetics, both previously unknown, at least consciously, among Eastern European Jews and frowned upon by the official bureaucracy of the community. Jews were encouraged to become active participants in politics, for example, volunteering help in times of crisis and war. Such activities, previously denied to Jews, accelerated during this period in nations such as Germany, which embraced enlightenment more quickly than others. Consequently, Jews participated more in the life of these countries. The first educated Jewish women appeared, along with some protests against the horrible oppression inflicted on Jewish women in the closed Jewish societies. In short, the "modernization" process was similar to the experiences of countries of the Third World today and what Russia experienced earlier.

To pursue this analogy further, the process of modernization is very painful in itself and is usually attended by inflated expectations. Young people repudiate the ways of their parents and are quite often rejected in return. They leave the comfortably warm nest of the extended family and the little town where everyone knows everyone and everything is predictable because everything is fixed by religion and custom. They expect that everything will be perfect in the new order. When perfection does not materialize and previously unthought-of difficulties arise, frustration and, often, disillusion follow. Two conflicting reactions then take place. There is a realization that modernization will not, contrary to expectations, solve all problems. At the same time, advances and improvements are taken for granted. In this frame of mind, it is not uncommon to indulge in nostalgic and romanticized images of a premodern society where everyone is sentimentally portrayed as happy. There follows a longing to restore the imagined idyllic past. The history of Europe during the last 100 to 200 years is replete with concrete examples of both tendencies existing before the rise of Zionism. The same two tendencies are recognizable throughout the Third World today. People try to retain social patterns that are incompatible with modernization while enjoying the advantages of modernization.

The combination of hope and frustration experienced by Jews entering the era of Enlightenment cannot be separated from the general political and social conditions in the countries of their residence. Two hundred years ago, the nations of Central and Eastern Europe generally faced modernization experiencing reactions similar to those experienced by Jews. The same contrasting tendencies were operative, one emphasizing the humanistic international and generally democratic, progressive spirit, and the other exclusivist, chauvinistic, reactionary characteristics. The two tendencies can be properly identified by their attitudes toward Jews. In a certain limited sense it remains true today that any state's or movement's posture about Jews may be a barometer of its progressive or reactionary character. The obverse is also true. Jewish attitudes in any given environment may be a general yardstick for measuring the progressivism or reactionism of any movement among Jews. The European reactionary movements made the anti-semitic claim that Jews cannot fully participate in the mainstream life of the country because their inherent "Jewishness" prevents them from becoming Frenchmen, Germans or Americans.

Addressing Anti-Semitism

There are two general philosophies for addressing anti-semitism or for confronting racism and chauvinism of any kind. On the one hand, they can be understood for what they truly are and not something inevitable which must be accepted. "You've got to be taught to hate and fear," as one line goes in a lyric in the popular American musical, *South Pacific*. This is an apt observation about these disreputable, social/political thought-patterns which are still too prevalent today. There is nothing inevitable about them, or "endemic," as Herzl labeled them. They can be and inevitably will be extirpated unless the slow agonizing efforts of progressive minds and spirits are doomed to a failure which would mark the failure of human development and aspirations to be better humans than we presently are. Mankind is gradually learning the hard lesson that living in a racist society is destructive not only of racism's victims but also its advocates and bad for an entire society. This is the lasting, universal testimony of Hitler's holocaust and Nazi Germany. The growing minority views of dissenters in Israel reflect the syndrome. History tells us that if racist societies cannot purge themselves, a common world consensus inexorably rallies to the support of the victims of racism and other varieties of oppression. Hapless victims of social/political evils will be rescued from dehumanizing policies and practices with support from out-group allies.

This is nowhere more apparent than in the struggle of Jews against anti-semitism. Jews did not—and could not—liberate themselves even if they wished; and regrettably, some in the Europe of pre-Enlightenment times did not wish to do so. They were liberated with the indispensable help of the more progressive forces of European and American societies which came to the conclusion that a society which oppresses Jews is a dangerous society for everyone. That inescapable logic proved more persuasive than any nostalgic or romantic feelings which may still have hankered for the closed and intimate inner-group relations of their past. It was not French Jews by themselves who defeated French anti-semites during the Dreyfus affair. It required a coalition of French progressives. Herzl and other Zionists completely misread the French situation in the last quarter of the nineteenth century. Neither did "the Jews" defeat the Nazis nor did they save European Jewry. The Allied Powers defeated the Nazis in World War II and they did so for their own purposes. Together with the pursuit of their own national political interests, all were motivated by a wish not to be Nazified themselves. Even if a Jewish state had existed in Palestine, there was no way that Jews alone could have defeated Nazism or any other form of anti-Semitism.

There is another pattern of reaction to the rise of anti-Semitism, not unlike reactions to other forms of racism and chauvinism. It consists of accommodating to it; the victims form their own mirror image of the phenomenon. This was basically the method Zionism used. Anti-Semites claim that Jews are "by nature" strangers forever and cannot be complete Americans, Frenchmen, etc. The overall Zionist ideological answer is essentially that the anti-semitic accusations are correct; that the very fact of Jews living in Europe or the United States makes them "abnormal." They can only become "normal" by living in a Jewish society. The anti-semites and other reactionaries look back nostalgically to the time when Jews were separated from the rest of the population. Zionists accommodate anti-Semitic longings for separation when they advocate a Jewish society to correct the "abnormal" state of the Jews and therefore eliminate anti-Semitism. Both anti-Semites and Zionism assume anti-Semitism is ineradicable and inevitable. Both argue that the very presence of Jews as a minority in any society causes anti-Semitism. According to Zionist thinking, this is to some extent beneficial because anti-Semitism reminds Jews of their "abnormal" condition. There have been continuous alliances of Zionist with some of the worst anti-Semites of recent times, from Herzl who allied himself with the Russian Minister of the Interior, Von Phleve, a notorious instigator of pogroms, to the Israeli governments of the 70's and 80's who allied themselves with the anti-Semitic Argentine junta which, according to Amnesty International, compelled Jewish prisoners to kneel before a picture of Hitler. These alliances reveal strong elements of ideological cooperation and cynical political opportunism.

Related to these is the Israeli policy concerning the apprehension of the notorious war criminal Adolph Eichmann by Israeli agents in Argentina in 1961. International law authorities contended justifiably that the proper jurisdiction for the trial should be Germany and the relevant law under which the trial should be conducted was that Eichmann's crimes were crimes against *humanity*. But the Israeli government, speaking through Ben Gurion, insisted that the trial be held in Israel under Israeli laws pertaining to crimes against *"the Jewish people."* The Israeli view prevailed against considerable international controversy. When the Israeli prime minister was pressed to explain his position he said it was important to dramatize anti-semitism to the Israeli population because they were showing signs of growing complacency about a phenomenon that was little evident in Israel's "Jewish society." It was necessary to demonstrate that anti-Semitism is "alive and well." The trial was aimed at intensifying and solidifying Israel's basic Zionist ideology that the world is anti-Semitic and Jews must be isolated to prevent persecutions.

The Common Denominator of State Zionism

The evidence and arguments submitted above illuminate the basic and consistent aims and fundamental ideological roots of all Zionist parties, despite important differences dictated by pragmatic policies. Zionism is essentially a reactionary movement. Its basic assumptions and aims resemble other exclusive, chauvinistic movements, including classical anti-semitism. It can be described as a mirror image of anti-semitism. Its ideal is the pre-modern state of affairs in which Jewish society was exclusively Jewish and isolated from non-Jewish contacts and influences. But it is and has been sufficiently pragmatic to be obsessed with the pursuit of power, as is the case of most recent reactionary movements. Zionism recognizes that the ideal must sometimes be modified in the interest of accumulation and consolidation of power. Zionism wants Israel not to be simply a ghetto, but a heavily armed ghetto. In an age in which ghettos are generally abhorred, the exclusiveness of Israel must be guarded by military might. In this way it can claim to be a victim of ostracism while at the same time discriminating against people who are not Jews.

Much of Israel's conduct and some of its self-proclaimed virtues are simply inverted forms of classical anti-semitic accusations against Jews.

Zionism was motivated, not by traditional inherent Jewish values or characteristics, but by rebuttals to anti-semitic allegations, as if Jews have a special obligation to prove they are a "nation like all other nations." The jibes of the anti-Semites were adopted in an inverted form and proclaimed to be true Jewish characteristics. When anti-semites accused Jews of being cowards and never working the land, the Zionist response was to try to demonstrate that Jews are "by nature" the best soldiers and the best farmers in the world. Common-sense answers, that people's acquired characteristics are determined by circumstances and change, were not considered. Indeed, one significant and informative way to analyze the whole Zionist enterprise is to see it as a response to anti-semitic ideas about Jews. Zionism incorporated these fallacious generalizations into its own ideology.

The basic character of Zionism has been and remains a worship of the past and the wish to restore a past in which Jews were separate, and because they were separate were supposedly "normal." As such, Zionism is indeed a recidivist Jewish movement. It is necessary to show what the past really was, for only by true historical knowledge can we understand the present, and to some extent the predictable future.

I express the sober hope that this contribution to understanding Zionism in its basic Jewish context will help people, particularly Jews, liberate themselves from its anachronistic influences which run contrary to the hopes and goals of continued emancipation and progress of all mankind.

NOTES

1. *Ma'ariv*, July 10, 1987.
2. Joan Peters, *From Time Immemorial*, New York: Harper & Row, 1984, offered false explanation for the phenomenon.
3. Talmud is the comprehensive term for combining the Mishnah (law) and Gemara (commentary) in one single unit. Talmud is applied specifically to two compilations: the Jerusalem and the Babylonian. Of the two the Babylonian Talmud is the most authoritative. Traditional Judaism regards the Talmud as deriving from God at Sinai and thus to be a complimentary, more fully explained expression of the same Divine law as the Bible.

   The Geonim were the heads of two major Babylonian academies of Sura and Pumbeditha who were both considered to be the authoritative spiritual and religious guides of the Jews. Geonim derived their authority by virtue of their prominence as teachers and expounders of the Talmud. Geonim compiled codes of Judaic law, the first of which was composed by Gaon Yeduhai of Sura between 756 and 777.
4. Philo was an Alexandrian philosopher who lived between 25 B.C.E. and 40 C.E. By combining contemporary Hellenistic philosophy and piety of Jewish belief in revelation and the Holy Scriptures, Philo became the first theological philosopher of Judaism.

   Maimonides' full name: Moses Ben Maimon, lived between 1135 and

1204. A medical doctor, he became a major philosopher of Judaism and codifier of Judaic law.

5. Karl Popper, *Open Society and its Enemies*. Princeton, NJ: Princeton Univ. Press, 1966.

6. "Ma'or Einaim" ("Light for Eyes") by Atarya Rossi, published in Italy in 1570 and promptly banned by many rabbis, including Rabbi Yoseph Caro, the famous author of *Shulkan Aruch*, for many Jews the still-operative compendium of redacted Halakha, or traditional law.

7. The eighteenth-century *Shevet Musar (The Scourge of Morality)*, published in Turkey, has been reprinted and is cited as authoritative in many books published in the 1960's, 1970's and 1980's.

8. Used by Menachem Begin after the massacres at Sabra and Shatila.

9. Not in such countries as Morocco or Yemen.

10. Middle East Information Project, (MERIP), Jan-Feb.,1988.

10

REFORM JUDAISM AND ZIONISM: EARLY HISTORY AND CHANGE

NORTON MEZVINSKY

It is difficult to reconcile differences between Reform Judaism and Zionism. These two philosophies were differently oriented and, as they developed, were basically antithetical to one another. By the end of the 1880s Reform Judaism had taken an official anti-Zionist stand that lasted for half a century. The Reform movement, however, changed in the twentieth century. The Columbus Platform of 1937 signalled that change. In less than a decade thereafter the Reform movement had embraced Zionism. Reform support of Zionism increased tremendously after the state of Israel came into existence in 1948.

This essay endeavors to reconsider the early anti-nationalist, anti-Zionist position of Reform Judaism and to reassess critically the early shift away from that original position.

From its inception Reform Judaism rejected Jewish nationalism. This rejection emanated from a new, Judaic theological formulation that differed inherently from Traditional Judaism. Affirming the existence of divine revelation in the Bible, Reform nevertheless denied the literal view that each and every word and idea in the Bible came directly from God. Reform also discarded the Traditional notion that Jews were unique as a people in the sense that God had obliged them to live their lives differently than other people. Reform extended another proposition of Traditional Judaism that Jews had been given a prophetic, universalist mission to bring God's message to all human beings. This message was moral and ethical; it beseeched all people to live according to principles of justice and mercy that would finally result in fulfillment of the Messianic promise of peace, brotherhood and righteousness. Jews, according to Reform, were then a "chosen people" only in the sense of being messengers of God's word but in no way did they constitute a nation.[1]

Reform Judaism was born in Germany in the aftermath of the French Revolution during the period known as the Enlightenment. Its intellectual leadership moved to the United States in the first half of the twentieth century.[2] Early Reform leaders, seeking unity among all human beings, wished to strip Judaism of its parochial features. Inspired by ideas of liberty, equality and fraternity, they believed that human beings, by employing reason, could and would be redeemed by adopting the democratic process. Some early Reform leaders even believed that Judaism would utimately disappear, because the coming rational, democratic world would no longer need Jews or Judaism to preach moral and ethical truths. Almost all early Reform leaders argued that their positions were logical extensions of earlier tendencies within Judaism. They viewed Judaism's historical development as dynamic and cited as supportive illustrations numerous changes that had occurred over a time period of centuries. They discarded as invalid previous religious laws for Jews that were dependent upon residence in a Jewish state for fulfillment and that had merely been suspended by Traditional Judaism during the many centuries of so-called exile or diaspora. Laws pertaining solely to Priests and Levites were examples.

Reform leaders explained that the ancient, nationalist period in the history of Judaism was temporary, perhaps necessary, at a certain juncture to better prepare Jews to carry the Divine message. They denied that Jews had been homeless and in exile since that time and insisted that Jews, not unlike other people, had made their homes in and had become citizens of various nation-states. Throughout the nineteenth century the founders of American Reform, convinced that Jews could and did live better lives in the United States than they could live anywhere else, were especially vehement on this point. Discrimination directed against Jews in the United States, when and where it occurred, was for them a minor problem that could be overcome within the democratic society. These early Reform leaders developed the idea that Jews constituted a religious community with the responsibility to bring the prophetic message to all people. Within this context, they argued, there was no basis whatsoever for Jews to attempt to create anew or to restore a separate Jewish nation-state.

The first Reform prayerbook eliminated references to Jews being in exile and to a Messiah who would miraculously restore Jews throughout the world to the historic land of Israel and who would rebuild the Temple of Jerusalem. The prayerbook likewise eliminated all prayers for a return to Zion.

In November 1885, nineteen Reform rabbis met in Pittsburgh and wrote an eight-point platform that one participant called "the most succinct expression of the theology of the Reform movement that had ever been published in the world."[3] The platform emphasized, among other things, that Reform Judaism denied Jewish peoplehood and Jewish nationalism of any variety. The relevant part of the platform in this regard read: "We recognize in the era of universal culture of heart and intellect, the approaching realization of Israel's great Messianic hope for the establishment of the kingdom of truth, justice, and peace among all men. We consider ourselves no longer a nation, but a religious community, and therefore expect neither a return to Palestine, nor a sacrificial worship under the sons of Aaron, nor the restoration of any of the laws concerning the Jewish state."

The Pittsburgh Platform reflected dominant themes in Reform rabbinic thinking for many subsequent decades; it was the most authoritative expression of American Reform until at least 1937. The Pittsburgh Platform succinctly presented the philosophical stand of what has been called "classical" Reform Judaism. In 1885, and for a lengthy time period thereafter, most Reform Jews were seemingly convinced that belief in Judaism in no way tempered their "Americanism." Together with most non-synagogue-affiliated Jews in the United States, they wished to diminish formerly recognized differences between Jews and non-Jews and considered the United States their legitimate nation-state. They were not inclined to view sympathetically, let alone to accept, Theodor Herzl's Zionist theory of the absolute existence of anti-Jewish anti-Semitism and his resultant advocacy of the necessity of Jews creating and living in an exclusivist nation-state of their own.

The philosophical evolution of Reform that led logically to a rejection of Jewish nationalism and Zionism is perhaps best illustrated by the individual case-example of Isaac Mayer Wise and his ideological development. Isaac Mayer Wise was the major spokesperson and organizing genius of the early Reform movement in the United States. The leading rabbi and the outstanding Jew of his day, Wise, although unsuccessful in his efforts to unite all Jews, largely succeeded in adapting Reform Judaism to the New World. He advocated religious reforms in Jewish thought and practice consistent with the idea of nineteenth-century democratic liberalism, of which he was a product. Throughout his adult life

Wise remained a staunch opponent of Jewish nationalism; he specifically opposed Zionism from its inception as being incompatible with the aims of democratic liberalism and Reform Judaism.

The ideological development of Isaac Mayer Wise, from which he developed his anti-nationalist fervor, is clear and unambiguous.[4] He was born on March 29, 1819, in Steingrub, Bohemia. At the age of four he began his studies under the direction of his father, a poor teacher, who operated his own primary school. By the age of six, Isaac Mayer, an obvious prodigy, was studying the Bible and Talmud. By the age of nine, after having learned everything his father could teach him, he went to study with his grandfather, a physician well-steeped in Jewish learning. In 1831, at age twelve and after the death of his grandfather, he went to Prague to study in a school famous for instruction in Talmud. He then became an outstanding student in Prague. In 1835 he journeyed to Jenikau and enrolled in Bohemia's most famous rabbinical school, headed by Rabbi Aaron Kornfield. At Kornfield's school Isaac Mayer studied secular as well as religious topics. He completed his formal education by attending the University of Prague for two years and the University of Vienna for one year, during which time he also worked as a tutor.

Wise became a rabbi in 1842; at the age of twenty-three, he accepted a rabbinical position in Radnitz, Bohemia. After marrying Theresa Bloch, a former student, in 1844, he continued to study and to advance intellectually. He was influenced by Gabriel Kiesser (1806-1863), the great jurist and parliamentarian, who heightened his awareness of nature and urged him to accept the need for political liberalism. He was also greatly influenced in religious liberalism by Samuel Hirsch (1815-1889). While attending a rabbinical conference in Frankfurt in 1845, Wise met, spoke with and listened to four noted religious thinkers: Abraham Geiger, Samuel Adler, Zachariah Frankel and David Einhorn, all of whom severely questioned many aspects of Traditional Judaism and, although not in full agreement with one another, established broad bases for Reform Judaism.

Wise soon realized that Radnitz was too small and isolated for him. Believing the United States to be a place where Jews would be receptive to the idea of Judaism as an evolving faith open to liberal and rational thinking consistent with the Enlightenment, he decided to emigrate to the New World. With his wife and little daughters he began a sixty-three day voyage in May, 1846, arriving in New York on July 23.

Isaac Mayer Wise served as rabbi of Congregation Beth-El in Albany, New York, for four years. In his desire to improve public worship, he introduced numerous reforms, including mixed pews for men and women, the full inclusion of women in the synagogue, choral singing and confirmation as a replacement for the Bar Mitzvah. Although continually facing opposition from the more traditionally-oriented, Orthodox element in his congregation, Wise continued to advocate and pursue changes and reforms in both faith and practice. In 1847 he originated the idea of a single ritual for the American Jewish community. In 1848 he called for a rabbinical meeting the next year to establish a union of congregations. This first call for a meeting failed. Having become a regular contributor to two American Jewish publications, he continued writing as well as speaking in order to argue the merits of this union proposal.

Wise in 1850 accepted an offer to become the rabbi of Beth Elohim in Charleston, South Carolina, an avowedly Reform congregation. He changed his mind, however, and finally refused the offer. Opposition to his Reform ideas increased at Congregation Beth-El. On the morning of the eve of Rosh Hashanah (the beginning of the High Holy Days) in 1850, he was dismissed as rabbi at a rump meeting of the board of directors. At services the next day a riot broke out.Shortly thereafter a minority of the Beth-El congregation left with Wise and established a new synagogue, Anshe Emet (Men of Truth). Anshe Emet was a congregation committed to Reform, the fourth such in the United States. (The other Reform congregations were in Charleston, Baltimore and New York.)

In 1854 Wise accepted the post of rabbi of Congregation B'nai Jeshuran in Cincinnati and stayed there the rest of his life. Soon after arriving in Cincinnati, he began to publish a weekly, *The Israelite*, later renamed *The American Israelite* , and a German supplement, *Die Deborah*. In both publications he advocated the centralization of Jewish institutions. He also established Zion College, which combined Judaic and secular studies. In 1855 Wise called for a rabbinical synod that, he hoped, would unite American Jewry by developing an overall authority for Judaism in the United States. His call prompted the convening of a rabbinical conference in Cleveland at which an intense debate between Orthodox and Reform rabbis erupted. Desiring to avoid conference failure, Wise sought agreement for a public declaration that would meet some of the minimal requirements of Orthodoxy but not violate the spirit of Reform. Wise's carefully worded declaration was finally accepted by the Orthodox and moderate Reform representatives in attendance. Wise, who presided at the conference, was overjoyed with the affirmative vote for the declaration. For him this signaled a forthcoming union of all congregations in the United States. He believed that Orthodoxy would ultimately bow to a Reform emphasis attached to Jewish tradition. Wise's joy, however, was short-lived. Orthodox rabbis, at first satisfied, became suspicious of Wise's intentions. Reform rabbis, more radical than Wise and led by David Einhorn in Baltimore, violently attacked the declaration as betraying Reform. Wise engaged in vigorous debate with both sides, but the synod idea quickly collapsed from lack of support.

Despite numerous setbacks Wise continued to advocate a union of congregations, a common prayer book and a college to train American rabbis. In 1856 he published *Minhag America*, a modified curtailment of the Traditional Hebrew ritual. He wrote extensively and discussed his ideas orally in repeated visits to Jewish communities throughout the United States.

After the Civil War Wise agitated again for a union of congregations. He attended the 1869 Reform rabbinical conference in Philadelphia and assented to the resolutions adopted there. Soon thereafter, he moved away from the substance of those resolutions, realizing that his identifying with too radical a stand would put him beyond his own dream for a comprehensive union of American synagogues under his leadership. During the next few years Wise carried on spirited debates with the more radical, Reform rabbis in the East. He called rabbinic conferences in Cleveland, Cincinnati and New York, which were boycotted by the more radical Reform rabbis. He also reissued his *Minhag America*.

In 1873 a part of Wise's dream became a reality. Delegates from thirty-four Reform congregations convened in Cincinnati on July 8 and organized the Union of American Hebrew Congregations (UAHC). Wise had wanted a union of all congregations in the United States; this was a union only of Reform congregations, mostly from the South and Midwest. Realizing the impossibility of bringing the Orthodox and Reform together at that time, Wise was happy with this development. He had contributed immensely; he was chosen the Union's first president.

For Wise the most important task for the Union was the establishment of a college to train rabbis. In July, 1874, the Union established Hebrew Union College, the first Jewish seminary in the United States; the formal opening occurred in October. Wise became president and taught as a member of the faculty. He spent the remainder of his life working at and on behalf of the college. He shaped its curriculum and supervised its administration; he ordained more than sixty rabbis. He was an excellent teacher. His classroom presentations were substantive and analytical. During his years as college president he was also able to write some of his more scholarly works.

Although Wise preferred one national organization for all American rabbis, he more realistically became the major advocate of a national organization for Reform Rabbis. The Central Conference of American

Rabbis (CCAR) was formally established in 1889. Wise was elected president and served in that post until he died.

Wise expanded his belief in the universalism of Judaism into a worldview, the major aspect of which was that God had established the United States as the symbolic model of nation-state freedom, equality and brotherhood. Jews and Judaism, he believed, should conform to this divine new order. He felt obliged to point them in that direction. His worldview negated Jewish nationalism. For Wise, Zionism especially was an anathema. He detested both the premise and conclusion of Zionism, i.e. that anti-Jewish anti-Semitism was an absolute condition in all nation-states wherein Jews constituted a minority and that a separate nation-state for Jews was thus a necessity. He openly expressed his opposition to Jewish nationalism and to Zionism in speeches and writings. His major vehicle of opposition in writing was the Anglo-Jewish weekly newspaper he published, *The American Israelite*, but he utilized the *Hebrew Union College Journal* and other publications.

Wise began to attack Jewish nationalism in the *American Israelite* by January, 1879. He specifically attacked what was to become the essence of Zionism: "... the colonization of Palestine appears to us a romantic idea inspired by religious visions without foundation in reality ... We take no stock in a dreamland; the idea of Jews returning to Palestine is not part of our creed. We rather believe it is well that the habitable become one holy land and the human family one chosen people."[5] In March, 1891, he stated that Israel's redemption could be achieved only by "the final redemption of Gentiles, their liberation from their fanaticism, their narrow-mindedness , their exclusiveness." He declared further: "... we want the equality and solidarity of mankind."[6] By the late 1890's, Wise filled the pages of the *American Israelite* with blistering condemnations of what he called "Ziomania."[7] He attacked Zionism as impractical and dangerous: "... The Herzl-Nordau scheme appears to us to be about as important to Judaism as was Pleasanton's blue grass theory to science or as is 'Christian Science' to medicine. Pleasanton's empiricism was at least harmless, but Herzl-Nordau's is so fraught with the possibility of mischief ... it becomes the duty of every true Jew to take an active part in efforts to destroy it."[8]

Disturbed by the first Zionist Conference, which met in Basle in 1897, Wise severely attacked Zionism in the December 1899 issue of the *Hebrew Union College Journal*.[9] He applauded the desire of some wealthy "Western Jews" to help their less fortunate and often-persecuted "coreligionists" in Eastern Europe and other places. He even praised philanthropists, like the Baron de Rothschild, who had doubts about Jewish emigration to Palestine but who nevertheless supported it as a means of relieving distress of Jews. Wise counseled these philanthropists to abandon the organizational framework of Zionism.[10] Zionism for Wise was at best a romantic, misguided nostalgia that would "brand us fossils and mummies, fit subjects for the museum."[11] Wise continued: "No normal man can believe that we Jews leave the great nations of culture, power and abundant prosperity in which we form an integral element, to form a ridiculous miniature state in dried-up Palestine; nor did Herzl or Nordau ever believe it. They evidently . . . had this in view, to expose the Jewish communities as foolish and sentimental phantasts; and in this they succeeded well to a large extent . . . We can never identify ourselves with Zionism."[12]

By the time of Wise's death in 1900 so many Jewish immigrants from Eastern Europe had poured into the United States that their number exceeded the number of Jews who had immigrated from Germany and Central Europe. During the first two decades of the twentieth century the great influx of these East European, Jewish immigrants completed a demographic change, underway since the 1880's, that greatly affected Reform Judaism.[13] With but few exceptions neither the first generation of East European Jews who were Traditional in belief nor those who might have been attracted by the religious liberalism of Reform established new or joined already existent Reform temples. Whether or not religious, East European Jews for generations had in varying degrees been discriminated against and persecuted by non-Jews as a separate and distinct people. Most East European Jewish immigrants believed that at least in this sense Jewish peoplehood was a reality. They obviously hoped and were guardedly optimistic that they would fare better in their new locale. Because of both their Old World and early New World experiences, however, few of them could be convinced that in the dominant non-Jewish society of the United States, Jews would be defined and designated by non-Jews solely as members of a religious community of believers in Judaism.

Many East European Jewish immigrants moreover, clung to what they considered to be positive historic and cultural aspects of Jewish peoplehood that transcended mere religious belief. Although only a small minority in the late nineteenth and early twentieth centuries believed fully in the essentials of and/or accepted the propositions of Herzlian Zionism, most of them were repelled by and viewed as nonsensical the classical Reform notion that Jewish peoplehood did not exist except in the sense of Jews being a religious community.

Although challenged by the rejection of most first-generation East European Jewish immigrants, Reform Judaism in the United States clung to its classical position, as outlined in the Pittsburgh Platform, until well into the twentieth century. Reform leaders, with but few exceptions, espoused a clear and staunch anti-Zionist position. No indications of even a minor shift towards Zionism within the Reform movement are discernible until the time of the Balfour Declaration in 1917. Such indications appear first at Hebrew Union College and thereafter in the UAHC and the CCAR.

From the late 1890's until the time of the Balfour Declaration the few Zionists who attained positions as faculty members or students at Hebrew Union College were able to exert little influence. Professor Caspar Levias is a good example. Levias was invited to defend Zionism before the CCAR in 1899. He declined that invitation, but he did write a manuscript that he submitted to the *CCAR Yearbook*. Informed that his manuscript had been rejected by the editors, he arranged to have it published in the *Hebrew Union College Journal*. (One year later the *CCAR Yearbook* published the same article.) In this article Levias attempted to refute three anti-Zionist arguments: 1) Zionism eliminated the "concept of mission of Israel"; 2) Zionism is a distortion of Messianic prophecy; 3) nationalism is evil.[14] This well-reasoned article won few, if any, new adherents. Other articles and editorials, written by faculty and student supporters of Zionism and occasionally published in the *Hebrew Union College Journal*, engendered little enthusiasm. The overwhelming majority of faculty and students at Hebrew Union College believed that Zionism was antithetical to the Pittsburgh Platform, which predicted the coming of a new order founded on brotherhood, peace and justice for everyone. Professor Louis Grossman summarized in 1899 what was to remain the dominant sentiment at Hebrew Union College for many subsequent years: ". . . A sober student of Jewish history and a genuine lover of his co-religionists sees that the Zionistic agitation contradicts everything that is typical of Jews and Judaism."[15]

Anti-Zionism so dominated the scene at Hebrew Union College in 1915 that President Kaufmann Kohler refused to allow Horace Kallen, a noted academician, to speak in favor of Zionism on campus. The students who had invited Kallen to speak appealed for help to Rabbi Stephen Wise. Wise, one of Reform's most prominent rabbis, traveled from New York to Cincinnati and arranged a meeting with Kohler for the students. Following that meeting Kohler agreed to a new policy, allowing any duly invited Jewish speaker to lecture on Zionism at Hebrew Union College. Kohler's first reaction, nevertheless, indicated the prevailing mood at Hebrew Union College.

Although no longer officially taboo, Zionist ideas remained extremely unpopular at the College following the Kallen incident. Most lectures and sermons on campus that dealt with this topic were anti-Zionist.[16]

The exceptional expression of Zionism evoked fierce rebuttal. It was in this context that President Kohler chose the October 14, 1916 opening exercises of the College to blast the defense of Zionism, made previously in a student sermon by James Heller, who later became a leading rabbi and president of the CCAR. In his speech, later published in the *Hebrew Union College Monthly*, Kohler asserted that "ignorance and irreligion are at the bottom of the whole movement of political Zionism."[17]

The number of students at Hebrew Union College who espoused Zionism increased after 1917. Two reasons are apparent: Enrolled in the College by then were a few students from families that were East European in origin and probably more amenable than were most American Jews of German origin at the time to accept certain aspects of Jewish nationalism. Secondly, the Balfour Declaration was undoubtedly a motivating factor. In spite of this, Zionists in the student body remained a minority in number for at least two subsequent decades.

Whereas Zionist influence was evident at Hebrew Union College by the end of the second decade of the twentieth century, it was hardly discernible in the leadership ranks of either the UAHC or CCAR. The Reform movement retained and continued its anti-nationalist, anti-Zionist posture. This was reflected in a petition, presented to President Wilson in 1919, titled "A Statement to the Peace Conference." Although not all of its three hundred signatories were Reform Jews, this petition reflected the then dominant Reform position on Zionism and Palestine.[18] The petition broadly asserted that the opinions expressed therein represented those of the great majority of American Jews in 1919. The petition denounced Zionist efforts to segregate Jews "as a political unit . . . in Palestine or elsewhere" and underlined the principle of equal rights for all citizens of any state, "irrespective of creed or ethnic descent." It rejected Jewish nationalism as a general concept and held against the founding of any state upon the basis of religion and/or race. The petition asserted that the "overwhelming bulk of the Jews of America, England, France, Italy, Holland, Switzerland and the other lands of freedom have no thought whatever of surrendering their citizenship in these lands in order to resort to a 'Jewish homeland in Palestine.' " Moreover, those Jews who were still being oppressed in certain nation-states, from which they were unable to emigrate, would likely be put into an even more precarious position by the creation of a Jewish state in Palestine that could be used by malevolent rulers "as a new justification for additional repressive legislation." The petition, noting that most inhabitants of Palestine were then non-Jews, suggested further that conflict between Jews and non-Jews could erupt if a Jewish state was created.

The rejection of Jewish nationalism as a general concept is reiterated repeatedly in the petition. Point 5 is unequivocal: "We object to the political segregation of the Jews because it is an error to assume that the bond uniting them is of a national character. They are bound by two factors: First, the bond of common religious beliefs and aspirations and, secondly, the bond of common traditions, customs, and experiences largely, alas, of common trials and sufferings. Nothing in their status suggests that they form in any real sense a separate nationalistic unit." This statement indicated that for the Reform Jews who signed the petition, the earlier classical Reform position of the Pittsburgh Platform had been expanded somewhat but certainly not to the point of accepting any type of Jewish nationalism.

The petition's final paragraph looked ahead, issued a hope but remained firm in opposition to the goal of Zionism: "As to the future of Palestine, it is our fervent hope that what was once a 'promised land' for the Jews may become a 'land of promise' for all races and creeds, safeguarded by the League of Nations which, it is expected, will be one of the fruits of the Peace Conference to whose deliberations the world now looks forward so anxiously and so full of hope. We ask that Palestine be constituted as a free and independent state to be governed under a democratic form of government recognizing no distinctions of creed or race or ethnic descent, and with adequate power to protect the country against oppression of any kind. We do not wish to see Palestine, either now or at any time in the future, organized as a Jewish state."[19]

Throughout the 1920's the shift towards Zionism continued at Hebrew Union College. Additional students announced their conversions to Zionism and began to stress the importance of the establishment of the Jewish state. Zionists, notwithstanding this, still constituted a distinct minority of the student body. Zionism seemed to creep into the College more subtly, as evidenced in 1928 when the College awarded an honorary degree of Doctor of Hebrew Letters to Chaim Weizmann, the then President of the World Zionist Organization. In awarding this degree, the administration, without itself overtly accepting or advocating Zionism, stressed what it considered to be Weizmann's positive role in advancing Zionism. The next year the *Hebrew College Monthly*, in response to the reorganization of the Jewish Agency for Palestine, editorially applauded the representatives of "all religious, cultural and economic strata in American Jewish life [which] have accepted at Zurich the principle of joint and open action in the cultural and economic rehabilitation of Palestine."[20] The editorial concluded with the statement: ". . . Many of us at the Hebrew Union College regard the Jewish Agency as a magnificent constructive endeavor, bound to imbue the rickety ideal of Kelal Yisrael with new strength and destined to transform the communities of the Disapora in countless ways."[21] The editorial stopped short of full advocacy of the Zionist goal of a Jewish political state in Palestine, but it probably represented growing sentiment among students at the time and thus illustrated movement towards Zionism at Hebrew Union College.

The pressures to stress more Jewish tradition and to increase the emphasis upon Jewish history at the College in the 1920's may have indirectly provided some ammunition for the case then being argued by the Zionist minority. The available evidence indicates that these pressures did not, as some commentators have attempted to argue, result from but that at most paralleled in some ways the advocacy of Zionism at the College.

Lay leaders of the UAHC continued to reject Zionism in the 1920's. They did not voice one word of support for Jewish settlement of any kind in Palestine until 1923. The UAHC resolution of support was limited but still had to be passed over the rejection of the Resolutions Committee.[22] In 1927 the 30th Council of the UAHC went somewhat further by deciding that it "heartily endorses the humanitarian efforts for spiritual and educational development and for agricultural settlements in Russia, Poland and Palestine."[23] The only discernible movement towards Zionism within the leadership of the UAHC during the 1920's was the concession to cooperate in the spiritual, economic and social renewal of a Jewish homeland in Palestine. The UAHC leadership more significantly continued to oppose Zionist activity, directed toward achieving an independent Jewish state in Palestine.

Throughout the decade of the 1920's only a small number of rabbis who made up the CCAR were Zionists. The great majority consisted of those who called themselves non-Zionists or anti-Zionists. This situation continued into the 1930's. In 1930 the inclusion of *Hatikvah*, which stressed Jewish nationalism and later became the national anthem of the state of Israel, in the *Union Hymnal*, a collection of liturgical music for use in all Reform synagogues, may have appeared at first glance to be a step towards Zionism in the CCAR. The next year a serious conflict within the CCAR developed over whether to keep *Hatikvah* in the *Hymnal*. The Zionist sympathizers urged inclusion as evidence of the Zionist goal for the future of Palestine. Anti-Zionists in the CCAR urged its deletion for the same reason. The vote of 54 to 41 to retain *Hatikvah* did not indicate a Zionist majority in 1931. Many who voted to retain were self-avowed non-Zionists, e.g. Julian Morgenstern, who merely thought it unethical to abrogate the inclusion decision of 1930.[24] Other non-Zionists who voted for inclusion in both 1930 and 1931 believed, as did Louis Witt, that "this hymn (is) expressive not so much of this or that 'ism' as of the indestructible hope of my people, of their yearning not for Zionism, but for Zion."[25]

When Rabbi Barnett Brickner delivered the conference sermon in 1932, he certainly did not represent the majority in his advocacy, but he may unwittingly have predicted what within a decade would become the dominant sentiment in the CCAR. Brickner suggested in his sermon that the time had arrived for Reform Judaism to change its attitude toward Zionism. Brickner argued that "history has proved that they (the early reformers) exaggerated the hope for the immediate messianic cosmopolitanism which they associated with political emancipation."[26]

In 1935, 241 Reform rabbis, members of the CCAR, published and signed a statement, titled "Rabbis of America to Labor Palestine", that urged and pledged support for the Histadruth and the League for Labor Palestine.[27] Rabbi Stephen Wise, pointing out that the signers represented more than half of the total CCAR membership, maintained that this statement was an expression of Reform rabbinical support for the concept of a Jewish National Home in Palestine. Many of those who signed the statement, however, did so more out of admiration for what they considered to be the social idealism of the Histadruth than for the program of the Zionist movement.

In 1935 the CCAR approved a controversial resolution that adopted a position of official neutrality on the issue of Zionism. This was the first official change in regard to Jewish nationalism since the adoption of the Pittsburgh Platform in 1885. The Neutrality Resolution stated: ". . . Acceptance or rejection of the Zionist program should be left to the determination of individual members . . . [The CCAR] takes no stand on the subject of Zionism, [but] will continue to cooperate in the upbuilding of Palestine, and in the economic, cultural and spiritual tasks confronting the growing and evolving Jewish community there."[28] The Zionists in the CCAR viewed this resolution as a major triumph, while anti-Zionists, although unhappy with the change in position vis-a-vis Zionism, understood the resolution as being something less than a complete Zionist victory. Some anti-Zionists, such as David Philipson, unhappily concluded that the resolution was the work of Zionist, "rabbinic politicians" and was from the outset never neutral.[29]

By the 1930's the influx of Jews of East European origin into congregations and the rabbinate had seriously affected Reform Judaism in the United States. A survey among forty-three Reform congregations, located in the largest centers of Jewish population in 1931, showed that nearly equal proportions of temple members were of East European and German origins.[30] The majority of Reform rabbis and a large number of the Reform organizational lay leadership were of East European origin.[31] This may have helped turn Reform towards Zionism, as certain observers have suggested. Some of those of East European origin were, as previously noted, more amenable to Jewish nationalism and Zionism than were many Jews of German origin. At the same time, however, others of East European origin were either opposed to or indifferent towards Zionism. Some outstanding Reform rabbis and lay leaders who became Zionists, on the other hand, were of German origin and came from classical Reform backgrounds.

A 1931 UAHC survey expressed concern about a move towards Zionism in the Reform movement. The report stated that "despite the traditional opposition of Reform Judaism to Zionism in the past, we find one member of every five families enrolled in the Zionist Organization of America or Hadassah."[32] The results of this survey, could also be cited as evidence that the Reform movement as a whole in 1931 was still far from being Zionist.

The Nazi persecution of Jews became the major influence in Reform Judaism's shift towards Zionism. Concern about Hitler and the Third Reich led a few Reform rabbis and lay leaders to re-examine their lack of sympathy for the Zionist cause as early as 1933. In that year the UAHC distributed a statement deploring the Nazi treatment of German Jews and criticizing the German people for not condemning unwarranted attacks upon Jews.[33] At its March 1935 biennial convention the UAHC publicly praised Reform Jews for providing aid for German Jews and, in observing that the crisis had worsened, stated that the task of providing relief had grown more formidable.[34] The UAHC then endorsed the efforts of the Jewish Agency in rebuilding Palestine.[35]

Within the CCAR the concern over Nazi persecution of Jews produced similar early results. Morris Newfield stated this concern in his 1933 presidential message. Newfield acknowledged internal CCAR disagreement on the subject of Jewish emigration to Palestine; he pleaded for compromise that would help salvage some portion of European Jewry.[36] Building upon Newfield's sermon, Abraham Feldman in 1934 urged his CCAR colleagues to rethink the Pittsburgh Platform on the eve of its fiftieth anniversary. Feldman argued: ". . . In 1885 Palestine did not occupy the place in Jewish life which it occupies today." He declared that the time had arrived for "a new statement, a new declaration of principles . . . [that would] recognize and reassert the spiritual and ethnic *Gemeinschaft* of Israel and take cognizance of the Palestine that is being rebuilt. . . "[37]

Responding to Feldman's appeal, the CCAR Resolutions Committee recommended that a symposium be held the following year (1935) to discuss the Pittsburgh Platform and to consider a reformulation of the philosophy and practices of Reform Judaism. The symposium of 1935 consisted primarily of papers dealing with God, Torah and Israel. Abba Hillel Silver, then a young rabbinical advocate of a Jewish state, and Samuel Schulman, a veteran anti-Zionist, presented papers on Israel. The Silver-Schulman debate was spirited and led to the previously mentioned Neutrality Resolution.[38] The 1935 symposium also laid the foundation for the appointment of a committee to draft a new set of Reform "Guiding Principles." The committee members were Samuel Cohon, James Cohon, James Heller, Felix Levy, David Philipson, Max Raisin and Abba Hillel Silver. Four of the six were avowed Zionists; one was favorably disposed towards Zionism; only David Philipson was an anti-Zionist. The die for the Columbus Platform of 1937 was cast.

The report of the committee evoked little discussion at the 1936 CCAR meeting. The official endorsement in 1937, which resulted in the Columbus Platform, passed easily; the only fierce debate was centered upon the statement on Zionism.

Only one-half of the CCAR members attended the 1937 convention, held at the Winding Hollow Country Club in Columbus, Ohio. A motion to refrain from adopting any platform at that time ended the morning session. The vote was an 81-81 tie; the CCAR President, Felix Levy, cast the deciding vote to defeat the motion. Only 110 rabbis attended the afternoon session. A personal report estimated that one-fifth of the registered rabbis opted to play golf rather than to participate in the debate and vote upon adoption of a new platform.[39] An afternoon motion to postpone adoption of the platform lost by a vote of 48 to 50. The new platform, which became the new "Guiding Principles of Reform Judaism", then passed by only one vote.

The significant section of the Columbus Platform dealt with Israel and reflected the language of the 1935 Neutrality Resolution. The text of that plank declared: "[Judaism] is the soul of which Israel is the body. Living in all parts of the world, Israel has been held together by the ties of a common history, and above all, by the heritage of faith. Though we recognize in the group-loyalty of Jews who have become estranged from our religious tradition, a bond which still unites them with us, we maintain that it is by its religion that the Jewish people has lived. The non-Jew who accepts our faith is welcome as a full member of the Jewish community. In all lands where our people live, they assume and seek to share loyalty and the full duties and responsibilities of citizenship and to create seats of Jewish knowledge and religion. In the rehabilitation of Palestine, the land hallowed by memories and hopes, we behold the promise of renewed life for many of our brethren. We affirm the obligation of all Jewry to aid in its upbuilding as a Jewish homeland by endeavoring to make it not only a haven of refuge for the oppressed but also a center of Jewish culture and spiritual life. Throughout the ages it has been Israel's mission to witness to the Divine in the face of every form of paganism and materialism. We regard it as our historic task to cooperate with all men in the establishment of the Kingdom of God, of universal brotherhood, justice, truth and peace on earth. This is our Messianic goal."[40]

The Columbus Platform did not settle the question of Zionism for Reform Judaism. In the first place, its ratification by no means made it certain that Reform Judaism would endorse and support Zionist efforts to establish a Jewish nation-state in Palestine. Secondly, the Columbus Platform was a statement by, for and of rabbis. Lay people did not necessarily have to accept it. Zionism as a political movement was not even debated officially within the UAHC until 1943, when holocaust concern was far more widespread and intense than it had been in 1937. The resolution, titled "Safeguarding Rights of Jews After World War II," passed by the 38th Council of the UAHC in 1943, was more limited than the Columbus Platform in its acceptance of Zionist emphases.[41] Thirdly, the Columbus Platform did not even finalize the position on Zionism in all Reform rabbinic circles. The number of rabbis present in Columbus when the final vote on the Zionist plank was taken represented only a small minority of the CCAR membership. Playing golf was seemingly more important for many rabbis who attended the 1937 Conference than was the vote on Zionism. The Zionist minority in the CCAR attained its victory in 1937 largely because of majority indifference.

On the one hand, the Columbus Platform provided the context for bitter struggle within Reform Judaism. Severe conflict over Zionism raged internally for over six years after the platform's ratification. Three happenings highlighted the conflict: 1) the CCAR's controversial endorsement by resolution in 1942 of the formation of a Jewish army in Palestine, 2) the Atlantic City meeting of non-and anti-Zionist rabbis in early June 1942 that led to the establishment of the American Council for Judaism and 3) the Beth-El Temple controversy in Houston, Texas, in the summer and fall of 1943 that resulted in a major Reform congregation's rejection of the Zionist plank of the Columbus Platform and adoption of a restatement of the anti-nationalist principles of the Pittsburgh Platform.

On the other hand, the Columbus Platform of 1937 was a turning point. Its Zionist plank, which repudiated the anti-nationalist mood and philosophy of the Pittsburgh Platform of 1885, established a new official basis for supporting Zionism. The internal conflict of the 1937-1943 period did not deter a growing number of Reform leaders from marching to the Zionist beat. Whether these individual leaders—lay and rabbinic—did so primarily out of personal conviction or because of varied mounting pressures upon them or because of other considerations, is interesting to ponder but almost impossible to assess with reliable evidence.

After 1943 the Reform movement actively supported the Zionist drive to establish a Jewish state in Palestine. Since the establishment of that state in 1948, the Reform movement has steadily increased its backing and intensified its support of both the Zionist movement and the state of Israel. The Reform movement has largely disregarded the principled resistance to this support of a few Reform rabbis, lay individuals and groups. It shunned the American Council for Judaism which, until 1967, during the time that Elmer Berger was its ideologue, actively advocated an anti-Zionist position and produced and distributed Reform-oriented material. It has refused to deal in any substantive way with Elmer Berger's penetrating, profound, Reform Judaic arguments against Zionism, presented in a great variety of books and articles. It has given almost no serious attention to those writings of Jakob Petuchowski, a leading Reform scholar and distinguished professor of rabbinics at Hebrew Union College, that have raised serious questions about the nature of Zionism and of a Jewish state. In these and other ways the Reform movement has attempted since 1948 to purge Reform Judaism of anti-Zionism.

The transition in Reform Judaism on the issue of Zionism can be well illustrated not only by developments within the movement but also by the transformation of certain major leaders. An excellent example is Julian Morgenstern who began as a staunch adversary of Zionism but later in his life accepted Jewish nationalism, endorsed the principle of Jewish settlement in Palestine and backed major Zionist propositions.

Morgenstern's opposition to Zionism was due in part to his early conditioning. Having moved to Cincinnati when seven years of age, he grew up under the influence of David Philipson, rabbi of the Mound Street Temple. Philipson, a staunch anti-Zionist, taught that endorsement of a Jewish nation in Palestine would imply political loyalty to that state instead of to the United States. This and other anti-Zionist arguments impressed young Morgenstern. As a student at Hebrew Union College a few years later, Morgenstern often argued against Zionism. Returning to the College as a professor of Bible in 1907, five years after his graduation, he remained an anti-Zionist for many subsequent years.

By the time that Morgenstern became the president of Hebrew Union College in 1921, his transformation on the issue of Zionism appears to have begun. He refused to sign petitions opposing the Balfour Declaration, circulated at Hebrew Union College between 1919 and 1921.

Although he maintained that he did not want to dignify the Zionist campaign by signing, he also stated that the substance of the petitions exceeded the parameters of his views.[42] His active opposition to Zionism thereafter diminished, and he became ambivalent. A few years later he participated in a Zionist Organization of America (ZOA) Convention and there emphasized that Judaism, although primarily a religion, was difficult to understand without appreciating the "consciousness of Israel as a unique people in the world." He expressed the hope that endorsement of Jewish peoplehood would help establish Reform Judaism's advancement "from its established position of our great honored pioneers and reformers of the nineteenth century."[43] In 1929 Morgenstern attended a Zionist-led rally at Plum Street Temple in Cincinnati to protest violence against Jews in the Arab riots in Palestine in 1929. He signed a petition, sent to Secretary of State Henry Stimson, which requested the British to increase their protection of Jewish settlements and not to deter Jews from equipping themselves for self-defense. The request was based on alleged grounds of "historic justice [due] to a people reft of its land, Jewish sacrifice during the World War, Jewish initiative and investment in Palestine and . . . Jewish martyrdom upon . . . its ancient soil."[44]

Why Morgenstern began to change his views is difficult to ascertain. There is little evidence to suggest that the small but steady increase of Zionist sentiment at Hebrew Union College in the 1920's was sufficiently significant to influence him. No single, motivating incident stands out. Morgenstern himself, over four decades later in retrospect, hinted that his own thought development and considerations of necessary adjustments to a changing world were responsible.[45] His explanation at best, however, lacked specificity. His lack of consistency in argument, evident until 1946, indicates that his transformation was not altogether rational.

In the 1930's Morgenstern continued to reject secular Zionism's denigration of religion and of the diaspora, the two cornerstones of his faith. For him there was no basis for Jewish identity without religion. In 1934 he declared that every American Jew had to decide whether to support wholeheartedly the cause of Jewish nationalism "with all the inevitable consequences of jingoism, suspicion, antagonism and warfare of one kind or another" or to advance the idea of Israel as "a united people dwelling in countless lands, yet bound together by the eternal imperishable band of a common religion."[46] Morgenstern further asserted that Jews had never lived in an environment as good as the United States "whose spirit is so closely akin to the eternal spirit of Judaism and of the Jewish people."[47] He believed in what he called an "American Judaism," an approach to Jewish life compatible with the major features of American culture. For him the Reform movement was the principle vehicle for the move towards "American Judaism." He worried about Zionism's ability to hinder movement towards "American Judaism." Only his devotion to Jewish unity allowed him at that time to leave the door open to a rapprochement with Zionism.

In 1935 Morgenstern opposed a proposal calling for a World Jewish Congress to represent World Jewry. This, he argued, would indicate acceptance of the negative concepts of Jewish separatism and racial nationalism. He viewed this proposal as a parochial Jewish extension of political nationalism, which he blamed for many of the world's ills. While conceding that Jewish nationalism in Palestine had some value, he viewed it as negative for American Jews, whom he regarded as a religious community.[48]

In the 1930's Morgenstern on balance continued to resist Zionism within the larger context of his repudiation of political nationalism, which he now vehemently attacked as being the major cause of the two world wars of the twentieth century. He acknowledged that political nationalism had once been a part of the Jewish existence, but he considered it historically incidental as well as dangerous and regressive in the twentieth century.

In his October 1943 opening day address at Hebrew Union College, Morgenstern rejected the claims of the Zionist movement to any major role in Jewish affairs. He asserted that Jewish nationalism in modern times had developed out of "sheer desperation and despair" and should not be accepted as a necessity. He argued that Israel was important for its religious insights and that Jewish peoplehood was meaningful only in religious terms. The Jewish people, he continued, enjoyed special distinction because of religious considerations and did not need a nation-state to fulfill its "God-given destiny". He concluded that it would be "foolish, sad and tragic for the Jewish people, which has dreamed the dream and proclaimed the message of world unity, to itself reject its message, faith and destiny and to seek for itself a salvation impossible of realization, an exploded theory of restored, racial statehood."[49]

The response to Morgenstern's speech by Reform Zionist leaders— lay and rabbinic—was fast and furious. The severity of the outburst stunned, but should not have surprised, Morgenstern. He had only one month earlier voted in favor of the CCAR Neutrality Resolution, reaffirmed that Zionism and Reform Judaism were not incompatible and supported the CCAR resolution urging the dissolution of the anti-Zionist American Council for Judaism. Outraged by the apparent fact that his speech was inconsistent with his previous positions and actions, Reform Zionist leaders charged the president of Hebrew Union College with having repudiated Zionism at a critical juncture, i.e. at the time that Reform Judaism was deciding whether or not to support the establishment of a Jewish state in Palestine. Several alumni of Hebrew Union College signed and sent a telegram, which they made public. In the telegram they deplored Morgenstern's remarks, especially his reference to Jewish nationalism being "practically identical with Nazi and Fascist theory."[50]

Influenced by the outburst of widespread disapproval, Morgenstern avoided any further public refutation of Zionism. During the next three years he experienced a metamorphosis. Close friends have suggested that he would not change his beliefs solely because of their being unpopular but that he needed to become "inwardly convinced" before doing so.[51] Whatever the reasons, he had radically altered his position on Jewish nationalism and Zionism by the fall of 1946.

In his opening address at Hebrew Union College in October 1946, Morgenstern offered his reassessment of Jewish nationalism. Although continuing to maintain that the character of Judaism was primarily religious, he asserted that an "unexplainable" kinship existed among Jews everywhere, superseding even the religious quality of Jewish life. He maintained that American Jews could survive only as a religious community, but he acknowledged that different conditions elsewhere might merit different adjustments. In this speech he obviously stopped short of advocating that all Jews needed to establish their nation-state in order to survive or to achieve their ultimate goal in a predominantly non-Jewish world. He still emphasized spiritual concerns, but he now agreed that "even though the fulfillment of historic Jewish destiny . . . lies in a direction which leads away from nationalism toward universalism, in its broadest and loftiest concepts there is nothing specifically un-Jewish in nationalism; it is quite within the bounds of reason and prosperity that a section of the Jewish people, dwelling anew in the land of its fathers, should under favorable and warrantable conditions, become once again a Jewish nation, independent and self-governing, wholly or conditionally, as the case may be."[52]

By 1946 Morgenstern appeared to believe that the establishment of Jewish sovereignty in Palestine was both inevitable and imminent. He said that Jewish sovereignty would be "blessed," because it would transform the issue of Jewish nationalism into a matter that was "only academic at the very most, and the issues will have passed from our control or influence completely."[53]

In 1947 Morgenstern further asserted that the aspiration for Jewish sovereignty was a legitimate, historical component of the Jewish spirit.[54] He even presented his new conceptual framework of Jewish nationalism.

He pinpointed the four major chronological periods of Jewish history as: 1) the conquest of Palestine to the Babylonian Exile, 2) the exile to 90 C.E. or 135 C.E., 3) the complete termination of national existence from 135 C.E. to the Enlightenment, 4) the Enlightenment to the present time. He emphasized that Jewish peoplehood was the common denominator of the Jewish experience throughout the whole of Jewish history; it was the only constant and fundamental concept of Jewish life to which all else was secondary and incidental.

The Zionist movement for Morgenstern thus now emerged as a legitimate response to a basic, historic principle of self-realization and fulfillment. Morgenstern adopted much of the major argument of the Zionist precursors of Herzl. He stated:"From Bar Kochba [135 C.E.] to Herzl there was no movement of political nationalism in the life of the Jewish people comparable to the present Zionist movement in magnitude and in realistic and positive character."[55]

Morgenstern was convinced that the vast majority of Jews supported Zionism and its program in 1947. He attributed this to the growing realization everywhere that the disasters in Europe and the instability in the Middle East had made it "absolutely essential" for Jews in Palestine to organize themselves politically. He concluded: "At heart we are all Zionists of a kind to a degree. This we realize clearly today as never before. We have learned anew and through pain and sorrow, our difficult and inseparable task is to devise a proper workable saving harmonization of universalism and particularism and of particularism necessarily expressing itself today as nationalism."[56]

Morgenstern's metamorphosis mirrored that of others in the Reform movement. He and these others performed a leap of faith; they did not, perhaps because they could not and still stay within the confines of the Judaism they espoused, present any rational, coherent case for their change in position. A few others within the Reform context changed differently. Morris Lazaron and Judah Magnes are representative examples. Lazaron, revered rabbi of the Baltimore Hebrew Congregation from 1915 to 1949, began as what he called a "spiritual Zionist" and then changed in the early 1930's and became a leading anti-Zionist.[57] Magnes, another distinguished American Reform rabbi who emigrated to Palestine in the 1920's and became the first president of the Hebrew University in Jerusalem, began as and remained a self-avowed Zionist but came to oppose political Zionism and the idea of creating an exclusivist Jewish state in Palestine.[58] The Reform movement welcomed and retained those who went through the Morgenstern type of metamorphosis but rejected those who changed in the Lazaron or Magnes manner.

That the Reform movement solidly supported Zionism by the time the state of Israel came into existence in 1948 is clear. That the differences between Reform Judaism and Zionism had been adequately reconciled by that time is not clear. Reform leaders maintained that, even with its diversity and development, Reform Judaism continued to maintain essential elements of its early formulation. This early formulation was, as previously noted, antithetical to Zionism. The rabbis who drafted the Pittsburgh Platform of 1885, reflecting many decades of Reform thinking and advocacy, anticipated a coming world of justice and freedom in which Jews would enjoy equal rights and privileges with all other citizens, wherever they lived. Zionism declared the opposite and stressed that anti-Jewish anti-semitism was an absolute condition of human existence, thereby necessitating the creation of a Jewish state, in which Jews would be able to survive and prosper by maintaining themselves as a majority of the citizenry. Early Reform Judaism regarded nationalism as the major cause of Jewish suffering. Zionism proposed nationalism as a solution to Jewish suffering. Early Reform Judaism predicated Jewish existence upon faith, stressing the belief that creative survival depended upon the acceptance by Jews of a "universal" mission to preach the ideals of justice, brotherhood and peace. Zionism based Jewish existence upon the concept of Jewish peoplehood. To sustain the Jewish people, political Zionism posited the creation of a state in which Jews would have absolute control and be granted rights and privileges denied to non-Jews. Early Reform Judaism stressed the religious-spiritual element among Jews and viewed ethnic differences as being of little significance. Zionism, as a secular nationalism, emphasized that ethnic bonds united all Jews and did not require any specific religious or cultural commitments.

Reform Zionist theoreticians did not advocate the total rejection of all early Reform concepts, nor were they content to assert only that the Nazi holocaust demonstrated the need for Zionism and the validity of its major premises. These theoreticians went further and attempted a philosophical union of Reform Judaism and Zionism. Samuel Wohl, a leading Reform Zionist rabbi, succinctly and typically presented this argument in 1943: "The Zionists cherish and put into practice in Palestine the universal teachings of prophetic Judaism."[59] Neither Wohl nor any other Reform Zionist advocate, however, demonstrated that the secular Zionists, many of whom were anti-religious and most of whom were particularly concerned only with what was best for the Jews, cherished the universal teachings of the prophets. Most religious Jews in the Zionist movement rejected the Reform interpretation of "prophetic Judaism."

Before 1948 Reform Zionists could hope that their conception of

Zionism would blossom after the state came into existence. That, however, did not happen. The state of Israel, created in the Zionist image, arose as, and has remained, a Jewish exclusivist state whose government has displaced, confiscated land from and denied basic human rights to the indigenous Arab Palestinian population.[60] Israel has not only become a military powerhouse but also one of the leading arms merchants in the world, selling tremendous quantities of armaments to other oppressive regimes in the world. Since the creation of the state, over seventy-five percent of the Israeli Jewish population has not been religious; a large percentage has been anti-religious. Israeli Jews who are not religious, as well as some who are, have consistently denigrated the diaspora. Antagonism between religious and anti-religious Jews has remained a serious problem in Israeli society. Religious Jews have repeatedly expressed their contempt for Reform Judaism and Reform Jews. Only Traditional Judaism has been officially recognized in the state of Israel. Only Orthodox rabbis have state authority to perform rabbinic duties. This is the blossom of Zionism in the Zionist state. The principles of Reform Judaism are not to be found here. None of this has deterred Reform lay and rabbinic organizations, most Reform congregations and a large number of individual Reform Jews in the United States and in a few other places from supporting ideologically, financially and politically the Zionist policies and practices of the Jewish state. The seemingly inescapable conclusion is that the Reform movement has thereby rejected the philosophical bases of Reform Judaism.

NOTES

1. For an introduction to the general philosophy and precepts of Reform Judaism see: David Philipson, *Reform Movement in Judaism* (New York: KTVA, 1967); Solomon B. Freehof, *Reform Jewish Practice and its Rabbinic Background* (New York: Union of American Hebrew Congregations, 1963); Jakob J. Petuchowski, *Prayerbook Reform in Europe* (New York : World Union for Progressive Judaism, 1968); *Reform Judaism: Essays by Hebrew Union College Alumni* (Cincinnati: Hebrew Union College, 1949); *Current Reform Responsa* (Cincinnati; Hebrew Union College, 1969); *Growth of Reform Judaism* (New York: World Union for Progressive Judaism, 1965).

2. See: Carl Becker, *The Heavenly City of the Eighteenth-Century Philosophers* (New Haven: Yale, 1932); Charles Vereker, *Eighteenth-Century Optimism* (Liverpool, England: Liverpool University Press, 1967); W. Gunther Plaut, *The Rise of Reform Judaism: A Sourcebook of its European Origins* (New York: World Union for Progressive Judaism, 1963); W. Gunther Plaut, ed., *The Growth of Reform Judaism; American and European Sources until 1948* (New York: World Union for Progressive Judaism, 1965); see M. Friedman, *Pilgrims in a New Land* (New York: Jewish Publication Society, 1948).

3. See: Barnett A. Elzas, "A Memoir of Alexander Kohut," *Yearbook of the Central Conference of American Rabbis (YBCCAR)*, vol. 35 (1925), p. 263; *Central Con-*

ference of American Rabbis (CCAR), *Sermons by American Rabbis* (Chicago: Central Conference Publication Committee, 1896), p. 260-61; David Philipson, *The Reform Movement in Judaism*, New York: C.J. Krehbiel, 1931), p. 355; Plaut ed., *The Growth of Reform Judaism: American and European Sources until 1948*, p. 31-35; Kaufmann Kohler's lectures on Reform Judaism, which were delivered in June and July 1885, and published as *Backwards or Forwards? A Series of Discourses on Reform Judaism* (New York: Stettiner, Lambert, 1885), was the most important and inspiring ideological statement for the rabbis at the Pittsburgh meeting.

4. For the most complete biography of Isaac Mayer Wise see: James Gutheim Heller, *Isaac M. Wise His Life, Work and Thought* (New York: Union of American Hebrew Congregations, (UAHC) 1965.) Also see: Israel Knox, *Rabbi in America: The Story of Isaac M. Wise* (Boston: Little-Brown, 1957; Max Benjamin May, *Isaac Mayer Wise* (New York: Putnam's 1916); David Philipson and Louis Grossman, *Selected Writings of Isaac Mayer Wise* (Cincinnati: Clarke, 1900); Isaac Mayer Wise, *Reminiscences*, translated and edited by David Philipson (Cincinnati: Clarke, 1901); Isaac Mayer Wise, *Pronaos to Holy Writ* (Cincinnati: Clarke, 1891); Isaac Mayer Wise, *Judaism: Its Doctrines and Duties* (Cincinnati and Chicago: Bloch, 1888).

5. See: *American Israelite*, vol. 32, no. 4 (January 24, 1879).

6. *American Israelite*, vol. 37, no. 38 (March 19, 1891),p.4.

7. See: "Editorial," *American Israelite*, vol. 45, no. 29 (January 19, 1899), p. 4.

8. Ibid. For additional discussion by Wise about Jewish nationalism in the *American Israelite*, see: vol. 42, no. 30 (January 23, 1896); vol. 44, no. 14 (September 8, 1898).

9. Isaac Mayer Wise, "Zionism," *The Hebrew Union College Journal*, vol.4, no.3 (December, 1899), p. 455-47.

10. Ibid.

11. Ibid.

12. Ibid.

13. The published material pertaining to Eastern European Jewish immigrants and their ideas is voluminous. Irving Howe, *World of Our Fathers* (New York: Simon and Schuster, 1976) and Moses Rischin, *The Promised City: New York's Jews: 1870-1914* (Cambridge, MA: Harvard, 1962) are the two best secondary sources. See the bibliographical essays in both books for citations of published works on various aspects of this topic.

14. See: Caspar Levias, "The Justification of Zionism," *The Hebrew Union College Journal*, vol.3, no. 3 (April, 1899), p. 169-175. 15. *The Hebrew Union College Journal*, vol. 4, no.3 (December, 1899), p. 72.

16. See: Harvey E. Wessel, "How I Became a Zionist at the Hebrew Union College," *Hebrew Union College Monthly*, vol. 6, no.6 (May-June, 1920).

17. Kaufmann Kohler, "What the Hebrew Union College Stands For," *Hebrew Union College Monthly*, vol. 3, no.1 (November, 1916), p.2.

18. See the appendix for the complete text of and full citation for "A Statement To The Peace Conference."

19. Ibid.

20. *Hebrew Union College Monthly*, vol. 17, no. 1 (October, 1929), p.4.

21. Ibid.

22. See: Union of American Hebrew Congregations (UAHC) Commission on

Social Action of Reform Judaism, *Where We Stand—Social Action Resolutions* (New York: UAHC, 1960), p.59. The Resolutions Committee voted 12 to 4 to defeat the resolution, but a majority of assembled delegates voted for the resolution.

23. *Yearbook of the Central Conference of American Rabbis (YBCCAR)*, vol. 3 (1928), p. 140.
24. See: *YBCCAR*, vol. 41 (1931), p. 115 f.f.
25. *YBCCAR*, vol. 40 (1930), p. 99.
26. *YBCCAR*, vol. 42 (1932), p. 178 f.f.
27. Pamphlet, "Rabbis of America to Labor Palestine," League for Labor Palestine, New York, 1935.
28. *YBCCAR*, vol. 45 (1935), p. 102, 110-112.
29. *YBCCAR*, vol. 455 (1935), p. 112.
30. Abraham Franzblau, *Reform Judaism in the Large Cities—A Survey.* (Cincinnati: UAHC, 1931).
31. Ibid.
32. Ibid.
33. The statement was entitled "Sympathizing with German Jews and Expressing Confidence in the U.S. Government's Attitude." See: UAHC Commission on Social Action of Reform Judaism, *Where We Stand—Social Action Resolutions*, New York, 1960, p. 60-61.
34. Ibid., p. 61-62.
35. Ibid., p. 62 "Enforcing the Efforts of the Jewish Agency in Upbuilding Palestine."
36. *YBCCAR*, vol. 43 (1933), p. 103-107.
37. *YBCCAR*, vol, 44 (1934), p. 178-189.
38. See: *YBCCAR*, vol. 45 (1935), p.260 f.f., 309 f.f.
39. See: Arthur J. Lelyveld,"The Conference View of the Position of the Jew in the Modern World," in Bertram Korn, ed., *Retrospect and Prospect—Essays in Commemoration of the 75th Anniversary of the Founding of the CCAR*, 1889-1964, (New York: CCAR, 1965), p. 1559-161.
40. See: *YBCCAR*, vol. 47 (1937), p. 94-114.
41. The following is the complete published text of the resolution, titled "Safeguarding Rights of Jews After World War II," passed by the UAHC in April, 1943:

"God uses men and people at great moments in history as the instrument of revelation. The Four Freedoms, the Atlantic Charter, collective security, common responsibility for a just and enduring peace enunciated by our President and his advisors and the leaders of the United Nations have practical goals which may be measurably realized. To their achievement we pledge our unreserved devotion. While the Four Freedoms must be applied to all persons of whatever faith, the Union of American Hebrew Congregations is deeply concerned with the fate of Jews in all lands who are suffering special hardships and even loss of life simply because they are Jews. We call upon our government and, through it, on the United Nations, to see that in the post-war settlement adequate provision shall be made to safeguard their rights, as well as the rights of all people who have been persecuted because of race or religion. We urge that adequate provision be made for their rehabilitation in new homes and in Palestine. We ask that our government use its good offices to see that Palestine is opened as quickly as possible for settlement of as many Jews as desire to go there and who can be taken care of."

42. See: Irving Levitas, "Reform Jews and Zionism, 1919-1921," *American Jewish Archives Quarterly*, April, 1962, p. 12.

43. See: Yonathan Shapiro, *Leadership of the American Zionist Organization, 1897-1930* (Champaign: University of Illinois, 1971), p.256.

44. See: Report of mass meeting at Plum Street Temple, August 29, 1929, in the *James G. Heller* Papers, American Jewish Archives, Cincinnati.

45. Julian Morgenstern, "What Are We Jews?," *CCAR Journal*, October, 1965.

46. Julian Morgenstern, Address at the opening Exercises of Hebrew Union College, September 29, 1934, *Julian Morgenstern Collection*, American Jewish Archives, Cincinnati.

47. Julian Morgenstern, Address, "The Task of the Hebrew Union College," October 7, 1944, p. 4. *Morgenstern Collection*. Also see: Julian Morgenstern, Address, "Unity in American Judaism, How and When?" September 22, 1945, p. 11, *Morgenstern Collection*.

48. Julian Morgenstern, Address, "Assimilation, Isolation or Reform?" *Contemporary Jewish Record*, April, 1942, p. 140. Also see: Julian Morgenstern, Address, "Judaism's Contributions to Post-War Religion," September 26, 1942, p. 17, *American Jewish Archives*, Cincinnati.

49. Julian Morgenstern, "Nation, People, Religion—What are We." *American Israelite*, October 21, 1943, p.1.

50. Telegram, Joshua Loth Liebman to Abba Hillel Silver, October 26, 1943, *Abba Hillel Silver Collection*, American Jewish Archives, Cincinnati.

51. See: Joshua Loth Liebman,"Kindles of Mental Lights," *Liberal Judaism* ,November, 1945, p. 22.

52. See: Julian Morgenstern,"Opening Day Address," in *Cincinnati Enquirer*, October 13, 1946, p. 3. See also: Morgenstern,"What Are We Jews?", CCAR Journal, October, 1965, p.20.

53. Ibid.

54. Julian Morgenstern, "With History As Our Guide," *YBCCAR*, volume LVII, 1947, p. 257-287.

55. Ibid., p. 280.

56. Ibid., p. 283. Also see: Published Letter from Morgenstern to the editor of the *Jewish Times* in Baltimore, January 2, 1948, p.5.

57. See the *Morris S. Lazaron Collection*, American Jewish Archives, Cincinnati, for the best material pertaining to Lazaron's ideas. Two representative articles, dealing with Zionism and written by Lazaron are: "Reform Judaism and Jewish Nationalism," *Baltimore Jewish Times*, January 2, 1931, p. 5 f.f.; "Rabbi Lazaron Berates American Zionists," *Baltimore Jewish Times*.

58. See: Norton Mezvinsky, "Humanitarian Dissent in Zionism: Martin Buber and Judah Magnes," in EAFORD and AJAZ, ed., *Judaism or Zionism?* (London: EAFORD and Zed, 1986), p. 98-119.

59. "Rabbi Wohl Replies to Dr. Morgenstern," *American Israelite*, November 11, 1943, p.1.

60. The evidence for and the analyses of the oppressive Zionist policies of the state of Israel are abundant. See for example: Noam Chomsky, *The Fateful Triangle* (Boston: South End Press, 1983); Uri Davis and Norton Mezvinsky, *Documents from Israel 1967-1973*; (London: Ithaca, 1975); Sabri Jiryis, *The*

Arabs in Israel (New York: Monthly Review Press, 1976); Naseer Aruri, ed., *Occupation: Israel Over Palestine* (London: Zed, 1984). The Israel Shahak collections of Israeli documents and articles from the Israeli Hebrew press, most of which have been translated into English from the original Hebrew, contain extremely valuable material in this regard and have been utilized by many commentators.

APPENDIX

A STATEMENT TO THE PEACE CONFERENCE [1]

As a future form of government for Palestine will undoubtedly be considered by the approaching Peace Conference, we, the undersigned citizens of the United States, unite in this statement, setting forth our objections to the organization of a Jewish State in Palestine as proposed by the Zionist Societies in this country and Europe and to the segregation of the Jews as a nationalistic unit in any country.

We feel that in so doing we are voicing the opinion of the majority of American Jews born in this country and of those foreign born who have lived here long enough to thoroughly assimilate American political and social conditions. The American Zionists represent, according to the most recent statistics available, only a small proportion of the Jews living in this country, about 150,000 out of 3,500,000. (*American Jewish Year Book* 1918, Philadelphia.)

[1] Handed to President Wilson on behalf of the signers by Congressman Julius Kahn on March 4th, 1919, for transmission to the Peace Conference at Paris. See above, p. 117, note 1. The statement was prepared conjointly by the Rev. Dr. Henry Berkowitz, of Philadelphia, Mr. Max Senior, of Cincinnati, and Professor Morris Jastrow, Jr., of the University of Pennsylvania.

At the outset we wish to indicate our entire sympathy with the efforts of Zionists which aim to secure for Jews at present living in lands of oppression a refuge in Palestine or elsewhere, where they may freely develop their capabilities and carry on their activities as free citizens.

But we raise our voices in warning and protest against the demand of the Zionists for the reorganization of the Jews as a national unit, to whom, now or in the future, territorial sovereignty in Palestine shall be committed. This demand not only misinterprets the trend of the history of the Jews, who ceased to be a nation 2000 years ago, but involves the limitation and possible annulment of the larger claims of Jews for full citizenship and human rights in all lands in which those rights are not yet secure. For the very reason that the new era upon which the world is entering aims to establish government everywhere on principles of true democracy, we reject the Zionistic project of a " national home for the Jewish people in Palestine."

Zionism arose as a result of the intolerable conditions under which Jews have been forced to live in Russia and Roumania. But it is evident that for the Jewish population of these countries, variously estimated at from six to ten millions, Palestine can become no homeland. Even with the improvement of the neglected condition of this country, its limited area can offer no solution. The Jewish question in Russia and Roumania can be settled only within those countries by the grant of full rights of citizenship to Jews.

We are all the more opposed to the Zionists, because they, themselves, distinctly repudiate the solely ameliorative program. They demand and hail with delight the " Balfour Declaration " to establish " a national home for the Jewish people in Palestine," *i. e.,* a home not merely for Jews living in countries in which they are oppressed, but for Jews universally. No Jew, wherever he may live, can consider himself free from the implications of such a grant.

The willingness of Jews interested in the welfare of their brethren to aid in redeeming Palestine from the blight of centuries of Turkish misrule, is no acceptance of the Zionist project to segregate Jews as a political unit and to re-institute a section of such a political unit in Palestine or elsewhere.

At the present juncture in the world's affairs when lands that have hitherto been subjected to foreign domination are to be recognized as free and independent states, we rejoice in the avowed proposal of the Peace Congress to put into practical application the fundamental principles of democracy. That principle, which asserts equal rights for all citizens of a state, irrespective of creed or ethnic descent, should be applied in such a manner as to exclude segregation of any kind, be it nationalistic or other. Such segregation must inevitably create differences among the sections of the population of a country. Any such plan of segregation is necessarily reactionary in its tendency, undemocratic in spirit and totally contrary to the practices of free government, especially as these are exemplified by our own country. We therefore strongly urge the abandonment of such a basis for the reorganization of any state.

OBJECTIONS TO SEGREGATION OF JEWS AS A POLITICAL UNIT

Against such a political segregation of the Jews in Palestine or elsewhere we object:

1. Because the Jews are dedicated heart and soul to the welfare of the countries in which they dwell under free conditions. All Jews repudiate every suspicion of a double allegiance, but to our minds it is necessarily implied in and cannot by any logic be eliminated from the establishment of a sovereign State for the Jews in Palestine.

By the large part taken by them in the great war, the Jews have once and for all shattered the base aspersions of the Anti-Semites which charged them with being aliens in every land, incapable of true patriotism and prompted only by sinister and self-seeking motives. Moreover, it is safe to assume that the overwhelming bulk of the Jews of America, England, France, Italy, Holland, Switzerland and the other lands of freedom, have no thought whatever of surrendering their citizenship in these lands in order to resort to a " Jewish homeland in Palestine." As a rule those who favor such a restoration advocate it not for themselves but for others. Those who act thus, and yet insist on their patriotic attachment to the countries of which they are citizens, are self-deceived in their profession of Zionism and under the spell of an emotional romanticism or of a religious sentiment fostered through centuries of gloom.

2. We also object to political segregation of Jews for those who take their Zionistic professions seriously as referring not to " others " but to themselves. Granted that the establishment of a sovereign Jewish State in Palestine would lead many to emigrate to that land, the political conditions of the millions who would be unable to migrate for generations to come, if ever, would be made far more precarious. Roumania — despite the pledges of the Berlin Treaty — has legally branded her Jews as aliens, though many are descended from families settled in that country longer than the present Roumanian government has existed. The establishment of a Jewish State will manifestly serve the malevolent rulers of that and other lands as a new justification for additional repressive legislation. The multitudes who remain would be subject to worse perils, if possible, even though the few who escape might prosper in Palestine.

3. We object to the political segregation also of those who might succeed in establishing themselves in Palestine. The proposition involves dangers which, it is manifest, have not had the serious consideration of those who are so zealous in its advocacy. These dangers are adverted to in a most kindly spirit of warning by Sir George Adam Smith, who is generally acknowledged to be the greatest authority in the

world on everything connected with Palestine, either past or present. In a recent publication, *Syria and the Holy Land,* he points out that there is absolutely no fixity to the boundaries of Palestine. These have varied greatly in the course of the centuries. The claims to various sections of this undefined territory would unquestionably evoke bitter controversies. " It is not true," says Sir George, " that Palestine is the national home of the Jewish people and of no other people." " It is not correct to call its non-Jewish in- habitants ' Arabs,' or to say that they have left no image of their spirit and made no history except in the great Mosque." " Nor can we evade the fact that Christian communities have been as long in pos- session of their portion of this land as ever the Jews were." " These are legitimate questions," he says, " stirred up by the claims of Zionism, but the Zion- ists have not yet fully faced them."

To subject the Jews to the possible recurrence of such bitter and sanguinary conflicts which would be inevitable, would be a crime against the triumphs of their whole past history and against the lofty and world-embracing visions of their great prophets and leaders.

4. Though these grave difficulties be met, still we protest against the political segregation of the Jews and the re-establishment in Palestine of a distinctively Jewish State as utterly opposed to the principles of democracy which it is the avowed purpose of the World's Peace Conference to establish.

Whether the Jews be regarded as a " race " or as a " religion," it is contrary to the democratic principles for which the world war was waged to found a nation on either or both of these bases. America, England, France, Italy, Switzerland and all the most advanced nations of the world are composed of representatives of many races and religions. Their glory lies in the freedom of conscience and worship, in the liberty of thought and custom which binds the followers of many faiths and varied civilizations in the common bonds of political union. A Jewish State involves fundamental limitations as to race and religion, else the term " Jewish " means nothing. To unite Church and State, in any form, as under the old Jewish hierarchy, would be a leap backward of two thousand years.

" The rights of other creeds and races will be respected under Jewish dominance," is the assurance of Zionism. But the keynotes of democracy are neither condescension nor tolerance, but justice and equality. All this applies with special force to a country like Palestine. That land is filled with associations sacred to the followers of three great religions, and as a result of migrating movements of many centuries contains an extraordinary number of different ethnic groups, far out of proportion to the small extent of the country itself. Such a condition points clearly to a reorganization of Palestine on the broadest possible basis.

5. We object to the political segregation of the Jews because it is an error to assume that the bond

uniting them is of a national character. They are bound by two factors: First, the bond of common religious beliefs and aspirations and, secondly, the bond of common traditions, customs, and experiences, largely, alas, of common trials and sufferings. Nothing in their present status suggests that they form in any real sense a separate nationalistic unit.

The reorganization of Palestine as far as it affects the Jews is but part of a far larger issue, namely, the constructive endeavor to secure the emancipation of the Jews in all the lands in which they dwell. This movement, inaugurated in the eighteenth century and advancing with steady progress through the western lands, was checked by such reactionary tendencies as caused the expulsion of the Poles from Eastern Prussia and the massacre of Armenians in Turkey. As directed against Jews these tendencies crystallized into a political movement called Anti-Semitism, which had its rise in Germany. Its virulence spread (especially) throughout eastern Europe and led to cruel outbreaks in Roumania and elsewhere, and to the pogroms of Russia with their dire consequences.

To guard against such evils in the future we urge that the great constructive movement, so sadly interrupted, be reinstituted and that efficient measures be taken to insure the protection of the law and the full rights of citizenship to Jews in every land. If the basis of the reorganization of governments is henceforth to be democratic, it cannot be contemplated to exclude any group of people from the enjoyment of full rights.

As to the future of Palestine, it is our fervent hope that what was once a " promised land " for the Jews may become a " land of promise " for all races and creeds, safeguarded by the League of Nations which, it is expected, will be one of the fruits of the Peace Conference to whose deliberations the world now looks forward so anxiously and so full of hope. We ask that Palestine be constituted as a free and independent state, to be governed under a democratic form of government recognizing no distinctions of creed or race or ethnic descent, and with adequate power to protect the country against oppression of any kind. We do not wish to see Palestine, either now or at any time in the future, organized as a Jewish State.

THE END

PRINTED IN THE UNITED STATES OF AMERICA

SELECTED BIBLIOGRAPHY

Abu Lughod, I., ed. *Transformation of Palestine*, Northwestern, 1987.
American Friends Service Committee. *A Compassionate Peace*, Hill & Wang, 1982.
Antonius, G. *The Arab Awakening*, International Book Center, 1976.
Aruri, N., ed. *Occupation: Israel Over Palestine*, Association of Arab-American University Graduates, 1983.
Avishai, B. *The Tragedy of Zionism*, Farrar Straus Giroux, 1985.
Avnery, U. *My Friend, the Enemy*, Lawrence Hill, 1987.
Begin, M. *The Revolt*, Nash, 1977.
Beit-Hallahmi, B. *The Israeli Connection*, Pantheon, 1987.
Berger, E. *Memoirs of an Anti-Zionist Jew*, Institute for Palestine Studies, 1978.
   Who Knows Better Must Say So!, Institute for Palestine Studies, 1970.
Brownlee, W.H. *The Lion that Ravages Palestine*, Americans for Middle East Understanding, 1983.
   The Rights of the Palestinians, Americans for Middle East Understanding, 1983.
Cervenka, Z. and Rogers, B. *The Nuclear Axis*, Times, 1978.
Chacour, E. and Hazard, D. *Blood Brothers*, Chosen Books, 1984.
Chomsky, N. *The Fateful Triangle*, South End, 1983.
   Pirates and Emperors, Amana, 1987.
   Towards A New Cold War, Pantheon, 1982.
Cohen, M.J. *Palestine and the Great Powers*, Princeton, 1982.
Collins, L. and LaPierre, D. *O Jerusalem!* Simon & Schuster, 1972.
Davis, U. *Israel: An Apartheid State*, Zed, 1987.
Domhoff, G.W. *Who Rules America Now?*, Prentice Hall, 1983.
Dye, T.R. *Who's Running America?*, Prentice Hall, 1983.
Eban, A. *Autobiography*, Random House, 1977.
El-Khawas, M. and Rabbo, S.A. *American Aid to Israel*, Amana, 1984.
El Kodsy, A. and Lobel, E. *The Arab World and Israel*, Monthly Review, 1970.
Elmessiri, A. *The Land of Promise*, North American, 1977.
Eveland, W.C. *Ropes of Sand*, Norton, 1980.
Feldman, R., ed. *The Jew As Pariah*, Grove, 1978.
Feuerlicht, R.S. *The Fate of the Jews*, Times, 1983.
Findley, P. *They Dare to Speak Out*, Lawrence Hill, 1985.
Flapan, S. *The Birth of Israel*, Pantheon, 1987.
   Zionism and the Palestinians, Harper & Row, 1979.
Goldmann, N. *Autobiography*, Holt, Rinehart & Winston, 1969.
Green, S. *Living By the Sword*, Amana, 1988.

Taking Sides, Morrow, 1984.

Gresh, A. *The PLO: The Struggle Within*, Zed, 1985.

Halpern, B. *Idea of the Jewish State*, Harvard, 1969.

Halsell, G. *Prophecy and Politics*, Lawrence Hill, 1986.

Heller, M.A. *A Palestinian State*, Harvard, 1983.

Herzl, T. *Complete Diaries*, ed., R. Patai, Herzl Press, 1960.

Hirst, D. *The Gun and the Olive Branch*, Harcourt Brace, 1977.

Irani, G. *The Papacy and the Middle East*, Notre Dame, 1986.

Jackson E. *Middle East Mission*, Norton, 1983.

Jiryis, S. *The Arabs in Israel*, Monthly Review, 1977.

Joseph, B.M. *Besieged Bedfellows: Israel and the Land of Apartheid*, Greenwood, 1988.

Kerr, M., ed. *The Elusive Peace in the Middle East*, SUNY, 1975.

Khouri, F.J. *The Arab-Israeli Dilemma*, Syracuse, 1985.

Kimche, J. *Seven Fallen Pillars*, Da Capo, 1976.

Kissinger, H. *Years of Upheaval*, Little Brown, 1982.

Kraines, O. *The Impossible Dilemma*, Bloch, 1976.

Laqueur, W. and Rubin, B., eds. *The Israel-Arab Reader*, Facts on File, 1985.

Lilienthal, A.M. *The Zionist Connection II*, North American, 1982.

　　What Price Israel?, Institute for Palestine Studies, 1969.

Lukacs, Y. and Battah, A., eds. *The Arab-Israeli Conflict*, Westview, 1988.

Lustick, I. *Arabs in the Jewish State*, Univ. of Texas, 1980.

Mallison, W.T. and S.V. *The Palestine Problem*, Longman, 1986.

Mamorstein, E. *Heaven at Bay*, Oxford, 1969.

Petuchowski, J.J. *Zion Reconsidered*, Twayne, 1966.

Quandt, W. *Decade of Decisions*, UCAL, 1977.

Rodinson, M. *Cult, Ghetto, and State*, Al Saqi, 1984.

Rokach, L. *Israel's Sacred Terrorism*, Association of Arab-American University Graduates, 1986.

Rubenberg, C.A. *Israel and the American National Interest*, Univ. of Illinois, 1986.

Said, E.W. *After the Last Sky*, Pantheon, 1986.

　　Covering Islam, Pantheon, 1981.

　　The Question of Palestine, Random House, 1980.

Said, E.W. and Hitchens, C. *Blaming the Victims*, Methuen, 1987.

Saunders, H.H. *The Middle East Problem in the 1980s*, American Enterprise Institute, 1981.

　　Other Walls, American Enterprise Institute, 1985.

Segev, T. *The First Israelis, Nineteen Hundred and Forty-Nine*, Free Press, 1985.

Shahak, I. *Israel's Global Role*, Association of Arab-American University Graduates, 1982.

Shalaim, A. *Collusion Across the Jordan*, Oxford, 1988.

Shehadeh, R. *Occupier's Law*, Institute for Palestine Studies, 1985.

Shiblak, A. *The Lure of Zion*, Al Saqi, 1986.

Shimoni, G. *Jews and Zionism*, Oxford, 1980.

Shipler, D. *Arab and Jew*, Times, 1986.

Smith, G.V., ed. *Zionism, the Dream and Reality*, Harper & Row, 1974.

Snetsinger, J. *Truman, the Jewish Vote and the Creation of Israel*, Hoover Institute, 1974.

Stevens, R.P. and Elmessiri, A.M. *Israel and South Africa*, North American, 1976.

Stone, I.F. *Underground to Palestine*, Pantheon, 1978.

Teveth, S. *Ben Gurion and the Palestinian Arabs*, Oxford, 1985.

Tivnan, E. *The Lobby*, Simon & Schuster, 1987.

Weizmann, C. *Trial and Error*, Greenwood, 1972.

Yaniv, A. *Dilemmas of Security*, Oxford, 1987.